AUGUSTINIANISM
AND MODERN
THEOLOGY

Uniform with this title :

The Mystery of the Supernatural

AUGUSTINIANISM AND MODERN THEOLOGY

Henri de Lubac, S.J.

Translated by Lancelot Sheppard

GEOFFREY CHAPMAN
LONDON DUBLIN MELBOURNE 1969

Geoffrey Chapman Ltd
18 High Street, Wimbledon, London SW 19

Geoffrey Chapman (Ireland) Ltd
5-7 Main Street, Blackrock, County Dublin

Geoffrey Chapman Pty Ltd
44 Latrobe Street, Melbourne, Vic 3000, Australia

This book was originally published under the title
Augustinisme et théologie moderne in 1965 by F. Aubier,
Editions Montaigne, Paris

This book is set in 11 on 13 point Baskerville

Printed in Great Britain by
Clarke, Doble & Brendon Ltd, Plymouth

Contents

Abbreviations

Denz.	Denzinger, *Enchiridion Symbolorum*
DTC	*Dictionnaire de théologie catholique*
JTS	*Journal of Theological Studies*
MScRel	*Mélanges de Science religieuse*
NRT	*Nouvelle revue théologique*
PL	*Patrologia Latina* (Migne)
RAM	*Revue d'ascétique et de mystique*
RB	*Revue biblique*
RevScRel	*Revue des sciences religieuses*
RHE	*Revue d'histoire ecclésiastique*
RSPT	*Revue des sciences philosophiques et théologiques*
RSR	*Recherches de science religieuse*
SC	*Sources chrétiennes*

This book is dedicated to the memory of
Father Jules Lebreton and
Father Joseph Huby

'. . . non temerario ausu Aquinatis mentem illustrandi, cum hac in re, luce clarissima de se fulgeat; sed potius animo cupientes, splendidam atque illimen Thomae doctrinam, ab obscuris vel impuris interpretationibus cernendi, quae temporum progressu ab aurea scholasticorum aetate recedentium circam illam succrevere.' J. SESTILI.

Introduction

'There is not a theologian who does not complain that the teaching of St Augustine, though praised by the Holy See, was dealt an incurable blow by the Constitution of St Pius V.' These are the words of Gerberon, the editor of the works of Baius and of the letters of Jansenius, echoing 'all the followers of St Augustine'.[1] Complaints apart, is the observation true? For there are many historians of theology—they are more numerous today than ever before—Catholics as well as Protestants, admirers or opponents, who hold that Baianism was the genuine consequence of Augustinianism, as to a great extent was the teaching of Luther, and still more that of Jansenius. According to these historians, Baius in his weighty exegesis of his favourite doctor, was not mistaken on the main point. As a slavish follower of the master whom he had chosen for his rupture with Scholasticism he made the error of disregarding all other sources of faith, or even certain aspects of Augustine's work, but he was not mistaken about certain of his more fundamental doctrines. On the contrary, according to Fr

[1] See Gabriel Gerberon, *Histoire générale du Jansénisme* ... (1700, 3 vols); J. B. Du Chesne, S.J., *Histoire du Baianisme* (Douai, 1731), preface; and *Renversement de la Religion* ... *par toutes les Bulles et Brefs donnés depuis près de deux cents ans contre Baius, Jansenius*, etc. (Rome, 1756; the author was Abbé Le Clerc). The quotations from Baius are made from Gerberon's edition (1696): *M. Baii* ... *opera omnia, cum bullis Pontificum et aliis causam spectantibus studio A.P.* (The *Baiana* are in the second volume.) On the history of the Baius affair: L. Pastor, *History of the Popes*, Eng. trans., vol. 17, pp. 287 ff. Miguel Roca, *Documentos ineditos en torno a Miguel Bayo*, 1560-82 (off-print from Anthologica Annua, Iglesia Nacional Española, Rome, 1953, pp. 304-476). Cf. Ed. van Eijl, *Revue d'histoire ecclésiastique*, 1953, pp. 889-91; 1955, pp. 499-542.

François-Xavier Jansen, the author of a brilliant and penetrating monograph about him, he must be blamed for being unable to 'resist' on occasion the 'fascinating genuis' of his master. The most that can be allowed is that his 'uncompromising exegesis' sometimes follows too closely the letter of St Augustine to the prejudice of the spirit; that he gives 'a systematically precise interpretation' of Augustine's ideas 'which they never had in the mind of their author', thus endowing Augustinianism with a 'coherence and an exactness which it never knew before'. As a result, when we find Baius himself complaining in his Apologia to St Pius V that the Bull, which censured his propositions, by the same token condemned not only the terms but also the very doctrines of the holy Fathers, we are obliged to admit that we have here something quite different from the mere recrimination of a professor upset at the condemnation of his teaching; and to be 'frank', we ought to add that 'in condemning Baius it seems as if the Catholic Church has definitely parted company with the doctor of Hippo'.[2] On this view theological thought has been set free 'from a majestic burden indeed' and with Baianism now acknowledged as a heresy Augustinianism was thereby made suspect and therefore harmless. Some Protestant author like Thomasius in his history of dogma, or more recently Harnack, might maintain that the Roman Church has progressively departed from Augustine's teaching to the extent of 'repudiating it energetically';[3] to show that he is not entirely right we should answer merely that his is an assertion for whose historial truth a Catholic, for whom the living

[2] François-Xavier Jansen, *Baius et le Baianisme* (Louvain, 1927), p. 17. Fr Jansen agrees, on the other hand, that Baius' doctrine is only 'pseudo-Augustinian', falsified on certain points, sometimes 'by omission and by exaggeration', and that if St Augustine could have known the 'Augustinianisms' of Luther, Baius and Jansenius, he 'would himself have condemned these illegitimate children of his genius, so great was his humble submission to the Church' (*op. cit.*, pp. 37, 70, 76, 169).

[3] As we know, it is a commonplace with many Protestant historians and theologians that the Catholic Church has become, to say the least, semi-Pelagian. See in the *Baiana* the assertions by Melchior Leydeckerus. Jurieu went so far as to say: '[In Molinism] the Roman Church tolerates plain unadulterated Pelagianism'. (Bossuet answers this complaint in his *Deuxième Advertissement aux Protestants*.) See below, p. 149.

tradition of his Church forms his rule of faith, 'can be excused from verifying'.[4]

That, it appears, was already Fr Annat's view, despite the fact that in 1652 he called one of his works *Augustinus a Baianis vindicatus*: 'By condemning the five propositions,' he remarked airily, 'the Pope did not bother to find out whether he was condemning St Augustine.' The great Arnauld was indignant at such a remark, terming it a 'blasphemy'.[5] He went too far. At least the opinion appears to be serious enough for it not to be adopted without careful examination. It certainly has the merit of making a break with a certain 'concordism' which, relying on rare, isolated, wrongly understood or over-emphasized passages, endeavours on occasion, according to the point of view adopted, either to 'save' St Augustine by reducing his teaching to what alone is held to be orthodox, or to base on his authority theories lacking sufficient support from other quarters. 'Concordisms' of this kind are no longer in favour nowadays and we may well be glad of it.[6] But should they involve St Augustine with them in their disgrace? Would a more rigorous method have led to our being obliged, since we understood him better, to give him up altogether? Notice that what is here at stake is not merely the memory of him who was given the title of 'Doctor of Grace': for even after the condemnation of Baius and Jansenius the Church has continued to give him this title, and she still insists on offering him to theologians as their guide. Clement VIII's forceful statements to one of the *de auxiliis* congregations are well known:

[4] Jansen, *op. cit*, p. 169. My study of Baius owes a great deal to this work; it is heavily documented and very illuminating on many points.

[5] *Réponse au Père Annat*, second Memoir (*Oeuvres*, vol. 19, p. 181; cf. pp. 196ff.).

[6] Compare, for example, the 'accommodated' exegesis of A. Gardeil, O.P., in 'La Puissance obédientielle de l'âme au surnaturel selon saint Augustin' in *La Structure de l'âme et l'expérience mystique* with J. de Blic, S.J., 'Le péché originel selon saint Augustin' in *Recherches de science religieuse*, 1926 and 1927 (it will be seen, moreover, that my interpretation of Augustinianism is appreciably different from what Fr de Blic seems to propose). Cf. Jansen's remark (*op. cit.*, p. 136): 'If the Augustine of the Catholic interpreters appears to be more in agreement with the ordinary teaching of the Catholic theologians, it may be asked whether he is sufficiently in agreement with the original and specific elements of Augustinian thought.'

'Sancti Augustini doctrina, quam et Ecclesiae doctrinam esse nemo vestrum ignorat.'[7] These statements have often been repeated since then, and Pius XI's encyclical *Ad salutem* is still remembered.

Of course, these are not *de fide* definitions. But they are at least clear indications of a view that has never been contradicted or modified. Nor does it follow that everything in St Augustine's teaching ought to be canonized, even on the subject of grace. At an early date tradition was able to make a proper distinction, and there is not one of his most fervent admirers who would not acknowledge in particular that there are marks of an excessive pessimism which, on one view, could be attributed to certain reminiscences from Manicheism. But some authors, it must be acknowledged, attach far too much importance to these reminiscences, without taking into account that Manichean pessimism and Augustinian pessimism draw their inspiration from opposite principles.[8] But to hold that Augustine's fundamental idea,

---

[7] Session of 20 March 1601, *Ex Actis Coronelli.* Cf. Aug. Le Blanc (Serry), *Historia congregationis de auxiliis* (1700), col. 388 and 402; and Petau, *Dogmata theologica,* vol. 1, bk 9, ch. 6. 'To have [St Augustine] on one's side,' concluded J. Leporcq in *Sentiments de saint Augustin sur la grâce,* preface, 'is tantamount to having the doctrine of the Church and the Gospel in one's favour.'

[8] Grotius, Richard Simon, de Launoy in the seventeenth century; in modern times, after Dom Rottmanner, Margival, Turmel, Humbert, even Paquier, again bring against St Augustine, with varying emphasis, the charge of Manicheism already laid against him by Julian of Eclanus. Cf. *Contra duas epistulas Pelagianorum,* bk 1, n. 4; bk 2, n. 1; *Contra Julianum pelagianum,* bk 1, c. 1-3: *Contra Julianum opus imperfectum,* bk 1, c. 59; bk 2, c. 9, bk 5, c. 32-3. St Augustine denied the charge: *Contra Julianum,* bk 1, c. 8. Cf. Patrice Larroque, *Examen critique des doctrines de la religion chrétienne,* vol. 1 (1860), p. 230: 'Without perceiving it St Augustine had returned to the Manicheism that he had previously held . . . and in his wake drew the Church which adopted his teaching. It is not always possible to drop one's early habits.' Note that Dom Rottmanner envisaged merely 'the doctrine of unconditioned predestination and the special salvific will as it was developed particularly by St Augustine in the last period of his life'. *'L'Augustinisme', étude d'histoire doctrinale* (Munich, 1892: French trans. by J. Libaert, in *Mélanges de science religieuse,* 1949, p. 31). Despite the prudence of its formulation the recent judgment of Jean Gaudemet is to be regretted, *L'Église dans l'empire romain* (1958), p. 490: 'In the dualism of the two cities there re-appears, perhaps, the memory of the Manichean doctrines.' Similarly A. Adam, 'Das Fortwirken des Manichaïsmus bei Augustin' in *Zeitschr. Kircheng.,* 69 (1958), pp. 1-25.

accurately formulated in all its logical purity, leads inevitably to heresy; that not only in actual fact, but with good reason, if understood in all the rigour of its terms, it was the begetter of the systems of Luther, Baius and Jansenius, seems an excessive paradox. It is true that 'the most Catholic of the Fathers' has more than once experienced 'the posthumous misfortune of finding errors and serious alterations in Catholic truth'[9] put forward under the cover of his name. But it remains to be seen whether this misfortune was fully deserved. After all, St Bernard and St Paul have suffered the same fate. 'Augustine,' remarked Facundus of Hermiane, 'could not do better than the prophets, the apostles, the evangelists, in saying words which the heretics have so often misused for the defence of their errors.'[10] For Baianism in particular, rather than an exaggerated Augustinianism,[11] would not be a systematized, rigid Augustinianism, taken to its ultimate conclusions, but a falsified version, a parody of it. Baius, and Jansenius after him, thinking that they were following St Augustine, may well have taken the wrong turning.

In this case, so far as Baius and Jansenius are concerned, if the point at which they went astray could be established with certainty, without condoning whatever should be condemned, and with no concessions to what was less a rigorist position than a

---

[9] Jansen, *op. cit.*, p. 138. Similar judgments are to be found in J. V. Bainvel's Introduction to *La théologie catholique au XIX* siècle* by J. Bellamy (1904), p. xlviii: 'Pius V in his fearless condemnation of Baius gave to theological thought . . . in one sense a new direction, but a more intransigent one, in face of the errors of modern times, than the old Augustinian one'; also P. Pourrat, *Histoire de la spiritualité chrétienne,* vol. 3 (1928), p. 4 Eng. trans. *Christian Spirituality*, vol. 4, Westminster, Md, 1955, p. 2): 'In later times Luther, Calvin, Baius, and Jansen drew monstrous conclusions from Augustinian principles.'

[10] *Liber contra Mocianum.* Cf. *Caractères des défenseurs du P. Quesnel* (Avignon, 1719), p. 91: 'There is nothing to astonish us here or lessen the respect that we ought to have for the doctor of grace.' François Bonal made the same remark on the subject of scripture (*Le chrétien du temps*, 2nd part, foreword): 'Where would the Church be if she had to give up all the scriptures that heresy has used to its own advantage and on which it has cast the infection of its own pernicious interpretations?'

[11] In *Revue des sciences religieuses* (1929) reviewing the work of Jansen here quoted, Jean Rivière compared the 'excessive Augustinianism' of Baius with the 'moderate Augustinianism of tradition'.

deadly narrowing of Christian thought, it might be possible to go beyond controversy and unilateral opposition. This is what the whole Church is seeking to do at the present moment in connection even with the Reformation itself, a state of affairs that is sometimes described figuratively by saying that we are coming out of the Counter-Reformation period and the viewpoints engendered by post-Tridentine theology. In such general formulas there is always some exaggeration. Nonetheless they are an expression of an actual situation. Thus in a more restricted, but still wide field, perhaps the time has arrived, while still profiting from the analyses to which several centuries of anti-Baianist and anti-Jansenist contest have given rise, as well as from the successive pronouncements of the magisterium, to return to a more synthetic mode of thought, to one more legitimately the heir of the patristic age and of the golden century of Christian theology.[12]

---

[12] Several signs seem to show that in fact the time has come, perhaps not for the necessary synthesis to be constructed, but at least for an attempt to be made to find it.

In this book I am reprinting a study which, with the title of 'Augustinisme et Baianisme', formed the first part of my *Surnaturel* (1946). The text has been carefully revised and there have been considerable additions. Since the writing of this new version, in which I have endeavoured to deal with all the points that have been put to me about it, various works have been published which I have been unable to take into account, at least to the extent that I would have wished. I should like to draw attention especially to the excellent thesis (for the Gregorian University) by Fr Alberto Arenas Silva, S.J., *Gratuidad e Immanencia de la Vision Beatifica en los Téologos Jesuitas*, estudio historico desde mediados del siglo XVI hasta mediados del siglo XVII (Bogota, 1963); and, quite recently, the important study by Étienne Gilson, 'Sur la problématique thomiste de la vision beatifique' in *Archives d'histoire doctrinale et littéraire du moyen âge*, vol. 31 (1964), 1965, pp. 67-88.

I

Baius

If, with a proper concern for method, we at first leave aside the assertions of the disciple and his master Augustine on the present state of fallen humanity—assertions which with Baius at least are obviously derived—we discover in both an apparently common principle. For Baius, as for Augustine, it is said, and this is at the origin of the whole question, man is so made that on any hypothesis to fulfil his destiny he has need of God's external help. For both of them, a state in which man would be left to his own wisdom and powers, in which he would have to develop and perfect himself unaided, is quite out of the question. In this sense neither of them has any room for the idea of 'pure nature'.[1]

It must be admitted that the resemblance is striking. Could it be that, as often happens, it is merely superficial? Beneath identity of formulation and, it could be said, of theory, we can perceive the diversity of inspiration. Actually it is a radical diversity which leads to many other differences and which, for the informed reader, changes an apparent resemblance into unyielding opposition.

By the principle stated above, Augustine declines to conceive a state in which man would be more self-sufficient, more independent of God; he rejects, even in thought, any system in which God would be less good and also less great. Baius, on the other hand, rebels at the idea of admitting that man, before sinning, must, in the matter of his salvation, give himself up to the good pleasure of his Creator. At once the conclusions part company. From a thesis which in its negative form seemed identical at all

[1] But this meaning, as we shall soon see, was not the only one.

1

points Augustine concludes that man can in no way escape the action of grace; Baius asserts that grace, save in a completely wrong sense, has nothing to do with man in the state of innocence : that by the law of nature itself man has strict rights over God, and thus indispensable divine assistance is no longer an action dictated by an overflowing of entirely gratuitous goodness, but the payment of a debt of justice. According to Augustine, the effect of this assistance is to bear us, to raise us to a blessed state in no way merited by created effort; according to Baius, it is only a necessary means placed at our disposal to enable us in a human way to gain merit which, in its turn, demands its reward. While in Augustine's view all, rightly speaking, is grace (although a distinction is to be made between one grace and another), in Baius' view grace itself does not deserve its name, because it serves nature. Lastly, where Augustine, following St Paul, states that love is the fulfilment of the law, Baius holds that observance of the law is the real love.[2] In this Baius is diametrically opposed to Augustine who, faithful to the New Testament, made the famous remark 'dilige, et quod vis fac'; Baius indeed returns to the former legalist idea of justice : 'In tantum iustus dicitur qui de lege Dei nihil unquam praetermisit.'[3] We can thus no longer talk of the relationship between God and man as a mystery of love; the whole thing has become a commercial transaction. Eternal life is offered to man on a basis of strict reward. Man demands, merits and claims; God provides the tool and pays the account, to the last penny : 'Sicut in impiis non est verisimile supplicium futuri saeculi fore infra delicti mensuram, sic in iustis minus verisimile est quod retributio praemii exuperet mensuram meriti.'[4]

---

[2] Compare Baius, proposition 32, with Augustine, in Psalmum 70, n. 1, or Enchiridion, c. 121 : 'Ad caritatem refertur omne praeceptum.'

[3] De Iustitia, c. 2 (vol. 1, p. 103).

[4] De meritis operum, bk 1; bk 2, c. 9 (in fine), vol. 1, pp. 25-34 and p. 44. See also propositions 13, 14, 15, 32, 33. Baius, says Du Chesne, analysing the treatise De meritis operum, compares 'heaven to a well-policed State in which commutative Justice renders to each according to his works in geometrical progression' (op. cit., p. 63). For the opposite view, see St Augustine, Enchiridion, c. 106 and 197; Contra Iulianum pelagianum, bk 4,

This is the governing idea evolved by Baius after long meditation on the works of his cherished master; according to Valère
André he had read the whole of St Augustine nine times and the
works on grace seventy times. Baius claimed to free his teaching
from the theories due to the influence of Aristotle and restore to
its original purity a doctrine whose corruption was caused by
Scholasticism. As a matter of fact, under the guise of an integral
material reproduction of the thought of Augustine no greater
deformation or travesty, no more total perversion of it, could be
managed. As Jansenius was to acknowledge[5] and as the Bull condemning the synod of Pistoia[6] declared, such an idea was not
derived from Augustine. It came from Pelagius.

Du Chesne, the author of *Histoire du Baianisme*, as impassioned
in its opposition to Baius as Gerberon, the editor of the *Baiana*,
is in his favour, clearly saw this point of capital importance. 'This
theologian,' he declared, 'attributes everything to nature in the
state of innocence, and nothing to grace : that is his crime.'[7] The
difference from Pelagius lies only in manner. The Baianist doctrine
concerning the primitive state of man might well be defined by
terming it impotent Pelagianism. Actually, according to Pelagius,
human autonomy consists in the fact that nature possesses its own
capacity before God; according to Baius it consists in the fact that
before God man has rights. Although therefore Baius is 'materially

in fine; *Epist.* 106 and 178, etc. Baius has no idea of divine charity which
is the foundation of the supernatural vocation of man and which, so to
say, includes the whole economy of salvation, whatever its conditions. Or
rather, he only thinks of it as a sort of alms, the result of scornful pity.
And so he rejects it as unworthy both of God and of man.

[5] *Augustinus*, vol. 2, *De gratia primi hominis*.

[6] 'Favens haeresi pelagianae' (Denz. 1516): 'a censure which sounds to us
like modest banter', says Fernand Litt, *La question des rapports entre la
nature et la grâce au synode de Pistoie*, 1934), p. 22. The relationship
between Baius and Pelagius has often been pointed out, for example by J.
Scheeben, *Préface à l'opuscule d'Ant. Casinius, S.J., Qu'est-ce que l'homme,
ou Controverse sur l'état de pure nature* (French trans. Cros, 1864, p. 14)
or by M. d'Herbigny, *RSR*, 1920, pp. 156-61. Similarly for the Jansenists:
L. Gallien, O.P., *Lettres théologiques touchant l'État de Pure Nature* (1745),
1st letter, pp. 48-50 and 116. Serry, the anti-Molinist, preferred to see the
connection with Molina : *Divus Augustinus divo Thomae . . . conciliatus*
(2nd ed., 1724), pp. 1-2.

[7] *Op. cit.*, p. 177. (The book was placed on the Index on 11 August 1733.)

in complete disagreement' with Pelagius, he is 'formally' in agreement with him.[8] Pelagius' man is prouder, more demanding, but neither displays the attitude of a son towards his father: 'Deus me hominem fecit, iustum ipse me facio'—the essence of Pelagianism is to be found in this proud formula. According to Baianism, the rational creature cannot by itself attain to its end, and hence there is discontinuity and obligatory recourse to divine intervention; but it can nevertheless claim this intervention and hence there is a persisting assertion of autonomy. What God bestows on it is not received as a gift; it is still something belonging to its nature, not a constituent of its nature, as Pelagius would have it, but a natural requirement.[9] Strictly speaking, it is not an integral part of this nature, but it is something indispensable to the integrity of this nature and therefore essentially required by it.

This appears clearly from the explanation forming the subject matter of the *De prima hominis iustitia*. Adam was created a 'living soul'; it obviously follows that he at once received the Holy Spirit, otherwise this soul would have been dead.[10] The integrity ensured by this gift of the Spirit was in no way something gratuitous for it was not a better good, but something whose absence would properly have constituted an evil, an evil against nature. It was therefore quite simply the natural state of man, it constituted his natural health, the health now restored by the divine physician.[11] 'Naturale non causae aut originis suae com-

---

[8] J. Scheeben. *loc. cit.*

[9] Cf. Le Bachelet, art. 'Baius' in *DTC*, vol. 2, cols 69 and 46.

[10] *De prima hominis iustitia*, c. 2: 'Ex quo manifeste sequitur, quod si Deus primo homini animam sine Spiritu Sancto dedisset, tunc non viventem, sed mortuam animam illi dedisset. . . . Sed non potest intelligi dedisse homini animam Spiritui Sancto destitutam, ne sic corpus vegetasse putetur, ut ipsa in se mortua fuisse credatur' (p. 53).

[11] *Op. cit.*, c. 4: 'Quod haec fuerit naturalis eius conditio, cuius semper necessario sit absentia malum, et non potius indebita quaedam humanae naturae exaltatio, qua ex bona melior fit . . . , non facile persuaderi sibi patientur' (p. 55). C. 6: 'Facile intelliges primae creationis imaginem, non supernaturalem et indebitam fuisse humanae naturae dignitatem, . . . sed potius naturalem hominis sanitatem, ad integritatem eius pertinentem . . .' (pp. 57-8). Cf. c. 10 (p. 61).

paratione dicitur, sed rei cui sit inest, ut ad naturalem eius integritatem pertineat, sitque eius absentia malum.' Aristotle himself acknowledged that everything which is natural does not necessarily spring from nature itself. When the latter needs it to avoid affliction and evil it becomes natural to it whatever its origin. Nothing that is essential for the completion of a being can be refused to it; it needs it absolutely. God must provide it.[12] Consequently 'the powers which lead to the ends and completion of nature are of supernatural origin but belong to nature. Supernatural and "owed" are not exclusive terms. For man before the fall eternal life . . . would not have been a gift of grace, but a reward.'[13]

Obviously, being more than a necessity here, the supernatural is misunderstood. The Holy Spirit only intervenes as a necessary means for entirely natural ends. Grace is the 'logical and necessary complement' of creation.[14] The power of God is placed at man's service for a human end. This is an inversion which is a perversion, and as we shall see, it underlies the whole system. Doctrinally, Baius' naturalism is the equivalent of Pelagius'. The only difference is the point of application or the way in which this naturalism occurs in both, and this difference is possibly more a question of temperament or mentality than of deep thought. Pela-

---

[12] *Op. cit.*, c. 11 : 'Sive ex natura e principiis tamquam efficientibus causis orta fuerit primi hominis iustitia, sive a Deo immediate illi collata (sicut plerique de anima rationali tradunt, quam tamen nemo supernaturalem esse arbitratur), adhuc tamen illi naturalis fuit, quia sic ad eius integritatem pertinebat, ut sine ea non possit salva consistere, miseriaque carere. . . . Sed ipse Aristoteles . . . non ea tantum naturalia . . . esse putavit, quae ex internis principiis tanquam efficientibus causis oriuntur' (p. 62). Cf. c. 6 : 'Mirum est quomodo quisquam dubitare nequeat, an sit homini naturale, quod tam evidenti ratione comprobatur ad primam eius nativitatem debere pertinere' (p. 57).

[13] Dr J. P. van Dooren, *Michael Baius, Zijn leer over de mens* (1958), p. 123 : 'and that by reason of the divine promise'.

[14] Cf. Jacques de Blic, S.J., 'Bulletin de morale' in *MScRel*, 1747, p. 101 : 'When Baius maintained in his lesser writings the thesis of grace *naturae innocenti debita*, the fundamental thought which he expressed in this way was certainly far less the idea of an aspiration of humanity to divine union or of a connaturality of the soul with the divine, than that of a need for the first man—to effect his justification—of the 'caritas Dei diffusa (in corde) per Spiritum sanctum". . . . It is this which for Baius makes necessary, and therefore owing to the complete creature, the logical complement of creation which is grace.'

gius, in St Jerome's phrase, thought that God had wound man up, once and for all, like a clock, and then gone to sleep; Baius' clock needs continually to be rewound. The perfect Pelagian would be the proud man who wishes never to owe anything to anyone. The perfect Baianist, on the other hand, would be the haggling litigant, always pleading poverty and claiming his due. Baius is a Pelagius turned beggar. Pelagianism means pure asceticism, Baianism pure juridicism. Both, each in his own order and his own way, holds a pure naturalism.

Necessarily, together with the supernatural the natural is no less misunderstood. From the philosophical point of view the incoherent, even barbarous nature of such a theory, together with its offensive character from the religious point of view, cannot be hidden. Like deism, its counterpart in the theoretical order, Pelagianism was already in an unstable position between complete recognition of the religious bond and absolute naturalism. By excluding God from human life it came very near to the denial of him or to transferring his attributes to man. The latent naturalism here is no less pronounced, but in addition it implies a radical extrinsicism : human nature, without being open to grace in the sense understood by authentic Christianity, since its end remains proportionate to its demands as a creature, does not possess that interiority without the existence of which there can be no connection with philosophy, since for its natural operation an intrusion from outside is required. Thus it can be said that if the spirit of Baianism will endure as long as man (and actually it has been very rightly discerned in the philosophy of Charles Renouvier, a thinker who had been hardly a student of Baius) at least the condemnation of Baius, as such, in its precise form as planned at the first Vatican Council, would have been principally of archeological interest.

Another doctrine closely related to Baianism is strict traditionalism, with its idea of an external revelation as indispensable to the development of reason. Is not Bonald's teaching concerning the necessity of a first revelation the exact parallel in the order of knowledge to the teaching of Baius concerning the need of supernatural aid in the order of action? Is it not true in both cases that the supernatural exists for nature, and not nature for the supernatural?[15] But traditionalism of this kind, at least in its strict form, no longer tempts anyone today. And what theologian or philosopher would wish, without frankly admitting the supernatural order in its absolute transcendence, to claim as necessary to human integrity gifts which nevertheless 'do not belong to the perfection of man's being'?

Yet there are many who profess admiration for the theologian of Louvain. His work, closely packed in short pithy sentences, displays a strongly systematic tendency. 'Admit his principle and he will seize on you, leading you on and pulling you down with him.' Thus wrote Jean-Baptiste Du Chesne some time ago,[16] recalling what Jansenius had written about Pelagius.[17] Similarly, in the eighteenth century, Abbé de la Chambre declared that Baius 'possessed a good mind; he was acute, methodical and

[15] Just as with Baius the supernatural is degraded by the fact that it is placed at the service of nature, with Bonald revelation is degraded by the fact that its primary object is to provide man with his initial share of natural knowledge; and just as with the former, nature is absorbed by the fact that the supernatural takes its place, so with the latter, reason is impaired by the fact that all autonomous development is refused to it. In both therefore we have a naturalism coupled with an extrinsicism (and not corrected by it). The supernatural is declared necessary to establish man in his complete nature and in the exercise of his strictly human activity; in this is its essential role. See the analyses of Robert Spaemann, *Der Ursprung der Soziologie aus dem Geist der Restauration, Studien über L. G. A. de Bonald* (Munich, 1959), especially pp. 58-62. The parallel could be continued with social traditionalism and its manner of understanding the relations of Church and State. Like the Baianists, the traditionalists came up against Jesuit theologians principally, and substantially blamed them for the same things. Just as Baius blamed them for reviving the semi-Pelagian heresy, one of the leaders (though one of the most moderate) of the traditionalist school in 1856 published a book against them under the title *La Tradition et les semi-pélagiens de la philosophie, ou le semi-rationalisme dévoilé.*

[16] *Op. cit.*, p. 179.

[17] *Augustinus*, vol. 1, *Praefatio in Pelagium*: 'Quemadmodum ansulae catenarum sibi innexae sunt et perplexae, ut qui unam arripuerit, etiam caeteras attrahat, ita in Pelagio tantillum dederis, danda sunt omnia; usque adeo, ut qui unicam anguis illius mortui palpitationem quovis verborum prestigio vel erroris minus perspecti fuco delusus, in sinu foverit, omnem ille veram gratiam extinguere . . . , scandalum crucis evacuare, . . . convincatur.'

hardworking', and even the condemned propositions, far from being 'disjointed', 'form a body of doctrine' which reflects the logical sequence of his thought.[18] Again, in our own times, Fr François-Xavier Jansen mingles admiration with severity : 'In my view, it is the exactness of his reasoning, which one cannot help admiring, that makes Augustinianism, as interpreted by Baius, into heretical doctrine.'[19] And still more recently, Fr Guy de Broglie has said : 'Si res aeque consideratur, fatendum . . . erit necessariam connexionem naturae innocentis cum gratia (si vere admittenda sit) non potuisse cohaerentius, neque lucidius neque sapientius exprimi quam apud Baium factum sit.'[20] Nothing could be truer, provided that the fundamental idea, which emerged above, is granted, si vere admittenda sit. Then all the rest follows quite coherently. In particular, the change from what is called Baius' surpralapsarian optimism to his infralapsarian pessimism seems perfectly logical.[21] His notion of the state of innocence governs his idea of the state following the fall.

Furthermore, positions which rightly seem to us unsound and to some extent lacking in depth, were enough in those days to attract minds weary of the intricacies and poverty to which only too often theological thought had degenerated. Baius' doctrinal simplicity could produce on them the effect of a real liberation, not unlike (if due allowance is made) the celebrated Cartesian cogito of the following century. They appreciated the straightforward treatises, free from the terms and questions of pure Scholasticism. Baius, by his entirely 'pragmatic' point of view, paying heed to the value of the act rather than to the dignity of the agent, might seem also

[18] Traité historique et dogmatique sur la doctrine de Baius et sur l'autorité des bulles des Papes qui l'ont condamnée (2 vols, 1739), vol. 1, pp. 152-3.
[19] Op. cit., p. 198.
[20] 'De gratuitate ordinis supernaturalis ad quem homo elevatus est' in Gregorianum, 29 (1948), pp. 448-9, note. I should have some reservations only on the 'sapientius', since wisdom cannot so easily be dissociated from truth as from the purely formal properties of coherence and lucidity.
[21] I do not therefore share the view of Fr d'Alès, RSR, 1928, pp. 539-40, when he speaks of the 'intense antinomies burdening this fleeting thought, . . . optimism in regard to the state of man before the fall, pessimism in regard to his state after the fall'.

to be in fortunate reaction against an exaggerated realism which actually tended to become materialism. Since the time of St Thomas Aquinas it was not only the idea of 'real distinction' which had become exaggerated. When Baius opposed those theologians who desired to measure merit 'non ex operis integritate, sed ex operantis dignitate',[22] he was probably wrong to accept such a dissociation from which he was to derive, in the opposite sense, an unacceptable doctrine, as we shall see later. But he was not its author. At all events, he had the virtue of opposing, albeit unilaterally, the morally dangerous idea according to which one and the same act, itself unchanged in its spiritual content, could change in value beforehand according to whether or not it was the act of a supernaturalized being. He rightly refused to admit that merit could automatically be derived from a dignity previous to the act, without reference to the inherent value of the act itself.[23] This refusal was similar to that which in the following century brought Pascal into conflict with Fr Sirmond.[24] It amounted almost to the Ockhamist doctrine, by which the saving value is attributed exclusively to the acts themselves, to the detriment of the *habitus*.[25] 'Personae operantis sublimitas in opere bono non auget rationem meriti, nisi quantum auget rationem

[22] *De meritis operum*, bk 2, c. 1 and 2. *Apologia*, in propositionem 42am.

[23] For example, there are the well-known explanations of the infinite cost of the sacrifice of Christ, in which there is no mention of his work of love, but only of 'the infinite dignity of the Victim'.

[24] Cf. the *5e écrit des curés de Paris:* 'And that Jesus Christ himself could have merited the redemption of the world by actions which charity could not have produced in him, as Fr Sirmond says.' But these are only caricatures of the ideas which are given expression, for example, in the wonderful passage by Meister Eckhart : 'Men should not always think so much about what they must *do*, they should think rather of what they must *be*. If only they were good and in accordance with their nature, their works would shine with great clarity. . . .' It is necessary to read a passage like this to feel by contrast the extent to which Baius' meagre thought lacks depth. But it should not be forgotten that the paradoxical summary, 'God loves the soul, not the external work', forms the nineteenth condemned proposition of Eckhart (condemned not as heretical, states John XXII's Bull, but as ill-sounding, or rash or suspect of heresy).

[25] Ockham, *In I Sent.*, dist. 17, qu. 1 and 2. I say merely 'almost', for although he insists on the act Baius does not disregard the role of the habitus : *De peccato originis*, c. 10 and 11 (vol. 1, pp. 10-12).

virtutis et boni.'[26] By this principle, the opposite of what Luther had just laid down,[27] and still more of what Nietzsche was one day to propound,[28] Baius probably tended towards a legalist religion, but at the same time, and we can be grateful to him for it, he blocked one of the sources of Pharisaism.

On the other hand, his thought appears as surprisingly limited and narrow, since it is confined to the bare bones of a subject to which he continually resorts. In this way, as by the content of his teaching, it is utterly different from Augustine's thought, which was wide-ranging, complex and very fruitful. Nothing in Baius recalls Augustine's wide human interests which are to be found even in the explanations of the most complex matters,[29] or that keen awareness of the mysterious depths of nature and grace. Nor is there any trace of those stimulating remarks, the overtones and undertones of which form the charm of the writings of the great doctor. Nor is there anything, as in the genuine Augustinian disciples who flourished in about the twelfth century, of those views on the collective destiny of humanity, of the interest in the pro-

[26] *De meritis operum*, bk 11, title of c. 7 (vol. 1, p. 41). See also the whole *De caritate, iustitia et iustificatione* (pp. 89-152).

[27] *De la liberté du chrétien*, 23 (*Les grands écrits réformateurs*, edited and French trans. by M. Gravier, p. 285): 'It is not works which make man good or bad, but it is man who. . . .' Cf. 4 (p. 257) and 13 (p. 269). Commentary on the Epistle to the Romans (ed. Ficker, p. 14), and so on.

[28] By his distinction between the egoism of the weak soul and the egoism of the noble soul. 'It is thought that there are acts which of their nature are good or bad. . . . But of itself an act is absolutely without value; what is important is to know who does it. The same offence can in one case be a higher privilege and in another a stigma.' Cf. the analysis by Fr de Montcheuil, 'Nietzsche et la critique de l'idéal chrétien' in *Mélanges théologiques*, pp. 163-7.

[29] See, for example, *De civitate Dei*, bk 2, c. 29, on the Roman virtues and on the natural principle of virtue, which awaits from true religion its purification and fulfilment; or bk 10, c. 32, on the 'universalis animae liberandae via'; *De doctrina christiana*, bk 2, n. 28 and 40, etc. Fr Fulbert Cayré has applied himself to throwing light on an aspect of St Augustine which is frequently misunderstood, what may be called his humanism or even his optimism: 'Contemplation et raison d'après saint Augustin' in *Revue de Philosophie*, 1930, p. 381. There is also some information in the works by H. Marrou, *Saint Augustin et la fin de la culture antique* (1930) and J. Wang Tsang Tsé, *Saint Augustin et les vertus des païens* (1938). Cf. G. Friedrich Klenk, 'Augustinus und die *Humanitas christiana*' in *Stimmen der Zeit*, 169 (1961), pp. 169-85.

gress of the City of God, of the wide all-embracing philosophy of history, nor of the mystical aspiration of the soul, the image of the Trinity, which finds its only rest in divine union. More different atmospheres are scarcely imaginable. This is no original genius that we have here, nor have we a true disciple.

Yet how could it happen that so ardent an admirer of St Augustine could in reality be so unfaithful to him? How could so wide a gap have occurred between his thought and his master's? And how could so sincere a Christian and one so attached to the Church fall into so serious a religious error?

The truth is that to understand an author it is not enough merely to read him There is no need to emphasize the fact that in the time of Baius historical criticism was still in its infancy, though just at that time it was making considerable progress with the Centuriators and Bellarmine. Baius himself did not give evidence of any great critical sense since he read 'sixty-nine times' the *Hypognosticon* (which as early as the ninth century had been denounced as spurious by Florus of Lyon)[30] without discovering in it the trace of any other hand besides Augustine's.[31] The real reason is that he fell a victim to his narrowly 'positive' prejudice, a prejudice entirely contrary even to St Augustine's method and particularly harmful when it concerned the study of a doctrine like his. With him especially, more perhaps than with others, it was necessary to make an effort to discern the spirit beneath the letter. In a praiseworthy endeavour to react against the abuses of the dialectical method, Baius came to share the illusion common at that time of those theologians whom the farseeing Dominic Soto described in these terms: 'Philosophiam abiiciunt, et . . .

---

[30] *Liber adversus Ioannem Scottum*, c. 18: '. . . quem libellum non esse eiusdem sancti Augustini et stylus ipse demonstrat, et sensus' (*P.L.*, 119, 238D). Cf. *De libero arbitrio*, c.11 (vol. 1, p. 86).

[31] On this work in very mediocre Latin (it contains solecisms like 'neminem nocuit nisi ipsum') which was for long attributed to St Augustine, see *P.L.*, 45. Bellarmine, even when teaching at Louvain, had been more clearsighted: *Dissertatio de praedestinatione*, n. 4 (Le Bachelet, *Auctarium Bellarminianum*, p. 42). The same cannot be said of Diego Alvarez, O.P., in his censure against Lessius (cf. Le Bachelet, *Prédestination et grâce efficace*, vol. 2, p. 152).

arbitrantur absque theseo per se posse, cum Sanctorum Patrum, tum etiam Sacrae Paginae adire volumina.'[32] In theology, as in religion itself, such a course if followed literally is illusory. Its systematic and exclusive application can only kill the spirit which brought it to birth. Instead of promoting a sound return to origins of the kind then shortly to be recommended by Maldonatus, it was at the bottom of all the unsound novelties of archaism. The kind of study by a change from the objective to the subjective meaning, then coming to be known as 'positive theology',[33] was certainly necessary, but far from being all-sufficient, at the outset it did not suffice even for itself. In this case Baius shared the illusion of a certain number of humanists and reformers.[34] In his endeavour 'to break with the system of Scholastic ideas'[35] he was only half successful. Unknowingly he was about to make use of a hybrid method.[36] On the pretext of avoiding the errors of his times he refused consciously to philosophize and did so unconsciously and in the worst possible fashion, and no one was more dependent on his own century. Like Luther, whose wide ranging mind he did not possess and of whom he appears to have taken little count, he laid himself open all the more to be led astray by certain contemporary ideas while he claimed to be inspired only

[32] *De natura et gratia*, bk 1, praefatio, p. 2 (Antwerp, 1550). Soto added, addressing the Fathers of the Council of Trent: 'Cui profecto malo nisi obviam publiciter occurratis, . . . totum brevi christianum orbem errores ebullire dolebimus.' Speculative theology, he concluded, is not to be abandoned but reformed.

[33] Positive theology was at first that of the 'positive doctors' who were principally the Fathers of the Church, the theology therefore before 'Scholastic' theology. It is thus that St Ignatius speaks of the 'positivi ac sancti doctores', whom he distinguishes from the 'recentiores', the 'doctores scolastici'. Cf. H. de Lubac, *Corpus Mysticum*, 2nd ed. (1949), pp. 365-76; R. Guelluy, *RHE*, 37 (1941), pp. 128-44.

In many cases the passage from one meaning to the other is unclear (as in certain uses of the word 'history'); thus, Jansenius, *Augustinus*, vol. 2, p. 10 BC, Liber proemialis, c. 9.

[34] H. M. Feret, 'Baius' in *Catholicisme*, vol. 1, col. 1174.

[35] G. P. van Dooren, *Michael Baius* (1958), p. 125.

[36] It was as a result of the same biassed method that certain humanists blamed St Augustine for being too much of a 'metaphysician'. Melanchthon too shared this illusion, as is shown by his inaugural address at the University of Wittenberg in 1518.

by the past. Luther did not understand St Paul, nor did Baius really understand St Augustine. Through Baius the Augustinian theory of merit without grace was to be falsified in the same way that through Luther the Pauline theory of faith without works came to be falsified.

Thus it was that speaking with Augustine about 'nature' and believing that he agreed with him, Baius understood this nature in an entirely different sense. There is no reason to dispute with him over his use of 'natura' and 'naturalis' following a very ancient tradition when 'the supernatural' is already employed; it could only be a question of words. But rejecting as derived from pagan philosophy the Scholastic definition of 'natura', he yet did not, as he imagined, return to the ancient idea; he did not understand this created nature as wholly steeped in and supported by the loving action of the Creator. Without his realizing it, Aristotle and Scholasticism had travelled the same road. It was impossible for him to forgo their legacy. It was the same with the correlative idea of 'grace' as with the notion of 'merit'. We need look no further than the theology of Duns Scotus, of William of Ockham, the interaction of one on the other, perhaps the new Stoicism, in short to the whole complex situation governed by a long history. It is these which enable us to understand the juridical meaning given to these terms in Baius. 'Whether one likes it or not it is impossible to avoid being influenced by the work of preceding generations.'[37] He owes much to these theologians although he scorns them, but he does not follow them right to the end. He does not hold with them, or at least not to the same extent, the idea of a sovereignly independent God—an idea which was on occasion the basis of the grandeur of their thought. They succeeded in preserving it through the concept—even if it is seen merely as a 'Scholastic subtlety'—of 'potentia absoluta'. He was no longer able to say with Ockham: 'Deus nulli debitor est quocum-

---

[37] Jean Orcibal, 'Dom Gabriel Gerberon' in *Revue d'histoire de l'Église de France*, 43 (1957), p. 221. Fr Anthony Levi makes a similar remark about Jansenius: 'La psychologie des facultés au XVIIe siècle' in *L'Homme devant Dieu* (1964), vol. 2, pp. 298-9.

que modo.'[38] Another influence outweighed theirs, that of Peter of Auriole,[39] which was at its greatest in the works of Gabriel Biel. But here again, the latter, while declaring that he followed Ockham's teaching 'frequentius', succeeded in maintaining the balance between extreme positions by means of the same distinction of 'potentia Dei absoluta' and the 'potentia ordinata'.[40] Baius upset this balance. The Pelagianism not long since denounced with some exaggeration by Gregory of Rimini as found in the nominalist doctors,[41] was now taken over by Baius. Far more than they, he really wished to introduce into the very idea of the relationships between the Creator and his creature the idea of a commutative justice. With Baius then we are at once far removed from the fifth century, further indeed than those he blames for departing from it. More especially we are far removed from the St Augustine of history as well as from the Augustine of Catholic tradition.

With Augustine and Catholic tradition there was still to be mention of 'vita aeterna', 'regnum caelorum', 'adoptio filiorum Dei', 'inhabitatio Spiritus sancti', and 'caritas Dei diffusa in cordibus',[42] and so on. But these expressions, which in Christian parlance 'clearly signified a deifying grace',[43] are obviously no longer so understood. They are no more than formulas devoid of meaning. Otherwise, how would it be possible at the same time to assert the presence of the Holy Spirit in human nature and

[38] *In I Sent,* dist. 41, qu. 1; dist. 17, qu. 1; Quodl. 6, qu. 1. Paul Vignaux was able to write in *Justification et prédestination au XIVe siècle,* p. 122: 'Limitless gratuity of divine action: everything that God does, he gives, he does not owe it. Ockham gives many arguments which astonish by the savagery of their logic: has he not placed his dialectician's fearlessness at the service of divine freedom?'

[39] For Peter of Auriole, cf. Paul Vignaux, *op. cit.,* pp. 54-7.

[40] Cf. Heiko Augustinus Oberman, *The Harvest of Medieval Theology, Gabriel Biel and Late Medieval Nominalism* (Cambridge, Mass, 1963), pp. 30-56.

[41] Biel took into account Ockham's criticism and even that of Gregory of Rimini: cf. Paul Vignaux, *Luther commentateur des Sentences,* pp. 51-3.

[42] Thus *De caritate,* c. 2 and 5 (pp. 90, 91, 94). *De peccato originis,* c. 3 (p. 4).

[43] Paul Dumont, S.J., 'Le surnaturel dans la théologie de saint Augustin' in *RSR,* 11 (1931), p. 533.

refuse to acknowledge a raising up of this nature in which the Spirit dwells? How could sharing in the sonship of the Word be the cause, as he laid down, merely of acts of wholly human merit? How could the act of obedience which every creature owes to his maker have the effect by its own power of bringing the creature right into the life of God? Under the combined influences already mentioned in his speculation Baius lost all understanding of the mystery of grace. Henceforth he might continue to use the traditional expressions; he could even protest against the 'innovations' of other theologians; but he was no longer in a position to discover the primitive idea behind the words. Not one line in the whole of his work has the same ring about it as many a page of St Augustine on the soul raised up by the divine presence. It is not merely a difference of atmosphere, it is one of doctrine. Lastly, without his realizing it, Baius was betrayed by his very vocabulary; he the uncompromising Augustinian went so far as to speak of the 'merit of perseverance', of that perseverance right up to the end in which his master Augustine sang the praises of the grace above all graces, 'gratia pro gratia', the unmerited 'gift' above all others.

In passing, we may draw attention to one of the points where Baius, despite his apparent fidelity to Augustine, is really unfaithful to the doctor's thought. In accordance with a tendency of his century, which on certain points Calvinism pushed to extremes—there have been many other instances of it in the history of the Church—Baius always argued as if the Old Testament had given us definitive light on the primitive state of man and his destiny. A verse from Genesis and another from Ecclesiasticus were enough for him;[44] with these two texts, which he repeats *ad nauseam,* he had found the answer to the puzzle. The New Testament is called upon neither to amend them nor complete them; it is not regarded as providing any new light on the relationship which is to unite man to God. For example, the 'mysterious plan' mentioned by St Paul at length with such enthusiasm, could not

---

[44] Ecclus 15:14; Gen. 2:17. *De meritis operum,* bk 1, c. 3. *Apologia S. Pontifici Pio V,* in prop. 2am et 4am, etc (vol. 1, p. 28; vol. 2, p. 81).

on this view be the secret of the destiny to which we are called by God; it has nothing to do with the end but only with the means. The 'spiritus adoptionis' of the Epistle to the Romans, the 'consortium divinae naturae' of the Second Epistle of St Peter, are only sorts of remedies granted by divine mercy to restore the nature of Adam and enable it thus to elicit its acts of obedience which will merit its reward. It is clear, then, that according to this idea Christ is only a 'restorer'. As his role is much reduced so his revelation is very much restricted. It is within the setting of the Old Testament, closed for ever, that his work is to be inserted. In short, Baius misunderstood the innovation that Christ represented. There is an apparent fidelity to St Augustine: in the latter's writing there are a great number of statements in which the two Testaments are set side by side and, so to say, on the same level, and in which the faith of the patriarchs and prophets is declared to be the same as that of Christ's apostles and disciples. Yet in fact there is infidelity: for Augustine's method was the precise opposite to that of Baius. Far from reducing the New Testament to the level of the Old, it was the Old Testament which in the passages in question he raised to the level of the New. He did not then look on it as the Jewish scriptures, but regarded it as retrospectively transfigured by the light of the Gospel. For Augustine the flower of the people of Israel already shared, in mystery, in the spirit of Christianity: 'in Veteri Testamento, de Novo'. Baius' Christian, on the contrary, was still sharing in the Jewish spirit.

Nothing shows more clearly the contrast between the two than the doctrine of Baius on perseverance. 'Nemo salvus fiet nisi merito perseverantiae':[45] Baius saves us, on a final analysis, just as if Adam had remained without sin, and as if by our own merits. The nickname given him by Louis Bail, 'the Pelagius of the earthly paradise',[46] does not therefore reveal the whole extent of

[45] *De meritis operum*, 1, II, c. 6. *Apologia*, in prop. 2am (vol. 1, pp. 40-1; vol. 2, pp. 80-1).

[46] *De beneficio crucis* (1653). In addition Ripalda, *Adversus Baium*, Disput. 3, sect. 1: 'Quasi Pelagii sententia in statu naturae integrae vera fuit, et solum damnata et falsa in statu naturae lapsae.' Cf. above, pp. xiv-xv.

his error. Of course, Baius admits that in our sinful world God's saving intervention is henceforth wholly gratuitous, 'indebita'. But since what constitutes this act in his view is, as we have seen, the mere fact of obedience to the law, it follows that its reward is heavenly glory and that the help and even the presence of the Holy Spirit, obtained through Christ's redemption, are solely its condition or at the most solely its instrument: 'Quemadmodum avis, fractis alis, volare non potest, ita nec homo destitutus Spiritu Sancto bene operari potest.'[47] Although this help and presence are now indispensable to enable the human subject to merit, they have no part in the substance of the meritorious act. They confer on it no excellence, no higher dignity. In other words, although grace is necessary for merit, it is not its intrinsic condition.[48] There is the further consequence that if an action in conformity with the law is done by a man before the remission of his sins, this action will not cease to be meritorious, a merit 'de condigno' on the same grounds as an action of the justified. To assert the contrary, notes Baius, would be to repeat the error of Julian of Eclanum.[49] These indeed are the very points on which Baius' colleague and opponent, Ravestein of Tielt, censures him in the letter of denunciation sent to the Catholic king in 1564.[50]

[47] 'Narratio brevis eorum verborum quae Lovanii in scholis theologorum intercesserunt inter magistrum nostrum Michaelem de Bay et Cornelium Gaudanum die 12 novembris anni 1580' (Roca, p. 475).

[48] Cf. H. M. Féret. *loc. cit.*, col. 1176.

[49] *De meritis operum*, bk 2, c. 4 (bk 1, c. 39). *De caritate*, bk 1, c. 7: 'Quod is animi motus, qui caritas dicitur, remissionem peccatorum praecedere possit' (pp. 96-100). Cf. the ninth proposition condemned as *plane haeretica* by the Sorbonne in 1560: 'Haereticus et schismaticus, et homo non pene infidelis, meretur quandoque de condigno vitam aeternam.'

[50] 'Baius has just published a paper on the merit of good works, in which orthodox theologians are sorry and pained to see that he undermines the foundations of the common teaching, according to which the good works of the righteous only merit eternal life by a merit *de condigno* in so far as they are the works not only of free will but of Jesus Christ himself and the Holy Spirit, who dwells in them, makes them holy, and raises them above nature. He also holds . . . that the good actions of those who are not yet justified which precede the forgiveness of sins can really merit eternal life, for the reason that they are in accordance with the law of God' (Letter to Fr Laurent Villavicentio, of the Hermits of St Augustine, Du Chesne, *op. cit.*, p. 63). Cf. *Histoire ecclésiastique* (continuation of Fleury), vol. 33, pp. 149-50 and 210.

However gratuitous the gift of God becomes after the fall, it is thus always reduced to the level of the natural. In paradise, the presence of the Holy Spirit was already necessary;[51] now this presence, no less necessary, is granted by pure grace; but neither now nor at the time of the earthly paradise, all things considered, does the reward go beyond our own human merit. Our merits are not gifts, not even the 'merit of perseverance'. As a result, in rewarding our merits God does not reward his gifts. Once again the most characteristic statements of Augustinianism have been turned upside down. Of course, St Augustine also said the mercy with which the just man will be judged, unlike the mercy which bestowed the first grace, will in some sort be the reward of his good works so that in this way eternal life will be granted to his merits by a just judgment:[52] but he said at the same time that such merits are the very fruit of grace and that good works possess a divine value of their own because they are not only conditioned but produced by grace. It was no play on the word grace: 'gratia vero, nisi gratis est, gratia non est'.[53] In short, what for St Augustine was true of Adam is also true of us—'sine gratia nec tunc ullum meritum esse potuisset'[54]—for Baius it is not truer of us than of Adam. The reversal is complete.

Augustine knew from experience what man is and what sin is,

[51] *De prima hominis iustitia*, bk 1, c. 1 : 'Quod primi hominis rectitudo non fuerit sine inhabitante Spiritu sancto' (vol. 1. p. 49).

[52] *Enchiridion*, c. 107: 'Vitam aeternam, quae certe (etiam nunc) merces est bonorum operum.' *De correptione et gratia*, n. 41: 'Tunc pro bonorum operum meritis iusto iudicio etiam ipsa misericordia tribuetur.'

[53] *De correptione et gratia, ibid.*: 'Confitendum est, ideo gratiam vitam aeternam vocari, quia de his meritis redditur, quae gratia contulit homini.' *De diversis quaestionibus ad Simplicianum*, bk 1, n. 3: 'Percipientis vero gratiam consequenter sunt bona opera . . . quae gratia pariantur.'

[54] *Enchiridion*, c. 106 and 107. These passages are concerned with the 'grace of the Creator', but this in Augustine's view is grace in the strict sense of the word; he does not confuse it with the 'grace of creation', which is only the gift of nature, although this is continually and freely renewed. He knows that this last is only called grace by a wrong use of the term: *Epist*. 178 ad Innocentium; *De correptione et gratia*, n. 32. The completeness of Adam's nature, which was already 'magna Dei gratia' (*Contra Iulianum*, 1, 4, *in fine*) was insufficient without further grace. *Epist*. 106: 'Natura humana, si in illa integritate in qua condita erat permaneret, nullo modo seipsam creatore suo non adiuvante servaret.'

but that was not the only reason that he understood the necessity of grace. His theology is not wholly 'infralapsarian'. He also realized the great gulf in any circumstances between the creature and the Creator, and the madness of the creature's dream, inspired by the Creator, to raise himself up to him for everlasting union. And in the revelation of Jesus Christ what he could see was principally the declaration that this mad dream could become a reality because it corresponded to the entirely gratuitous plan governing creation.[55] Nothing of all this seems to have provoked an echo in the solid but narrow head of Michel de Bay. It was a whole world that was closed to him. The smallest glimpse of this world, in which St Augustine's soul flourished as in the atmosphere natural to it, would have revealed to him both the pettiness and the irreligious nature of his system.

He rejected any idea of a 'supernaturale quoad essentiam', and that, as Fr X. Le Bachelet has clearly shown,[56] was his fundamental error. When he comes to speak of the 'novitas vitae' it is never by allusion to a sanctifying grace revivifying the whole being to its very depths; by it he means only the 'iustitia legis', obedience to the law by one who hitherto had disobeyed it,[57] in other words, the 'opera virtutum'.[58] Among the propositions condemned by St Pius V the twenty-first runs as follows: 'Humanae naturae sublimatio et exaltatio in consortium divinae naturae debita fuit integritati primae conditionis, et proinde naturalis dicenda est, et non supernaturalis.' This proposition, already formulated and noted as 'heretical' by the first censure of the theological faculty of Alcala,[59] has the advantage of bringing out clearly the

[55] Cf. Étienne Gilson, *Philosophie et incarnation selon saint Augustin* (Montreal, 1947).

[56] 'Baius' in *DTC*, vol. 11, col. 110.

[57] *De iustitia*, c. 3: 'iustitiam huius vitae duabus constare partibus, remissione videlicet peccatorum . . . et vitae novitate; quae posterior pars in Scripturis sacris iustitia legis nuncupatur' (p. 104).

[58] *De iustitia*, c. 4 (p. 105). *De iustificatione*, c. 8 (p. 152).

[59] 31 March 1565: the faculty of Salamanca, on 3 August 1565, reproduced it, marking it merely as 'erroneous' (Miguel Roca, *Documentos inéditos en torno a Miguel Bayo*, 1560-82, pp. 323 and 335; *Anthologia Annua*, n. 1, Iglesia Nacional Española, Rome, 1953). Cf. E. van Eijl, 'Les censures des universités d'Alcala et de Salamanque et la censure du pape Pie V contre Michel Baius (1565-7)' in *RHE*, 48 (1953), pp. 719-76.

absurdity of the doctrine. But its terms were not those written by Baius. As Fr Juan Alfaro has explained, if it was desired to formulate it in his own terminology and according to the logic of his system, it should have been expressed differently.[60] Although Baius actually uses the word 'exaltatio' he does so not to adopt the idea that it signifies, but expressly to reject it. This is clear from the twenty-sixth proposition which is a textual reproduction of the title of chapter 6 of his *De prima hominis justitia*. The title of the chapter runs: 'Integritas non fuit indebita humanae naturae exaltatio, sed naturalis eius conditio.'[61] Thus in one of his Apologiae he was to complain that his text had been changed for the purpose, he said, of making his teaching hateful.[62] (It is known of course that the compilation submitted to the pope was not composed from the works of Baius alone, but also from those of John Hessels, his close friend and principal follower, of various Franciscans, and also from the lecture notes and notes of oral debates; the bull mentions neither names of authors nor titles of books.) In addition, he could never have written the twenty-first proposition in those terms. Its words clashed too obviously to be taken together, and Baius could never have brought himself to use them in this way, however much he was dominated by his idea of 'nature'. The whole idea would finally have given way before his faith, whose demands in the contrary sense would at last have

[60] 'Sobrenatural y pecado original en Bayo' in *Revista Española de Teologia*, 12 (1952), p. 3.

[61] Cf. p. 55. It is therefore incorrect to summarize the teaching of Baius as follows, though it is so summarized in *Analyse de l'Augustin de Jansénius* and many other authors: 'Baius teaches that God could not fail to raise the angel and the first man to a supernatural state; that this raising was a necessary consequence of their creation' (p. 44).

[62] *Michaelis Baii . . . Apologia S.P. Pio V* (1569): 'Collector more suo sententiam hanc longe aliis verbis, alioque sensu expressit, quam in libello continetur: ibi enim tantum dicitur, quod primae creationis integritas, cuius absentia est malum, non fuerit indebita humanae naturae exaltatio, sed naturalis eius conditio. Ipse vero Collector de divinae naturae consortio adiunxit, quae voluit, ut rem odiosam faceret. . . . Non enim dixi (quod me etiam dixisse calumniatur) humanae naturae sublimationem esse dicendam naturalem, et non supernaturalem . . .' (*Baiana*, p. 92). The propositions in question, numbers 21-4, are aimed at the teaching of *De prima hominis iustitia*, though they do not reproduce the exact text. See Le Bachelet, *loc. cit.*, col. 60.

been clearly perceived. Or at least to satisfy both, Baius, whose honesty is above suspicion, would have done the same as most others : he would have sacrificed logic, and faith which, according to a phrase of Crétineau-Joly, prevailed over pride in his heart and would have prevailed over error in his mind.[63] Yet it is only too certain that his previous refusal to admit an 'exaltatio' of human nature, a refusal which, in regard to both the term and its meaning, set him in opposition to all the great doctors,[64] by the same token doomed him to incomprehension of the essential gratuitousness of the gift of God. He asked ingenuously for this gratuitousness to be demonstrated, 'solida ratione, et non tantum scholastica traditione'.[65] Actually, on the basis of his negative assumption it was impossible. But by this negative assumption he shut himself off not only from a scholastic tradition, but even from the tradition of the Church.

It has been said, and I think rightly, that 'what makes the propositions of Baius erroneous is their systematic meaning in the context of his teaching'.[66] Certainly this series of sixty-nine propositions does not constitute a synthesis; one or other of them, like

[63] On the views of Baius, several new points are to be found in the documents published in 1953 by Miguel Roca, loc. cit., for example, pp. 417-22, letter from Morillon to Granvelle, Brussels, 16 October 1675. From the same author also : Génesis histórica de la bula 'Ex omnibus afflictionibus' (Madrid, 1956).
[64] See for example St Bonaventure, In II Sent., dist. 29, art. 1, qu. 1 : 'Secundum vero genus acceptationis non potest non esse gratuitum, tum propter gratuitam Dei condescensionem, tum propter creaturae exaltationem ultra terminos sive status naturae. . . . Creaturae etiam sublimatio in tali acceptatione, ultra statum naturae repertitur. . . .' And dist. 27, art. 1, qu. 3 : '. . . humanam exaltationem, ex qua homo ea quae Dei sunt excellenter participat. . . . Homo per illam inhabitationem sublimatur et ad magna conscendit.' See also the Summa of Alexander of Hales, p. 11, qu. 91. membr. 1, art. 3, 1, resol. : 'Haec autem sublimatio creaturae rationalis est supra naturale complementum. . . .'
[65] Apologia S.P. Pio V (Baiana, p. 92). Cf. the twelfth proposition condemned by the new censure of the faculty of Alcala (20 June 1567) as blasphemous and erroneous : 'Deus non potuisset ab initio hominem creare sine Spiritu sancto et charismatibus Spiritus sancti.' I have not been able to find these words in the De peccato originis from where the censure alleges they were taken; but they undeniably express Baius' ideas.
[66] Jansen, op. cit., p. 198. Cf. E. Amann, 'Semi-Pélagiens' in DTC, vol. 14, col. 1847.

21

the example that we have just seen, even requires a sort of translation for it to be included. Baius himself protested on several occasions: to Morillon (Granvelle's vicar-general) in 1568,[67] to Pius V in 1569,[68] to the bishops and to the University of Louvain in 1570,[69] and so on. And it was not always mere cavilling; more than once his protests were justified.[70] Nevertheless, as a whole, the propositions were chosen sensibly. Often they reproduce the actual titles given by Baius to his chapters; many of them give expression not to approximations or remote consequences but to the fundamental principles of his teaching. In particular, it was not without reason that the first twenty propositions were taken from the *De meritis operum*. This small work is not the first in date and it is as short as the others. By itself it is insufficient to explain the whole genesis of the system. Logically, a general explanation should not be begun with this work but with *De prima hominis iustitia*. Nevertheless, it reveals the governing idea of its author. Its owner possesses, so to say, the whole of Baius, obviously not because it contains all his teaching, but because it reveals his mind. And to read it is to be reassured. Although on almost every page of this candid booklet, where we encounter the 'curia caelestis' organized according to strict justice like a 'respublica bene

[67] Letter from Morillon to Granvelle, 20 June 1568: 'I found him still angrier this time, . . . complaining . . . that the articles have been badly assembled, . . . and that none of those in the Bull are his.' Morillon continues: 'I answered Bay that he was very wrong to complain that the Bull contains no articles that are his, since that was in his favour, showing that the Bull was not made for him alone, for he is also not mentioned in it' (*Baiana*, p. 71). Cf. the previous letter from the same to the same of 2 January (Roca, pp. 367-8).

[68] *Apologia brevis*: in sententiam 52am: 'Collector valde dormitavit'. *Baiana*, p. 136, in sent. 20am: 'Collector male refert' (p. 91). There is a further complaint by Baius, protesting the sincerity of his submission: to Granvelle, 13 October, 1575 (M. Roca, p. 415).

[69] 'This Bull contains about forty propositions which never even occurred to my mind.' Baius' supporters continued to protest; cf. *Baiana*, p. 233: 'Ex quibus nemo non intelligere valet, quanta fuerit eorum qui huiusmodi sententias collegerunt . . . , adversus M. Baium aemulatio, audacia, ac nequitia, imo et erga Sanctam Sedem irreverentia. . . .'

[70] Cf. Ed. van Eijl, 'L' Interprétation de la bulle de Pie V portant condamnation de Baius' in *RHE*, 50 (1955), pp. 499-542. Jean Orcibal, 'De Baius à Jansénius: le *"Comma" Pianum*' in *RevScRel*, 36 (1962), pp. 115-39; Boissard, *ibid.*, pp. 140-53.

constituta',[71] Augustinian formulas are repeated, the spirit of
Augustine is manifestly absent. And so to avoid the danger of
Baianism, there is no further temptation to part company with
St Augustine. We can quite safely pronounce against Baius the
verdict pronounced in the twelfth century against Gerland,
another unfortunate Augustinian, by his opponent Hugh Metel:
'Confidis in verbis Augustini: ne confidas. Non est tecum. Erras
tota via. Asseris quod ille asseruit, sed non sentis quod ille sensit.
Ut video, rodis crustam, sed non tangis micam. Auctoritati Augustini niteris, sed deciperis. Augustinum enim quem tibi parasti
advocatum, si bene investigaveris, reperies tibi contrarium.'[72]

A few examples, bringing out certain of the 'deceptions' of
Baius, will be ample confirmation of this verdict. On the three
points of doctrine—formation of the soul by the Holy Spirit, the
hypothesis of an entirely natural merit, and his assimilation of
'free' with 'voluntary'—we shall catch him red-handed.

At first sight the concept of 'natura integra' seems to correspond fairly closely in Baius to St Augustine's idea of 'mens formata'. The soul, according to St Augustine, cannot be fully
'formed' without God's justifying action: 'in ipsa vita nostram
mentem iustificando formare non potest nisi Deus'.[73] Just as it is
not the body that causes the body to live, but a principle that is
higher than the body, so it is not the soul which causes the soul
to live but a principle superior to the soul.[74] In other words, the
human soul is not completed until it has received the 'forma
filiorum Dei'; it is not really 'formed' until it has become 'dei-
form'. But St Augustine is far from denying that, before reaching
this stage, the soul is already complete, in a certain sense. It is
already living, although its life is without form before becoming
the life of 'wisdom and blessedness'; it is 'life' before becoming

[71] Bk 1, c. 2 (vol. 1, p. 26).
[72] *Epistula quarta ad Gerlandum de sanctissimo Eucharistiae sacramento* (*P.L.*, 188, 1273-4).
[73] *De Trinitate* (Bibl. aug. 16; cf. pp. 576-8, note by P. Agaësse).
[74] *Confessions*, bk 10, c. 6 and 20. *De civitate Dei*, bk 19, c. 25 and 26. *In Ioannem*, tract. 23, n. 5.

'light'. Cut off from any influx of grace, by its natural properties and by its very being, at least inchoately, it is the image of God. Even were it to be positively turned away from the Word, living a 'foolish and wretched life', this image of God would be deformed, effaced, but not wholly destroyed. At all events, by reason of his rather loose terminology[75] it seems that for a correct interpretation of St Augustine we must distinguish, at least in the abstract, a twofold degree of 'formation' of the soul : a first degree to be called the natural or essential formation, and a second degree, the supernatural or spiritual formation.[76] The first, which in relation to the second is only 'informitas' and 'imperfectio', corresponds to the 'exordium' and 'creatio'; the second corresponds to the 'conversio' of the creature which becomes perfect by its adherence to the creator. Thus, when St Augustine tells us that the soul is not self-sufficient the assertion does not mean that for the living of its own created life it needs to have recourse to powers outside itself, but that, without being able to do so, it tends to self-transcendence in order to live a higher life, a life which is not solely its own.

Baius overlooked these distinctions. In his view human nature can only be whole, complete in its essence, through the Holy Spirit. Wishing to accept only the second degree of the 'formation' of the soul, in actual fact he understood it after the manner of the first. Unaware that he is misusing the language of some of the Fathers, he places 'the natural dignity of man' in this second degree.[77] This creates an imbroglio which Scheeben attempted to disentangle :

Baius claims that in man there is no image of God that is natural by being derived from the principles of nature,

[75] The principal explanations regarding the creature 'without form' and 'formed' are given by St Augustine in *De Genesi ad litteram*, bk 1, n. 9-32 (cf. bk 8, n. 23-7) and more shortly in the *Confessions*, bk 13, n. 2-6. See also *Enchiridion*, c. 51. According to Augustine's ideas the notion of 'form' is analogical (cf. C. Couturier in *Rech. de Philosophie*, 1, p. 68).

[76] E. Gilson, *Introduction à l'étude de saint Augustin*, pp. 161-2. Cf. Sestili, *De naturali intelligentis animae capacitate atque appetitu intuendi divinam essentiam* (1896), pp. 81-2. On the *anima formata* according to St Thomas: *Prima*, qu. 106, art. 1, ad 3um; *De veritate*, qu. 2, art. 1, ad 15um.

[77] *De prima hominis iustitia*, bk 1, c. 1 (vol. 1, p. 52); cf. c. 2.

and so he denies that image based on the nature of man which we call natural. It is as if he said that our soul is not spiritual in its essence, but only 'psychic', in the Gnostic meaning. But since for it to be complete and perfect there must be in man's nature a certain likeness to God, Baius calls 'natural' what in this sense is in reality 'supernatural'. By this means alone he ensures not that what is already formed is raised to a higher form, but that what has no form receives one by grace.[78]

St Augustine revealed the completion of nature in its being made supernatural. Baius, on the other hand, reduces the supernatural to the natural. He transforms a spiritual doctrine into an ontological thesis. It is true no doubt that Augustine's teaching has ontological implications, but Baius' ontology, which is entirely physical, has no spiritual implications. The basis of Augustine's thought is mystical, that of Baius is naturalist. The formulas are often similar, the difference being principally one of viewpoint and tendency. But this is often the case with fundamental disagreements. When St Gregory writes 'Anima in corpore vita est carnis, Deus vero vita est animarum',[79] and when St John of the Cross says in his turn 'The lack of God, who is the death of the soul . . . since he alone is my life, may he give me my life',[80] they are faithfully repeating St Augustine because the attitude of mind is the same. They raise man above his own nature by first abasing him humbly before God. Baius' approach is the direct opposite: he makes use of the Holy Spirit for the sake of nature; it is to establish this nature in itself that he calls for the intervention, informing us, moreover, that if he could he would willingly do

[78] Casinius, *Qu'est-ce que l'homme?*, introduction by Scheeben (French trans. by Cros, 1864, p. 27).

[79] *In Ezechielem*, bk 2, hom. 5, n. 9. Gregory adds: 'Si igitur tantae est magnitudinis ut comprehendi non possit vita vivificata, quis intellectu comprehendere valeat quantae maiestatis sit Vita vivificans?' (*P.L.*, 74, 990). Cf. *In septem psalmos paenitentiae*: 'Anima, sanctae Trinitatis fide formata' (*P.L.*, 79, 551).

[80] *Spiritual Canticle*, stanza 2 (English trans. *The Complete Works of St John of the Cross* translated by E. Allison Peers (London, 1943), vol. 2, pp. 40 and 42).

without it. The gifts received by Adam he wants to become his property; it was for the purpose of being a 'living soul' that Adam, at his very creation, received his Holy Spirit.[81] Man, according to Baius, thus claims to make use of God to develop and perfect his own nature; once he has done so, he remains man, just as he was beforehand. A lion does not cease to be a lion because it has eaten human prey. But one who, on an impulse of unselfish generosity, from the very depths of his being gives himself to God finds his completion in God. The first, according to Baius, on the supposition that the Holy Spirit is willing to come and quicken him, would lay hold of this divine principle only to maintain natural life within himself; the other has actually entered into supernatural life.

It is all very well for Baius' man to acknowledge that he is not self-sufficient; this is not humility, it is merely further arrogance on his part since he demands that the Spirit of God himself should come to bestow on him his completeness ('integritas'). But at the same time this is a base for ambition, for by this supernatural means only a natural end is intended, just as vision is the natural function of the eye.[82] Such a man is in the same category as those doubly misguided men stigmatized by Ruysbroeck 'who desire to achieve blessedness within the limitations of their own nature'.[83] Deliberately he is enclosed within himself. It will be noticed that

[81] *De prima hominis iustitia*, c. 2 (vol. 1, pp. 52-3): 'God,' said a Jansenist author of the eighteenth century in the same frame of mind, 'could not make a perfect body without all its parts; he could not make an intellectual creature without giving it his grace' (*Abrégé de la Sainte Bible en forme de questions et de réponses familières*, by Dom Robert Guénard, of the Congregation of St Maur, 3rd ed., Rouen, 1711). And Swerts, explaining the teaching of Baius: 'primae integritatis partes, ipsam naturam in suo esse constituentes' (Berti, vol. 8, p. 382).

[82] *Apologia S.P. Pio V*, in prop. 21am: 'sicut visus diceretur supernaturalis in illis, quibus divina virtute per miraculum esset restitutus' (vol. 1, p. 92). Actually the comparison is St Augustine's (*De gestis Pelagii*, c. 3, etc), but it does not refer to the same point.

[83] *The Book of the Highest Truth*, c. 4. The error of the Beghards here criticized by Ruysbroeck was however quite different in its actual tenor. Cf. the third proposition condemned by the Council of Vienne in the second Clementine, bk 5, tit. 3, *De haereticis*, c. 2. The judgments of theologians on Baius' naturalism are to be found collected in Berti, *Augustinianum systema de gratia . . . vindicatum*, dissertatio 2a, c. 1, paragr. 1.

with Baius there is scarcely ever any question of the beatific vision, he is not interested in this order of things. Once again, if he denies so obstinately the primary gratuitousness of the supernatural order and is very surprised that all do not share his view, it is because more radically he denies the reality itself. Belleli was not very wrong, despite the indignant protest with which Saléon received his remarks, when he said in effect that while St Augustine rejected the idea of a state of pure nature, Baius, on the contrary, recognized no other.[84] Sylvester Maurus had already made a similar remark about Jansenius.[85] M. Fernand Litt likewise points out that if 'for Baius there is very little separating nature from what forms for us the supernatural order, . . . such an idea could just as well be explained by too modest an idea of the order of grace as by too optimistic an idea of the order of nature'.[86] It is time now to reverse the judgment of certain historians whose views were summarized at the beginning of this chapter. Baius, far from declaring 'pure nature' impossible—if by this is understood not only a being created without exemption from conscupiscence or any other 'preternatural' gift, but a being whose end is strictly natural[87]—in reality declared it to be the only one possible.

[84] Berti in fact defended Belleli against Saléon with some alacrity (*De disciplinis theologicis*, vol. 8, p. 422). But it should be acknowledged that Belleli and his followers were apt to accuse Baius in order to be more distinctly separated from him. See below, chapter 9.

[85] *Opus theologicum*, vol. 2, bk 6, tract. 7, qu. 44 (Rome, 1687): 'Ostenditur Iansenium solum voce tenus negasse possibilitatem purae naturae, re autem ipsa concessisse puram naturam fuisse de facto in Adamo et in angelis.'

[86] *Op. cit.*, p. 16.

[87] These two meanings of the expression *pura natura* gave rise to two problems which are frequently solved by reference to each other and which ought to be carefully distinguished. See below, chapter 4, p. 109-11. On the meaning of the celebrated proposition 55 of Baius', 'Deus non potuisset ab initio talem creare hominem, qualis nunc nascitur', which has often been referred to, though without reason, in discussions about finality, cf. Le Bachelet, *loc cit.*, col 71-3. In chapter 5 of *De peccato originis* (p. 6) from whence it has been taken almost literally, it is a question solely of carnal concupiscence. The refutation of it by the doctors of Louvain in the declaration of 1586 also speaks only of preternatural gifts (*Baiana*, pp. 166-7). And obviously there was no question of anything else. In a passage of *De prima hominis iustitia*, c. 8 (p. 59) Baius quickly rejects the idea of a natural

Despite the words used, this is a judgment which is only an apparent paradox. There is no better way, I believe, of defining the disagreement between Baius and St Augustine.

A second example will clearly demonstrate the kind of subtle deformation to which, unwittingly, the disciple constantly subjects the ideas of his master.

In the *De meritis operum,* Baius writes: 'Natura humana, etiam Spiritu sancto destituta, si Dei mandata illibate servaret, esset de praemio secura.'[88] He draws his argument from the following text of Augustine: 'Natura generis humani . . . si potest sibi sufficere ad implendam legem perficiendamque iustitiam, de praemio debet esse secura, hoc est de vita aeterna. Non enim iniustus est Deus, qui iustos fraudet mercede iustitiae.'[89]

Once again the resemblance is obvious. But it is also obvious that this, for St Augustine, is an impossible and quite absurd assumption, for it amounts to saying that 'without God man might nevertheless perform a divine work'. The opponent at whom he was aiming claimed that unbelievers could really do good. He answers: if it were so, they would have eternal life, for God is just. But in what does this good consist? Augustine does not say what he says elsewhere: there is no real good which, as it tends to God, does not have God for its author. So he only accepts the hypothesis because it has been formulated by the objector, a legitimate method of argument and quite usual. But by its very nature, he holds, it is inconceivable and contradictory, and he is constantly arguing against the dissociation which it

beatitude 'cuius neque locus, neque ratio in Scripturis sacris invenitur, sed a vanis et otiosis hominibus (iuxta Pelagii sensum) ex Philosophia confingitur'. This passage does not appear to have shocked Baius' first opponents, nor even to have aroused their attention; in any case the bull of condemnation contains no sign of it.

[88] Bk 2, title of c. 3 and c. 2: 'Bono operi, non ex praevia aliqua dignitate operantis, sed ex natura et qualitate boni operis, vita debetur aeterna' (vol. 1, pp. 36 and 37). *Apologia*, in prop. 42am *(Baiana,* p. 102).

[89] *De natura et gratia,* c. 2. It might also be thought that St Augustine means here to speak of the apparent unbeliever, to whom only explicit faith in the redemption would be wanting; if this were the case the 'sibi sufficere' would not have to be understood in the sense of 'without grace'. But that is a very improbable interpretation.

implies.[90] Baius, on the other hand, sees the 'indwelling' of the
Holy Spirit, in supernatural exaltation, in adoption into the state
of child of God, only as a mere extrinsic condition enabling the
meritorious act to be effected (with no influence whatever on the
nature of this act). And so he can postulate such a dissociation as
perfectly thinkable, or even actually capable of realization. He
does not find it in the least offensive. After all, in his view all
merit is natural, and even all justice. The 'supernatural' exists for
him only in its mode: for Adam it was a mere precedent condition; for us, in addition, it is gratuitous and miraculous. But
whatever form divine collaboration may take the result remains
human.[91] Grace precedes the act of the just man, but it cannot be
said to 'inform' it; it makes it extrinsically possible, but it does not
sustain it intrinsically: 'opera sanctorum . . . non ulterius egent
gratia Christi ut sint vitae aeternae meritoria, sed illis sufficit
gratia quae praecedit ut fiant.'[92]

Baius suffers from a similar delusion in thinking that he is
reproducing St Augustine's teaching about freedom. Both of
them indeed work out equivalence between freedom and volun-
tariness. But Baius lays down that 'whatever is voluntary is free',
while St Augustine said 'only that is voluntary in the full sense of
the word which is free, only the free act has the right to be
called voluntary'. The difference is obvious: one defines volun-
tariness by means of freedom, the other does the precise opposite.
St Augustine says for example: 'Voluntas nostra, nec voluntas
esset, nisi esset in nostra potestate. . . . Monstruosum (est) eumdem
hominem dicere: necesse est ut ita velim, qui necessitate super-
posita auferre nititur voluntatem; si enim necesse est ut velit,
unde volet, cum voluntas non erit?'[93] And he said also: 'Illae
animae, quidquid faciunt, si natura, non voluntate faciunt, id est

[90] For example, *De spiritu et littera*, c. 3.
[91] *De prima hominis iustitia*, c. 6 ('Quod vera iustitia fuerit primo homini
naturalis') 9, 10, 11. *De meritis operum*, bk 2, c. 3 (vol. 1, pp. 57, 60-3,
37-8).
[92] *Apologia* in prop. 2am (vol. 2, p. 81); words taken from the Second
Council of Orange, but with the emphasis of the sentence reversed.
[93] *De libero arbitrio*, bk 3, c. 3, n. 8 (Bibl. august., 6, p. 340).

si libero arbitrio et ad faciendum et ad non faciendum motu animi carent. . . .'[94] Far from reducing freedom to the level of the will understood in too wide and incorrect a way, he exalts the human will—that is, the reflective will, not just the spontaneous will or mere volition—and is willing to recognize it as such only in the exercise of a truly royal freedom.[95] How therefore could the thirty-ninth proposition in any way be Augustinian: 'Quod voluntarie fit, etiamsi ex necessitate fiat, libere tamen fit'? Of course it is not found in so many words in Baius. Chapter seven of *De libero arbitrio,* which includes formulas not unlike it— 'Quod libertati a servitute sit impertinens, utrum actio sit in volentis potestate'—does not mention the human will under the rule of sin but the state of the blessed who can sin no longer. Baius does not fail to point this out in his defence,[96] and it is only right to add that on this point he is in substantial agreement with St Augustine, as indeed with the Gospel and the whole of Catholic tradition. Nevertheless, he merely contrasts this higher freedom, 'libertas a servitute', with the 'libertas a necessitate' which he finds realized in Adam in his state of innocence; whereas for St Augustine where this 'plena et perfecta libertas' is found, 'nullum est vinculum necessitatis, quia libertas est caritatis'.[97] This difference of terminology is an indication of a difference of attitude. Further, it remains true that the condemned proposition also expresses Baius' view concerning the will of sinful man; it is also true that he constantly speaks of 'free will' in connection with a will that cannot desire the good or overcome any temptation;

[94] *De duabus animabus,* c. 12, n. 17 (Bibl. aug., 17, p. 100).

[95] Cf. on this subject A. Martin, *Augustini Philosophia,* pars 5a, c. 47-9 (ed. J. Fabre, 1863, pp. 656-62) and J. Martin, *Saint Augustin,* 2nd ed., pp. 176-9. Cf. Gregory of Valencia, *Commentaria,* vol. 1 (3rd ed., 1603), p. 1171: 'Recte docet Damascenus . . . liberum arbitrium re non differre a voluntate. Hoc ipsum videtur quoque sensisse Augustinus.'

[96] *Baiana,* p. 101. Cf. *De libero arbitrio,* c. 4-7 (pp. 76-80). He had used the same method of defence against the censure of the Sorbonne which had condemned this proposition: 'Libertas et necessitas eidem conveniunt respectu eiusdem; et sola violentia repugnat libertati naturali' (2nd proposition; *Baiana,* p. 11).

[97] *Tract. in Ioannem* XLI, n. 13 (*P.L.,* 35, 1699); *De natura et gratia,* n. 78 (*P.L.,* 44, 286).

and so it remains true, finally, that he identifies 'more or less what is simply voluntary with what properly is free',[98] which makes his position that which was condemned in Jansenius.[99]

With just as much reason, therefore, one might deduce from St Augustine's maxim 'Dilige et quod vis fac' the immoral principle cherished by various Beghards, the followers of Molinos and the false mystics of all periods.[100] The misinterpretation would be the same in both cases.[101] Yet again, it is as if St Thomas Aquinas were blamed for having taught that a 'free act is a human act' by making him say thereby that 'man's every act is free of its nature, and it is enough for an act to be man's for it to be called free', whereas he means on the contrary that only 'a free act is really, fully human, and that this alone of the acts of man is rightly called human'.

As we saw in connection with Adam, Baius' position was Pelagian. In this case the freedom of fallen man amounts in his view, if a comparison is needed, approximately to what it was for Plotinus. According to Plotinus, writes Régis Jolivet, 'men are wicked despite themselves. Nevertheless, they are responsible for their actions, because they do them of themselves, that is, the necessity to which they are subject is not external to them but internal.'[102] It is indeed ironical that in desiring to follow St

[98] Le Bachelet, *loc. cit.*, col. 82. As with St Augustine, in this case Baius could be compared with St Bernard whose authority he also likes to invoke (thus concerning charity: *De caritate*, bk 1, c. 2 and 7; vol. 1, pp. 90 and 99). St Bernard's formulas are close to his, but then their author takes care to make us appreciate the paradox: cf. *In Cantica sermo 81*, n. 7-9 (*P.L.*, 183, 1174-5).
[99] Cf. propositions 66 and 67. See also *Baiana*, pp. 169-70. As we know, Jansenius' theory was approved by Leibniz: *Théodicée*, 3rd part. n. 208-12.
[100] Examples in Henri Busson, *Les sources et le développement du rationalisme*, pp. 317-18, 339-40. St Augustine, *In primam Ioannis*, tract. 7, n. 8 (ed. Paul Agaësse, *S.C.*, 75, p. 328).
[101] I take for granted here, as previously, the classic interpretation of this maxim, an interpretation indeed which is in agreement with the general teaching of St Augustine. In fact, the maxim refers directly not to the love of God but to the love of our neighbour. Marie Comeau, 'L'évolution de la sensibilité de saint Augustin' in *Cahiers de la Nouvelle Journée*, 17 (1930), pp. 43-4. P. Agaësse, *op. cit.*, pp. 80-1.
[102] *Le problème du mal chez saint Augustin*, p. 101. Cf. *Enneads*, III, 3, 5.

Augustine alone, Baius finds himself in the position of adopting one after the other the doctrines of Augustine's principal opponents.

Note. A critic thought that in an earlier version of this chapter I was putting forward a distinction between two sorts of claims to the supernatural, the one called 'ontological' and the other 'juridical', and that while ascribing the latter to Baius, I kept the former as my own view. In reality, such a distinction never entered my mind, any more than it came from my pen. It seems clear to me, and probably to everyone else as well, that a claim of nature could only be ontological (and, as I said, in my view any claim must be excluded). If, in emphasizing Baius' naturalism, I also spoke of juridicism in his connection, it was as a psychological explanation to characterize the way in which he put forward the claims of created nature. The spirit in which he understands the relationship of moral activity with God who rewards it is to be found also in his idea of the relationship of nature with the God who completes it. It does not seem to me that this is a caricature. The same point has been recently made by Fr Féret.[103] Baius understood the gift of the Spirit to innocent nature as being owed to it, and not as a gratuitous gift: '*debitum* ex naturali exigentia et conditione naturae humanae, non gratuitum Dei beneficium'. Quite certainly, in his view there was something lacking in man which, without belonging to him essentially, was indispensable to him as the logical complement of his being, just as wings were necessary to a bird to fly; and so his Creator owed it to him. Such was the idea which in Baianism was shrewdly substituted for the traditional idea of our divine vocation. In this way the supernatural was reduced to the natural level. In condemning this system the Church did not condemn an imaginary error.

If this first chapter is still not clear enough the continuation of this book will show plainly, I think, that the distinction between

---

[103] *Loc. cit.*, col. 1174: 'In his case it is even possible to speak of an attitude of mind that was more juridical than evangelical or theological, as often happens when a great religious, or at least a great metaphysical mind does not keep in check a certain obstinacy.'

two sorts of claim is not mine; in my view, which is that of every Catholic, any idea of a claim of created nature in relation to the supernatural should be absolutely excluded.

In 1958 J. P. van Dooren put forward a partially new interpretation of Baianism. Without questioning the usual way in which Baius' ideas on the completion granted to Adam are understood, this writer believes that Baius would have allowed in addition to this completion a real ontological raising up or exaltation of human nature. The passage on which this interpretation is principally based occurs in *De prima hominis iustitia,* book 1, chapter 9, *in fine* : 'alterum esse nobis naturale . . . , alterum vero supernaturale, id est naturae nostrae indebitum, et creatoris munificentia nostrac integritati ad ornatum liberaliter adiectum'.[104]

The following is a fuller version of the same passage and will enable the reader to judge the correctness of this interpretation :

> Ponatur enim (disputandi gratia) Adam cum sua posteritate talis permansisse, qualis initio conditus est, atque pari facilitate Deum agrosque coluisse, quis nunc coniectaret alterum esse nobis naturale, id est, ex ipsa generatione atque nativitate concessum, alterum vero supernaturale, id est naturae nostrae indebitum, et creatoris munificentia nostrae integritati ad ornatum liberaliter adiectum?[105]

[104] *Michael Baius, Zijn leer over de mens,* p. 22; cf. pp. 90-8.
[105] *Baiana,* vol. I, pp. 60-1.

2

Jansenius—I

The Augustinianism of Jansenius is even more generally accepted than that of Baius. Bayle wrote:

> It is certain that the Roman Church is committed to the system of St Augustine and this is the cause of embarrassment to it and even ridicule. It is quite obvious to anyone who examines the matter without prejudice and with the necessary understanding that the doctrine of St Augustine and that of Jansenius, Bishop of Ypres, are one and the same; the fact that the Roman Court boasts of having condemned Jansenius and of retaining Augustine's teaching in all its glory is certainly cause for indignation.[1]

Richard Simon thought the same, and fundamentally it is the opinion of more than one historian of our own times. There is no difficulty in accepting that the modern *Augustinus* contains a more active poison because it contains a 'heavier concentration' of the doctrines which were scattered throughout the works of the great doctor.[2] Actually, the heavy folio volumes of the Bishop of

---

[1] *Dictionnaire*, art, 'Saint Augustin', section E, and art. 'Jansenius', section H.

[2] H. Margival, *Richard Simon*, c. 3. Cf. Lucien Ceyssens, O.F.M., 'Jansénisme en Belgique' in *RHE*, 51 (1956), p. 172, n. 1: 'It would have been enough, I think, to say that Jansenius' theories were condemned, whether or not they agreed with those of St Augustine. It is the distinction between condemned Jansenism and authorized Augustinianism which was at the root of the difficulties. Jansenius may well have been mistaken about the teaching of St Augustine but, after studying it for twenty years, he certainly knew more about it than most of his opponents.'

Ypres, no more than the shorter treatises of the theologian of
Louvain, did not succeed in reviving Augustine's teaching. Jansenius, Lancelot tells us,[3] 'had read St Augustine more than ten
times, and the works on grace against the Pelagians more than
thirty times, and this at a time when hardly anyone had read or
understood them.' Yet, despite all the attraction of literal exegesis
and the astonishing textual knowledge that he displays, he too, as
I hope to show, achieves only a 'conscientious misunderstanding'.[4]

It may seem that at the basis of Jansenius' teaching there is an
error opposite to that to be found in Baius. While the latter
understood the relationship between God and the creature—even,
on a final analysis, in our present world—on the pattern of a
balance sheet or a labour contract, Jansenius seems hypnotized
by the biblical image of clay in the hand of the potter. He sub-
ordinates everything to the vision of a God, terrible in his almighty
power, who knows no law, is accountable to no one, saves one,
damns another, according to his own good pleasure. Both failed
in their different ways to appreciate the sublime novelty of
Christian revelation; the first to a great extent misunderstood the
mysterious end to which this revelation calls us, while the second
entirely overlooked the way of love which it sets before us. Both,
by certain of their tendencies, were men of the Old Testament—
'in novo, non autem de novo Testamento'. Baius, however, seems
chiefly to have kept to the mentality of those Pharisees who,
drawing up a sort of legal agreement between God and man,
spent their lives in perpetual lawsuit, with all their hopes set on
obtaining a sentence of justification when it came to judgment.
Jansenius, on the other hand, seemed rather to have inherited
something of the character of carnal Judaism, which was also
Mohammed's,[5] namely, the fanatical narrowness of one who

---

[3] *Mémoires touchant la vie de Monsieur de Saint-Cyran,* vol. 1 (1738), p.
104.
[4] The phrase is Maurice Blondel's, 'Le jansénisme et l'antijansénisme de
Pascal' in *Revue de Métaphysique et de Morale,* 1923, p. 137.
[5] 'Mohammedan propositions', remarked Richard Simon of the condemned
propositions.

believes himself to be the Lord's chosen one.[6] The former tended really to do away with the idea of grace; the latter in some sort exaggerated it, regarding it as a manifestation of power all the more adorable the more arbitary and tyrannical it appeared. In the last place, although both also tended to dissolve the unity between God and man which consists essentially in the mystery of Christ, it was surely because one sets up man before God claiming his rights, while the other does away with him entirely.

These differences are undeniable, at least from a certain viewpoint. They would appear to be more real still and perhaps more radical if instead of considering Jansenius alone we took into account as a whole the vast religious and moral movement to which his name remains attached. Far more than in the *Augustinus,* the origins of this movement are to be found in the soul of Jean Duvergier de Hauranne, Abbé de Saint-Cyran. Now Saint-Cyran seems hardly interested in Baius' primary assumption regarding the primitive state of man. In the short treatise *De la Grâce de Jésus-Christ, de la liberté chrétienne et de la justification,* which he wrote at Vincennes shortly after the posthumous publication of his friend's large work, probably to bring the principal points within Arnauld d'Andilly's grasp, it is remarkable that he says nothing of the state of pure nature treated at length by Jansenius;[7] further, it is some time before he mentions the state of innocence, in contrast to our own. His usual point of view is entirely direct and concrete. Before all else in theology[8] he concentrates on the awesome nature of the mysteries of faith, on the rarity of grace, on the fact that Jesus Christ died for a small

[6] François Bonal, *Le chrétien du temps* (1655), part 2, p. 4: 'This teaching boasts and is convinced that it is defending the grace of its enemies, because it takes it away from almost the whole world.' Cf. E. Tobac, *Le problème de la justification dans saint Paul,* p. 11.

[7] Cf. Jean Orcibal, 'La spiritualité de Saint-Cyran avec ses écrits de piété inédits' (Les origines du Jansénisme, 5, 1962), pp. 81 and 233.

[8] On the contrary, 'Augustine can only keep to the severity of his principles when he argues in the abstract. When faced with actual beings his charity prevails; he is incapable of resigning himself to the death for ever of any living soul': M. Comeau, *Saint Augustin interprète du quatrième évangile,* p. 217.

number only. 'As the sun makes sacred days and secular days,
summer days and winter days, so God has made some men to be
saved and holy, and others ungodly, to be damned.'[9] For him,
far more than a deduction this is a sacred intuition. 'Not one drop
of grace for the pagans!' he exclaims in a sort of ecstasy. God's
wrath 'appeared for four thousand years before the Incarnation,
and after it still continues both in the larger part of the world
outside the Church and among those many Christians who have
forfeited the grace of their baptism'. 'God does not often speak to
the soul; usually it is once only, and then in an instant, and as it
were in passing.'[10] These austere views Saint-Cyran found charm-
ing. On a visit to the schoolboys of Port Royal he could not for-
bear from teaching them that Virgil was damned.[11]

Of course, traits of this kind do not take us far towards the
definition of a man's thoughts, especially of one whose genius
was not without contrast, whose ideas fluctuated and whose
language was inclined to excess and paradox. He said of himself
that in him 'fire and water were gathered together', a fact which
inclined him to 'contradictory utterances'.[12] These traits are only
mentioned here to show that Saint-Cyran's religious outlook was
very different from that of the Bishop of Ypres. It has been said,
possibly with some exaggeration, that they conducted a 'dialogue
of the deaf' and that there was a fundamental misunderstanding
between them. At least it should be remembered that although
both appealed to St Augustine,

as representatives of two opposing mentalities they did not
read him in the same way. Jansenius, whose approach was
intellectual, sought a scientific solution of the precise problem stated in academic terms. Saint-Cyran, however, was

[9] *De la grâce de Jésus-Christ* (Orcibal, *op. cit.*, p. 240). Cf. Ecclus 33 : 7-12.
[10] In Orcibal, *op. cit.*, pp. 251 and 91.
[11] Lancelot, *Mémoires*, vol. 1, p. 39. Thus some distinctions must be
made before we accept what Lancelot says about the *Augustinus*: 'M. de
Saint-Cyran's great unction could have softened many of the expressions
and put them out of reach of his enemies.'
[12] Cf. Fr Michel de Certau's careful observations in 'De Saint-Cyran au
Jansénisme, conversion et réforme' in *Christus*, 39 (1963), pp. 399-417,
especially pp. 401-9.

concerned with the more practical level; . . . in his view
the return to Augustinian spirituality was the means to
enable the primitive Church to flourish again in the seventeenth century.[13]

This was his 'great plan'. The *Augustinus,* whose preparation
he had encouraged, and in which he had to some small extent
collaborated, did not arouse his enthusiasm. Yet his friend's final
conclusions, drawn up in secret, were in accordance with his
initial intuition. And so he asked Arnauld to defend them. By
this means he ensured their success by inspiring them with his
enthusiasm. It is to Saint-Cyran that Jansenism owes all its
greatness. It also owes him its success. Without him and without
Arnauld, whom he sent into battle, it might only have been a
school of theology or some 'professors' heresy', not a very dangerous kind, and a worthy object of Campanella's scorn.[14]

It remains true, however, that the theology of Jansenius came
at a particular moment to justify, in the name of St Augustine,
the religion of Saint-Cyran. The *Augustinus* was to serve as the
very backbone of Jansenism. Now its author, though it is too
seldom noticed, was actually far from admitting the doctrine
according to which God is an almighty power who in determining his creature's fate has no other rule than that of his own
power. Everything that he appears to say in this sense presupposes the world of the fall. As with St Augustine before him, it is
on sinful man and not on God himself that he bases his ideas on
predestination. This is not the invention of Jansenius, as some of
his opponents have wrongly asserted, including even a famous
historian and disciple of Calvin;[15] nor is he, as others have said in

[13] Jean Orcibal, *Saint-Cyran et le Jansénisme* (1961), p. 46; cf. pp. 47-50.
See the fine portrait, possibly a little apologetic but very detailed, sketched
by Jean Orcibal in 'Jean Duvergier de Hauranne, abbé de Saint-Cyran et
son temps' (*Les origines du Jansénisme*, vol. 2, 1947, pp. 595-657): 'Les
deux Saint-Cyran'.

[14] Cf. Léon Blanchet, *Campanella* (19), p. 89. See also Sainte-Beuve, *Port-
Royal* (Hachette ed.), vol. 1, p. 35. Jean-François Thomas, *Le problème moral
à Port-Royal* (1961), pp. 29-41.

[15] Sainte-Beuve said of Port-Royal that 'on points concerning grace it
was near to Calvinism': bk 2, c. 131 (ed. de la Pléiade, vol. 1, p. 657).

his defence or perhaps for malicious reasons, a disciple of St Thomas.[16] On the other hand, it was not for nothing that, through Jacques Jansson, principal of the College of Adrian VI at Louvain where he went for the completion of his studies, and perhaps also through the Franciscan Florent Conrius,[17] he was almost the immediate heir to the thought of Baius.[18] In 1621 he feared 'that they would play the trick on him in Rome that had been played on others', an obvious allusion to the condemnations of 1567 and 1579.[19] He took up his pen, he says, 'ad excusandas apophases magistri nostri Michaelis'. On several occasions he argues about the bull of St Pius V, giving examples of other doctrines also judged to be 'scandalous' or 'offensive to pious ears' which it is nevertheless legitimate to hold.[20] There are some who say even that he first called his work 'Apology for Baius' and a first-generation Jansenist, Feydeau, praised him for having defended the cause of his predecessor.[21] That the teaching of Jansenius was compared with that of Baius is not therefore merely the result of Jesuit 'tactics' as a recent scholar seems to suggest.[22]

[16] Cf. A. de Meyer, *Les premières controverses jansénistes en France*, p. 14: 'Those who assert the direct dependence of the *Augustinus* on Calvin have misunderstood the teaching of St Augustine.' Jean Laporte, *La doctrine de la grâce chez Arnauld*, p. 432, makes a similar remark: 'The difference between Arnauld's conception of grace and that of Thomism is, fundamentally, that physical premotion, attributed by the Thomists to both states of human nature, belongs, according to Arnauld, to the grace of the Redeemer.'
[17] Cf. Jean Orcibal, *Correspondance de Jansénius* (1947), p. 59, n. 4.
[18] Leopold Willaert, S.J., *Les origines du Jansénisme dans les Pays-Bas*, vol. 1 (1948), p. 340: 'There, under the master's supervision, he was imbued with the teaching of Baius.' Cf. pp. 80 and 339. In the *Augustinus*, vol. 2, p. 276 AD, Jansenius expressly appeals to the authority of Jansson's interpretation of the Bull against Baius.
[19] Letter to Saint-Cyran, 5 March 1621 (Orcibal, p. 69).
[20] *Augustinus*, vol. 2, pp. 272-7, and 402-4; vol. 3, p. 304.
[21] *Catéchisme de la grâce* (1650), preface. Cf. Du Chesne, *Histoire du Baianisme*, pp. 300 and 301.
[22] Lucien Ceyssens, *Sources relatives aux débuts du jansénisme et de l'antijansénisme*, 1640-3 (Louvain, 1957), p. 29. The work is valuable for the numerous unpublished documents it contains; the first in which there is any question of this comparison attributes it not to a Jesuit but to Sylvius (p. 49, Letter of Jean le Pessier, S.J., 8 April 1641).

'The dependence of one on the other is undeniable', says another scholar.[23]

The foundation stone laid by Jansenius for his doctrinal edifice is also a thesis concerning the primitive state of human nature. In consequence, if in the Jansenist movement we look not merely to its actual inspiration but also to the teaching to which it appeals for its authority, and if in this we make the effort to go back from the consequences displayed throughout it (and often watered down) to the principles succinctly enunciated in the first work, we shall be obliged to observe that Jansenism is the exact continuation of Baianism. Although it tones down slightly some of its statements, it actually strengthens it as a whole, endowing it, as Du Chesne points out, 'with body, consistency and colour'.[24] Urban VIII saw this clearly when, in the bull *In eminenti,* he condemned the *Augustinus* as 'containing and renewing the articles, opinions and sentiments condemned' by Pius V.[25]

It is true that Jansenius begins by rejecting energetically the opinion 'of Luther and Calvin', by which original righteousness was as natural to the first man as health is to the animal or coldness to water. 'The Bishop of Ypres,' noted Arnauld in his *Seconde Apologie,*[26] 'never so wronged grace as to believe that

[23] F. Claeys Bouuaert, *L'ancienne Université de Louvain, études et documents* (Louvain, 1956), p. 155. '(Cornelius Jansen) entered Louvain in 1602, was placed first at the end of the philosophical course in 1607, and during the course of his eight years of theological studies gradually adopted the principal tenets of Michael Baius.'

[24] *Op. cit.,* p. 186.

[25] The Bull was prepared by Albizzi, assessor at the Holy Office, who adopted the opinion of the consultors on this subject, especially that of Hilarion Rancati. Details given in Albert de Meyer, *op. cit.,* p. 128, and especially L. Ceyssens, 'Jansénisme et antijansénisme en Belgique au XVIIe siècle', *RHE,* 51 (1956), pp. 143-84. Ceyssens is severe on Albizzi and somewhat daring in his judgment: 'Albizzi's intransigence frustrated the first and best opportunity of avoiding the great misfortune that was to fall upon the Church. A little good will and a little understanding, on occasion a little charity and courage would have sufficed for there never to have been any question of Jansenism or anti-Jansenism' (p. 172). Isaac Habert, as early as 1644, was of a different opinion: *Défense de la foi de l'Église . . . ,* p. 11: 'The Jansenists' heat and lack of discretion, coupled with the distrust that they have for everyone, discredited Jansenius. . . .'

[26] Bk 2, c. 16 (*Œuvres,* vol. 17, p. 167).

without it either the angels or the first man in the state of innocence could do anything good'. The magnificent 'balance' of the
primary state was not obtained without a sufficient grace.[27] Baius,
on the other hand, in speaking of grace, admitted that it was in
a wrong sense, but Jansenius states that it was to be understood
as 'a real grace', a 'supernatural grace'. In this case, he declares,
it is even a dogma of faith.[28] But when he comes to describe this
grace, when he wants to explain what was the state of humanity
before the original fall, despite his obvious efforts to avoid
the rock on which his master foundered, in the end he follows
him.[29]

Of course, as he again emphasizes, grace was not due to
Adam's merits nor was final glory within the reach of his natural
efforts : but were not both nevertheless postulated by essential
claims? He comes close to asserting it when, after saying that
God owes it to himself to grant his help to the being whom he
has just created, he assigns as reason for it not so much the sub-
limeness of the end to which God destines him, as the weakness of
the creature which, brought out of nothingness, always retains an
inclination for nothingness. Again, we can judge by the commentary by Feydeau, one of the most careful of Jansenius' disciples : 'The Creator was not obliged by any consideration of the
merits of the creature, who did not yet exist and who consequently
had no merit, but *as he could not make a perfect body which had
not all its parts,* so he could not make an intellectual creature in
that order without giving his grace to it.'[30] In the same spirit
Quesnel exclaimed : 'Gratia Adami est sequela creationis, et erat
debita naturae sanae et integrae.'[31] On the other hand, and it is

[27] *Augustinus, De gratia Christi Salvatoris,* bk 3, c. 5 : 'Amissum est enim
illud pristinae integerrimaeque voluntatis aequilibrium, per quod ei, non
sine gratia sufficiente, aderat posse, si vellet, ita ut velle et nolle in eius
libero (non sine gratia) relinqueretur arbitrio' (vol. 3, p. 113C).

[28] *De gratia primi hominis,* c. 10-12 (vol. 2, pp. 53-6).

[29] Cf. *Analyse de l'Augustin de Jansénius* (1721), pp. 44-5 and 420-2.

[30] *Catéchisme de la grâce,* c. 1, p. 10.

[31] 35th condemned proposition; cf. the 34th. Cf. Fernand Litt, *La question
des rapports entre la nature et la grâce de Baius au synode de Pistoie* (1934),
pp. 67-74.

logical, once endowed with this necessary adjunct Adam's nature was exalted to the extent of needing grace only as a means at its sovereign disposal, as a mere instrument in the service of its free will. 'In the state of innocence,' says Feydeau again, 'the will, being sound and free, applied grace and caused it to act.'[32] Arnauld says something similar : 'The free will of the angels, which was the first cause moving grace and causing it to act when it would, with grace doing nothing else but following it, had the principal part in the action.'[33] And although it is therefore true that a certain supernatural element is not here denied, at least the notion of it, as in Baius, is singularly misrepresented.

Now it is from this initial misrepresentation that all the rest derives. What results, in fact, is that latent naturalism in the explanation of the 'state of integral nature' : grace is not necessary to ensure the efficacious co-operation of human freedom in a more than human work, since free will is already present, fully constituted in its proximate power of acting, before its intervention. And from this too, in the state of fallen nature, comes that determinism short of which there can be no avoiding the impiousness of Pelagius. For if in that case freedom retained some power, grace would always be used by it as an instrument, and it would then have to be admitted that Pelagianism, which in paradise was to some extent true, would continue to be true in the present world. Like Baius, therefore, we should be playing on the word 'free', calling 'free' anything which could be said to be voluntary on any grounds whatever, even when determined on evil, and the idea of freedom would be corrupted in the way the idea of grace was above. Lastly, from this there derives equally inevitably, in the 'state of redeemed nature', that opposite determinism, the result of an always efficacious grace which, as an external power, makes up for the fallen powers of the will but does not restore them—a holy enjoyment of the same kind and in all respects

[32] *Catéchisme de la grâce*, p. 7.
[33] *Seconde Apologie*, l. 2, c. 16 (*Œuvres*, vol. 17, p. 71). Cf. Saint-Cyran, *De la grâce de Jésus-Christ*: 'Adam's grace placed him in dependence on himself, for he made his grace act according to his own will' (Orcibal, p. 236; cf. *Pensées, ibid.*, pp. 224-5).

like the enjoyment of carnal concupiscence. Maurice Blondel remarks:

> When man falls, he falls in his entirety, and all of a piece. And he cannot be rescued from the mire save by an experienced attraction, by the domination of an opposite and entirely holy concupiscence. Grace remains extrinsic; it does not fall into the promiscuity of a wholly corrupt nature; it is for this reason that for the saving action to be effected an attraction must be felt and experienced. And this opens the door to illusions and deceptive exaltations of the individual consciousness.[34]

Thus everything, right up to these final consequences in the psychological and spiritual order,[35] is governed by the theory concerning the relationship of grace and free will in Adam. Jansenius himself acknowledged indeed that this was the principal point. Subsequently several of his opponents saw it clearly. A further observation provides additional confirmation of it: while on other points, such as nature, the distribution and efficacy of the grace of Christ, considerable differences among Jansenist

[34] *Loc. cit.*, p. 142. *Cf.* Anthony Levi, 'La psychologie des facultés au xviie siècle' in *L'Homme devant Dieu*, vol. 2 (1964), p. 298: 'Once Jansenius had introduced the maxim "quod amplius nos delectat, secundum id operemur necesse est" in the fourth book of the *de gratia Christi*, he seems constantly to imply that the delectation of grace effects in the soul an attraction that can be felt.'

[35] An interesting criticism of this aspect of Jansenism will be found in G. de la Baule le Blanc de la Vallière, *La lumière du chrétien* (1963) quoted by Henri Bremond, *Histoire littéraire du sentiment religieux en France*, vol. 4, p. 568, note. Yet it would be wrong to lend too much weight to certain phrases, like this one of Nicole's in *Traité de l'oraison*, p. 497: 'In the absence of grace, that is, in the state of aridity. . . .' In these spiritual matters words, of which there are too few for the many slight shades of meaning, can easily be deceptive. In connection with the 'game of love' by which God gives the soul the sweet feeling of his presence and then withdraws it, Bl. Henry Suso writes: 'Tender Master, teach me how to behave myself in these alternations of grace and abandonment' (*The Little Book of Eternal Wisdom and the Little Book of Truth*, translated with Introd. and notes by J. M. Clark, 1953, part I, c. 9). In the sixteenth and seventeenth centuries 'grace' was often used in the sense of 'favour' in a psychological context: cf. remarks on this subject by Michel de Certeau, S.J., *Mémorial du bienheureux Pierre Favre* (1960), pp. 23-4.

writers, and especially between Arnauld and Nicole, as well as a whole series of attenuations and variations, may be discerned, yet on this point they remained in complete agreement. But where they are mistaken is in thinking that they are repeating the teachings of St Augustine. This or that feature may have been taken from genuine Augustinian texts, as was the case with some of the propositions of Baius. Some of the summaries or analyses of the *Augustinus* on matters of detail can be perfectly accurate. The opponents of Jansenius, who had not always read St Augustine carefully enough, or who allowed themselves to be carried away by the heat of controversy, were not always aware of this and did not acknowledge it sufficiently. But these material borrowings, this literal accuracy, notwithstanding, Augustinianism has here again been skilfully corrupted. St Augustine makes use of a formula to answer, with many qualifications, some difficult question; Jansenius seizes on it, sets it up as a principle and with almost geometrical precision deduces a system from it. From a passage which merely alluded to a specific problem, from an argument which referred to a precise point under discussion, he thought he could derive the essentials of the Augustinian theory on the nature of man. We should not be surprised to learn that after this Augustine seems to him to 'become a little remote'.[36] But instead of this causing him any hesitation over the accuracy of his interpretation, he soon forgets all about this remoteness and pushes on with the same fearlessness. If necessary he will be more faithful to Augustine than Augustine is to himself. And in the end, using this method, his whole edifice was to be built on a misinterpretation. Under his leadership the Jansenists might well repeat, in its extremist form, the language of the earlier Augustinians and with them curse 'the enemies of God's grace'; the agreement was really only verbal, the two parties were talking of different things.

From this point of view consistently adopted throughout this book the problem is almost entirely centred on one passage. It

[36] 29th Letter to Saint-Cyran, 28 February 1622 (Orcibal, p. 117).

concerns the interpretation to be given to chapters 11 and 12 of the book *De correptione et gratia,* in which St Augustine compares the relationship between grace and freedom in Adam in the state of innocence and in us sinners.[37] It is the thorny question of 'adiutorium sine quo non' and of 'adiutorium quo'. This Augustinian distinction of the two 'aids' had already been used to advantage by Calvin against the decrees of the Council of Trent. The Dominican Peter de Soto had also advanced it in an exchange of letters with Ruard Tapper in which Du Chesne thought he could discern the timorous origins of Baianism.[38] (The assumption seems to have been gratuitous, as a colleague of De Soto's, Cardinal Orsi, subsequently showed.)[39] More than once it had been referred to in the controversy on grace and predestination between the theologians of the Society of Jesus and the congregations *De auxiliis.*[40] At about the same time in his commentary on the first book of the *Sentences* Estius, who at Louvain had been the pupil of Baius and Hessels, had unsuccessfully attempted to produce an original explanation.[41] Jansenius now had recourse to it, and in it he rediscovered so to say the whole of Baius. Throughout the interminable Jansenist controversy the contrasting of 'medicinal grace' and 'healing grace' or 'versatile grace' and 'determining grace' was to play a part similar to that played by the distinction between the two meanings of scripture in the Lutheran controversy. Like Luther with the *De spiritu et littera,* the defenders of the *Augustinus* clung to the *De correptione et gratia.* And this was not a bad choice, if we are to believe Fénelon

[37] Fr Charles Boyer has produced an annotated edition of this work, Pontificia Univ. Gregoriana, Texts and Documents, theological series, 2 (1932).

[38] Peter de Soto, 2nd letter, 26 May 1551 (Du Chesne, pp. 12-14).

[39] *De Petro a Soto et Jud. Ravesteyn liber apologeticus* (2nd ed., Rome, 1761), pp. 117-19. In any case it is certain that Peter de Soto did not hold the naturalism of which Baius was soon to show signs. In his second letter to Tapper he wrote: 'Omnis gratia, sicut sola revelatione Dei cogniscitur, ita sola eius liberalitate donatur; unde non est debra alicui, vel consequens naturam.'

[40] Le Bachelet, *Prédestination et grâce efficace,* vol. 1, pp. 205 and 253-4; vol. 2, pp. 66, 166 and 268.

[41] See also *In II Sent.,* dist. 25, n. 7 (Paris, 1680, p. 269).

who is in his *Instruction* in dialogue form remarks to the Jansenist whom he brings on the scene, 'You have made the best possible case for your party'.[42]

St Augustine, it should be observed in the first place, did not have to contend with a supralapsarian naturalism, like that of Baius, but with a directly infralapsarian naturalism. As the doctrinal expression of something actually experienced, Pelagianism denied the necessity, or at least misunderstood the real function of grace in the present state—and that was the only one envisaged —of humanity. In his anti-Pelagian writings, therefore, it was this present state and the present function of grace that Augustine had primarily in view. In judging it together with scripture and the tradition of the Church, he examines his personal experience which he interprets in the light of his own philosophical reflection. At the outset he does not investigate the primitive state of the first man as a matter of curiosity—nothing would be more opposed to the general spirit of his theology—but he merely seeks to define it after the event, in comparison with and for a better understanding of our own.[43] Even if his explanation does not prove entirely adequate he can hardly be blamed for it, since it is certainly difficult to state precisely what exactly the first state of innocence was, and not to go wrong at some point.

But is it really right in this case to plead attenuating circum-

---

[42] *Instruction pastorale en forme de dialogues sur le système de Jansénius* (*Œuvres*, 1823, vol. 15, p. 385). Cf. *Augustinus, passim*, especially *De gratia primi hominis*, cc. 15ff. In the same way Cardinal de Noris attached great importance to *De correptione* : *Historia pelagiana*, bk 1, c. 23 (1673), p. 143 : 'Hic quidem liber parvus mole est, sed doctrina maximus, totus mysteriis refertus, universam divinae gratiae oeconomiam oculis subiicit, ut iure merito aureus a doctissimis nuncupetur. Docet in eo sapientissimus Antistes . . . diversam esse gratiam hominis innocentis et reparati : esse illam adiutorium quo fit ut possimus bene agere si volumus, hanc vero reapse facere ut velimus; unde una est adiutorium sine quo non, altera adiutorium quo; ita enim humana voluntas indeclinabiliter et insuperabiliter agitur. Ego quidem hunc librum soleo appellare clavem, qua ad universam Augustini de divina gratia et libero arbitrio doctrinam aditus aperitur. . . . The Dominican J. H. Serry, who refuted at length the Jansenist interpretation, very rightly refused to see in it the key *par excellence* to Augustinian teaching on grace : *Divus Augustinus divo Thomae . . . conciliatus* (2nd ed., 1724), especially pp. 174-7.

[43] *De correptione et gratia*, c. 26 : 'Hic exoritur alia quaestio. . . .'

stances as several commentators do? Are we obliged to resign ourselves to the fact, as if the distinction between 'adiutorium sine quo non' given to Adam and the 'adiutorium quo' bestowed on us is difficult to maintain in all its consequences? According to Jansenius this celebrated distinction whose terms St Augustine merely borrowed from the treatises on rhetoric, which were themselves derived from the Stoic vocabulary,[44] was fundamental. He quotes it as many as one hundred and seventy times (Dechamps counted them).[45] It is, he says, of the same importance to the doctrine of grace as axioms are to geometry. It is the immovable foundation on which the whole edifice rests; it is the only key giving access to the writings of St Augustine; it is the light for want of which we shall falter like a blind man in full daylight, the thread always to be held lest we go astray as in a labyrinth.[46] Arnauld too lays stress on it and comments on it at length in the analytical synopsis which he made of the *De correptione et gratia,* a work, he remarked, 'in which this divine teaching is divinely explained'.[47] We can grant them that it is really of importance, although St Augustine only formulated the distinction on one occasion towards the end of his life in 426 in a short work composed for a particular occasion.[48] But how is it to be understood? Are Jansenius and Arnauld right in regarding the 'adiutorium sine quo non' as the equivalent or their 'gratia sufficiens' or 'parva' which, contrary to what it is now, would in

[44] Cf. A. Solignac, S.J., 'La condition de l'homme pécheur d'après saint Augustin' in *NRT*, 78 (1956), p. 362.

[45] *Tradition de l'Église catholique* (1688), avertissement, n. 8.

[46] *De gratia primi hominis*, c. 17.

[47] *Analyse du livre de Saint Augustin de la correction et de la grâce* (Paris, Antoine Vitré, 1644; republished in 1690 by François Muguet). As is well known the insertion of this work in the edition of St Augustine by the Maurists provoked an outcry. F. A. Zacharias, S.J., 'De adiutorii sine quo non et adiutorii quo vera germanaque notione Diatriba' (in his *Thesaurus*, vol. 5, pp. 637-51) says: '. . . quam etiam Maurini Patres, sancti Augustini editores, indignantibus bonis omnibus, libro illi praemittere non dubitarunt, etsi deinde saniore consilio avulsa ab ipsis est.' An account of the matter can be read in Dom Ingold, *Histoire de l'édition bénédictine de saint Augustin*, and in Dom Butler *Benedictine Monachism* (1924), pp. 273-7.

[48] Following Arnauld's example, it should be compared with a passage in *De dono perseverantiae*, c. 13.

paradise have been sufficient in all truth?[49] Were they right to regard the 'adiutorium quo' as the synonym of their 'delectatio victrix' or 'gratia efficax per se'?

The question has been dealt with on many occasions, but it certainly seems as if 'the last word has not been said' about it.[50] No novel solution is offered here. Nevertheless, my excuse for returning to the subject once more is that I endeavour to approach it from a somewhat newer angle. What was of primary interest to most of Jansenius' opponents, particularly as the problem closely affected their own internal controversies on the efficacy of grace, was the 'adiutorium quo' : that is, the help which, with good reason, they refused to identify with a grace 'efficax per se'. The point of view of immediate interest to them does not now appear to be the best way of judging the teaching of Jansenius and of its fidelity to that of St Augustine. Beyond the problem of grace the discussion should be directed, I believe, to the far wider and more fundamental problem of the 'supernatural'. Thus my principal concern here is the 'adiutorium sine quo non' : it is the primitive and enduring relationship of man with God, leaving out of account the modifications introduced by original sin and its consequences. In accordance with the reasoning of the *Augustinus* itself it is, therefore, the Augustinian idea of the grace of Adam that it is important to clarify.[51]

For St Augustine the grace enjoyed by Adam was only a help without which perseverance would have been impossible, while

[49] Arnauld, *Réponse au Père Annat*, second memoir: 'It has pleased Molina . . . to offer us for the real grace that Jesus Christ came to give to men to heal their weaknesses and their ills, that which was only the characteristic of the first man in his health and strength' (*Œuvres*, vol. 19, p. 189). Cf. *Cinquième lettre d'un docteur de Sorbonne . . . touchant les hérésies de XVIIe siècle* (1715), pp. 69-70.

[50] Athanase Sage, A.A., 'Les deux temps de la grâce' in *Revue des études augustiniennes*, 7 (1961), p. 209; the Jansenist context has caused 'a suspicion of unorthodoxy which has not yet been removed from it' to fall upon this doctrine.

[51] Despite different points of view, the interpretation that will be proposed here comes near, at least partially, to that put forward in 1932 by Fr Charles Boyer in his *Essais sur la doctrine de Saint Augustin*, pp. 206-36 : 'Le système de saint Augustin sur la grâce, paraphrase du *De correptione et gratia*.'

now the justified receive the very help which causes them to
persevere, the strength which wins perseverance. But if he makes
so clear a distinction between the two positions, it is on his view
perhaps less because Adam possessed a sounder and more robust
nature than the justified now (although obviously this consideration must be taken into account) than because we know that
Adam actually sinned : 'acceperat posse si vellet, sed non habuit
velle quod posset, nam si habuisset, perseverasset';[52] while the
justified, by definition, do what is good and are saved, for here
it is a question only 'of the saints predestined to the kingdom of
God by divine grace'.[53] In any case it is by no means because this
sounder and more robust nature would have enabled Adam to
act in less dependence on God. Everything in Augustine's religious thought is against such an inversion of roles, just as everything in his metaphysical ideas rejects the opposition between
grace and free will, or to use terms less likely to be misunderstood,
between the activity of the creature and the efficacious influence of the Creator. Indeed, in dealing with the hypothesis
of Adam's perseverance, it is very noticeable what emphasis St
Augustine lays on the idea that Adam did not win it or obtain it
himself but would have received it as a gift.[54] And in a similar
passage of the *Enchiridion,* it is again noticeable that the distinction that he makes between the 'grace' belonging to our
present state and the 'merit' characteristic of the innocent creature
does not prevent his also asserting that establishment in the good,
which is perseverance, ought to be understood entirely as a gift
received.[55]

Moreover, the whole thing appears quite clearly in connection
with the angels. St Augustine himself in this same book, *De cor-*

[52] *De correptione et gratia,* c. 31. Cf. *De peccatorum meritis,* bk 1, c. 37 :
'. . . facile posset custodire si vellet. '
[53] *Op. cit.,* c. 39. Cf. St Thomas, *Prima Secundae,* qu. 109, art. 10, ad 3um;
Secunda Secundae, qu. 139, art. 4, ad 2um.
[54] The word (accepit, accepisse) occurs as much as five times in a few
lines.
[55] *Enchiridion,* c. 105-106. Fr Sage, *loc. cit,* pp. 210-12, drew attention to
this passage in which 'the comparison between Adam's grace and that of
Christ is already beginning to take shape', but it is still 'in the background'.

reptione et gratia, invites us to compare their case with man's. 'It would have been a great merit for Adam', he writes, 'if he had wished to persevere in his good will, as did the saints and angels who persevered. . . . For if this help had been wanting to the angel or to man at the moment of their creation. . . .'[56] Now if among the angels some persevered and not others, this was no doubt a result of their free will,[57] but this reason, which is obvious, nevertheless fails to explain everything, as in all logic it should, in accordance with the interpretation given by Jansenius of the 'adiutorium sine quo non'; for it is a question here, just as with Adam, of beings whose nature is still complete. And all has not yet been said on the subject when we have recalled that the good angels made better use than the bad angels of the grace which was also offered to them. The mystery goes deeper than that. Here again is what St Augustine says: 'Isti aut minorem acceperunt amoris divini gratiam, quam illi qui in eadem perstiterunt; aut, si utrique boni aequaliter creati sunt, istis mala voluntate carentibus, illi amplius adiuti ad eam beatitudinis plenitudinem . . . pervenerunt.'[58]

This passage from the *De Civitate Dei* was more than a little awkward for the 'faithful disciples'. It gave too large a role to the first grace and as a result (in their view) too small a one to 'sound and robust' freedom. 'You would have to be the Bishop of Ypres', wrote Arnauld, that is, to have penetrated as deeply as he into the teaching of St Augustine, 'by untiring study and consummate piety, to find the real meaning of this passage.'[59] We can guess

---

[56] *De correptione et gratia,* c. 11, n. 32. St Fulgentius says the same, *Ad Trasim.,* bk 2, c. 3: 'The same grace which raised man who fell by sin, preserved the good angels from this fall; this same grace which preserved the good angels from the wounds of sin, also cured man of the wounds which sin had caused in him.' The passage was quoted by Hugot, the anonymous (Jansenist) author of the work *Instruction sur les vérités de la grâce et de la prédestination, en faveur des simples fidèles* (2nd ed., Avignon, p. 82).

[57] *De correptione et gratia,* c. 10, n. 27: 'Ceteri autem per ipsum liberum arbitrium in veritate steterunt.'

[58] *De civitate Dei,* bk 12, c. 9, n. 2; cf. n. 1: '. . . profecto et bonam voluntatem, qua meliores essent, nisi operante adiutorio Creatoris habere non possent.'

[59] *Seconde Apologie,* bk 2, c. 17 (*Œuvres,* vol. 17, p. 176).

what subtle arguments were required to obtain this 'real meaning'. Jansenius was obviously in difficulties: 'Cum ista (these words of Augustine) doctrinae hactenus ex ipso traditae tam perspicue repugnent, ut capitalem ictum infligere videantur, neque ullibi legatur illum quem citavimus retractasse locum, non segniter explorandum est. . . .' In opposition to most of the 'recentiores' he then contrived a laborious explanation : the additional help mentioned by St Augustine in this passage came after the choice which ensured perseverance to the good angels; it consisted quite simply in their certitude that they had no longer to fear a fall.[60] This was an explanation that was improbable on three counts. In the first place, such a certitude by itself would not be a help; and it would be a very curious 'help' since it was given 'post perseverantiam', 'in praemium istius permansionis', to beings who were no longer 'viatores' but who had already definitively settled in the everlasting happiness that their perseverance had earned for them.[61] In the second place, the good angels are said by Augustine to have been 'amplius adiuti'; this assumes that the others too were 'helped', although to a lesser degree, and yet there could be no question in their case of experiencing a perseverance that they were not to have. Lastly, there is the third improbability; it is expressly said that it is by taking advantage of this further help that the good angels 'ad eam beatitudinis plenitudinem, unde se numquam casuros certissimi fierent, pervenerunt' : whence it happens that the latter—the blessedness, which is not distinguished from the certitude that their perseverance is assured

---

[60] Jansenius, *De gratia primi hominis et angelorum*, c. 18 (*Augustinus*, vol. 3, pp. 69-70). Among the 'plerique recentiores' against whom he is arguing, he expressly mentions Bellarmine and Vasquez.

[61] *Loc. cit.*: '. . . in illa sua libertate ceciderunt, hi permanserint, et in praemium istius permansionis amplius adiuti, praescientiam numquam futuri sui casus acceperint. . . . Verba ista . . . loquuntur enim de adiutorio, quod per ipsam aeternam felicitatem illa permansione promeritam, eis datum fuit; non de illo, quod eos perseverare faceret, et ad illam beatitudinis plenitudinem pervenire. . . . Manifeste significat, post perseverantiam Angelorum eos qui steterunt esse magis adiutos quam qui ceciderunt. . . . Et ne quis illud "maius adiuti" ad illud tempus referret, quo viatores ad beatitudinem tenderent. . . .'

—is not identified with the former, that is, with help given them to reach it.[62]

In reality therefore the passage seems clear enough in all essentials. And we are not surprised to find that Isaac Habert, one of the first opponents of the *Augustinus,* in his *Défense de la foi de l'Église et de l'ancienne doctrine de Sorbonne* (1644) quoted this passage without feeling any need to add the slightest comment.[63] It is easy to apply it to the case in point. 'Concerning the angels Augustine asks the same question as that concerning man's sin, and he concludes that to persevere the faithful angels needed a special grace that the sinful angels did not receive.'[64] In the *De Civitate Dei* it is therefore between the angel who sinned and the angel who persevered that St Augustine makes comparison : in the same way, in the *De correptione et gratia,* the two terms which he opposes are not exactly Adam the sinner and a sinner now, nor Adam before his sin and a righteous man now; it is rather, on the one hand, Adam who sinned, and on the other, the righteous man who now perseveres.[65] This is the foundation of his distinc-

[62] Jansenius is very arbitrary in his comparison of this passage with one in bk 11, ch. 13, where it says : '. . . post illorum ruinam illis certa scientia suae sempiternae felicitatis accesserit. . . .' The passages are in perfect agreement, but they do not speak only of the same thing. On the one hand (in bk 12) it is a question of a help given to the good angels at the time when the bad ones fell; on the other (in bk 11) it is a question of the certitude acquired by the good angels after the fall of the bad as well as after their own victory. This certitude is recalled by the passage in bk 12 (and it is for this reason that St Augustine himself refers back to the preceding book), but as having to be obtained after this choice for which the good angels are said to have been 'amplius adiuti'. Of such a help there was not and there could not have been question in the passage of the eleventh book.

[63] P. 26. The book is a reply to the first *Apologie de Jansénius* by Arnauld.

[64] G. Bardy, note on the *De civitate Dei,* bk 12, c. 9, n. 2 (Bibl. aug., 35, p. 498).

[65] *De correptione et gratia,* n. 33. In his *Études sur saint Augustin* (1932), p. 228, Fr Charles Boyer wrote : 'The *auxilium quo* is that by means of which a being perseveres to the end, at least after the last return to justice', and this last qualification gives a sense which is acceptable, at least in the case of man; but when Jansenius applied it to the angel, whose destiny is, for St Augustine, fixed by one sole act, it does violence to the thought of his teacher. But in 1947 Fr Boyer seems to have adopted this interpretation himself (*Gregorianum,* 20, p. 390) : 'It is an obvious mistake . . . to speak of the special help afforded the good angels at the moment of the victory, according to the *De Civitate Dei.* . . . This help came afterwards, it is the reward of

tion between the two helps: 'Itemque ipsa adiutoria distinguenda sunt. . . .'[66] And it is this which enables him to state: 'Haec prima est gratia quae data est primo Adam; sed haec potentior est in secundo Adam.'[67]

St Augustine's statements concerning this twofold grace or this twofold help thus leave open 'the question of knowing whether Adam, even before his fall, had not to receive, in the event of his persevering, another kind of *auxilium quo*'.[68] Nevertheless, such a negative and cautious solution does not manage to avoid a misleading parallel with modern ideas—which do not have an exact equivalent in St Augustine—of sufficient and efficacious grace.[69] Perhaps this solution should be left aside, as I shall endeavour to show a little further on.

For it does not clear up everything. But in many another passage of St Augustine's works, especially in this eleventh chapter of *De correptione,* we find another distinction which, without corresponding exactly with the one that concerns us, does nevertheless throw light on its meaning. Adam, we are told, like us needed grace to perform good deeds, but we need in addition a previous help to dispose us to do so. Adam's eye was sound (we can recognize the comparison from which Baius was wrongly to derive a theory), ours must first be cured.[70] Love of justice is not predominant in us as it was spontaneously in him. If therefore

their fidelity and their entry into blessedness such that perseverance is assured. Comparison with the parallel passage of the *De correptione et gratia,* n. 32, and also the connection between the ideas, require this interpretation.' I think that M. Bardy's more recent interpretation is preferable, or at least it is clearer.

[66] *Op, cit.,* n. 34.
[67] *Op. cit.,* n. 31.
[68] Guy de Broglie, S. J., 'Pour une meilleure intelligence du *De correptione et gratia*' in *Augustinus magister,* vol. 3 (1954), p. 330.
[69] Cf. Charles Boyer, *Études sur la doctrine de saint Augustin* (1932), p. 209: 'What is more common in the history of doctrinal exegesis than the introduction in good faith of an erroneous idea into ancient texts by giving words of another period a sense that they only acquired later, or by the hasty search for the solution of present problems in works of great authority, no doubt, but which only treat these questions implicity or indirectly?'
[70] See also *De natura et gratia,* n. 29 and n. 56; *Enchiridion,* c. 106 and c. 107; *De perfectione iustitiae,* n. 9: 'Sicut ergo non est opus sanis medicus, sed male habentibus, ita non est opus liberis liberator, sed servis.'

we take the word 'grace' in the whole breadth of meaning with which it is endowed by theology nowadays, we ought to say, lest we misinterpret St Augustine's thought, that grace is not more necessary to us, basically, than it was to Adam, nor has it to make up for our strength or take the place of our will.[71] Properly speaking, it does not lead us further, but it comes to seek us further away—and further down. 'Maioribus donis adiuvanda remansit infirmitas.'[72] In other words, 'the *adiutorium quo* is of its nature' in the first place 'a grace of victory over sin'.[73] Since we have fallen, grace must begin by raising us up.[74] This is the specific role of the grace of Christ, and it is also one of the aspects of that providential reality which allows us to speak of 'felix culpa'. The grace of Christ as a matter of fact does not work in us in the same way as the grace of paradise worked (or would have worked) in Adam; it is more abundant, 'greater', 'more powerful', and we can be sure—even before considering, as we did just now, the work that was accomplished—that the divine goodness is more favourable to us today and the divine condescension more marvellous towards us than it ever was towards the man who had just come from the hands of the Creator : 'Ille in bonis erat, quae de bonitate sui conditoris acceperat . . . , in quibus prorsus nullum patiebatur malum. Sancti vero in hac vita, ad quos pertinet *liberationis haec gratia,* in malis sunt, ex quibus clamant ad Deum : libera nos a malo.'

In other words, despite appearances,[75] it is not quite accurate

[71] Cf. Athanase Sage, 'La grâce du Christ, modèle de notre grâce' in *Revue des études augustiniennes,* 7 (1961), p. 29 : 'With what vehement indignation does Augustine refuse to deny free will. . . . "Quis nostrum dicat quod primi hominis peccato perierat liberum arbitrium de genere humano?" (*Contra duas litteras Pelag.,* 1, 5). The role of grace is to set free. . . .'

[72] *De correptione et gratia,* n. 29; cf. n. 32. Fulgentius, *Epist.,* 15, n. 16 : 'Liberum vero arbitrium, quod fuit in primo homine sanum ante peccatum, nunc in filiis Dei propria quidem infirmitate concutitur, sed maiore divini muneris gratia sublevatur.'

[73] A. Sage, 'Les deux temps de grâce', *loc. cit.,* p. 225.

[74] *C. Iulianum opus imperfectum,* bk 1, c. 82 : 'Homo quamdiu stetit in bona voluntate liberi arbitrii, non opus habebat ea gratia, qua levaretur cum surgere ipse non posset; nunc vero, in ruina sua. . . .'

[75] Especially *De correptione,* c. 10, n. 27 : 'Saluberrime confitemur Deum . . . sic ordinasse angelorum et hominum vitam, ut in ea prius ostenderet

to assert that according to St Augustine grace had only to work in Adam as the mere power (which in fact it did) while it has to operate in us in an additional way as 'the will and the deed'. Once at least, in the work against Julian of Eclanum, St Augustine expressly lays down the contrary :

> Quomodo verum erit, fecit Deus hominem rectum? An rectus erat non habens voluntatem bonam, sed eius possibilitatem? Ergo et pravus erat, non habens voluntatem malam sed eius possibilitatem? Et a seipso illi est voluntas bona, falsumque scriptum est : Praeperatur voluntas a Domino, et : Deus in vobis operatur et velle.[76]

There are then texts from scripture, referring to our present state, which St Augustine does not scruple to apply even to the state of primitive innocence. It is not true that for him grace which must now be operative would only then have been cooperative, wholly in dependence on the will of man. But it is true, nevertheless, that without being in itself more marvellous than in the earthly paradise, it is now doubly 'gracious' and assumes, as it were, a miraculous character which hitherto it did not possess.[77] And it is true again that in Adam the attraction of the light (as Malebranche indeed noticed) had no need as with us to be felt, though this does not imply by any means that this light did not need to make itself attractive : for to St Augustine, divine light in itself was already

quid posset eorum liberum arbitrium, deinde quid posset suae gratiae beneficium iustitiaeque iudicium.' After the explanations above, the implications of this text appear to be limited, though there is no need to have recourse to any *effugium*.

[76] *Contra Iulianum opus imperfectum*, bk 5, c. 57. See the commentary by Merlin, *Véritable clef des ouvrages de saint Augustin contre les Pélagiens*, p. 58, and compare this with Jansenius, *Augustinus*, vol. 3, 'De gratia Christi salvatoris', bk 2, c. 26.

[77] St Augustine on one occasion applies, as if parenthetically, his theory of seminal reasons of the second order to the grace of Christ by which the sinner is saved : *De Genesi ad litteram*, bk 9, n. 33. He does so on account of the 'miraculous' character of this grace. It would be an unwarranted extension to appeal to this theory to solve the problem of the relationship between nature and the supernatural. There is a good analysis of the principal passages in A. Darmet, *Les notions de raison séminale et de puissance obédientielle chez saint Augustin et chez saint Thomas* (Belley, 1934). See below, chapter 6.

an attraction of its nature: 'Trahit Christus revelatus a Patre: quid enim fortius desiderat anima, quam veritatem?—Docendo delectat.—Ista revelatio, ipsa est attractio.'[78] This superior attraction, this delight to which Adam himself was subject, was the pure 'delight in the truth'. As of its nature there was nothing 'sensible' in it, it did not impair his free will. Now it is essentially this which Christ still effects in the depths of our hearts. From man in a state of innocence to man redeemed by Christ, there exists therefore through all the undeniable differences a profound continuity which was misunderstood by Jansenius and later by Pascal.[79]

As for the distinction between the grace of the two states, notwithstanding the differences that are known to exist in other respects, is this not the distinction explained by St Thomas when he spoke of the 'auxilium Dei moventis', the help necessary in any circumstances, and the 'auxilium gratiae naturam sanantis', which in the case of us sinners must precede it?[80] St Thomas, using a formula which can be taken as an accurate exegesis of St Augustine and a refutation in anticipation of Jansenius, stated: 'Homo post peccatum ad plura indiget gratia quam ante peccatum, sed non magis.'[81]

[78] *Tractatus in Ioannem*, tr. 26, n. 5. The whole of this paragraph is a commentary on *De natura et gratia*, n. 56. Cf. *De correptione*, n. 37: '. . . a weakness which needs to be helped by greater gifts.' The fifty-seventh chapter of the *Enchiridion* is also very illuminating in its brevity: 'Homo in paradiso ad se occidendum relinquendo iustitiam idoneus erat per voluntatem; ut autem ab eo teneretur vita iustitiae, parum erat velle, nisi ille qui eum fecerat adiuvaret. Sed, post illam ruinam, maior est Dei misericordia, quando et ipsum arbitrium liberandum est a servitute, cum dominatur cum morte peccatum.'

[79] M. Comeau, *op. cit.*, p. 208: 'In the very passage on which Pascal thinks to rely for his theory of victorious delectation (*Writings on Grace* in Brunschvicg ed., vol. 2, pp. 226 and 230-1; Augustine, *In Ioannem*, tract. 26, n. 5), the victorious charm which irresistibly attracts the soul is represented as a revelation of the truth, a sovereign proof for the soul, as well as delight for the heart.'

[80] *Prima Secundae*, qu. 119, art. 3.

[81] *Prima*, qu. 95, art. 4, ad 1um: '. . . quia homo etiam ante peccatum indigebat gratia ad vitam aeternam consequendam, quae est principalis necessitas gratiae; sed homo post peccatum super hoc indiget gratia, etiam ad peccati remissionem et infirmitatis sustentationem.' And *In II Sent.*, dist. 29, art. 2, ad 3um: 'Homo post peccatum indiget gratia ad plura quam ante, sed ad iustitiam habendam non minus indigebat gratia ante quam post; et ideo gratia operante indiguit ante peccatum, sicut et post.' The answer

One thing at least is certain. By reason of several very clear statements by St Augustine himself as well as of his intrinsic idea of the relations between free will and grace[82] and of his other explanations on the difference between Adam's first state and our own, it is impossible to admit that his 'adiutorium sine quo non' is the equivalent and nothing more of the 'sufficient grace' with which Jansenius seems to wish to endow only the father of our race. For the same reasons, neither can his 'adiutorium quo' be likened to efficacious grace by itself, which Jansenius held to be the only one that God would grant through Jesus Christ to the few chosen ones taken from the mass of reprobates, this being the only grace from which they could not even derive profit but merely benefit in an entirely passive way. Fr Daniel was quite right to say in his *Défense de saint Augustin,* which is not aimed directly at Jansenists:[83] 'It is deceiving the faithful to say in general that St Augustine here characterizes the grace of both states in such a way that he only recognizes in the state of innocence graces which can be resisted, and in the state of corrupt nature only necessitating graces.' The distinction between the two

'ad secundum' explains the matter with further conceptual details which are no longer Augustinian: Adam, like us, needed the *infusio gratiae,* but not the *remissio culpae.* (To what extent Adam at first made use of this grace and was established in the positive state of justice are further questions to which St Augustine and St Thomas do not answer in the same way.) And it must be acknowledged that the continuity between Adam and us is clearer in St Thomas, while in St Augustine it is the contrast, because the viewpoint of both is not the same, St Thomas concerning himself particularly with the metaphysical view of the problem of grace, which remains unchanged in the various different states, while Augustine is obliged to maintain and explain against Pelagius the doctrine of original sin and its consequences. There is a similar explanation in Hugh of St Victor (*PL,* 176, 273); Bellarmine, *De gratia primi hominis,* bk 1, c. 4; cf. c. 7: 'Laetiore gratia donatus fuit Adam, nos potentiore' (the words are Augustine's); Bossuet, *Traité du libre arbitre,* c. 5 (Lachat, vol. 25, especially pp. 453-4).
[82] *De gratia et libero arbitrio,* c. 15; *De spiritu et littera,* c. 30. *Epist.* 157, c. 2, nn. 8-10. *Epist.* 194, c. 2, n. 3; etc. In the *De correptione* itself, see c. 8. On the entirely interior relationships of grace and free will in the thought of St Augustine, M. Jacquin, O.P., 'La question de la prédestination aux Ve et VIe siècles' in *RHE* (1904), pp. 744-5.
[83] *Œuvres,* vol. 2 (1724), p. 270. This *Défense* was drawn up in answer to Launoy's work, *La véritable tradition de l'Église sur la Prédestination et sur la Grâce,* in which St Augustine was attacked as an innovator and as the ancestor of heretics, especially of Jansenius.

helps cannot bear such a meaning, because, on its author's view, the problem to be solved was quite different from the problem of efficacious grace, the subject of bitter discussion between Catholic as well as heterodox schools. In *De natura et gratia* for example, in which he examines precisely the hypothesis of a state of integrity and health—that is, a state governed by the 'grace of Adam'—St Augustine says quite simply : 'Et tunc esset *adiutorium* Dei, et tanquam lumen sanis oculis, *quo adiuti* videant, scilicet praeberet volentibus.'[84] As Malebranche again clearly saw, what the Doctor of grace sought to establish against Pelagius was not the irresistible nature of grace, but merely the necessity.[85] Meanwhile developments of the controversy and the internal logic of the problem led him to bring into the foreground the question that for long had been at the back of his mind, namely, that of final perseverance and predestination.[86] In reality it was this necessity of a grace which by definition had at the same time to be gratuitous that had troubled the monks of Hadrumetum, and it was to calm their worries that St Augustine had sent them the book *De correptione et gratia.*[87]

To cut short not only any false solution, but above all any false problem, it is important to repeat that St Augustine's thought, however subtle it was, has no more to do with our distinctions between efficacious or sufficient grace than with our distinctions between sanctifying grace and actual graces. It 'is not involved in our modern controversies'. The Doctor of grace was concerned only 'with the Manicheans and Pelagians'. To give way to the temptation 'to compare his *adiutoria* with the *auxilia*' mentioned by a more recent theology would certainly lead to misinterpretation of him and would result in 'contradictions or

---

[84] *De natura et gratia*, n. 56.

[85] 'Première lettre touchant celles de M. Arnauld', nn. 30ff., etc. Cf. Henri Gouhier, *La philosophie de Malebranche*, p. 180.

[86] *De dono perseverantiae*, n. 55 : 'Puta me ita posuisse donum Dei esse, etiam perseverare in finem, ut hoc antea (i.e. before the *De correptione*), si me non fallit oblivio, tam expresse atque evidenter, vel nusquam vel pene nusquam scripserim.' Cf. *art. cit.*, p. 28.

[87] *Epist.*, 194 ad Sixtum; *De correptione*, nn. 1-4.

dilemmas which, in the end, whether desired or not, would be a justification of Jansenism'.[88]

These last remarks, although as a whole they are negative like those which preceded them, will nevertheless help us to understand more accurately the meaning of the two Augustinian aids. In laying down the distinction between them what exact problem was the author of *De correptione* seeking to solve? It has already been hinted at here and it will now probably appear more clearly. The Oratorian Jean Leporcq, a disciple of Thomassin and a great specialist in the works of St Augustine, came to soundly established conclusions in his voluminous work against Jansenius.[89] The chapter in which the distinction occurs is devoted, remarks Leporcq, to perseverance to the end. In the discussions on grace in which he was involved, this problem of perseverance was a matter of increasing concern to Augustine. Adam's nature was righteous: this is Augustine's teaching; to understand it properly we should remember that this righteousness went hand in hand with a close union with the Creator, and that Augustinian 'nature' is not exactly what was intended by the scholastic 'nature' of Baius or Jansenius. As a result of this righteousness, to fulfil his destiny Adam did not need a special help in addition to the helps that God had granted him for each of his acts. This supplementary help, which is now indispensable for us to be saved, far from comprising prevenient grace alone, consists in the whole of the means, interior and exterior, used by God to lead his chosen ones unerringly from justification up to final perseverance. That is the 'adiutorium quo': a help which, by definition given only to the predestined, sets them free from evil for ever; 'liberationis haec gratia': a help which without necessarily preventing their falling into sin during their mortal life—no one is exempted from praying daily for the forgiveness of their debts—prevents their remaining in it to the end, from giving

[88] A. Sage, *loc. cit.*, pp. 209, 221, 224-6.
[89] *Sentiments de saint Augustin opposés à ceux de Jansénius* (1682). See also Charles Boyer, *op. cit.*, pp. 217-19.

themselves up to 'this sin which leads to death';[90] in the last place, it is a help which gives not merely a will, but a will to persevere.[91]

Jean Leporcq is not alone in maintaining this interpretation. It is that of the Capuchin Charles-Joseph, the author of a translation of the *De correptione,* which appeared in 1683.[92] With some slight modifications it was also Fr Annat's,[93] Petau's and Thomassin's.[94] 'The help *quo,*' says the last-named, 'is nothing else than the multitude, variety, the coming together of several helps by which Providence leads and watches over its chosen ones with so much gentleness, wisdom and strength that they persevere right to the end; or, if they fall, that unerringly they raise themselves up from their sins.'[95] Merlin in his *Véritable Clef*[96] and the

[90] 'By this grace they receive so great a freedom that although so long as they live in this world they are obliged to fight against the attractions of sin, into which they sometimes fall, for which they say every day, "Lord, forgive us our sins", nevertheless they will never give themselves up to that sin which leads to death.' Nor does that mean that a future 'elect' can only commit small sins; he could fall into what we call the state of mortal sin, by committing what St Augustine calls *crimina* (which he contrasts, as being more serious, with simple *peccata*): *Enchiridion,* cc. 54-5.

[91] *De correptione,* c. 13, n. 39: 'Haec de his loquor, qui praedestinati sunt in regnum Dei.' Cf. Fénelon (*Œuvres,* vol. 2, p. 182). See below, at the end of chapter 3, Note on the *De correptione et gratia,* p. 93. See also Boyer, *op. cit.,* p. 226.

[92] 'Although St Augustine states that the grace which he mentions is efficacious it is not the nature of this grace always to be efficacious, as some have thought; but he is speaking here of the grace of God which is always efficacious and so always produces its effect' (p. 377).

[93] *Augustinus a Baianis vindicatus,* bk 7, c. 6, sect. 8.

[94] Cf. Daniel, *op. cit.,* vol. 2, pp. 270-83. In an analogous sense, the theses of the Paris Jesuits, *Jesuitarum Parisiensium theses de gratia Christi Salvatoris,* 21 February 1685, 1: 'Relicta regia via, quae in Augustini scriptis ostio tantummodo referato, valde manifesta est, ad diverticula nova et periculosa divertit, qui docet gratiae sanitatis et medicinalis verum et genuinum discrimen esse, quod gratiae sanae voluntatis in eius libero arbitrio relinqueretur, ut eam, si vellet, desereret, aut ea, si vellet, uteretur; gratia vero lapsae aegrotaeque voluntatis, nullo modo in eius relinquatur arbitrio, ut eam deserat aut arripiat. . . .' In Aug. Le Blanc (Serry), *Historia congregationum de auxiliis* (1700), appendix, col. 455-6.

[95] *Mémoires de la Grâce,* c. 60.

[96] 1732, p. 73: 'The help *sine quo non* must belong to the providential order observed by God in regard to Adam and the angels before their sin, in the distribution of the means of salvation, just as the help *quo* is the providential order observed by God now in regard to the predestined.'

Lettres d'un docteur de Sorbonne à un homme de qualité touchant les hérésies du XVIIe siècle[97] repeated it a century later, and Zaccaria was to explain it in his *Diatribe* on the two helps[98] and Bergier in his Dictionary.[99] Other interpretations have been put forward which more or less link up together. It has been asserted for example that in addition to the helps like those given to Adam ('sine quo non') God now dispenses other graces too ('quo') which are unerringly efficacious. This kind of exegesis is untenable. It aims rather at correction of the teaching of Jansenius than at close examination of the text of St Augustine, and it has the disadvantage of seeking in this passage, like Jansenius, a direct solution to the problem of the efficacy of grace. Estius was hardly more successful when he contrived to make the help 'sine quo non' correspond to habitual grace, and we can understand why the 'Doctor fundatissimus' after setting out on so fruitless a quest, was finally discouraged. In the end he declared that such an obscure distinction could be given up since it did not possess the authority of scripture, nor of the other Fathers of the Church, and it was not followed by St Thomas.[100] A wise conclusion in practice, but insufficient for the historian.

Fénelon, for his part, was principally concerned to show that the Augustinian distinction did not create 'a diversity of species' between two graces, 'so that one by its nature or essence includes the good will of man and the other . . . leaves man still indifferent to himself'. In his first *Lettre au Père Lamy sur la grâce et la prédestination* he repeats roughly Leporcq's interpretation, which

[97] Vol. 1 (1711). *Abrégé des sentiments de saint Augustin sur le système de Jansénius,* pp. 377-411 : 'It has been shown quite clearly that St Augustine in the passages quoted by Jansenius certainly did not claim to explain the nature of graces of the present state of mankind; and that he merely pointed out the difference of the grace given to Adam to maintain him in his state from the grace given to us now for us to persevere to the end.' Cf. pp. 391-2, and 397-8. See also the analysis of the *Augustinus* of Jansenius (1721), p. 334: 'There is no way of explaining the help by which, *auxilium quo,* except by understanding it in the sense of the innovators.'
[98] *Op. cit.* (above, p. 47, note 47), especially c. 2, 3 and 4.
[99] *Dictionnaire de Théologie, art.* 'Augustinianisme' (Besançon ed., 1830, vol. 1, p. 261).
[100] *In I Sent.,* dist. 41, sect. 14.

he had consulted. By the help 'quo', he considered, 'God, pre-destining in Jesus Christ certain men whom we call elect, makes ready for them certain means which, without taking away the will for good by their own nature or essence, are nevertheless pro-portionate to the need of the human will, and so fitted both to persuade man and inspire him to will, so that he wills effec-tively'.[101] A few years later, Fénelon without leaving this view aside, brought out more clearly the relationship of the 'adiutorium quo' with final perseverance. This was in his great *Instruction pastorale en forme de dialogues sur le système de Jansénius* where he dealt with the question at length. There as always he shows a thorough and varied knowledge of his author. Nevertheless he does not fully describe Augustinian thought when he makes this 'adiutorium quo' consist somewhat narrowly in 'a quick death' because, he says, 'as life is evil, death is the grace of deliver-ance'.[102] Although he bases his explanation on a previous passage of *De correptione,* in which St Augustine speaks actually of the righteous who by the grace of God 'mortis celeritate subtrahun-tur',[103] Fénelon is mistaken, or he is in danger of misleading us by too abrupt a short-cut in thinking that 'the great Doctor obviously confines the *adiutorium quo* to the last moment alone', to that 'decisive moment when the end of this life finds a man really persevering', to 'the end itself which suddenly arrives by the mercy of God'.[104] The *Lettre au Père Lamy* was more satis-fying.

Nevertheless, this last explanation contains certain elements

[101] *Œuvres,* vol. 3 (Versailles, 1820), pp. 307-8.
[102] *Œuvres,* vol. 15 (Paris, 1823), pp. 380-464. Daniel gives a good summary of Fénelon's twofold explanation. In his view, the *adiutorium quo* 'consists principally in that auspicious providence of God which causes all things to co-operate for the salvation of his elect, which upholds them, raises them up again by his grace, prevents their straying or brings them back when they have strayed, causes them to die or preserves their lives according as he thinks it serves their salvation, and takes them always in favourable con-ditions' (*loc. cit.,* p. 280).
[103] *De correptione,* c. 7, n. 13, and c. 8, n. 9: 'Sicut ergo coguntur fateri, donum Dei esse ut finiat homo vitam istam, antequam ex bono mutetur in malum.'
[104] *Loc. cit.*

worthy of note. For like St John when he scans the depths of souls to discern in them beneath passing appearance their definitive attitude to the light, and like St Paul when he praises the unerring ways by which God leads his chosen ones, St Augustine, in his reflections on grace, takes a synthetic view of human life, and to form a judgment on it is apt to look at it from its end. With him this is as much a habit of his philosophical manner of thought as the result of his meditation on the Bible. It is also, so to say, an instinct of his mystical genius. We know how important it is to remember this in considering his teaching on the salvific will,[105] or, in another sphere, in studying his teaching on the Church.[106] It has also to be remembered for a full understanding of the 'adiutorium quo' which is soon to be realized, and so to say gathered together in the final help, the 'donum perseverantiae': it is as if St Augustine were following in himself, as he approached his own end, the transformations of divine action in the continuity of an ever more pressing appeal.[107] Is not the definition which he gives of the 'adiutorium quo' in the eleventh chapter of the *De correptione* ('the help which imparts blessedness')[108] already fitting for the 'gift of perseverance'? In spirit he crosses the last boundary, even to the extent that finally the difference which he emphasizes so strongly appears as less that between Adam's state and the present state of the righteous than that between the state of earthly paradise and the heavenly state. As a matter of fact, on the same page on which occurs the distinction that Jansenius was to falsify, as we have seen, he wrote: 'Prima libertas voluntatis erat, posse non peccare; novissima erit multo maior, non posse peccare. Prima immortalitas erat, posse non mori; novissima

---

[105] Cf. van Crombrugghe, '*La doctrine sotériologique de saint Augustin*' in *RHE* (1904), p. 501.

[106] *De civitate Dei*, bk 19, c. 17: 'Civitas caelestis vel potius pars eius quae in hac mortalitate peregrinatur. . . .'

[107] The *De correptione* belongs to 426, the *De praedestinatione sanctorum* and the *De dono perseverantiae* to 428 or 429. Augustine died in 430. This comparison of the *adiutorium quo* with the *donum perseverantiae* was outlined by Daniel, *Défense de saint Augustin, loc. cit.,* pp. 281-2.

[108] N. 34. The whole of the following chapter is devoted to the subject of final perseverance.

erit multo maior, non posse mori. Prima erat perseverantiae potestas, bonum non posse deserere; novissima erit felicitas perseverantiae, bonum non posse deserere.' It is in this final state, this perfect freedom and happiness, this everlasting stability that, in the 'adiutorium quo', as in its cause, Augustine exults by anticipation.[109]

The 'adiutorium quo' is an eschatological grace, already present, it is 'a grace culminating in the gift of final perseverance'; 'final perseverance is the measure of its extent and defines its boundaries'.[110]

It can be said that in this way St Augustine solves the twofold problem raised by the Pelagian controversy. With his unique idea of the 'adiutorium quo' in reality he unites the two ideas for which he fought so hard; on the one hand the idea that man without divine grace cannot attain to the perfection of justice and, on the other, the idea that even with grace he cannot attain to it absolutely here below. Increasingly, under the influence of the controversy, the contrast between the sinner and the just man, or between man of the old Law and man of the new, gave place in his mind to another : the comparison between man who on earth struggles against evil and the one who in the 'fatherland' is entirely set free. Right at the end, in his incomplete work against Julian, he wrote : 'Nec ipsa lex nova . . . testimonium est liberae, sed liberandae potius voluntatis.'[111] As happened in other encounters, it was by means of a very questionable piece of exegesis that he was able to achieve this development of his teaching. At the time when he wrote his *Questiones ad Simplicianum* he could still

[109] Although Fénelon restricts the field of the *adiutorium quo* unduly, seeing it as an 'early death' which places man 'beyond the temptation of his earthly pilgrimage', and ensures his eternal salvation by taking away his free will, he is not far from the truth in his view that 'this special help is the gift of final perseverance alone, which is only given to the elect, by the end alone'. More accurately, Augustine only mentions it in connection with the elect

[110] A. Sage, 'Les deux temps de la grâce', *loc cit.*, pp. 219-20 and 230.

[111] Bk 6, c. 15. This is the view already in n. 33 of the *De correptione*: 'Now, because the final benefits will be greater than the first, does that mean that the first were nothing, or very little?'

understand the sinner's plaint mentioned in St Paul on the good
that despite his desire he had not the strength to accomplish.[112]
But later he came to think that this painful inability was also the
position of the Christian, even of the 'spiritual man'.[113] This
second interpretation, which is a continuation and deeper investigation of the first rather than a substitute for it, constitutes the
whole theme of the treatise *De perfectione iustitiae* in which he
refutes Celestius who claimed that man could exist without sin.
His refutation is not purely and simply a denial, but he asks:
When and how can this state of perfect justice be realized? That
is what Celestius had not understood. Augustine's final answer
was given by the 'adiutorium quo', the help through which we
are enabled 'perficere bonum', to arrive 'ad saturitatem
iustitiae', to possess at last in all perfection health of soul, justice,
freedom, charity—which obviously can only take place in heaven,
'quando videbimus Deum sicuti est'.[114]

In these circumstances are we, with some historians, to talk of
determinism? Must we once again stir up the ghost of Manes?
We might just as well attack St John the Apostle whose teaching
is well known on the opposition of light and darkness, on the man
who, born of God, sins no more,[115] on the judgment that has
already been given, and on those who 'went out . . . but they were

---

[112] Quaest. 1, n. 11: 'Velle adiacet mihi, perficere autem bonum non
invenio: istae voces sunt sub lege hominis constituti, nondum sub gratia;
non enim quod vult facit bonum, qui nondum est sub gratia.'

[113] He wrote in his *Rectractationes,* bk 2, c. 2, n. 1: 'Longe postea etiam
spiritualis hominis (et hoc probabilius) esse posse illa verba cognovi.' Cf.
Contra Iulianum pelagianum, bk 2, c. 8-9; bk 3, c. 26.

[114] *De perfectione iustitiae,* n. 7-9; n. 16: 'Quod neque nos negamus;
quando autem possit, et per quem possit, hoc quaeritur'; cc. 17ff. As we know,
this Augustinian idea of justice, in opposition to the Pelagian idea of im-
peccability, is regarded by Merlin, the sometimes over-subtle continuer of
Petau, as the 'real key to the works of St Augustine against the Pelagians' (it
is the title of the first part of the book called *Réfutation des critiques de M.
Bayle sur saint Augustine,* Paris, 1732). Like Jansenius on the subject of the
adiutorium quo, in presenting his work to the reader he says that he has
made a 'discovery', the 'fortunate and solid consequences' of which will be to
throw light on Augustinian doctrine even in its slightest details. See also
Mémoires de Trévoux, December 1736, pp. 2605-16.

[115] The author of the *Exercices du Pénitent* (1737) relies on the text from
St John: 'Omnis qui natus est ex Deo, peccatum non facit.'

not of us. . . '.[116] Like the Evangelist whose keen perception found
its continuation in him, Augustine sees in the present moment
more than its momentary reality; he refuses to consider a passing
reality otherwise than in its relationship to the final state. But all
the same he is far from reducing to mere spectres the vicissitudes
of this world, with the alternatives of good and evil which follow
one another in men's consciences; right up to the end, he hopes
or fears the conversions or perversions which are always possible.[117] With St Paul he can recognize the insurmountable duality
which is the Christian's lot in this world: 'Aliud quippe volumus
quia sumus in Christo, et aliud volumus quia sumus adhuc in hoc
saeculo.'[118] He is able when necessary to discern the two viewpoints
of time and eternity, and while maintaining the pre-excellence of
the second, which is that of divine fore-knowledge,[119] he does not
fail to acknowledge the reality of the first.[120] This is a frequent
theme of his and it recurs in the *De correptione*.[121] Commenting
on St Paul's terrifying phrase, 'Dedit eos in reprobum sensum', he
explains: 'Ea est caecitas mentis; in eam quisquis datus fuerit, ab
interiore Dei luce secluditur; *sed nondum penitus cum hac in vita
est.*' So long as the eighth day, the day of judgment and of consummation, has not dawned the alternation of darkness and light
does not cease.[122] Those who afterwards repeated his profound
statements in order to obtain from them a despairing theory on

[116] 1 John 2:19; 3:9; John 3:18.
[117] *De correptione*, n. 26 and 40. The *adiutorium quo*, although it does not
prevent momentary lapses, establishes a man finally in a state of impecca-
bility: now we have just seen that St Augustine does not admit such a
state as possible on earth. See also *Enchiridion*, cc. 54-5; *Epistulae ad Galatas
expositio*, n. 47; *Expositio quorumdam propositionum ex epistula ad
Romanos*, c. 13; *In Ioannem*, tract. 1, n. 6, etc.
[118] *In Ioannem*, tract. 81, n. 4 (*CSEL*, 36, 531).
[119] 'In illa ineffabili praescientia Dei multi qui foris videntur, intus sunt,
et multi qui intus videntur, foris sunt.'
[120] 'Sunt filii Dei qui nondum sunt nobis et iam sunt Deo; et rursus sunt
quidam qui filii Dei propter susceptam vel temporaliter gratiam dicuntur a
nobis, nec sunt tamen Deo' (*De baptismo*, bk 5, n. 38; bk 4, n. 4). Cf. *In
Ioannem*, tract. 45, n. 12; *In epist. primam Ioannis*, tract. 3, n. 4, 5, 8, 9.
De perfectione iustitiae, n. 39. Cf. *Epistulae ad Gal. expositio*, n. 47, etc.
[121] C. 9, n. 20 (*PL*, 44, 928).
[122] *In psalmos*, 6, n. 8; see the whole sermon.

'the stability of Christian justice'[123] were to show their powerlessness to raise themselves up to the summit where he dominates, without denying it, the dispersal of time. It was for their benefit that Tauler seems to have uttered the words which he addressed to certain unintelligent hearers of his teacher Eckhart : 'Not long ago a teacher spoke to us of these things, but you did not understand him. He spoke to you from the point of view of eternity, you understood him from the point of view of time.'[124]

'Many people,' Tauler went on, 'understood him in accordance with their senses and they became infected with poison.'

---

[123] Cf. this hymn in the *Exercices du Pénitent*, p. 478 :

> All those who lay their troubles on Jesus
> Feel their ills flee at his voice;
> But how fearful to fall again;
> He cures no one twice.

Or Nicole himself, usually so moderate: *Essais de morale*, vol. 12, on the epistle for the sixth Sunday after Pentecost, n. 8.

[124] Sermon for the day before Palm Sunday. English trans. by J. M. Clark, in *Meister Eckhart: An Introduction to the Study of his Works with an Anthology of his Sermons* (1957). 'The most imponderable things about St Augustine is his rhythm and it comes to an end with him', wrote E. Przywara (quoted by H. Urs von Balthasar in *Le visage de l'Église,* French trans., 1958, p. 19). This is true, not only of his style but also of his thought.

3

Jansenius—II

In the introduction to the second volume of his *Augustinus* Jansenius, in defining theological method, complains of the disastrous effects caused by the intrusion of philosophical reasoning, the mother of all heresies, and contrasts it with the 'memory' or the study of tradition. Many theologians before him, particularly Bérulle, had dreamt of a renewal of theology by simpler and more spiritual means. At Louvain itself, since the time of Erasmus, the abuses of Scholasticism had occasioned more than one attempt at reform. Earlier still, French humanists like Clamanges, Fichet or Gaguin, tried to return to the tradition of Alcuin and St Bernard, which was inspired by St Augustine.[1] But the originality of Jansenius consisted in his reacting against Scholasticism in a very pig-headed and scholastic way and in understanding the tradition that he wished to revive in a sense that was not only strict but also narrow-minded.

He rejected outright the 'gossips of the schools' who were guilty of introducing a 'strange maze of opinions' and had 'corrupted theology' so thoroughly that it was a wonder that the whole Church had not followed them in falling into error. Only the 'old way' was in his view 'that of truth', and this way was that of St Augustine alone.[2] His veneration for the doctor of Hippo, that

---

[1] Cf. Henri Gouhier, R. Guelluy, *art. cit.*, *RHE*, 37 (1941). L. Willaert, *Les Origines du Jansénisme dans les Pays-Bas catholiques* (1948). Étienne Gilson, *La Philosophie au moyen âge* (1944) (English trans. *History of Christian Philosophy in the Middle Ages*, 1955); Anthony Levi, 'La psychologie des facultés au XVIIᵉ siècle', *loc. cit.*, pp. 301-2.

[2] To Saint-Cyran, 5 March 1621 (Orcibal, pp. 69-70). Expressions of this kind are still treated with some respect by certain historians for whom 'the old theology' or 'the old theological traditions' seem to be confused with Augustinianism, and Augustinianism, or at least that of the seventeenth century, with the teaching of Jansenius.

'divine mind', that 'doctor of doctors', was the result of an exclusive enthusiasm. Baius had not disdained to learn from some other Latin Fathers; on occasion, he was even led to cite the authority of St Irenaeus or St Cyril of Alexandria.[3] But Jansenius was far more uncompromising. In the face of his scorn of the Greek Fathers Isaac Habert exclaimed : 'Non solum indignor, sed etiam obstupesco!'[4] In fact, to Jansenius literally nothing counted besides Augustine's teaching; he was the one sun in the doctrinal heaven; he alone had elucidated the four great mysteries of faith —the Trinity, the Church, baptism and grace. He was comparable to St John and St Paul. As St John explained the divinity of the Word, so Augustine explained the grace of Christ in which the whole of the New Testament could be found. His work was a real Gospel which was to be read with the same humility and in the same submissive spirit as the scriptures were to be read. None of the early Fathers could offer anything comparable.[5] Jansenius confessed that in reading him he was seized 'sacra quadam admiratione et pavore'. He swore to devote his life to the spread of the light which he had received.[6] By a process of reduction not unlike one experienced in our own century, once Augustine was acknowledged to possess all the qualities characteristic of the other doctors, instead of extending his investigations Jansenius set about studying the truth in him alone. And just as he did not consult the earlier Fathers, neither did he concern himself with the theologians who came afterwards. St Augustine had fixed the boundaries beyond which those who ventured could only go astray. With the exception of the few points subsequently defined by the authority of the Church, everything which from the very depths of revelation baffled him will always baffle us; in him, therefore, Jansenius

[3] A. Morillon, 23 December 1567 (Roca, p. 362). *De prima hominis iustitia*, bk 1, c. 1 (Gerberon, vol. 1, p. 50).

[4] *Theologiae graecorum Patrum*, p. 2.

[5] *Augustinus*, vol. 2, Liber proemialis, cc. 7-20 (pp. 7-28); vol. 3, *De gratia Christi salvatoris*, bk 6, proemium (pp. 253-5). Fénelon blamed him for this exclusivism : *Instruction pastorale. . .* , 17th letter (*Œuvres*, Paris, 1823, vol. 16, pp. 3-60).

[6] *Augustinus*, vol. 2. Liber proem., c. 17 (p. 16 E). To Saint-Cyran, 14 October 1619; 15 October 1620; 11 February 1622 (Orcibal, pp. 58, 65, 110), etc .

could hear the whole of tradition.[7] 'Unum (Augustinum) pro omni materia theologica sufficere aiebat.'[8] We are even assured that by dint of continually rereading him Jansenius knew him by heart.[9] In any case, despite the example bequeathed him by Baius—'attentione acri et adnotatione diligenti'[10]—he did not always read him aright. His disciples, for their part, imitated his exclusive attitude,[11] and most of them only read the ancient doctor through the eyes of the 'new Augustine'.[12] Following his example, the whole party proclaimed far and wide 'the heavenly doctrine of St Augustine', as formerly the Jews cried 'The temple of the Lord, the temple of the Lord', but they understood him no better than the Jews in their blindness could understand the scriptures.[13]

We can hardly be surprised at this if we notice in what spirit and under the influence of what particular concerns Jansenius

[7] *Augustinus*, vol. 2, Liber Proem., c. 11 : '. . . cum inter omnes Ecclesiae Patres ac Doctores unus ille sit . . .' (p. 12 BC); c. 23 : '. . . nemo limites illius (theologiae christianae) notitiae . . . propius invenisse videtur ac fixisse, quam Augustinus, quos terminos ab illo fixos, qui accuratioris alicuius doctrinae praetextu, praetergredi nituntur, nimium felices habendi sunt, si non in humanarum opinionum labyrinthis sine tali duce aberrantes, proprias imaginationes pro scientia ex fide derivata mirentur . . . quidquid scientiae ex fidei fundamentis per rationem eliciendae sanctum istum latuit, etiam posteros latuisse (arbitrandum est) . . .' (pp. 20-1).

[8] *Synopsis vitae auctoris (Augustinus*, init.).

[9] *Renversement de la religion*, vol. 1, p. 478.

[10] *Synopsis vitae auctoris.*

[11] Jansenius, one of them wrote, was raised up by God 'ut fax veritatis ab Augustino in Ecclesia accensa, et humanae philosophiae nebulis seorsim involuta, restitueretur, et caligines illae dissiparentur, et S. Augustinus splendori suo redderetur.' In exam. proposit. excerpt., 4 (quoted by Fr Annat, *Augustinus a Baianis vindicatus*, 1652, p. 438).

[12] When Habert, desiring to uphold the orthodoxy of the Greek Fathers, gave quotations which proved awkward for the party (*Theologiae graecorum Patrum vindicatae circa universam materiam gratiae*, 1646), Gerberon replied, in *Histoire générale du jansénisme*, vol. 1 (1700), p. 185 : 'Habert had forgotten that he was a son of the Latin Church, and that the Latin Church does not refer its children to the Greek Fathers but to St Augustine to find out what they ought to believe about the mysteries of grace.' (Cf. *DTC*, vol. 8, col. 469, art. 'Jansénisme'.) Previous centuries provided similar examples. According to Richard Simon, Thomas Bradwardine (1290-1349), 'one of the most rigid and fervent Thomists there ever was', had a 'sovereign disregard for the Greek Fathers': *Critique de la Bibliothèque des auteurs ecclésiastiques de M. Du Pin* (1730).

[13] Fénelon, *loc. cit.*, pp. 122 and 131.

approached his author. 'The doctrinal basis of Jansenism', it has been said, 'is not, properly speaking, a particular view of pre-destination, nor even of freedom; it is an optimistic idea of the normal state of the reasonable creature.'[14] We have already seen in what this optimism—the word is possibly not very well chosen —consisted. St Augustine, we have also seen, viewed matters from quite another angle. Throughout his contest with Pelagius his starting-point was situated in actual humanity in its present state, and that was already the method that he used at the time when, reflecting on his own history, he came to the point of criticizing Manichean or neo-Platonist ideas as erroneous or ineffective. Of this his *Confessions* are the abiding witness. On the other hand, his metaphysical genius was freely exercised in treating of God, the creature, predestination and Providence, without confining his view to one or another state of man.[15] If like St Paul he was led to deal with the first man and the state of innocence, it was by way of contrast with the present situation; what he says about them is not a cardinal point of his teaching but appears rather as a set of conclusions derived from it. In anthropology, his field of direct observation and his real centre were, as for St Paul again, man as sinner or as redeemed by the grace of Christ.[16] The view-point of Jansenius, always an individual one, is precisely the contrary, as a mere glance at the plan of the *Augustinus* clearly shows. Following a system which among the medieval theologians was popular as a teaching method, Jansenius, the despiser of scholastic theologians, borrowed it from them and fell into the trap. At the outset he postulated the state of Adam and deter-mined *a priori,* according to philosophical views uncritically accepted and remote from Augustinianism, the role that grace had to play in it. Now since this theory was false—the 'optimism', or rather the naturalism, characterizing it being in direct line of

[14] J. Paquier, *Le Jansénisme* (1909), p. 130.

[15] Cf. P.-J. Thonnard, 'Le prédestination augustiniennes' in *Revue des études augustiniennes,* 10 (1964), pp. 97-123.

[16] More than in connection with this problem of grace and the supernatural, this remark is important for reducing St Augustine's authority on the questions of human origins, paradise and the first sin, to its right proportion.

descent from Baius—the whole of his teaching is vitiated by it.

Actually, once it was admitted as a starting-point that the earthly paradise was placed under the rule—regarded as the ideal —of a sufficient grace which man had at his disposal like an instrument, there was no way, apart from falling into the semi-Pelagian error, of avoiding in our present world grace which was efficacious of its nature. For medicinal grace could no longer be understood as really curing and freeing the will; remaining external to the will, it came to take its place. If therefore not everything was attributed to the will, something was necessarily attributed to it that was external to the will. This was a formidable dilemma which puzzled not only the Jansenists. The two similar cases of Malebranche and Thomassin make this clear, though in a somewhat more attenuated form.

By his *Traité de la Nature et de la Grâce* (1680) Malebranche hoped 'to bring back many people who had gone over to Jansenius' opinion'.[17] He too contrasted the 'grace of the Creator' with the 'grace of Jesus Christ'. The former was a 'grace of light', the latter a grace of 'feeling' or 'delectation', for light 'cannot cure a heart wounded by pleasure; this pleasure must cease, or another take its place'; to rescue sinful man from his wretchedness the grace of feeling must be set against concupiscence. Nevertheless, while 'the light leaves us interiorly free, pleasure exerts influence on our freedom', it 'lessens' it, causing us to 'love the good rather from a love of instinct and impetuosity than from a love springing from choice and reason'. As a result, while the grace of the Creator enlightened a perfectly free man, that of Jesus Christ is efficacious of itself in weakened man. But, as 'concupiscence has not entirely destroyed freedom', this grace, efficacious by its nature, has not to be efficacious right to the end : it 'is not wholly insuperable'; by setting 'pleasure against pleasure' or 'horror against horror' it sets us free, 'restores us almost to equilibrium and by this means we are in a state to follow our light in the

<hr/>

[17] *Correspondance inédite* (ed. E.-A. Blampignon, 1862), p. 9, to Abbé B. : 'It will be found, I think, that this subject has already been thoroughly discussed without agreement being reached.'

movement of our love'; henceforth, we can merit by going 'as it were, further' than we are 'invincibly urged by pleasure', acting from a 'pure and reasonable love'.[18]

After striving to prevent the publication of the *Traité* Arnauld opposed Malebranche bitterly in a controversy which lasted upwards of twelve years until 1694. According to Arnauld, Malebranche firstly fell into 'Luther's heresy with his love of instinct and feeling', then 'into that of Pelagius with the movement of free love and reason', whence it followed that 'our merits are not the gifts of God'.[19] Fénelon urged by Bossuet to write a *Réfutation du système du Père Malebranche sur la Grâce*,[20] somewhat more shrewdly observed that Malebranche held a view of grace that was too narrowly paralleled by the idea of concupiscence; as a result, in his desire to avoid the error of Jansenius, he had to fall back on the opposite view and maintain that to be meritorious our action must go further than a prevenient 'delectatio' impels it, so that we go forward by ourselves toward the real good. Opposed on all sides, put on the Index, the *Traité* was condemned in 1689-90, and one of the reasons, urged as especially serious, was its agreement with Molinism and Quietism.[21]

It should however be noticed, lest we attribute to Malebranche a position too glaringly in contrast with Jansenism, that in saying that consent must be the act of the will alone, at the point where prevenient grace (and necessitating grace) ends he does not mean 'the will and the deed', but only 'the consent to the will and the deed'; for he bore carefully in mind that the will and the deed

---

[18] *Traité*. . . , Second discourse, 21-31; Third discourse, 13, 18-23, 29, 34.

[19] Summary by Ginette Dreyfus, *Malebranche, Traité* . . . , *Introduction philosophique* (1958), pp. 113-16. Malebranche replied that his principles, on the contrary, destroyed this heresy right to its foundations.

[20] 1687; it remained unpublished until 1820, perhaps because Bossuet, who at first termed Malebranche a heretic, had been reconciled with him. For the historical detail and the principles involved see the thesis by Fr Yves de‧ Montcheuil, *Malebranche et le Quiétisme* (1946), as well as the Introduction referred to by G. Dreyfus.

[21] G. Dreyfus, *Introduction* . . . , appendices 1 and 2 (pp. 166-73). On the contrary idea of Malebranche and Fénelon regarding pure or disinterested love: Yves de Montcheuil, *op. cit.*, pp. 309-24, 'L'argument de la grâce'. Cf. Ely Carcasonne, *Fénelon, l'homme et l'œuvre* (1946), p. 124.

are themselves both from God. By its agreement the will which acts allows itself simply to go where God takes it.[22] In addition— and here we touch on a fundamental point underlying the whole of this book—Malebranche's idea of nature is very near the Augustinian idea; at least it is much nearer to it than that of Jansenius and most of the Scholastics. Without being false to his thought, we can therefore say that nature which, to merit, must go further than it is impelled by medicinal grace, in reality only obtains the strength for this further effort from another grace. Despite these various qualifications it must be nevertheless confessed that Malebranche's position is at least 'delicate'[23] and that he is by no means a safe interpreter of St Augustine. Malebranche read him as a Cartesian just as Jansenius, despite his protests, read him as a Scholastic; it was inevitable that, like Jansenius, Malebranche should to some extent misinterpret Augustine.[24]

For his part, Thomassin, faced with the same difficulty, summarized the contrast between innocent nature and fallen nature in the following terms: 'Adamo certe adhuc stanti permiserat Deus clavum et moderamen omne sui, et perseverantiam denique finalem. Atqui, nulla ex eis rebus metimus merita, quae non nostra posita sunt in potestate. Angeli denique et Adamus auxiliis sibi concessis moderabantur, nunc illa nobis moderantur.'[25] In this passage we can discern, couched in a Latin more to the taste of

---

[22] It remains to be seen whether such a distinction, which makes consent (to which free will is likened) something entirely negative, is fully intelligible.

[23] Yves de Montcheuil, *op. cit.*, p. 324: 'What is given to the intensity of delectation is taken away from freedom. In the present state of man merit and danger go together; Malebranche is therefore caught between the fear of exposing man too much and that of lessening his merit, the source of his future happiness. The point of balance is difficult to determine.'

[24] And see also Henri Gouhier, *La philosophie de Malebranche et son expérience religieuse* (1926), pp. 142-56. Lucien Labbas, *La grâce et la liberté dans Malebranche* (1931). Geneviève Rodis-Lewis, *Nicolas Malebranche* (1963), pp. 244-54.

[25] *Consensus scholae de gratia* (in Vivès ed., vol. 6, p. 56). Thomassin adds: 'Nostrum ergo nunc aliquid minus est, nec tanti est meritum nostrum, ubi Deus centies a nobis repulsus, a nobis repugnando fatigatis vix tandem extorquet assensum.' Cf. *Dogmata theologica,* praefatio: 'Non perseverante enim Adamo in ea quam acceperat gratia . . . , opus fuit . . . alio ac validiore gratiae adiutorio, quo qui donarentur, invictissimae perseverarent' (vol. 1, p. 6).

the end of the period of Louis XIV, the distinction of the two helps 'sine quo non' and 'quo', but with a tendency on this occasion towards Jansenius' interpretation. Of course, the 'learned Oratorian mediator'[26] had an entirely different idea from the sectarian theologian of the efficacy of what he still calls 'insuperabile adiutorium', so that the similarity is less real than at first appears. Nonetheless, it is undeniable that here again, and in the opposite sense from Malebranche, the equilibrium is upset.

Whether the bias is towards one side or the other, there is always, whether pronounced or latent, the same initial assumption on the position of Adam, governed by the same idea—the same error—on the role of grace in relationship to free will. On a final analysis it is an error on the supernatural itself, on the mystery of divine adoption. Admitted or not, predominating or hinted at, it is always the naturalist thesis: created nature is regarded as perfect in itself, not necessarily beyond all divine help (Baius and his followers actually call for this help) but outside that relationship with God which makes it open and raises it above itself. But Jansenius, an uncompromising logician, has taken the theory to its logical conclusion, both in its fundamental principle and its consequences. His supralapsarian 'optimism' has determined his practical pessimism. Like St Augustine he understood literally St Paul's phrase, 'Having been set free from sin you have become slaves of righteousness', without, as Augustine did, noticing the Apostle's qualification which follows immediately: 'I am speaking in human terms, because of your human weakness.'[27] He sees the grace of God now reigning over the ruins of a nature formerly master of itself.

But is this really grace in the Christian sense of the word? Sometimes it appears as an instrument under the complete mastery

---

[26] This is the title given him by the *Nouvelles ecclésiastiques*. Cf. Pierre Clair, *Louis Thomassin, étude biographique et bibliographique* (1964), p. 79.

[27] Rom. 6:18-19. St Augustin, *Enchiridion*, c. 30: 'Ad iuste faciendum liber non erit homo, nisi a peccato liberatus, esse iustitiae caeperit servus. Ipsa est vera libertas propter recti facti licentiam, simul et pia servitus propter praecepti obedientiam.' Similarly, Baius, with his legalistic attitude, took the expression 'lex fidei' of Rom. 6:27 literally; St Augustine on the contrary very differently, *De spiritu et littera*, c. 10.

of man, and sometimes as an invading power taking the place of all natural activity and reducing him whom it 'sets free' to a new slavery. How can we recognize in this that initiative of creative Love, which precedes the human effort that it has itself set in motion in order to make it efficacious or restore it to its first rectitude, and which brings about the marvellous union of which the Incarnation of the Word is at once the pledge and the exalted model?[28] Yet to Augustine this was pre-eminently the mystery of grace, a mystery which assumes different forms but remains fundamentally the same in various states of humanity. To him, man and God were not two powers in confrontation, nor two individuals who are strangers to each other. He was aware of divine transcendence; he had even experienced the instinctive repulsion of the sinner and of the being imbued with nothingness which doubles, so to say, the distance naturally separating the finite from the infinite. But with St John and with all humble Christians he believed in Love. He had even experienced the irresistible strength of its appeal, which was capable of filling all the depths. Lastly, there was no question for him of opposition between nature and grace, but of inclusion; there was no contest, but union. It was not a matter for man of annihilation but of closest unification and transformation. There was the great principle dominating everything in which his soul found expression: 'Deus interior intimo meo.' And thus, for him as for St Paul, even in our fallen world—in this world in which evil desire is so closely bound up with our being that it is, one might say, what is most characteristic of us—the grace of Jesus Christ becomes holy desire in order the better to vanquish evil desire[29] and is not in all points

[28] Saint-Cyran with his spiritual instinct was nearer than Jansenius to the authentic tradition. *De la grâce de Jésus-Christ*: 'God associates the will which does good with the unity of his working, and it can be said of God working by the power of grace with the soul and through the soul, that their works are indivisible and are peculiar to God and the soul, as all theologians teach: "opera sanctae Trinitatis ad extra sunt indivisa" ' (Orcibal, pp. 238-9). Similarly St Bernard and Bérulle (*Grandeurs de Jésus*, discours 7, n. 4) who quotes 1 Cor. 6:17: 'Qui adhaeret Domino, unus spiritus est.' Cf. Origen, *In 1 Cor.*, frag. 39, 60 (*JTS*, 9, p. 510).

[29] *Opus imperfectum contra Iulianum*, bk 2, c. 217: 'ut delectatio peccati iustitiae delectatione vincatur'.

the direct opposite of nature. By its principal characteristics it is in direct contrast with it. It is not exterior to the soul, but interior, not a disintegrating force but one making for unification, not making captive, but really setting free. The 'amor iustitiae' which it engenders is something quite different from the tyrannical attraction of the passions.[30] This is why, without in any way diminishing the action of God, St Augustine could say : 'Adiutor noster Deus dicitur (Ps. 41 : 9), nec adiuvari potest, nisi qui etiam aliquid sponte conatur.'[31] And again, concerning conversion and the act of faith, after mention of the exterior and interior helps from God : 'Profecto et ipsum velle credere Deus operatur in homine, et in omnibus misericordia eius praevenit nos; consentire autem vocationi Dei, vel ab ea dissentire, propriae voluntatis est.'[32] In this way an assertion like the following gains it full force and meaning : 'Secundum gratiam Dei, non contra eam, libertas defenditur voluntatis.'[33]

Thus the question was not exhausted when, in the wake of St Augustine the dichotomy 'caritas-cupiditas' was established. It was still necessary to understand it and not endow charity with the features of cupidity.

Here, especially, words are deceivers. 'Arnauld was not wrong,' wrote Jean Laporte, 'when he claimed that St Augustine's followers had understood better than any other theological school this idea of charity or love which forms the very essence of the Christian religion and its beauty.'[34] Of course, it is certainly not because it claimed an exalted place for charity that Jansenism is

[30] *Contra duas epistulas Pelagianorum*, bk 1, c. 10, n. 22 : 'cum ipsa delectatio boni, qua etiam non consentit homo ad malum, non timore paenae sed amore iustitiae (hoc est enim condelectari) nonnisi gratiae deputanda sit'; cf. *De correptione*, n. 4 : 'cum dilectione et delectatione iustitiae'.

[31] *De peccatorum meritis*, bk 2, c. 5, n. 6.

[32] *De spiritu et littera*, c. 34, n. 60. Formulas as clear as this are not to be found in the *De correptione*, where the thought becomes more unilateral; but there is no contradiction in them, and the idea can be discerned beneath these words of n. 4 for example : 'Intelligant, si filii Dei sunt, spiritu Dei se agi (Rom. 8 : 14) ut quod agendum est agant. . . . Aguntur enim ut agant, *non ut ipsi nihil agant.*'

[33] *De correptione*, n. 17.

[34] 'Pascal et la doctrine de Port-Royal' in *Revue de métaphysique et de morale*, 1923, p. 261.

to be condemned, and the *Dictionnaire des livres jansénistes* was at least ill-advised when it blamed Jansenists for saying that the rule of Christianity is the rule of love.[35] The Venerable Vincent Huby was not a Jansenist for saying that 'Paradise is the kingdom of charity, and charity alone can give entrance to it'[36] nor St Ignatius Loyola for writing, 'Charity, without which we cannot win eternal life, is that love which makes us love the Lord our God for his own sake, and all else for his love'.[37] Would to heaven that all the latter's sons had been more mindful of it in their theological speculations! Nor is Jansenism to be condemned for extolling the triumphant attraction of celestial delectation: an anti-Jansenist, another Jesuit, Blessed Claude de la Colombière, extolled it too,[38] just as in our own days Fr Rousselot has.[39] Up to this point both sides, under the common patronage of St Augustine, agree without difficulty. If the phrase 'gratia victrix', which Jansenius claims to have read 'non raro' in Augustine's works,[40] seems not to figure in them, the phrase 'delectatio victrix' certainly does.[41] But a metaphor is not a theory. What exactly is the nature of this 'delectation'? Whence does it come? How is it victorious? Over what or whom? In what does its success consist? Here are several questions which involve as many points of doctrine, and to which the disciple does not always answer in the same way as the master.

To avoid the error for which the Jansenists were blamed it is not necessary to have recourse to Fénelon's interpretation according to which St Augustine, in those passages in which he mentions 'delectatio victrix', never meant to speak of a delectation consequent upon deliberate choice of the will, or at least coincident

[35] 1755 ed., vol. 2, p. 59; the criticism of a work of 1720 on the Sunday Epistles and Gospels.

[36] *Œuvres*, (1761), p. 234.

[37] Letter to Martin Garcia de Onaz, June 1532.

[38] Sermon for Pentecost, 3rd point.

[39] 'La grâce d'après saint Paul et d'après saint Jean' in *Mélanges Grandmaison, RSR*, 1928.

[40] *De gratia Christi Salvatoris*, bk 2, c. 24 (vol. 3, p. 82); cf. Liber proemialis, c. 21 (vol. 2, p. 19).

[41] *De peccatorum meritis et remissione*, bk 2, c. 19, n. 22: 'Intelligemus Deum etiam sanctis aliquando non tribuere certam scientiam vel victricem delectationem. ut cognoscant non a se sed ab illo eas esse.'

with this deliberate choice; on this view it was only a matter of 'the free and meritorious will' which is required.[42] This interpretation, which is repeated by the *Dictionnaire des livres jansénistes*[43] and, curiously enough, maintained even by Arnauld—who on this subject is finally in formal opposition to Jansenius[44]—is no doubt somewhat forced, although it is not without some textual support.[45] The emphasis laid on the element of deliberation seems scarcely compatible with the spontaneous movement of the will as understood by St Augustine. Such an interpretation, although its intention is different, implies a misapprehension similar to that of Jansenius who insisted on the undeliberative character of Augustinian 'delectatio'[46] and, practically speaking, identified it with grace. Jansenius 'committed the initial error of actualizing apart, as if they were things, the different stages of an analysis which in reality are inseparable'; he 'reasons always as if *delectatio* in the will were a different element from the will

[42] *Lettres sur la grâce et la prédestination*, letter 1, qu. 2 (*loc. cit.*, p. 302).

[43] Ed. of 1755, vol. 1, p. 240: 'Although it is true that St Augustine often gives the name of delectation to grace, it is no less true that he often uses the word "to delight" or "delectation" as it is always used in the scriptures and Latin authors, for a rational and deliberate delectation, for the free choice which it pleases the will to make. It is in this sense that we are accustomed to say when we prefer one thing to another: "hoc eligo, hoc volo".' See also J. Cerpani, S.J., 'De caelesti ac terrena delectatione disputatio polemica' in Zaccaria, *Thesaurus theologicus*, vol. 5, pp. 497-525.

[44] He ends with the complete rejection of the idea of indeliberate delectation, opposing 'the opinion of those who see grace as a triumphant delectation which is an indeliberate and not a free motion of the will' (*Œuvres*, vol. 8, p. 620; cf. p. 689). He says again, referring to the explanations given by St Augustine, St Bernard, St Thomas, etc: 'in all this we can see neither *qualitas fluens*, nor *actus indeliberatus*, in which the Bishop of Ypres has made triumphant delectation to consist; in this he is certainly wrong' (vol. 3, p. 636).

[45] *Fragmentum epistulae ad Maximum* (*PL*, 33, 752): 'Iam desiderate implere iustitiam multo vehementius atque ferventius quam nequissimi homines voluptates carnis desiderari solent . . ., ut non solum onerosum non sit, verum etiam delectet abstinere a voluptatibus omnis corruptionis.' But *De spiritu et littera*, n. 5 (44, 205); *De diversis quaestionibus ad Simplicianum*, bk 1, 2, 22 (40, 128), etc. Similarly for the famous passage in the commentary on the Epistle to the Galatians, n. 49, provided that it is read in its context: 'quod enim amplius nos delectet, secundum id operemur necesse est'.

[46] *De gratia Christi Salvatoris*, bk 4, c. 11 (vol. 3, pp. 184-8). All the texts to which Jansenius appeals for the direct proof of his thesis refer not to holy delectation but to concupiscence.

itself'. For him '*delectatio* is the cause of volition', while for some of his opponents it is its effect. Étienne Gilson puts it more accurately when he tells us that 'according to St Augustine delectation is only love which is itself only the interior bias of the will which in its turn is but free will itself'. Thus the attraction experienced by the will 'could not endanger its freedom since it is the choice itself in which freedom is affirmed'.[47]

Since this fundamental point was not understood, Jansenius, for all his display of Augustinian erudition by an overwhelming accumulation of texts, nonetheless falsified his author. Quite often, in fact, it is enough to look up the texts in question to see that this is so. The word 'victrix', for example, does not, as Jansenius thought, mean that grace masters the will—although it could master it in another way than that which he explains.[48] His mistake can be rectified perhaps, the scandal lessened, when it is stated that the stronger of the two delectations encountered prevails 'by a moral but efficacious necessity';[49] but the true meaning of Augustine's ideas is not thereby restored. When he speaks in connection with grace of a 'delectatio victrix' what he means fundamentally is that this grace enables the human will to overcome concupiscence, free will to overcome sin, the spirit to overcome the flesh. 'Victoria qua peccatum vincitur, nihil aliud est quam donum Dei, in isto certamine adiuvantis liberum arbitrium.'[50] On our own we shall be vanquished in the struggle; but when we are helped by the grace of God, by Jesus Christ our Lord, the strength of health returns to us and the attraction of

[47] E. Gilson, *Introduction à l'étude de saint Augustin*, 2nd ed. (1953), pp. 210-11. Cf. *De gratia Christi Salvatoris*, bk 7, c. 3: 'Delectatio efficit voluntatem et libertatem, hoc est, facit velle et libere velle' (vol. 3, pp. 309-11). See also Burnaby, *Amor Dei*, p. 233. In this Origen had preceded Augustine: Hans Urs von Balthasar, *Parole et mystère chez Origène* (1957), p. 133.

[48] That is why I do not rely on Fr Guy de Broglie's expression, although it seems to me true in itself, in which he shows in the *auxilium quo* a certain type of grace that is 'triumphantly victorious'. 'The proper effect of grace' is what Fr Rousselot rightly called it, in connection with the 'delectatio victrix': 'La grâce d'après saint Jean et saint Paul' in *RSR*, 18 (1926), p. 102.

[49] Thus Louis Habert, *Theologia dogmatica et moralis . . .* (Paris, 1709). On Habert: R. Tavenaux, *Le Jansénisme en Lorraine*, pp. 133 and 180-5.

[50] *De gratia et libero arbitrio*, c. 4. *De spiritu et littera*, c. 29, n. 51.

righteousness is in us the victor over everything that inclines us to sin.[51] In this way we overcome the 'mala concupiscentia'.[52] We master all earthly attractions.[53] The grace of Jesus Christ, which must never on any account be thought of apart from the Incarnation itself,[54] is therefore liberating: 'gratia liberatrix, gratia liberans, gratia liberationem pollicens'.[55] It is victorious, not over us, but 'in us, not over free will, but over sin and all the obstacles heaped up in our way by the sin of the world'.[56] By setting him free, it endows man with the power of overcoming the world: 'ut vincatur hic mundus'.

Thus the more St Augustine's thought is examined in its different phases and details the more coherent it appears. The various concepts in which it is cast successively are connected with one another; passing from one to the other they all converge on a single point. The idea of 'delectatio victrix' is analogous though not entirely identical with that of the 'adiutorium quo' as with that of the 'donum perseverantiae'. This all-powerful delectation is that of righteousness which is to be found in the higher part of the soul: 'delectatio iustitiae, delectatio mentis'.[57] The victory of

[51] *Contra Iulianum pelagianum,* bk 5, c. 7: 'Dum hic vivimus, ubi caro concupiscit adversus spiritum, et spiritus adversus carnem; quae (libido) non vincitur, si nullum cum ea geritur bellum'; bk 2, c. 9: '. . . nisi adiuvet nos gratia Dei per Iesum Christum Dominum nostrum, ne sic etiam mortuum peccatum rebellet, ut vincendo reviviscat et regnet. . . .' *Enchiridion,* c. 22, n. 81: 'Profecto vincimur, nisi divinitus adiuvemur, ut non solum videamus quid faciendum sit, sed etiam, accedente sanitate, delectatio iustitiae vincat in nobis earum rerum delectationes. . . .'
[52] *Enchiridion,* c. 31, n. 118: 'vincente delectatione iustitiae'.
[53] Cf. *De peccatorum meritis,* bk 2, n. 32: 'victricem delectationem'.
[54] *De verbis Apostoli,* sermo 8: 'Venit Deus homo per gratiam liberatricem. . . .'
[55] *Fragmentum epistulae ad Maximum. Contra Iulianum opus imperfecttum,* bk 1, c. 79: 'Hoc si intelligatis, non aliud intelligetis esse arbitrium laudabiliter liberum, nisi quod fuerit gratia Dei liberatum.' Cf. *In psalmum* 67, n. 13: 'ut bonum opus fiat non timore, sed amore; non formidine paenae, sed delectatione iustitiae. Ipsa enim vera et sana libertas.'
[56] A. Sage, *art. cit.,* p. 31. Cf. *De correptione,* c. 35.
[57] *De verbis Apostoli,* c. 2: 'Inter omnia quae te delectant, plus te delectet ipsa iustitia.' Sermo 159: 'delectationi carnis, delectationem mentis praeponere'. *Enchiridion,* c. 22, n. 81. Cf. *Sermo* 353. *In psalmum* 57, n. 4: 'Veniet enim gratia Dei ut delectet te iustitia', etc. It is here a question neither of Jansenist delectation, nor of the 'feeling' or 'instinct' of Malebranche. Cf. *Bibl. august.,* vol. 9, pp. 396-8, note by A.G. (Gaudel).

which it is the sign obtains the perfection of righteousness in the fulness of freedom. 'Victoria est finis certandi,' said the *De vera religione*;[58] and right at the end the *Opus imperfectum* was to echo the same thought: 'Aliter gratia certantem facit atque adiuvat, aliter victorem sine hoste ullo, vel externo vel interno, in aeterna pace conservat; ista laboriosa militia est in praesenti saeculo, illa beata requies in futuro.'[59]

The celebrated adverb 'insuperabiliter' and the similar adverbs used by St Augustine on various occasions are by no means the signs of a tyranny of grace. This appears clearly if they are carefully replaced in their context. By words like these St Augustine has no intention of saying what Jansenius makes him say: 'Adiutorium Christi determinat ac praedeterminat etiam physice voluntatem, ut velit et ardentius velit.'[60] For Augustine the problem was to imbue our weak wills with the strength without which they would succumb to the grievous temptation encountered at every step: 'inter tot et tantas tentationes infirmitate sua succumberet.'[61] The problem was not to ensure the continual sinlessness of the will, but the rightness of its final steps, it perseverance in good. In this connection Augustine writes: 'Subventum est igitur infirmitati voluntatis humanae, ut divina gratia indeclinabiliter et insuperabiliter ageretui.' There is here no allusion whatever to a sort of struggle between grace and the will, as if the latter, despite all its efforts, were outmanœuvred and must in the end be vanquished. The sentence continues with these words which Jansenius' supporters pass over or omit to quote:[62] 'et ideo,

[58] C. 53, n. 102.
[59] Bk 2, c. 106.
[60] *De gratia Christi salvatoris*, bk 8, c. 3 (*Augustinus,* vol. 3, p. 346).
[61] *De correptione et gratia*, n. 38, cf. n. 35: 'I admit with St Augustine,' says Fénelon very rightly, 'a grace which makes the will invincible to temptation, and not a grace that is invincible to the will': *Instruction pastorale en forme de dialogues* (*Œuvres,* Paris, 1823, vol. 15, p. 156). It is therefore against Jansenism, and not against the Christianity of St Augustine and the Catholic Church, that an Orthodox theologian was able, very properly, to write: 'Grace does not constrain (as *insuperabilis* and *indeclinabilis*); it does not transform man into a thing, an object of creation' (Sergius Bulgakov, *Le Verbe incarné,* p. 298).
[62] Cf. Laporte, *op. cit.,* p. 360. Cf. the speech by Degola at Port-Royal-des-Champs, 29 October 1809: 'It was believed at Port-Royal that man, always

quamvis infirma, non tamen deficeret, neque adversitate aliqua vinceretur'; and a little further on in the same paragraph we read : 'Infirmis servavit Deus ut, ipso donante, invictissime quod bonum est vellent, et hoc deserere invictissime nollent.'

There again Jansenist interpretations are faulty. Whatever Arnauld may say,[63] and he here follows Jansenius faithfully, or whatever Dom Rottmanner may seem to say,[64] it is clear that it is not grace which is termed invincible in relation to the will : it is the will itself by the working of this grace. St Augustine explains this by an example. Such, he tells us, was Peter's faith : free, strong, persevering, invincible in all temptation, by reason of the Lord's prayer.[65] Further, this invincibility of the will strengthened by grace, this 'insuperabilis fortitudo', is not to be understood as a sort of metaphysical attribute, but it must be seen, on the contrary, in the way in which cupidity acts when left to itself.[66] On the other hand, it is always to be envisaged in relation to the last end. Just as in the 'adiutorium quo' St Augustine saw a gift which was only applicable to the predestined, so now he applied 'the properties of inevitability and invincibility not to grace but to the will of man who perseveres to the end'.[67] Or rather, according

free to resist grace, never resists when God, by the victorious delectation of charity, works efficaciously on his heart.' In A. Gazier, *Histoire générale du mouvement janséniste,* vol. 2, p. 174. That is a moderate and not unambiguous formula.

[63] *Œuvres,* vol. 8, p. 361; translation of *De correptione,* c. 12: grace is made 'victorious' over the human will 'by an invincible power'.

[64] *Loc. cit.,* p. 42.

[65] *De correptione et gratia,* c. 8, n. 17: 'Quando rogavit ergo ne fides eius deficeret, quid aliud rogavit, nisi ut haberet in fide liberrimam, fortissimam, perseverantissimam voluntatem? Ecce quemadmodum secundum gratiam Dei, non contra eam, libertas defenditur voluntatis. Voluntas quippe humana non libertate consequitur gratiam, sed gratia potius libertatem, et ut perseveret delectabilem perpetuitatem et insuperabilem fortitudinem' (*PL,* 44, 426). The same interpretation in Mausbach, *Die Ethick des heil. Aug.,* p. 35 and Boyer, *op. cit.,* pp. 227-8.

[66] Cf. *De diversis quaestionibus ad Simplicianum,* bk 1, n. 10: 'Quae duo, scilicet tanquam natura et consuetudo, coniuncta, robustissimam faciunt et invictissimam cupiditatem.'

[67] *Lettres d'un docteur de Sorbonne . . . touchant les hérésies du XVIIe siècle* (1711), vol. 1, p. 393; cf. pp. 404-5.

to the commentary by Fr Daniel in *Défense de saint Augustin*,[68] 'these terms fall under this gift (of final perseverance) considered along its whole range'. In other words the properties of inevitability and invincibility are also applicable to the grace of perseverance, but only in so far as this grace is opposed to the snares of the enemy, not to the resistance of the will.[69] And these properties, on a last analysis, are those of free will itself in its higher and definitive state. They are those of the blessed who have entered on the final Sabbath : 'Nec ideo liberum arbitrium non habebunt, quia peccata eos delectare non poterunt. Magis quippe erit liberum, a delectatione peccandi usque ad delectationem non peccandi indeclinabilem liberatum.'[70]

It must also be acknowledged that the maxim 'Regnat carnalis cupiditas, ubi non est Dei caritas' is authentically Augustinian.[71] It does not make a theologian Jansenist to refuse to admit in conformity with this maxim that there is actually in man a sort of neutral zone, the domain of a *tertium quid* which, without being bad, possesses only a purely natural value, with no efficacy for salvation. Augustine would never admit that there could be actions which were 'steriliter boni'. He never conceived a situation intermediate between that of the old man and that of the new. But what is more serious and a complete misreading of the passage quoted in support is to understand charity as an inverse con-

[68] *Recueil* . . . , vol. 2 (1724), pp. 281-2 : 'Thus the *indeclinabiliter, insuperabiliter* and *invictissime,* which are misused to show us that according to St Augustine grace forces the will, do not apply to the actual graces of the predestined, which—and this is *de fide*—they can resist and which only form a part of the gift of final perseverance; but these terms apply to this gift viewed in its whole extent, and as comprising several things which do not actually depend on us, and especially with reference to this capital point, which consists in being taken from this world when we are in a state of grace, and not to be taken when we are in a state of sin.' Also, by the same author : *Dissertation théologique sur cet axiome de saint Augustin* . . .: '*Quod amplius nos delectat, secundum id operemur necesse est*' (vol. 3, pp. 368-83).

[69] Cf. St Bernard, *De diversis sermo* 11, c. 1 : 'Haec est libertas nostra qua Christus nos liberavit, ut nulla penitus creatura avellere nos, aut vim facere possit.'

[70] *De Civitate Dei,* bk 22, c. 30, n. 3.

[71] *Enchiridion,* c. 117; or *Sermo* 14, n. 1 : 'Sicut cupiditas facit hominem veterem, sic caritas novum (Mai, *Nova Patrum bibliotheca,* p. 27, etc.).

cupiscence; as if, between heavenly delectation which causes the soul to experience its true happiness, and earthly delectation which produces the illusive pleasures of this world, there were only a difference of object not of nature, as if both were made, so to say, of the same stuff,[72] as if concupiscence did not tend to the distraction, dismemberment and collapse of the being which it possesses by externalizing it, whereas charity interiorizes it and unifies it in God : 'colligens me a dispersione in qua frustratim discissus sum'.[73] What is more serious is misunderstanding of the humble course of 'caritas inchoata' in the soul of the sinner as well as the sublime ascents of the 'caritas perfecta' in the soul of the mystic and the saint.[74] The misinterpretation amounts to the transformation into a narrow and niggardly rigorism of perhaps one of the most fluid and comprehensive doctrines that ever was, in any case one that takes into account in the fullest manner the complexities and hidden depths of the spiritual life.

However glaring these misapprehensions, it is still true that there is great danger of falling into them when St Augustine's teaching on the supernatural is sought solely in his writings concerning the controversy on grace. Not that there is any need to dispute the

---

[72] As Fr Grou pertinently pointed out, 'he who knows only the pleasures of the senses and whose soul is immersed in material things cannot understand that there are other pleasures of a higher order, similar pleasures for the soul, and spiritual in nature, as it is' (*Morale tirée des Confessions de saint Augustin*, 65). Cf. a similar idea in Gregory of Nyssa (*PG*, 44, 772A): 'pathos' in the incorporal beings is 'apathos'.

[73] St Augustine, *Confessions*, bk 2, n. 1; cf. bk 1, n. 3 : 'colligis nos'.

[74] Cf. *De natura et gratia*, c. 70, n. 84; *Contra duas epistolas Pelagianorum*, bk 2, c. 8, n. 21 : 'The doctrine of the two loves, taken from St Augustine and hatefully travestied' (Pierre Charles, 'Les civilisations non chrétiennes et l'amour du prochain', *Semaine sociale de Paris*, 1928, p. 198). Another consequence of this travesty could be the reduction of all spirituality to 'penance', with an obsession about salvation and damnation. This helps to explain the frenzied agitation of the Jansenist party against Fénelon in the controversy over disinterested love.

It seems that on this point Baius remained nearer to St Augustine. Cf. *De caritate*, c. 7, 8 and 9 (*Caritatis initium = initium bonae voluntatis*); *Apologia* to St Pius V, ad 18m : 'Invenitur in fide et paenitentia, aliisque bonis operibus Catechumenorum, quae in iis Deus operatur, licet nondum inhabitans.'

importance of these works, or to see their contents as the exaggerations of old age or the result of controversy. Despite undeniable exaggerations of this kind, despite the severity and narrowness which formed the price of the struggle, their significance is great, nor do they require correction by means of the previous writings: Augustine's teaching had already taken shape, so far as its main features were concerned, before the stir caused by Pelagius and it never deviated from this standard. But these writings from the end of his life should not be considered in isolation. They must be seen in the context of the whole of Augustine's work; more especially they must not be asked to perform a task for which they were not intended. They were intended principally, and this stands out clearly, to show the difference between two systems of grace, the one concerning Adam before his fall, and the other concerning us now. On the strength of this elementary observation Arnauld, repeating Baius, Jansenius and all belonging to his party, wrote: 'The famous difference between the grace of the angels and the first man, and that of Jesus Christ, is the key to the whole theology of St Augustine in this matter.'[75] And again: 'The fundamental maxim of his whole teaching, which is the difference between the two graces of the Creator and the Redeemer, of the will healthy and strong before sin, and of the will sick and weak after sin. . . .'[76] If this 'matter', if this 'teaching', is grace, understood in the narrow sense, strictly speaking the statement is correct. But if it is taken to refer to the whole body of teaching for which, in modern theology, the usual term is 'the supernatural', Arnauld is completely wrong. Speculations about Adam have been used by many theologians to elaborate their conception of man and God, of nature and its end, to study in some sort the supernatural in its pure state, that is, without the complications introduced by the contingent factor of sin. This method, which has its advantages, was not St Augustine's. His constant teaching was that grace is necessary to restore freedom,

[75] *Œuvres*, vol. 19, p. 445.
[76] Vol. 17, p. 167. See also Du Pin, *Mémoire historique*, manuscript quoted by Carreyre, *DTC*, vol. 8, col. 478, art. 'Jansénisme'.

to heal nature; but how does he understand this freedom, this nature? This is the real question, and the anti-Pelagian treatises are not sufficient to provide an answer to it. In them discussion is strictly confined to the matter in hand: Augustine is opposing the adversaries of the 'grace of Christ'.[77] These treatises, of course, do not give the naturalist answer which Jansenius, reading through the eyes of his master Baius, thought that he could detect in them; but the contrary answer, which is authentically Augustine's, must principally be sought elsewhere. It is spread throughout his whole work. Of course it is not to be found formulated in definitive and explicit theses. In a work composed so unsystematically but of such concrete inspiration, the most fundamental ideas are always those which are not so explicitly formulated as the others; they govern the whole work[78] but there is no occasion for them to be clearly reflected, though they find expression through many another idea. In any case, it is clear that all really profound thought is inevitably deformed if its fundamental implications are not seized.

A further difficulty arises from the fact that the answer which is sought is not to be found in St Augustine in the terms that we would use today. His theological language is very different from ours. The treatise *De Deo elevante* is of quite recent composition. As correlatives of the word 'nature' the very words 'supernatural' and 'grace' have an exceedingly complex history. The principal use of the latter term by Augustine is to designate atonement for sin by the merits of Christ, a fact which favoured the misapprehensions of several of his commentators. In his works, as in the whole

[77] *Contra Iulianum Pelagianum,* bk 4, c. 3: 'Inimici gratiae Dei quae datur per Iesum Christum Dominum nostrum.'

[78] If at one and the same time we endeavour to grasp Augustinian teaching in all its aspects, 'we perceive', says Maurice Blondel, 'that it is pregnant with an idea of the supernatural that is both theological and philosophical, which has perhaps never been clearly explained' ('Pour la quinzième centenaire de saint Augustin' in *Revue de Métaphysique et de Morale,* 1930, p. 464). In this connection a remark by Fr Lagrange is applicable: 'After Luther, Jansenius, Baius and many Jansenists misunderstood Augustinian thought because they relied on his expressions without taking into account the general meaning' ('Le commentaire de Luther sur l'Épître aux Romains', *RB,* 1916, p. 100).

theological tradition deriving from him, the idea of grace brings to mind more directly the idea of mercy rather than that of liberality, the idea of *forgiveness* rather than that of a mere *gift*. In *grace* there is the idea of doing a favour, and 'act of grace'. Grace, then, is in the first place and almost always, when it is a question of interior help, medicinal grace, or the grace of the Redeemer; it is the 'gratuita liberatio',[79] the 'gratia donans peccata', the fruit of that merciful action by which God plucks us from the 'mass of perdition'.[80] In contrast with the present fallen state in which we have need of this special help to raise us up, the state of innocent man is always termed 'natural'; [81] on the other hand creation itself can be called 'grace', 'quadam non improbanda ratione'.[82]

Once again, of themselves these words are of small importance; after all, in the *Confessions*, the principal source to which we must constantly return to understand St Augustine's mind on these

[79] *De dono perseverantiae,* c. 8, n. 19.

[80] *De correptione et gratia,* n. 26, 28 and 40. Cf. *In Ioannem* tract. 3, n. 9. *Ad Simplicianum,* bk 1, n. 7. Fulgentius of Ruspe, *Epist.,* 11, n. 39: 'Haec vero libertas . . . gratuita Dei miseratione confertur.'

[81] See for example *Retractationes,* bk 1, n. 25; *Epistula* 118, *ad Innocentium*; *De Civitate Dei,* bk 12, c. 1. Also St Prosper, or St Leo: *In nativitate Domini sermo* 4, n. 2; *De ieiunio decimi mensis sermo* 1. Cf. Fulgentius, *Epist.,* 17, n. 46: 'Potest igitur Deo donante homo in Deum naturaliter credere. Arbitrium itaque hominis sanat Deus atque illuminat, ut homo in Deum naturaliter credat.' As the latest witness to this tradition, there is St Bonaventure, *In Hexaemeron,* bk 7: 'Haec est medicina, scilicet gratia Spiritus sancti', or *Soliloquium de quattuor mentalibus exercitiis*: 'Diligenter considera quam generosae a summo artifice sis facta per naturam, quam vitiose a tua voluntate deformata sis per culpam, quam gratiose a divina bonitate saepe reformata sis per gratiam' (Quaracchi, vol. 8, p. 30). There are also examples in St Thomas, etc. Cf. D. Soto, *De natura et gratia,* bk 1, c. 22; Petau, *De lege et gratia libri duo adversus doctrinam Iansenii* (1648), etc.

If the theologians who refuted Baius and Jansenius are altogether right when they denounce the equivocation in regard to the word 'natural', as indeed is being done in this book, it must yet be acknowledged that their positive attempts to explain the meaning of this word in the ancient writers are founded on a somewhat unsubtle exegesis and above all are lacking in historical perspective. The ancient concept of 'nature' cannot be simply reduced, as it is by some, to that of 'historical' (by contrast with 'essential') nature, an idea that has been popular in these last centuries.

[82] *Epist.,* 177, in which Augustine explains the matter very clearly. *Confessions,* bk 13, n. 4: '. . . et quod utcumque vivit, et quod beate vivit, non deberet nisi gratiae tuae. . . .'

matters, the actual word 'grace' is hardly to be found a dozen times, and not always in the meaning of interior grace.[83] In this case St Augustine must be allowed the benefit of his own defence of St John Chrysostom against the Pelagians : 'Vobis non litigantibus, securius loquebatur.'[84] No more for him than for his predecessors, the Greek Fathers, was created nature, made in the image of its Creator, what it became for many after the beginning of the period of a separate philosophy—or perhaps right at the very start it should be called a separate theology. To the extent that the soul was 'formed', in that it was already more, if it can be so described, than the substance of mind, he saw the human soul as illuminated and strengthened by God's unceasing action. As his whole thought was steeped in a supernatural atmosphere, he did not constantly feel the need, as we do nowadays, to work out a 'supernaturalist' vocabulary. But if we are to understand his real thought, it is enough to note that he more than any other held the entire dependence, in all circumstances, of the rational creature on his Creator;[85] that this dependence was, on his view, not a yoke of wretchedness, but the sign of a greatness that is in some way infinite, since it raises the creature up to God; that lastly he showed that the foundation, the law and the end of everything was in Love. After this, in contrast with us sinners, he speaks of the 'merits' of man in a state of innocence,[86] but it still

[83] 'Gratia' is usually employed to designate a providential occurrence : *Sermo* 99, n. 6; *De praedestinatione sanctorum*, n. 15; *De spiritu et littera*, c. 34, n. 60; *In psalmum* 81, n. 1. Dom H.-M. Rochais, O.S.B., points out that for Defensor of Ligugé, whose terminology is governed by that of the authors whose maxims he reproduces, '*auxilium Dei* means properly speaking what theologians now call grace, while *gratia* designated the gifts and talents which the Lord entrusts to us for us to make them bear fruit'. Defensor of Ligugé, *Scintillarum Liber* (*SC*, 77, 1961), introduction, p. 12.

[84] *Contra Iulianum pelagianum*, bk 1, n. 22. Similar remarks could be made on the use of the words 'faith' and 'reason'. Often St Augustine relates faith to the state of intellectual infirmity to which sin has reduced us. He does not admit, however, that in the earthly paradise rationalism would have been the truth. See below, chapter four.

[85] It is this profound awareness of the creaturely condition which causes him to reject any idea of 'merita naturae bonae' : *Contra duas epistolas Pelagianorum*, bk 11, c. 2, n. 3 (the parallel with 'merita voluntatis bonae').

[86] *De praedestinatione sanctorum*, n. 31: 'Humana merita . . . quae perierunt per Adam' : *Contra Iulianum opus imperfectum*, bk 12, c. 37.

remains true that he never attributes to man in any good work either the initiative or the principal role.

Not only free will, which may be used well or badly, but also good will, which can never be used badly, can only come from God. If our free will, by which we can do good or evil, nevertheless comes from God because it is a benefit, and our good will comes from ourselves, it will follow that what we have of ourselves is of greater value than what is given by God, which is the height of absurdity : this can only be avoided by acknowledging that good will is a gift of God.[87]

There is nothing in this, it will be noticed, that implies the fall. It is a universal principle. 'Non se ipse homo, sed Deus bonum hominem fecit'.[88] 'Ab eo autem est omnis salus, a quo est omne bonum.'[89] For 'if all that is good comes from God, it follows that the good use of free will, which is a virtue and which counts as a greater good, also comes from God'.[90] And so it would be pointless to seek in good will anything which is ours and does not come to us from God.[91] Even the desire of good can only come from him who alone is the Good.[92] Of Adam it must be said : 'Vivebat fruens Deo, ex quo bono erat bonus.'[93] The insistence on the point

[87] De peccatorum meritis et remissione, bk 2, n. 118. The same reasoning about Adam in Contra Iulianum opus imperfectum, bk 5, c. 57 : 'ut per se ipsum bonus sit homo, non per Deum, aut certe melior per seipsum quam per Deum.'

[88] De perfectione iustitiae, n. 10. De gratia Christi, n. 26 : 'ut agant quod bonum est, ab illo aguntur qui bonus est'. Cf. Second Council of Orange, canon 19 (Denz. 192) and the Indiculus of Celestine (Denz. 131).

[89] De vera religione, c. 18, n. 36. See also De civitate Dei, bk 12, c. 9, n. 1; In psalmum 70, Sermo 2, n. 6; Enchiridion, c. 1, etc. Harnack noted this aspect of Augustine's teaching and acknowledged its implications, but, as was his custom, to show a contradiction : Eng. trans. Outlines of the History of Dogma (1957), p. 235.

[90] Retractationes, bk 1, c. 9, n. 6.

[91] De peccatorum meritis, bk 2, c. 18, n. 28.

[92] Contra duas epistulas Pelagianorum, bk 2, c. 9, n. 21.

[93] De Civitate Dei, bk 14, c. 26; cf. c. 13. Enchiridion, c. 106 : 'Etsi peccatum in solo libero arbitrio erat constitutum, non tamen iustitiae retinendae sufficiebat liberum arbitrium, nisi participatione immutabilis Boni divinum adiutorium praeberetur.'

is monotonous but it is also significant. Actually, whether it concerns man in his innocence or man the sinner, the salutory act which completes the divine image in him is always a real creation —a creation of the spiritual being 'which is the real existence', as Bérulle was to say. Man, of course, cooperates in this—and the conditions under which he cooperates may vary—but, of absolute necessity, God is always its real author.[94] By the first creation he endowed the being with nature; he produces, fosters and renders its activity efficacious, he presides over its development. But for this accession to another kind of being effected by the free effort of the moral will, for this passing to another order, a further creative cycle must begin—it is a higher gift, of supereminent gratuity, by the effect of which the created spirit, transcending its nature, enters the supernatural order. 'Tunc efficimur vere liberi, quando Deus nos fingit, id est format et creat, non ut homines (quia iam fecit), sed ut boni homines simus.' But since man has rejected the gift, this new creation must now be a recreation. It must begin by forgiveness and for this reason it merits more especially the name of grace: 'quod nunc gratia sua facit, ut simus in Christo Iesu nova creatura'.[95]

From the calm reflections of the young convert of Cassiciacum down to the heated controversies of the old bishop, the basic thought of the Doctor of Grace remains constant: it is entirely 'supernatural'. Investigation quickly shows that he is also 'very much more than the vanquisher of Pelagianism'.[96] Or rather, he

[94] *In psalmum* 58, sermo 2, n. 11: 'Si omnino nihil eram antequam essem, nihil te promerui ut essem. Fecisti ut essem, et non tu fecisti ut bonus essem? Dedisti mihi ut sim, et potuit mihi alius dare ut bonus sim? Si tu mihi dedisti ut sim, et alius mihi dedit ut bonus sim, melior est ille qui mihi dedit ut bonus sim, quam ille qui mihi dedit ut sim.'
[95] *Enchiridion,* c. 31, cf. *De Trinitate,* bk 8, n. 3-5; *De peccatorum meritis,* bk 2, n. 30; *De Genesi ad litteram,* bk 1, n. 9: 'Ipsa pro sui generis conversione ad creatorem, formam capit et fit perfecta creatura'; bk 9, n. 27. Cf. William of Saint-Thierry, *Epistola ad fratres de Monte Dei,* n. 91: 'factum animum vel iam perfectum' (Davey, p. 134). That in St Augustine's view the moral act was a real creation, necessitating grace, was clearly seen by the Jansenist Hugot: *op. cit.,* pp. 77-81.
[96] Rousselot and Huby, *Christus,* 1st ed., p. 808. The authors mean that St Augustine is not only the doctor of grace. But it can also be understood of the doctor of grace himself.

is the vanquisher of that everlasting Pelagianism which he had already encounted under various forms in his excursions into the systems of Manes and Plotinus,[97] and whose spirit was to be revived, sheltering under their own formulas, in the theses of Baius and Jansenius. In opposition to those teachers who only humble man to so great a degree in his present wretched state because they first exalted him unduly, proudly—and indeed basely—in his primitive 'healthy' condition, we hear Augustine's heartfelt cry:[98] 'Absit ut sit vel dicatur voluntas bona, quae in seipsa, non in Domino gloriatur.'[99]

---

[97] See *Contra duas epistulas Pelagianorum*, bk 2, n. 3, the parallel between Pelagians and Manicheans. As we know, it was with Plotinus in view that in his *Confessions,* fifteen years before the beginning of the great controversy, Augustine discovered the definitive formulas which were to scandalize Pelagius.

[98] *Contra Iulianum Pelagianum,* bk 4, c. 3; *Epist.,* 104, n. 81: '*Ipse fecit nos, et non ipsi nos.* Hoc enim non ad eam naturam qua homines sumus, cuius naturae idem creator est, qui caeli et terrae, siderum omniumque animantium; sed ad illud potius referendum est quod Apostolus ait: *Ipsius enim sumus figmentum*'; and n. 85: 'necesse est autem ut parum diligat Deum, qui non ab illo, sed a seipso bonum se arbitratur effectum. . . .' Gregory of Rimini understood St Augustine better than Baius and Jansenius were to do, or their disciples: *In II Sent.,* d. 29.

[99] Another example of Jansenius' real infidelity to his master. In bk 3 of the *Augustinus,* c. 5-8, Jansenius relies on 'six hundred passages' of Augustine to establish that the ancient Israelites were all 'guilty of prevarication'. The whole of the Old Testament was nothing else 'than a sort of great comedy' in figure and its reality was 'a state of sin and death'. God never granted a single Jew the slightest *gratia sufficiens* or *adiuvans,* and, to make sure that not one of them would succeed in being saved, he even sent them an 'impedient grace': 'Status veteris Testamenti figurativus et propheticus non afferebat Iudaeis gratiam sufficientem, sed potius *impedientem*' (c. 8; pp. 119-22). It is in this sense that Jansenius understands St Augustine's *De catech. rudibus,* c. 4: 'In veteri Testamento est occultatio Novi, in Novo manifestatio Veteris.' Jansenius understands Augustine's dialectical categories in a purely historical sense, and he understands those of Paul in the same way. Furthermore, he chose the texts, refusing to read those concerning the 'righteous of the Old Testament', the men 'of the New Testament under the Old', and so on. (Augustine distinguishes three 'great periods, ante legem, sub lege, sub gratia, all three of which included elect': A. Sage, *Revue des études Augustiniennes,* 7, pp. 228-9.) On the will to save and predestination: Agostino Trapè, O.S.A., 'A proposito di Predestinazione' in *Divinitas,* 1963, pp. 243-83; Athanase Sage, A.A., 'La volonté salvifique universelle de Dieu dans la pensée de saint Augustin' in *Recherches augustiniennes,* 3, 1965, pp. 107-31.

Note on the
De Correptione et Gratia, c. 10-14

The problem of efficacious grace could not be dealt with in these chapters because there is no question in them of the conjunction of grace and the will for a specific action. St Augustine does not deal with good actions but with perseverance in good; he does not envisage the righteous action, but the perfection of righteousness. The two 'aids' which he distinguishes are both, according to his own expression (n. 34), an 'adiutorium perseverantiae'. Among all the various points of view which one after the other are forced upon their author by the circumstances of the discussion there is a common purpose connecting these three works : *De perfectione iustitiae, De correptione et gratia* and *De dono perseverantiae.* They explain each other perfectly.

What nevertheless forms the difficulty of the chapters which we are examining here is the fact that in the comparison which they make between Adam and the justified, two problems are involved together, two contrasting points are combined.

1. Adam was established 'in bonis', while now man is born 'in malis' (n. 30). Hence 'maioribus donis adiuvanda remansit infirmitas' (n. 37). God seeks fallen man *lower*; it is this previous aid, which *ex hypothesi* Adam did not need, which in the highest sense of the word deserves the name of grace (although there is mention of grace for Adam in n. 29 and n. 31), because it is bestowed not only by liberality but by mercy. This grace comes from the redemptive Incarnation by which God lowered himself to our wretchedness.

2. But Augustine also considers the fact that Adam sinned while the saint perseveres. The latter therefore needs a help to take him *further,* to the point which Adam did not reach—a grace, then, which by definition Adam did not receive since it is essentially the grace of perseverance and Adam did not persevere.

This second point of view remains vaguer and more implicit in the *De correptione*. He does touch on it however in some passages: thus in n. 32: 'Acceperat (Adam) posse si vellet, sed non habuit velle quod posset; nam si habuisset, perseverasset.' It cannot be left out of account without misrepresenting St Augustine's thought and without making him contradict himself.

The confusion is increased by the fact that certain words are used, successively or together, with different meanings, according to whether they are used in connection with one or other of the two problems just mentioned. For example, 'gratia potentior' is thus named because it must come to seek out man lower (first comparison), or because it takes him further (second comparison) —n. 31. The 'gratia liberationis' concerns either the first deliverance which restored us more or less 'in bonis', healing our free will to bring us back to the state of doing good, or the total deliverance which is the entrance into eternity. In one sense, indeed, these two deliverances are only one, because no one here below is wholly restored to the primitive state of innocence: even the greatest saint is only 'delivered from evil', set free from concupiscence, at his death.[1]

The distinction between the grace of the two states consists, as we have seen, in the fact that the first gave Adam the necessary *power*, the second goes so far as to make the saint *will*. The preceding explanations enable us to follow more closely the precise meaning of this distinction.

When it is a question of the second problem alone there is no special difficulty; since the result is not the same, it is not hard to see that the grace is different—if, apart from any physical influx, every good result in the order of moral activity must in the last resort be attributed to a grace.[2] But, particularly in nn. 31 and

[1] A unity and duality which are likewise to be found, objectively speaking, in the New Testament. Cf. *De vera religione*, c. 7, n. 12: '. . . spiritualis populi gratiam, quod Novum Testamentum vocatur.'

[2] Even among those who have most successfully managed to make out the meaning of the *adiutorium quo*, there are few who have paid any attention to this second problem and so understood the precise implications of the *adiutorium sine quo non*. The trouble, as was pointed out above, was that the controversies of the seventeenth century placed the question of the actual

32, it is also a question of the first problem. Here are we not concerned with the 'grace efficacious of itself' which is to be found in the 'adiutorium quo'? By no means. It must be remembered that St Augustine's thought is here synthetic as it usually is, and that he is not concerned to analyse a particular act. In this first problem, the marked difference between Adam's state and our own is this : to will the good we now need a special, added, previous help, while Adam for his part had received this once for all as a whole, and thus had no need to receive it again. This is what is said in n. 32 : 'Dederat homini Deus bonam voluntatem . . . dederat adiutorium. . . . Nunc autem quibus deest tale adiutorium, iam paena peccati est . . .'; hence the necessity now of a further gift : 'Nunc autem per peccatum perdito bono merito, in his qui liberantur factum est donum gratiae. . . .' This was explained by St Thomas in the *Prima Secundae,* qu. 109, art. 2.[3] However,

efficacy of grace in the foreground. Nevertheless, Cardinal Orsi and—if his interpretation is correct—as early as the sixteenth century, Peter de Soto, whose teaching he was explaining, had seen (though at the same time they mistakenly likened the two helps in Augustine to efficacious and sufficient grace) that if Augustine did not mention the *adiutorium quo* in connection with Adam, it was because Adam had actually succumbed to temptation. Orsi complained that in one place Du Chesne had erroneously copied Soto's text, and he suspected an ulterior motive: 'Id incauto lectori persuasum voluit Duchesnius, adiutorium sine quo non et adiutorium quo ita, ex Soti sententia, esse invicem secernenda, ut alterum naturae innocentis proprium esset, alterum naturae corruptae; ut neque secundum hominem primagenia virtute et iustitia praeditum sustineret, neque primum profligatas per peccatum humanae naturae vires instauraret, aut saltem medicinalis Christi gratiae pars haberetur; quo certe nihil magis a Soti mente ac proposito alienum : qui ut aperte (quod postea demonstrabimus) adiutorium quo etiam naturae innocenti necessarium fuisse docuit, ita adiutorium sine quo a praesenti corruptionis statu neutiquam eliminit' (*De Petri a Soto et Iodaei Ravesteyn . . . liber apologeticus,* c. 5, 1. 1, n. 2; 2nd ed., 1761), p. 117. And p. 347: 'Ad superandas diaboli tentationes, ad reipsa perseverandum, et ad exercitium bonorum operum, opus fuit homini innocenti, non modo adiutorio sine quo, seu gratia sufficiente, sed etiam adiutorio quo, seu gratia efficaci. . . .' If the theologians who refuted Jansenius have paid less attention to this aspect, is it not because most of them were Molinists and they unconsciously feared to provide their Thomist opponents with a weapon in favour of efficacious grace?

[3] A similar explanation was given by 'several very Catholic theologians': 'the *auxilium sine quo* is *gratia actualis adiuvans,* and the *auxilium quo* is *gratia actualis excitans.* Although he had need of an *auxilium adiuvans,* Adam did not need an *auxilium excitans*' (*Analyse de l'Augustin de Jansénius,* by Abbé ***, 1721, pp. 334-5).

this good will possessed by Adam was not given to him, nor did he personally possess it as his very own; although it was received under other conditions, with him as with us, it was a gift of God, and a gift which remained 'unnaturalizable'. St Augustine had no need to repeat it—any more than St Thomas in the article quoted above—because it was not his purpose at that point. But even here he allows it clearly to be understood : 'Dederat homini Deus bonam voluntatem.' The following chapter will show this.

4

Adam's Prayer

Jansenius, as we have seen, thought that he was being true to St Augustine's teaching when he claimed that man, in his state of innocence, had need only of a 'sufficient grace', a mere 'versatile' instrument entirely at the service of his free will, and that as a result the merits of this man would have been entirely human merits. This, it seemed, implied leaving out of account important passages concerning grace which gave to man not only the power but the will and the deed, and also explanations relating to the analogous case of the angels considered at the time of their testing. It also meant forgetting that in the fifth century, in the face of the Pelagian error, the problems raised for the theologian were quite different from those of the seventeenth century, and the meaning of words like nature and grace—especially nature—had evolved considerably in the course of twelve hundred years. Lastly, the very fact of confining the investigation to works dealing with the Pelagian controversy meant neglecting essential elements of information on the fundamental thought of St Augustine.

Nevertheless, however careful we are to emphasize the very clear indications showing that St Augustine cannot be interpreted in a Jansenist sense, at every moment there crops up some further passage which once more calls the whole matter in question, so greatly does Augustine's blunt clarity appear suddenly to support this interpretation. It is then to be wondered whether the accusation of naturalism, formulated by Augustine against the followers of Pelagius—'latent inimici gratiae in laude naturae'[1]—did not contradict the Augustinian teaching on the state of innocence, as it was certain that it did the teaching of Baius and Jansenius.

[1] *Contra duas epistulas Pelagianorum,* bk 2, n. 1.

Two series of passages are particularly impressive. In the first St Augustine seems to be telling us that humility is the virtue proper to sinful man, while Adam could boast of his merits; in the others he assures us that Adam had no need to pray since his natural powers sufficed for everything. A man without humility or prayer : could such a monstrosity be the Augustinian ideal of man?

Adam had no need to pray. The wretched state to which we have been reduced by sin alone makes prayer necessary for us. It was unknown in the earthly paradise and so, in the normal course of events, it should have always remained. However strangely that may sound in our ears, St Augustine asserts it on several occasions. Three passages especially are very explicit and merit consideration.

1. *De natura et gratia,* n. 62.

We are not considering here, says St Augustine, that grace in which man was created, but the grace by which he is saved. This second grace alone is to be asked, implored by prayer : 'libera nos a malo'. Man possessed the first grace by the very fact of his existence, the other we must seek to heal our wounds and recover our nature in its original integrity.[2] What could be more foolish, he remarked, shortly before this, than to pray in order to be able to do what is already in our power?[3]

2. *Contra Iulianum opus imperfectum,* bk 6, chapter 15.

To punish man for the pride which caused him to sin, God

[2] 'Non tunc de illa gratia quaestio est, qua est homo conditus; sed de ista, qua fit salvus per Iesum Christum Dominum nostrum. Fideles enim orantes dicunt: Ne nos inferas in tentationem. Ecce quod vitium naturae humanae inobaedientia voluntatis inflixit. Orare sinatur, ut sanetur. Quid tantum de naturae possibilitate praesumitur? Vulnerata, sauciata, vexata, perdita est. Gratia ergo Dei, non qua instituatur, sed qua restituatur, quaeratur; quae ab isto sola clamatur non esse necessaria, cum tacetur. . . .'

[3] N. 20: 'Nam quid stultius, quam orare ut facias quod in potestate habes?' (Adam was not specially in question here.)

imposed the law of prayer. By virtue of his original union with God Adam's will was naturally free; our own now is in bondage; it must be set free and for this it needs the external help of grace. Now this work of liberation is never complete so long as our present life lasts; hence the necessity of continual prayer to obtain an abundance of grace. Adam could keep his innocence by his own efforts; but for us, whose nature is impaired, it is by praying rather than by using our powers that, according to God's own will, we have to continue the struggle.[4]

3. *Enarratio in psalmum 29*, nn. 16-18.

In paradise Adam saw the face of God and this for him was a continual motive for joy. He was established in abundance, lacking nothing since he enjoyed God himself. But since man's sin, God has turned his face away from him. Turned out of paradise, in exile and in want, man who formerly had only to praise God had now to implore him in tears.[5]

The simple analysis of these passages already enables us to perceive that Augustine's Adam is not that monster of self-sufficiency that we might have feared for an instant. For a clearer view of the meaning we must endeavour to see the fundamental idea more explicitly. It is only implicit, because St Augustine's purpose was not to emphasize the element of continuity between Adam's state and our own, both creaturely states, but only the

[4] 'Et quoniam vitiari per se ipsum potuit, non sanari, legem etiam pravus accepit, non per quam corrigi posset, sed per quam se pravum esse, et nec lege accepta a se ipso corrigi posse sentiret; ac sic, peccatis non lege cessantibus, sed praevaricatione crescentibus, deiecta et contrita superbia, humillimo corde auxilium gratiae desideraret. Nec ipsa lex nova . . . testimonium est liberae, sed liberandae potius voluntatis. . . . Unde et Apostolus ait: Oramus autem ad Deum, ne quid faciatis mali. Quod si ita esset in potestate, quomodo fuit ante peccatum, priusquam esset natura humana vitiata, non utique posceretur orando, sed agendo potius teneretur. Ideo in hoc agone magis nos Deus voluit orationibus certare, quam viribus.'

[5] Iam . . . nolebat videre faciem Dei, ad quam gaudere consueverat. Abundantia erat, quando constitutus est homo in paradiso, quando nihil deerat illi, quando Deo fruebatur. Avertit ergo faciem Deus ab illo, quem emisit foras de paradiso. Iam hic positus, clamet et dicat: Ad te, Domine, clamabo, et ad Deum meum deprecabor. In paradiso non clamabas, sed laudabas; non gemebas, sed fruebaris; foris positus, geme et clama.'

contrast between them, in other words between the state of innocent man and that of sinful man. What is of immediate concern
to us here, however, is to grasp this element of continuity so as to
obtain a right idea of Augustine's concept of man and his fundamental relationships with God.

Now, if for Augustine Adam's attitude was not and had not to
be one of prayer, it is to be understood only by giving the word
prayer, as we shall see, a restricted meaning. For his attitude had
certainly to be one of thanksgiving and of continual humility.
Augustine does not tell us that Adam had no need of God's help
to do good. He says merely that he did not lack this help. Adam
found it naturally, as something normally at his disposal, and
always, as it were, within his reach, without having to ask for it
first. He did not have to seek God, because God was already near
to him. 'Rectorem habebat, non liberatorem quaerebat.'[6] Moreover, this divine help which he had continually at his disposal
was not possessed by Adam as his own property, as a treasure
that he could make his own with no thought of its donor; this
gift always remained a gift, this power of doing good was a divine
power,[7] so that man had to remain always in thanksgiving and
humility. Otherwise he would at once fall into untruth and God
would withdraw his presence.

The 'oratio', which St Augustine tells us that Adam had no
need to use, was therefore only 'postulatio'—'non utique posceretur orando'—it was petition for something remote.[8] Grace was
there, near at hand, proffered, already even within the will, predis-
posing it to good : in this sense Adam had no need to ask for it,
he did not have to pray. This precise kind of prayer was useless
to him. He did not feel 'passions at war in his members'. 'In illo
beatitudinis loco', he did not have to cry, 'Lord deliver me from

[6] *Contra Iulianum opus imperfectum,* bk 3, c. 110.
[7] Cf. *De Civitate Dei,* bk 14, c. 26 : 'Vivebat fruens Deo : gaudium verum
perpetuebatur *ex Deo* in quem fragrabat caritas de corde puro. . . .'
[8] It must be admitted that this restriction given to the meaning of the word
oratio, orare, is the result of controversy, at least in part. In the heat of
controversy with Julian Eclanus, Augustine produced an argument *ad
hominem* which consisted in inferring from his opponent's teaching a shocking
conclusion : 'With your teaching on freedom you abolish prayer !'

evil!'[9] As Martin de Barcos wrote: 'Prayer is not, properly speaking, a raising up of the mind to God, nor a familiar conversation of the soul with him; for in heaven the mind is lifted up to God and there is familiar conversation with him and yet there is no prayer there for there is nothing more to ask of him.'[10]

But our own prayer (itself the effect of a first grace) is principally a prayer of petition: 'orent ut quod nondum habent accipiant.'[11] It is the prayer of the sick man imploring health, of the shipwrecked mariner crying for help, of the man condemned who prays for mercy. In the first place, it is the cry of our poverty and distress. We need grace in the sense that to begin with we are deprived of it, we have need of it.[12] We must beg spiritual benefits in prayer, like the poor man who begs his bread: 'Omnes enim quando oramus, mendici Dei sumus, ante ianuam magni Patrisfamilias stamus, imo et prosternimur, supplices ingemiscimus.' In asking we implore the first remedy for our ills.[13] Adam had not to ask for this remedy. He needed God no less fundamentally than we, but he did not have to pray and beg, for God was with him; God fulfilled his need at the same time as he caused him to be born. We are by nature in want, Adam by nature was in a state of wealth. But beneath this diversity of state one thing remained identical which was clearly and strikingly shown in Augustine. This is man's complete powerlessness without God. Beneath this difference one duty remains the same: the avowal of this powerlessness, the recognition that all comes to man from

[9] *De correptione et gratia*, c. 11, n. 29.

[10] *Réflexions de l'abbé Philérine sur l'écrit de Philagie* (i.e., Mère Agnes), p. 57. And pp. 3-4: 'The blessed see and understand far better than we the mysteries and truths of God, and so form incomparably more fervent and stronger affections than we do, but because they moan no more and have nothing more to desire or ask of God, neither do they pray, according to all the Fathers, just as they are not prayed for, but they pray only for us, as we do ourselves.'

[11] *De correptione et gratia*, c. 11, n. 29.

[12] *Contra duas epistolas Pelagianorum*, bk 1, n. 5: at the present time 'natura humana divina indiget gratia'. Compare what Gregory of Nyssa says, *In Cant. canticorum*, homily 2 (*PG*, 44, 796): '*Gegone to katarchas ho anthrōpos oudenos tōn theiōn agathōn endeēs. hōn ergon ēn phulaxai monon ta agatha, ouchi ktēsasthai.*'

[13] *Sermo* 131, c. 7: 'remedium orationis'.

God, even what he has not had to ask for; it is the acceptance of total dependence. Beneath the differences in the manner of prayer there remains one and the same fundamental attitude, the humble attitude of prayer.[14]

St Gregory the Great said the same thing in a passage of his *Moralia in Iob* : Adam had no need in paradise of the 'assiduitas precis', because 'salutis bonum ex ipsa sua conditione percepit'.[15] And at a later date St Anselm said : 'Man then ate of the bread of the angels, for which now he goes hungry. He was filled, while we now feel the want of it. He enjoyed abundance, and we are in a state of poverty. He possessed in joy the wealth which he subsequently wretchedly abandoned, while we are suffering from our poverty. . . .'[16]

The passages in Augustine about Adam are made clearer by his explanations on the state of the elect. The last state of things corresponds with their beginnings, and paradise, magnified, is to be found again in heaven. No one surely will think that according to St Augustines' idea the heavenly Jerusalem was a Pelagian city. In connection with prayer he speaks of the elect as we have

[14] Even in our present condition certain states of prayer offer some resemblance to Adam's prayer. Cf. St Jane de Chantal, *Œuvres,* vol. 4, p. 737 : 'Going forward with eyes closed, leaning on my Beloved, not wishing . . . not even asking him anything, but remaining quite lost and resting in him.' See also the *Mémoires* of Joseph Arnaud (ed. Jean Bremond, vol. 2, 1951, pp. 64-5) : 'It is clear that when we have arrived at the end we have no more need of the means. In the active life prayer is an efficacious means to reach our end. That is why our Lord desires that ceaselessly we should ask for his kingdom to come, for his will to be done. But when this kingdom has come and the will of God has been accomplished according to the request that we have made, we must not be surprised if the disposition we have for prayer ceases. "It follows from this that in this state we pray no more", someone will object. On the contrary, we pray in a far more perfect and effective manner. For in that state, one will pray for us in his silence, and his prayer will be more valuable than the prayer of all those men together who are in the active life or the state of life proper to them. . . . That is what is meant by *sine intermissione orare*.'
[15] *Moralia in Job,* bk 35, c. 17, n. 44 (*PL,* 76, C-D).
[16] *Proslogion,* c. 1 : 'Manducabat tunc homo panem angelorum, quem nunc esurit. . . . Ille ructabat saturitate, nos suspiramus esurie. Ille abundabat, nos mendicamus. Ille feliciter tenebat, et misere deseruit; nos infeliciter egemus, et miserabiliter desideramus . . .' (*Opera omnia,* ed. Fr Sal. Schmitt, vol. 1 (1946), p. 98).

heard him speak of Adam : 'Again a little time and we shall see Christ; we shall see him there where we have no longer to pray, no longer to question, because there will remain nothing more to desire, because there will be nothing hidden to seek.'[17] Certainly there will be no more questions to ask, although beatific knowledge must not be confined to knowledge of ourselves. The idea of such narcissism is obviously absurd. In the same way in heaven there will be no more prayer, though this does not mean that we are to obtain a sort of independence from God! But what shall we have still to ask for when all our desires are satisfied? God will then make us like himself, we shall see him as he is, and his glory will be made manifest. Prayer, that is petition, request, presupposes a certain need; in heaven there will be no need, for it will be perfect satisfaction.[18] Yet this is not quite accurate for here such language is inadequate. For once satiated we could withdraw from the divine banquet and claim henceforward to be self sufficient. In reality, we shall never cease to receive. And yet, neither can it be said, without qualification, that we shall not be satisfied; for in this case we should still be in want. Together with scripture we must say both, in order to rule out the exclusiveness of either one. It will be no longer satiety or want, but rather a perpetual satisfaction.[19]

[17] *In Ioannem* tract. 101, n. 6: 'Modicum, et videbimus eum, ubi iam nihil rogemus, nihil interrogemus, quia nihil desiderandum remanebit, nihil quaerendum latebit.'

[18] *In Ioannem* tract. 102, n. 3: 'In futuro enim saeculo, cum pervenerimus ad regnum, ubi similes ei erimus quoniam videbimus eum sicuti est, quid petituri sumus, quando satiabitur in bonis desiderium nostrum? Unde et in alio psalmo dicitur: Satiabor cum manifestabitur gloria tua. Petitio namque alicuius est indigentiae, quae ibi nulla erit haec satietas erit.' Cf. Rabanus Maurus, *De videndo Deum*: 'Sic quoque et nos erimus, quando ad ipsum fontem vitae venerimus. Erit enim nobis delectabiliter impressa sitis simul atque satietas. Sed longe ab ista siti necessitas, longe a satietate fastidium, quia et sitientes satiabimur, et satiati sitiemus.'

[19] *In psalmum* 85, n. 24: 'Et satiat te, et non te satiat. Mirum est quod dico. Si dico quia satiat te, timeo ne quasi satiatus velis abscedere: quomodo de prandio, quomodo de caena. Ergo quid dico? Non te satiat? Timeo rursus, ne si dixero: non te satiat, indigens videaris, et quasi inanior exsistas, et minus in te sit aliquid quod debeat impleri. Quid ergo dicam, nisi quod dici potest, cogitari vix potest? Et satiat te, et te non satiat: quia utrumque invenio in Scriptura. . . .'

It was also said that another Adam did not have to pray—despite the numerous Gospel texts which apparently assert the contrary—and that he, still less than the elect, could not be explained by a certain natural sufficiency. For was not he, more than anyone, dependent in his human nature on the Godhead whose human nature, without belonging to him for a single instant, was entirely assumed by the Person of the Word? Now St John Damascene speaks of Christ as St Augustine speaks of Adam : 'His soul had no need to raise itself up to God, since it was already hypostatically united to him; with far greater reason then he had no need to ask for anything at all, since he himself was God.' If Jesus appeared sometimes to address a prayer of petition to his Father it could only have been as an example for us by giving expression to the feelings that should be ours.[20] This christological question need not be discussed here; it is enough to point out the analogy between St John Damascene's statements and those of Augustine. And in our own day Fr Lagrange, commenting on the sayings of Jesus about the devil that cannot be cast out save by prayer, observes pertinently that Jesus had nevertheless cast out this devil without himself uttering any prayer : 'It was because his Father always heard him.'[21] One day it will be the same for all his disciples : 'in illo die me non rogabitis quidquam.'[22] And even here below, at certain privileged moments this day begins to dawn. This is what St Seraphin of Sarov says :

> When he deigns to visit us we must stop praying. After all, what good is it to say, 'Come and make your dwelling with us and cleanse us from all evil and save our souls, O my God', when this Comforter has already come to us to save

[20] *De fide orthodoxa,* bk 3, c. 24.

[21] *L'Évangile de Jésus-Christ,* p. 263 (on Mark 9:14-28). Malebranche seems to say the contrary, but it is really a question of terms : '(Jesus Christ's) prayers are always heard : his Father refuses him nothing, as scripture tells us (John 11:42). Yet he has to pray and to desire if he is to obtain, because . . . all creatures, and even Jesus Christ regarded as man, are of themselves only weakness and powerlessness' (*Traité de la Nature et de la Grâce,* second discourse, 12; in G. Dreyfus, *Œuvres complètes,* vol. 5, 1958, p. 72).

[22] John 16:23.

us, who trust in him and invoke his holy name in order to receive him with humility and love in the temple of our souls which hunger and thirst after his coming?[23]

In a series of similar passages St Augustine seems to say again that what obliges us to humility is solely our sinful state. Would whatever is removed from the corruption of sin be therefore so much loss, even rightfully, for humility? And through reaction against infralapsarian pessimism, if we would remain faithful to Augustinian philosophy, are we making ready, whether we like it or not, for a resurgence of human pride? What we have just seen on the subject of prayer should disabuse us of this idea. But a more direct answer is possible to the question that is here raised.

It is quite clear that as a result of sin, even of original sin alone, we must be humble, and *for an additional reason*. But must we be *humbler*? Would the creature in the state of innocence have the right to be less humble, perhaps not to be humble at all?

It is in precisely this sense that Baius and his successors Jansenius, Arnauld and Quesnel[24] interpret St Augustine's ideas on the subject. Innocent man, they explain, was healthier, stronger, freer. In this way he acquired, if he determined to do good, more merit on his own account from which he could derive legitimate pride: 'gratia Adami non producebat nisi merita humana'. Now, on the contrary, since grace itself effects all good in us, we are obliged to give to God all praise and glory: 'God,' said Arnauld, 'to stifle

---

[23] *Entretiens sur la doctrine du Saint Esprit*; quoted by E. Behr-Sigel, 'La prière à Jésus' in *Dieu Vivant*, 8, p. 92.

[24] Quesnel, thirty-fourth condemned proposition. Cf. De la Font, *Principes de morale établis sur l'Écriture sainte* (1709): 'The first man, in the happy state of original justice in which he was created, had an uprightness of mind and heart which were enough for him in leading his life, and he had no need of any other light save that of reason.' Quoted in the *Dictionnaire des livres jansénistes,* vol. 3 (1755 ed.), p. 306. For St Augustine, on the contrary, 'Adam, in the very completeness of his nature, was bathed in a light of grace': Athanase Sage, 'La grâce du Christ, modèle de la nôtre' in *Revue des études augustiniennes,* 7 (1961), p. 27.

man's pride (the evil pride of rebellion, not the good pride of original pleasure in self) which was the cause of his downfall, no longer wills that he should glory in his merits'; and he made him incapable of all good without the help that St Augustine calls 'adiutorium quo', to show clearly that he leaves nothing to man alone. The good works performed by men no longer constitute human merits like those of Adam who in his state of innocence could do good actions 'praevia et dominante voluntate'. And so men no longer have the right to glory in their good deeds as Adam glorified in his own.[25] Henceforth God alone is to be glorified in his saints!

Jansenius was so well pleased with his explanation that he thought that the Augustinian teaching, restored by him to its original vigour, would cause a revival of Christian humility in the Church. We are told of this by the author of his *Life*: 'rem istam ingentis momenti et fructus in Ecclesia esse censebat, nec vitam perfecte spiritualem formari posse, nisi ad illam doctrinae sancti Augustini normam, christianam tamen praecipue humilitatem in ea fundare'.[26] Possessed by the same thought Arnauld

---

[25] *Remarques sur les contradictions du Père Thomassin* (*Œuvres,* vol. 10, pp. 446-8). Thomassin 'admits . . . with St Augustine that the angels owed their predestination to their merits, and that they owed their merits to their own powers, although aided by an *auxilium sine quo non.* And thus he acknowledges that for God to have removed from men all occasion of pride, and for him to have left them no opportunity for glorying in their own merits, it was necessary for grace to be all their merit, that is, that they had no more merits than by means of the *adiutorium quo*—"pedissequa iam et famulante, non ut antea praevia et dominante voluntate". Now the just merit by all their good works; and so all their good works were no longer to be human merits as Adam's had been (for if they were, as St Augustine agrees, they would be able to glory in them, and God does not wish them to do so), but entirely divine merits.'

Thomassin's observations here approved by Arnauld were as follows: 'Nec de ipsa perseverantia boni voluit Deus sanctos suos in viribus suis, non in ipso gloriari, qui eis non solum dat adiutorium, quale primo homini dedit sine quo non possint perseverare si vellent, sed in eis etiam operatur et velle. Ad humilitatem ergo lapsis pernecessariam, contemperata est et haec gratia quae merita ipsa donat, et haec praedestinatio, quae merita antevertit et gratiam praeparat qua donentur. Ex adverso autem periclitaretur humilitas, si suis meritis praedestinationem, si suis viribus merita sua deberet' (*Dogmata theologica,* bk 8, c. 4).

[26] *Augustinus,* init.: 'Synopsis vitae auctoris'.

relied principally on two passages of St Augustine, one from the *De correptione et gratia,* the other from the *De dono perseverantiae.* In the first passage we find: '. . . ac per hoc, nec de ipsa perseverantia boni voluit Deus sanctos suos in viribus suis, sed in ipso gloriari'.[27] Must we not conclude, asks Arnauld, that Adam, if he persevered, would have been able to glory in himself and not in the Lord? And do we not find, he adds, quite similar teaching in *De dono perseverantiae* where it is explained for us that since all that draws us nearer to God is henceforth the work of grace there is nothing left from which we may derive glory?[28]

This in fact is the conclusion that would have to be drawn from these passages if, as these writers assume, everything that Adam possessed independently of redeeming grace he did by the fact of his nature and his own activity, independently of his union with God. But, once more, such an assumption is surely contrary to the thought of St Augustine as it is implicit throughout his works and explicitly stated on many occasions. With regard to the two passages put forward by Arnauld it must be said that they do not bear the meaning attributed to them by him and his followers.

Consider in the first place the passage from the *De dono perseverantiae.* It can only be used as an argument if a sentence is changed. Explaining the Lord's Prayer St Augustine had just said: 'Si ergo alia documenta non essent, haec dominica oratio nobis ad causam gratiae, quam deferimus, sola sufficeret: quia nihil nobis reliquit, in quo tanquam in nostro gloriemur. Siquidem et ut non discedamus a Deo, non ostendit dandum nisi a Deo, cum poscendum ostendit a Deo.' It is therefore, according to St Augustine, the Lord's Prayer itself which by the petition 'et ne nos inducas in tentationem' leaves us nothing in which to glorify ourselves. But if the quotation is begun, as it is in several writers,[29] only at the words 'Nihil nobis reliquit', it seems that the

[27] *De correptione et gratia,* c. 12, n. 38.
[28] *De dono perseverantiae,* c. 7, n. 13.
[29] Cf. Jean Laporte, *La doctrine de Port-Royal,* 2, 'Exposition de la doctrine (daprès Arnauld)', 1, 'Les vérités de la grâce (1923), p. 372.

subject of the sentence is 'Deus' and that the verb 'reliquit' contains an allusion to a first state in which God would actually have let us glorify ourselves. This really amounts to a partial misunderstanding, because the rest of the passage compares the state of man before and after sin.[30] But it will be noticed, on the other hand, that the only point on which this comparison rests is a negative one; by the power of his free will Adam could 'draw back', but Augustine does not say that he could go forward. This is the teaching which was handed down in the Augustinian school by the celebrated axiom: 'Stare poterat, pedes movere non poterat.'[31] In its actual form the axiom is not Augustine's, as was thought in the Middle Ages. It is none the less an accurate expression of his thought. Adam, therefore, could be proud of nothing positive; he could ascribe to himself no good work as being his and not God's.

If Arnauld forces the meaning of this passage it is also because he interprets it in the light of the chapter of *De correptione* on the two helps. He is keen on such a comparison.[32] But his reasoning on this chapter is still more faulty than his exegesis of the passage in *De dono*. St Augustine said: 'Nec de ipsa perseverantia boni voluit Deus sanctos suos in viribus suis, sed in ipso gloriari.'[33] Therefore, continues Arnauld, if Adam had persevered in the good, he could have gloried in his powers, and not in God. On this view, he had persevered with the simple 'adiutorium sine quo non', while for the perseverance of the saints the 'adiutorium

---

[30] 'Qui enim non infertur in tentationem, non discedit a Deo. Non est hoc omnino in viribus liberi arbitrii, quales nunc sunt: fuerat in homine antequam caderet. Post casum autem hominis, nonnisi ad gratiam suam Deus voluerit pertinere, ut homo accedat ad eum; neque nisi ad gratiam suam voluit pertinere, ut homo non recedat ab eo.'

[31] Peter Lombard, *Sentences,* bk 2, dist. 29, n. 1: 'Ante peccatum homo . . . non habebat quo pedem movere posset sine gratiae operantis et cooperantis auxilio, habuit tamen quo potuit stare.' Albert the Great, *Summa theologiae,* p. 2a, tract. 14, qu. 90, n. 1: 'Dederat enim (Deus Adae) unde posset stare, sed non unde proficeret ad meritum', etc. And there are many other passages of this kind.

[32] *Œuvres*, vol. 10, pp. 448ff. See also Pascal, *Écrits sur la Grâce* (Brunschvicg, vol. 11, pp. 222-3).

[33] *Loc. cit.*

quo' must intervene. In reality this development of Augustine's thought is only a deviation. Arnauld based his conclusions on an interpretation of the two helps which, if I am not mistaken, is untenable. God has willed that his holy ones should glory in him alone; does this mean that Adam could have gloried in himself alone, as the only real artisan of his victory? By no means. Augustine definitely does not imply this. According to him Adam ought also to have gloried in God, without whose grace he could not have performed the good actions necessary for his perseverance. He could also, though secondarily, glory in himself since his unimpaired nature from the outset would have served as the active support of the divine work in him. All the same, this would in no way have diminished what was due to God; for Adam would have regarded this unimpaired nature, with all its powers, as a gift continually renewed, from the Lord. To put it more accurately, therefore, we can say that Adam would have gloried in his powers and in his Lord, and the more in his Lord than in his powers, but that he would not have gloried in himself at all, or regarded himself as in any way apart from his Lord and independent of him.[34] In other words, just as much as the attitude of every saint living in a state of redeemed nature, that of a saint living in the state of unimpaired nature, as it was conceived by Augustine, would have been one of complete humility.[35]

[34] In other words: Adam had strength, health and free will. But whence came this health and strength, whence this free will, always ready for doing good? He was more his own than we are, he really belonged to himself; but for that reason he was more 'open' to God, more imbued with the presence and action of God. So that it could be said that he possessed himself less, that he was less his own because he belonged more to God. But in neither sense is an antithesis to be found, for this is not in conformity with Augustinian thought.

[35] Cf. Léon Bloy, *L'Invendable,* p. 85 : 'I think that Humility, like Purity, Beauty, Knowledge, Understanding and all the others have been destroyed by the Fall. I am sure that Adam and Eve in paradise were humble, just as they were pure, beautiful, powerful and immortal, that is, in a way that is absolutely incomprehensible even for the saints.'

It remains true none the less that the frailty of our present state is a valuable safeguard for us against the temptation to pride to which Adam fell. *Contra Iulianum,* bk 4, n. 11 : 'Infimitas admonitio est non superbiendi', and n. 28.

Coram Deo, ubi nulla iactantia est.[36]

Once again, the case of the angels provides us with confirmation. The good angel did not undergo the fall or the redemption. His order of grace was essentially the same as that of the first man. Did he therefore attribute to himself a particular role in his perseverance? According to Jansenius and Arnauld he ought to have done so. Now the angel in glory, St Augustine tells us, is light 'non in se ipso sed in Deo'.[37] He was well pleased not in himself but in his Creator: 'Si eo modo sibi placeret mens angelica, ut amplius seipsa quam creatore suo delectaretur, non fieret mane, id est, non de sua cognitione in laudem creatoris assurgeret.'[38] Likewise, the vision in which Augustine delighted is available for all without distinction because the reason forming the basis of hope derives not from angels or men, innocence or its recovery, but from God: 'Tanta satiabitur (animus) visione et tanta inflammabitur caritate superioris boni, ut ad seipsum sibi placendo deficere ab illius dilectione non possit.'[39] Again, it is concerning the angels that we are told: 'Qui gloriatur, nonnisi in Domino gloriatur, cum cognoscit non suum, sed illius esse, non solum ut sit, verum etiam ut nonnisi ab illo bene sibi sit, a quo habet ut sit.'[40] A humility founded only on an avowal of the powerlessness to which original sin has reduced free will would not be Christian humility. This is the humility which the editor of the *Augustinus* attributes to Jansenius.[41] It is not that of Augustine. The City of God, as contemplated by the latter, is not divided into two parts of which one, that of the redeemed saints, would be lost in humble gratitude while the other, that of the innocent angels who persevered, would know that they owed to themselves a part at least of their triumph. This was an equal humility in each case, differing only in its manner and emphasis. It is the same with

[36] *In psalmum* 7, n. 4.
[37] *De Civitate Dei,* bk 11, c. 9.
[38] *De Genesi ad litteram,* bk 4, n. 49.
[39] *Contra Iulianum Pelagianum,* bk 4, c. 3.
[40] *De Genesi ad litteram,* bk 11, c. 8, n. 10.
[41] *Augustinus, Synopsis vitae auctoris.*

Adam and the Christian; the former had not the right to be less humble than the latter ought to be, but while humility now, pleading for grace, seems at first sorrowful and bewailing its lot, that of the first age, without being less, could from the outset manifest its joy and gratitude.

Here again we should remember one of the essential features by which St Augustine differs from those who regard themselves as his principal disciples—although this difference seems not to be clear in all its force to those critics who cling to the literal sense. The central viewpoint, which he always adopts, concerns the man of today, sinful man, Augustine of Tagaste and Hippo, whose chains were broken by the grace of Christ. We should understand that everything which he states concerning man in a state of innocence is affirmed by contrast; it is as it were a second phase of his thought, arranged schematically on occasion and simplified, without a return to the fundamental points that are obvious in his view, which he has often explained and which nothing could call in question. When he seems to tell us that Adam merited by his own efforts, or that by his nature he had the right to enter in possession of the kingdom of heaven, we should be able to see the implication of such assertions in proper prospective. They merely meant that Adam, to fulfil his destiny, had no need either of 'extrinsic help' or of remedial and redemptive grace. God, as we saw, without having to rectify Adam's action, did not cease to 'direct' it.[42] In a similar case, St Gregory of Nyssa, when he taught that without the disorder introduced into his being by original sin man would be perfect by the very fact of his creation, was far from meaning to assert that the creative act alone was enough to establish man in his final perfection; he only meant to deny, on the hypothesis of a world without sin, the necessity of development in a purely temporal sense.

[42] Abbé Gourlin (d. 1775), although an ardent Jansenist and an 'appellant', speaks very wisely on this question in his *Tractatus de gratia Christi* (it appeared anonymously, published by Abbé Pelvert), vol. 2 (1781), p. 88: 'Absit . . . ut eximius humilitatis praedicator senserit licitum fuisse primo homini in seipso gloriari, cum e contrario multoties inculcet eum, nonnisi de se praesumendo, in peccatum incidisse.'

111

With these remarks in mind we should be able to discern, running right through the great Catholic tradition, those fundamental constants which are affected neither by divergences of school nor diversity of viewpoint, neither by the differences of emphasis made necessary by various errors, nor by variations of terminology in the course of the centuries. For St Thomas, for example, and still more for the theologians coming after him who followed his tradition, Adam in the state of innocence needed grace, he prayed, he had faith.[43] For St Augustine, however, it seems—at least from certain passages—that this same Adam could, for the decisive step, do without grace, that he did not pray, that he did not have to believe.[44] Yet there is no contradiction between the two doctors. For if by grace is understood the remedy for the wound of sin, by prayer petition for help that is still not at hand, by faith obscure belief wholly based on external evidence[45] and also concerned primarily and fundamentally with the events of salvation which took place in time,[46] then these things must be expressed as they are by St Augustine in the passages to which I have just referred.

[43] *Secunda Secundae,* qu. 5, art. 1 : 'Tam in angelis viatoribus quam in Adamo in statu innocentiae fuit fides.' *Prima,* qu. 62, art. 1 ; qu. 95, art. 1.

[44] St Augustine's vocabulary is not quite so fixed as that. Regarding Adam's faith he says, for example : 'In statu innocentiae (habebat homo) gaudium verum, quod perpetuabatur ex Deo, in quem flagrabat caritas de corde puro, conscientia bona, et fide non ficta' (*De Civitate Dei,* bk 14, c. 26). Cf. St Ambrose, *In Lucam,* bk 7 : 'Adam nudatus est, mandati caelestis custodia destitutus, et exustus fidei vestimento, et sic lethale vulnus accepit' (G. Tissot, *SC,* 52, p. 33). St Fulgentius, *Epist.* 17, n. 26 : 'Exspoliatus vestimento fidei'; regarding grace, *ibid.,* n. 14 : 'Deus primum hominem ad suam imaginem gratuita bonitate bonum fecit. . . . Si autem gratia excidisset. . . .'

[45] Cf. Hugh of St Victor, *De Sacramentis,* bk 1, part 6, c. 14 : 'Cognovit homo creatorem suum non ea cognitione, quae foris solum et auditu percipitur, sed ea, quae potius intus per spirationem ministratur. Non ea quidem, qua Deus modo a credentibus absens fide quaeritur, sed ea quae tunc per praesentiam contemplationis sicuti manifestius comebatur.' Peter Lombard, *Sentences,* bk 2, dist. 23. Even for this life, William of St Thierry told the Carthusians of Mont Dieu, 'Aliorum est Deum quaerere . . . , vestrum est sapere' (n. 11 ; Davy, p. 74).

[46] Thus William of St Thierry, following St Augustine : 'Fides autem maxime est rerum temporaliter pro nobis gestarum, per quam corda nostra mundantur, ut ad aeterna non credenda, sed intelligenda, idonea inveniantur. In qua si fideliter nos agimus, et fides meretur veritatem, et mutabilitas transit ad creditae rei incommutabilem veritatem . . .' : *Speculum fidei* (PL, 180, 383 D).

For in this sense completed nature excludes grace, divine union excludes prayer, and infused contemplation or the 'vision' (*species*) excludes faith. Thus, following Peter Lombard, the *Summa* of Alexander of Hales finds no difficulty in saying that Adam, in his first state, 'non habuit fidem in ratione fidei'.[47] St Bonaventure even calmly asserts that the state of innocence, which did not comprise extrinsic 'hearing' ('ex auditu') or 'knowledge by enigma', did not there include faith, any more than it included the perfect vision.[48] But if the assertion of grace is in opposition principally with that of the sufficiency of created nature, if the attitude of prayer is essentially the contrary of natural pride, if faith is distinctive principally of a certain state of understanding which excludes rationalist autonomy without reaching the fulness of beatific vision, then it is St Thomas' language that we must adopt. In that case we shall say that the knowledge possessed by Adam, according to the traditional idea, was 'comprised within the limits of faith';[49] we shall say that he already had need of grace to perform good actions and that prayer was his first duty.

While emphasizing the inferiority of the knowledge of faith, 'a strange and essentially imperfect act' at the rational level,[50] St

---

[47] *Summa Theologica*, n. 694 (Quaracchi ed., vol. 4, p. 1103): 'Dicendum quod Adam in primo statu non habuit fidem in ratione fidei. Et hoc patet, si quis consideret comparationem cognitionis quae per fidem est et cognitionis quae erat in Adam ante peccatum, ad cognitionem gloriae. Cognitio enim quae est per fidem evacuatur adveniente gloria; cognitio vero Adae de Deo non evacuatur adveniente gloria, si stetisset, sed perficeretur.'
[48] *In II Sent.*, dist. 23, a. 2, qu. 3: 'Nota quod quadruplex est modus cognoscendi Deum, videlicet per fidem, per contemplationem, per apparitionem et per apertam visionem. . . . Primum igitur et ultimum genus cognitionis statui innocentiae non competebat: primum, propter cognitionem aenigmaticam et propter hoc quod cognitio fidei, ut plurimum, est ex auditu. . . .'
[49] Thus Estius, *In II Sent.*, dist. 23, n. 6: 'Primus homo cognoscebat Deum quadam altiori cognitione quam nos eum cognoscimus, adeo ut cognitio illius, quamvis intra limites fidei comprehensa, quodammodo media fuerit inter cognitionem praesentis status et cognitionem patriae, qua Deus per essentiam videtur' (Paris, 1680, p. 221). He refers to *Prima,* qu. 94, art. 1, *De veritate,* qu. 18, art. 2; *In II Sent.*, dist. 23, qu. 2, art. 1.
[50] Pierre Rousselot, *L'Intellectualisme de saint Thomas,* 2nd ed. (1924), pp. 190-2.

Thomas nevertheless takes pleasure in showing faith as the sketch or the germ of vision, the 'substantia beatitudinis', the 'inchoatio rerum sperandarum'.[51] He likes to see in it a 'praelibatio quaedam illius cognitionis quae in futuro beatos faciet'.[52] He even says that faith will not be made void absolutely in heaven as hope will be, because 'cum visione patriae convenit in genere'; only its obscurity or enigmatic character will disappear.[53] From a similar point of view St John of the Cross, who always maintains the spiritual element in faith, says further, 'When the faith of this life gives place to the clear vision of God, then the substance of faith, stripped of its veil of silver, will shine like gold'.[54] St Augustine would apply all this to what he calls 'understanding of the faith' or more simply 'understanding', as his disciple St Bonaventure was to apply it to 'contemplation'. 'Fides quaerit, intellectus invenit.'[55] As for 'fides' itself he gives contrary emphasis, following a passage from St Paul, to the opposition with 'species', just as he emphasizes the opposition of 'spes' and 'res' : 'Modo enim credimus, tunc videbimus. Cum credimus, spes est in isto saeculo; cum videbimus, res erit in futuro saeculo. . . . Mundantur autem corda nostra per fidem, ut possint esse idonea

[51] *Secunda secundae,* qu. 4, art. 1, *In Hebr.* Cf. Spicq, 'L'exégèse de Hebr. XI par saint Thomas d'Aquin' in *RSPT,* 31 (1947), pp. 231-2.
[52] *Compendium theologiae,* c. 1; *ibid.*: 'per modum cuiusdam inchoationis'.
[53] *Prima Secundae*; qu. 67, art. 5: 'Quidam dixerunt, quod spes totaliter tollitur, fides autem partim tollitur, scilicet quantum ad aenigma, et partim manet, scilicet quantum ad substantiam cognitionis. Quod quidem si sic intelligatur, quod maneat non idem numero, sed idem genere, verissime dictum est: fides enim cum visione patriae convenit in genere, quod est cognitio. . . .' (And all knowledge of God can be called vision: cf. *In II Sent.*, dist. 23, qu. 2, art. 1.) At the resurrection, Origen asserted, in the same sense, there will be perfect knowledge, the completion of faith, that is, its fulfilment rather than its abolition : *In Ioannem,* vol. 10, n. 27 (Preuschen, p. 221).
[54] *Spiritual Canticle,* stanza 12 (See E. Allison Peers ed., *op. cit.*, vol. 2, p. 257).
[55] *De Trinitate,* bk 15, c. 2, n. 2. For a more thorough investigation of the subject, see J. M. Le Blond, *Les conversions de saint Augustin* (1950), I, c. 3 and 4 (pp. 89-138).

capere speciem.'⁵⁶ Very rightly there has been mention of the 'twofold Augustinian equation between knowledge and a vision on the one hand, belief and non-vision on the other'.⁵⁷ 'Creduntur abstentia.'⁵⁸ This is said again in the *De Trinitate* with some emphasis.

Quando ista peregrinatione finita, qua peregrinamur a Domino, ut per fidem ambulare necesse sit, species illa succedet, per quam videbimus facie ad faciem, sicut modo non videntes, tamen, quia credimus, videre merebimur, atque ad speciem nos per fidem perductos esse gaudebimus. Neque enim iam fides erit, qua credantur quae non videntur; sed species qua videantur quae credebantur.⁵⁹

Such differences between the two doctors are not absolutely constant. St Thomas has more than one passage in which faith is envisaged rather like a substitute for reason;⁶⁰ there are others again where the continuity that he allows between faith and vision is only continuity 'in genere cognitionis'.⁶¹ On the other hand, Augustiniansm does not find the same contrast as Thomism between the 'creditum' and the 'scitum'; and St Augustine himself could say : 'Sed intelligens omnis etiam credit.'⁶² The Scholastics did not fail to offer subtle distinctions on the matter. Here is a single example taken from the *Summa* of Gerard of Bologna :

⁵⁶ *In psalmum* 123, n. 2. *In psalmum* 120, n. 6. *Sermo* 38, c. 2, n. 3. Cf. 2 Cor. 5 : 7. William of Saint Thierry, *Speculum fidei*: 'Videbitur, cognoscetur, non credetur' (*PL*, 180, 395B); 'a fide ad speciem transeatur' (396A).
⁵⁷ J.-Fr Bonnefoy, *La nature de la théologie selon saint Thomas d'Aquin*, p. 35.
⁵⁸ *Epist.*, 147, n. 3.
⁵⁹ *De Trinitate*, bk 14, c. 2, n. 4 (Bibl. Aug., 16, p. 350). There are further texts in P. Th. Camelot, O.P., 'A l'éternal par le temporel' in *Revue des études augustiniennes*, 2 (1956), pp. 163-72. By the same author : ' "Quod intelligimus debemus rationi", note sur la méthode théologique de saint Augustin' in *Hist. Jahrbuch*, 77 (1958), pp. 397-402.
⁶⁰ For example, *Secunda Secundae*, qu. 2, art. 4.
⁶¹ See above, footnote 53.
⁶² *De utilitate credendi*, c. 11, n. 25: 'Invenimus primum beatorum genus ipsi veritati credere, secundum autem studiosorum amatorumque veritatis, auctoritati: in quibus duorum generibus laudabiliter creditur' (*PL*, 42, 83).

Addunt quod fides est de tali obiecto quoad id de obiecto quod est obscurum, intellectus vero quoad id quod est clarum de eo, visio vero patriae quoad id quod de obiecto clarius restat. —Haec autem additio est valde incompetens, quia, si fides et intellectus ac visio sint tota aliud, et de re vel obiecto, tunc frustra laboratur vel ab eis vel ab aliis ad declarandum quomodo fides et intellectus ille vel visio quaeque stare possint simul, vel non; quia constat quod, si non sit de eodem secundum idem, simul stare possunt. . . .[63]

On the other hand, with a little ingenuity the two forms of language that we have been examining can be harmonized without difficulty by means of certain explanations. This is done, for example, by Eudes Rigaud[64] and the *Summa* of Alexander of Hales; they distinguish 'fides oenigmatica' which is ours now from 'fides lucida' which was Adam's in paradise and Christ's in his humanity on earth; or again, faith by 'auditus exterior' and faith by 'inspiratio interna'.[65] The same was done by later commentators on St Thomas. One wrote: 'Fides semper manet in quantum est fundamentum spiritualis aedificii, id est ratione cognitionis, non autem ratione aenigmatis.' Another said: 'Fides potest dici semper manere, ratione visionis Dei succedentis ei in patria.'[66] Yet it is more than a question of language here. The differences that we have noticed undoubtedly have real significance. They are an indication, at least in certain cases, of two trends in theological thought—two trends whose roots, or first signs, could probably be shown to lie in the two ways of understanding (and firstly of interpreting) the passage of St Paul in the

[63] *Summa,* qu. 8, n. 3; ed. Paul De Vooght, *Les sources de la doctrine chrétienne* . . . (1954), pp. 400-9. Obiectio secunda et ad secundum.
[64] *In II Sent.,* dist. 29-9-2. (J. Bouvy, *Rech. de théol. anc. et méd.,* 28, p. 92).
[65] *Summa,* n. 512 (Quaracchi, vol. 2, p. 540). While insisting on the obscurity of faith and the absence of its object, St Augustine spoke of the 'oculi fidei' (*In psalmum* 134, n. 24, etc.) and we have just seen that St Thomas adopted (*Secunda Secundae,* qu. 67, art. 5) the distinction between faith *quantum ad aenigma* and *quantum ad substantiam.*
[66] Texts from Sylvius and Billuart, quoted by A. Gratry *De la connaissance de Dieu,* vol. 1, 2nd edition (1854), p. 262.

thirteenth chapter of 1 Corinthians.[67] But—and this is of the greatest importance—for all that they do not destroy the unity of tradition.

[67] 1 Cor. 13 : 13 : 'Nunc autem manent. . . .' The historical study of the twofold exegesis of this verse has been done, for the patristic period, by Fr Paul Henry, S.J. See also Hans Urs von Balthasar, *Theologie der Geschichte,* Eng. trans. *Theology of History* (1959), p. 149; *Parole et mystère chez Origène* (1957), pp. 20-4; *La gloire et la croix,* vol. I, pp. 113-15. For St Paul's actual meaning: Dom. M.-Fr. Lacan, 'Les Trois qui demeurent' in *RSR,* 1958.

5

Conservative Thomism in the Sixteenth Century

Although a number of theologians still regard St Augustine as the ancestor of Baius and Jansenius it does not always mean that the differences which I have endeavoured to emphasize are wholly hidden from them. It appears to me, rather, that they are wrong in their location of the precise point of doctrine which makes Baianism and Jansenism a heresy. In this sense, their mistake is doctrinal rather than historical. For there are several propositions which these two 'Augustinians' held in common with their great doctor, and which are contested by other theological schools. But it would still be necessary to know if these propositions, considered in themselves, are always worthy of condemnation. If, for example, the heresy of Baius and Jansenius consists, as has been maintained, in not admitting a 'purely rational morality' or in having a 'dynamist'[1] idea of charity, or in thinking that original sin is something other than a mere withdrawal of grace, leaving nature absolutely intact and, so to say, restoring man to his normal state, or even that the soul, as a result of the act of creation, is the image of its author just as the unrational creatures are his vestiges[2]—then, yes, St Augustine is indeed their master

[1] Jansen, *op. cit.,* p. 89; cf. pp. 59-97. On the opposition between charity and cupidity, see above, chapter three. In this opposition Saléon claimed to see the fundamental idea of Baianism; but this means he found the purest Baianism in the works of Belleli and Berti—and also, he could have added, in the works of St Augustine. See Saléon, *Baianismus redivivus,* and Berti's answers.

[2] Jansen, *op. cit.,* p. 62. This last idea does not obviously appear to be specifically Baianist or even Augustinian. There is no theme more widespread nor more constantly to be found in Scholasticism, the patristic period,

and St Augustine was wrong. But such historically questionable assertions do not bear on the essentials of Augustinianism nor on the essence of the condemned doctrines.

There is at least one idea, the charge continues, governing all those just enumerated, which connects them together to form a single whole that is certainly heretical : this is the idea that Adam's primitive state was a natural one, not in the sense that it was without grace, but in the sense that to be defined accurately it would not have needed the contrast of a possible state of 'pure nature' as it is understood by the theologians. Now, is not this very point an Augustinian idea ? Baius hardly did more than make it explicit and systematize it and then in his turn Jansenius insisted on it. This idea, it is added, which had hitherto remained more or less latent, emerged clearly in the sixteenth century as a result of avowed opposition to scholastic theology. Then its poison was clearly seen and an anathema had to be pronounced against it. On the other hand, it became easier to avoid it; 'it was one of the better results of the Baianist controversy that once for all there was established the possibility of what is called the state of pure nature'.[3] And so the dangerous germs of Augustinianism were killed at the source.

Perhaps no one was concerned to see whether, by this verdict, together with St Augustine the whole of Christian tradition, with the Greek Fathers at its head, and to some extent including even

modern theology or ancient theology. See, among hundreds of other examples, Bellarmine, *De gratia primi hominis,* c. 2, or Gregory of Valencia, *Commentaria,* vol. 1 (3rd ed., 1603), col. 1221 and 1226 : 'Est (homo) vere ac proprie Dei imago, ut est natura intellectuali secundum mentem praeditus. . . . Homo, ut est praeditus natura intellectuali secundum mentem, Dei imago est, non modo ut Deus est natura sua, sed etiam ut est personis trinus.'

[3] Jansen, *op. cit.,* p. 28; cf. p. 31 : 'A purely natural religion' is inconceivable for Baius. Further on, the writer is even alarmed at the fact that 'Augustinianism still finds some support; a group of theologians does not hesitate to assert that in the created will there is a natural appetite or desire for the clear vision of God. This thesis, which stated in this way lends itself to misunderstanding, they believe to be found in certain passages of St Thomas, those precisely which Jansenius put forward to exclude any end for man that was lesser than the beatific vision' (pp. 143-4). Cf. Du Chesne, *Histoire du Baianisme,* pp. 177 and 356-7.

St Thomas, was in danger of being declared unorthodox. But without for the moment going back any further than the time of Baius it is possible, I believe, to show that this idea of pure nature, as it is understood by modern theology, is a systematic idea, quite legitimate no doubt and perhaps useful, but recent. In any case, the traditional dogmas defended by the condemnations of St Pius V and Urban VIII are not necessarily bound up with it, and it is possible that they have not been sufficiently taken into account.

In the first place, reread the seventy-nine propositions condemned by St Pius V in 1567; there is not one of them whose contradictory proposition does not assert or merely assume the concrete possibility of an order of things in which man, left by the Creator to his own powers or enjoying 'natural' helps, would have been able to lay claim only to an inferior destiny, limiting his reasonable desires to a purely 'natural' happiness. Nor, for the explanation of certain propositions, is there any need here to have recourse to the concluding formula of the Bull. From this it emerges, at least negatively, that each proposition is not necessarily bad in itself, taken in separation from the others, but only if it is taken from within the whole system from which it was extracted.[4] Suarez was wrong when, in his impatience to cut short certain bad and over-subtle arguments of the Baianists, he refused to adopt this wise rule of interpretation.[5] The other censures, without having the same authority as the Bull, are also relevant in this connection. That of the Sorbonne (1560) attacks principally the theories concerning free will and sin; those of the Spanish faculties are directed against various articles—the eucharist, indulgences, charity, justification, the pope, the Council of Trent, predestination and so on, with no attempt to see a connection

[4] *Ibid.*, p. 198.
[5] *De Gratia*, proleg., vi, c. 3, n. 11: 'Concludo (propositionum) sensum non aliunde, quam ex verborum proprietate regulariter sumendum esse. . . . (To understand them there is no need to have recourse to the system of Baius.) Alioqui non fuisset aequa censura ad assertorem relata, et ad opera eius, si assertiones damnandae tali modo verbisque ita in contextu ipso operis vel sermonis continerent . . .' (Vivès, vol. 8, p. 291).

between them.[6] Obviously, 'pure nature' did not concern the first opponents of Baius to any great degree.[7]

Actually Baius himself scarcely mentioned it. The celebrated proposition 55 (formerly 53) taken from *De peccato originali*,[8] as we have seen, only called in question concupiscence and the gift of integrity or completeness, that is, it concerned only the original state of man, as Baius himself explains very clearly in his *Apologia* to St Pius V in 1569[9] and in his declaration of 1570 before the Faculty of Louvain.[10] This emerges with equal clarity from the *Explicatio* given by the Faculty,[11] and it was so understood by everyone. The *De meritis operum,* which is rightly to be considered as one of Baius' major works, shows, as we have also seen, a thoroughgoing misunderstanding of the supernatural considered as the deification of man;[12] yet never for a moment is there any question, in one sense or the other, of a world in an entirely

[6] In the censures published in 1953 by Miguel Roca, *op. cit.* (Alcala and Salamanca, 1565; Alcala, 1567), the censors merely followed, as usual, the order of Baius' works. Again, in 1569, the same thing occurred with the long reply to Baius' *Apologia.*

[7] However, in the declaration signed by the professors of the Louvain theological faculty, in which the errors of Baius are repudiated, the possibility of an order of things in which God would have left man in the status of servant without raising him up to the dignity of son, is clearly stated: 'Doctrinae eius quam certorum articulorum damnatio postulae visa est, brevis et quoad fieri potuit ordinata et cohaerens explicatio', c. 2 and 3, in *Baiana,* pp. 163-4. (It is thought that this text was drawn up by John of Lens, who seems to have been at first a disciple of Baius, and then to have turned against him, and finally to have joined him again to help him draw up the censure against Lessius in 1587 or 1588.)

[8] Baius claims that it was 'male collecta' (*Baiana,* p. 110): 'Haec sententia in libello non habctur, nec ad verbum, nec ad sensum, sed potius indicatur contrarium' (p. 136). Gerberon goes further: 'male fide collecta'; and he adds: 'Ipse pater Ripalda fatetur eam non haberi in Michaelis Baii operibus' (p. 230). But it is, as a matter of fact, quite untrue. Cf. Le Bachelet, *DTC,* vol. 2, col. 71-2.

[9] *Baina,* p. 110: 'Deus non potuisset ab initio esse auctor peccati originis, in quo iuxta fidem catholicam omnes concipimur. . . .'

[10] *Baiana,* p. 145.

[11] *Doctrinae eius,* etc., 4 (*Baiana,* pp. 166-7).

[12] In his Apology to St Pius V, Baius could find no other method of defence to justify the propositions taken from this short work, than to offer explanations which show his error more clearly. See *In propositionem nonam,* and the corresponding remarks in the declaration by the theological faculty, *Baiana,* p. 161. Or else he withdraws: 'Non asseritur, sed refertur inter sententias quae a Catholicis disputantur.'

natural state which would be in opposition to that actually chosen by the Creator. Such an hypothesis is merely touched on in the eighth chapter of the first book of *De prima hominis iustitia* where Baius attacks it in passing;[13] but, and this is very remarkable, the Bull of condemnation makes no mention of it, not even to reject in this connection the affinity with Pelagianism, and it is possible to agree with Baius in his criticism without at the same time adopting any of his positive ideas.

If, as some have asserted, Baius' principal error consisted in the denial primarily of *this sort* of 'pure nature' and consequently in the destruction of the foundations of dogma and in opposition to a unanimous tradition, we come up against a curious problem. It is this: how could the innovator, at least to some small extent, have been entirely without the idea of innovating? Time and again he declares that he is only repeating the teaching of the Fathers, as in his remark about a letter by Morillon to Granvelle where his ideas were treated as mere dreams: 'Antiqua Patrum doctrina novis Theologis somnium est ac deliramentum!'[14] Of course he was wrong, but we have seen above the misunderstanding by which he was able sincerely to believe it. On the other hand, how are we to explain so complete a delusion on such a definite point? Or, indeed, how could so fundamental a truth be so generally disregarded in orthodox theology?

Actually, the idea of a complete order of 'pure nature' was not at that time so old or of such doctrinal importance as some recent theologians are somewhat too ready to suppose. Its appearance in theology dated only from a very short time previously and it was very far from being regarded as established by all. It would be interesting to follow in detail the stages by which it gradually came to be recognized.

'Pure nature' with some theologians was at first, it seems, one

---

[13] *Baiana*, p. 70.

[14] '. . . quasi videlicet homo non fuerit naturaliter ad hoc conditus, ut soli Deo serviret, et postea beatitudinem possideret: sed ut in naturali quadam vivendi ratione, quae neque peccatum esset, neque regni caelestis meritum, vitae suae cursum transigens, tandem naturalem quamdam beatitudinem acciperet, cuius neque locus, neque ratio in Scripturis invenitur sed a vanis et otiosis hominibus (iuxta Pelagii sensum) ex Philosophia configitur' (p. 59).

of those numerous abstractions which, since the time of William de la Mare, medieval speculation was fond of introducing, and more particularly, one of the numerous results of the 'potentia Dei absoluta' which the new schools, not without a certain excess, were wont to enumerate. It was an abstract hypothesis, and did not imply the rejection of the traditional view on the end of the created soul. Thus the nominalist John Bockingham could write on the one hand: 'Revera videtur mihi mirabile quod Deus non possit de potentia sua absoluta facere creaturam rationalem, nisi sit digna clara Dei visione vel in peccatum mortali' (sic) while continuing to assert on the other, 'Deum clare et perfecte videre et videndo amare . . . est finis et felicitas creaturae rationalis'.[15]

Secondly, the case of children dying unbaptized, to whom the beatific vision could not be granted and whom the theologians felt unable to declare damned in quite the same way as sinners, was to result in the hypothesis being advanced—a concrete hypothesis, but one within our own world—of an intermediate state. By analogy the case was envisaged—this was entirely hypothetical —in which the first man could have died before receiving the infusion of sanctifying grace, and consequently before having to make the moral choice, which was original sin. St Thomas himself had envisaged the two cases. His successors continued to do so.[16]

[15] *Super Quatt. Sent.*, qu. 6, conclusio 8, dubium 3; and qu. 1., concl. 8 (Cf. Juan Alfaro, *op. cit.*, pp. 355-7 and 337.) On the idea of *potentia absoluta* towards the end of the Middle Ages see my *Le Surnaturel* (1946 ed.), 2nd part, chapter four. Henri Rondet, *Gratia Christi* (1948), pp. 240-1. Ch. Baumgartner, *La grâce du Christ* (1963), p. 106. M. de Gandillac in Fliche and Martin, *Histoire de l'Église*, vol. 13 (1951), pp. 340, 447-8, 467. For an example of this kind of hypothesis in post-Tridentine Scholasticism: Gregory of Valencia, *Commentaria theologica*, vol. 2 (Lyon, 1603), col. 958 and 959 (with reference to Vitoria and Soto.) Cf. Elzearius Bonke, *Doctrina nominalistica de fundamento ordinis moralis* . . . (1944), p. 30: 'Negari quidem non potest tum apud G. de Ockham quam apud G. Biel inveniri multas exaggerationes quibus tendentia omnipotentiae divinae ad ultimum limitem extendendae et accentuandae certe ansam dat.'

[16] Thus Thomas of Strasbourg, *In IV Sent.*, bk II, dist. 33, qu. 1, art. 3, concl. 2, ad 1m: 'Illi qui decedunt in peccato originali solo, non sunt frustra; quia, quamvis non consequantur finem supernaturalem, consequuntur tamen, finem naturalem. Possunt enim habere evidentiorem contemplationem, quam quicumque philosophus unquam habere potuit in hac vita; quae quidem contemplatio est naturalis finis hominis virtuosi.' Or Petrus Paludus, *In IV*

But it concerned an exceptional case, having in view beings who
had not reached their normal development. It was generally
thought that such beings, at the time of their death being 'sine
culpa nec gratia', were as a result in the after-life 'sine poena nec
gloria', that is, 'in statu neutro'.[17] There was no mention in their
case of 'natural blessedness' but only of a 'carentia beatitudinis'
which however would be for them only a certain 'paena negativa'.
In this connection Fr Alfaro quotes in particular Michael Aiguani
(died 1440), a commentator on the *Sentences*. If the first man
had died with only original justice, says Aiguani, in answer to
more rigid theologians who equated any privation of the vision
of God with the 'summa damnatio', he 'would have been numbered neither among the damned nor the elect'. In such a case,
'carentia visionis non fuisset sibi damnatio; sicut si angelis, qui
steterunt, Deus non contulisset gratiam aliam quam in creatione
acceperant, non fuisset eis damnatio carentia visionis, quam modo
habent'.[18] More paradoxically, Giles of Rome thought that children who died unbaptized before coming to the use of their free
will had really to suffer the penalty of damnation without being
deprived of their natural end and natural blessedness.[19] It will be
noticed that at the forefront of hypotheses of this kind there was the
special situation of an individual at the moment of his death (or of
the angel at the moment when his choice fixed his state), not that
of a whole world, not the destiny of the nature to which this individual belonged. How could one agree just to consign to 'damnatio' a being who obviously could not receive the 'visio' and yet who
was not burdened with any 'culpa'? This was, as de Vitoria has
pointed out, the 'tacita obiectio multorum'.[20] Those who en-

Sent., dist. I, qu. 5, concl. 3: 'Homo qui formaretur de limo terrae et
moreretur sine gratia et culpa, careret visione divina, quod tamen non esset
ei poena, sed natura' (Alfaro, pp. 382-3 and 273).
[17] Thus the nominalist William Rubio, *Super Quatt. Sent.*, bk IV, dist. 1,
qu. 4; and bk 11, dist. 32, qu. 1 (in Alfaro, pp. 350-3). Or J. Bockingham,
loc. cit.
[18] *In Sent.*, bk 2, dist. 30, qu. unica (Alfaro, op. cit., pp. 391-2).
[19] *In Sent.*, bk 2, dist. 32, qu. 2, art. 2 (Venice, 1581, p. 470).
[20] *In Primam Secundae*, qu. 81, art. 2: 'Respondendum est tacitae obiectioni
multorum, quod est mirabile de misericordia Dei quod velit damnare pueros.'
Vitoria offers three answers; the third depends on the supernatural character

deavoured to supply an answer were sometimes in more than a little difficulty.

At the beginning of the seventeenth century again we find Gregory of Valencia admitting that children dying in original sin must suffer an interior pain 'ob carentiam divinae visionis'. He takes comfort in thinking that their pain must be lightened by the fact that they understand that this privation is not due to their own fault. Gregory had indeed put forward the hypothesis of an intellectual creature which God, by virtue of his 'absolute power', had not ordained to a supernatural end; but he did not feel able to apply it to this case because these children belonged to human nature, to our nature; the desire to see God ('propensio naturalis ad Deum videndum') was therefore natural to them.[21] Fifteen years later the Dominican Diego Alvarez (died 1635) took the hypothesis further: it was no longer an individual or individuals, it was 'man' whom he supposed dying without having sinned gravely, and he supposed that he was without sanctifying grace (as Aiguani had done) but also without original justice (the two things for a Thomist going hand in hand). This man, created and dying 'in puris naturalibus', without either grace or sin, would enjoy a 'natural beatitude' but nevertheless he would not be 'satiatus positive', since he would not cease to have a 'naturalem capacitatem ad visionem beatificam'. Alvarez, then, could only allow him a 'negative' satiety, thanks to a distinction between the strictly natural appetite which remains in him and the act of desire elicited which, actually, goes no further than the natural blessedness obtained.[22] Although he does not explicitly raise here the question of finality, which in the evolution of ideas then in process puts him behind Molina or Suarez, and

of the vision of God. What in us would be 'poena' would, in beings created 'in puris naturalibus', be called 'passio naturalis'. Cf. Bricio Torres, S.J., *Los Maestros de Salamanca* . . . (1959), p. 36.

[21] *Commentaria theologica* (Lyon, 1603), vol. 2; disput. 6, qu. 17, punctum 4 (col. 692). Cf. vol. 1, disp. 4, qu. 14, punctum 1 (col. 984-5) in which the hypothesis of a spiritual creature whose finality is natural is only introduced in reference to the hypothesis of a creature that cannot sin.

[22] *Disputationes theologicae in Primam Secundae S. Thomae* (1617), Disp. 25, n. 2: '. . . esset tamen satiatus negative, quia videlicet de facto nihil aliud appeteret, nec posset appetere actu elicito.'

even several of his colleagues, Báñez in particular,[23] this opponent of Molinism is very close to the Molinist idea of 'natura pura'.

Lastly, the third stage, the third origin forming the most determining factor : the idea of 'pure nature' was virtually part of the speculations of the Humanists who in the fifteenth century developed the idea of a natural religion, as it was soon to be found, for example, according to certain historians in the *De optimo reipublicae statu deque nova insula Utopia* by Thomas More.[24] It had been implied for a long time past in the naturalist tendencies and in the separatist theories of the Paduan philosophers. It could also be inferred from the neo-Platonist doctrines. Some theologians were impressed by it. While St Thomas criticized, though at the same time excusing and pitying, the 'ancient philosophers' who had not known the true end of man, these theologians came to think that the end conceived by these heirs of the ancient philosophers must be for man his natural end.[25] The idea is fully and decisively stated for the first time in the work of Denys Ryckel, known as Denys the Carthusian (died 1461),[26] who on two occasions initiates *ex professo* a refutation of the teaching and arguments of St Thomas. It began to appear less clearly, or rather it crept in, as a sort of implicit outline, under cover of a refutation of the Scotist theory, in the works of two previous Thomists. The first was one Thomas Anglicus who has not yet been identified with certainty.[27] He was the author of an enigmatic *Liber propugnatorius,* of uncertain date, which was published for the first time at Vicenza in 1485. The second is

[23] Báñez, *In Primam Secundae* (*Commentarios ineditos*, ed. V. Beltrán de Heredia, vol. 1, 1942, pp. 81 and 128-9).

[24] In 1516. Cf. the edition by M. Delcourt (1942), pp. 184-7.

[25] On the development of the idea of natural transcendent beatitutde, see below, chapters six and seven.

[26] I return to this below, chapter seven.

[27] Fr Mandonnet suggested Thomas of Jorz (d. 1310); Fr Pelster named Thomas of Sutton (of the same period); the attribution seemed unlikely to Mgr Schmaus; Mgr Glorieux put forward as an hypothesis the name of Thomas of Wylton whose literary activity is placed between 1312 and 1322. See also Alfaro, *op. cit.*, pp. 218-21 and pp. 261-3; texts, pp. 212-15.

Bernardo Lombardi (died c. 1332), a commentator of the *Sentences*.[28]

Cajetan, like Denys the Carthusian, with whose teaching his own, at least in its negative aspect, shows a strong resemblance,[29] is much more explicit. He had studied in Padua from 1491 to 1496 and had subsequently taught there. He must have come across the *Liber propugnatorius* there; it was then a weapon in the hands of the Paduan Thomists in their heated controversy against what one of them, Silvester Prieras, author of a polemical *Malleus in falsas assumptiones Scoti,* called the 'argotizatiunculae' of Duns Scotus.[30] The fact is that he sets to work, like Thomas Anglicus and Lombardi, using the expedient of a refutation of the Scotist positions. But his principal originality, particularly in connection with Denys the Carthusian, is that he puts forward his thesis as an explanation of the thought of St Thomas. From Denys to Cajetan, in the space of less than half a century a complete reversal took place. Swiftly followed by two of his colleagues, Koellin and Javelli,[31] he originated an explanation of the texts of St Thomas which, in essentials, was to continue, with some slight shifts of emphasis, among many of the commentators of the *Summa* and theologians down to our own century. According to Cajetan, man can have a really natural desire only for an end which is connatural to him; in speaking of a desire to see God face to face St Thomas could only speak of the desire awakened in man as he is considered by the theologian, that is, he states clearly, in man actually raised up by God to a supernatural end and enlightened by a revelation.[32]

[28] Alfaro, *op. cit.*, pp. 221-2: 'Al rechazar Lombardi la teoria escotística acerca de lo sobrenatural, rechaza implícitamente la inclinación natural de la potencia receptiva hacia las perfecciones sobrenaturales.'

[29] Fr Alfaro enumerates six important points on which he observes an 'extraña coincidencia' (p. 299).

[30] *Malleus in falsas assumptiones Scoti contra S. Thomam in Primo volumine Sententiarum,* dedication (in Alfaro, p. 216). See below, p. 141.

[31] On this group of three commentators, see below, chapter six.

[32] See the judgment on this subject by Fr J. M. Alonso, C.M.F., 'Lo natural y lo sobrenatural' in *Revista española de Teologia,* 1953, p. 68: 'La verdadera perspectiva, la histórica, la concreta, la teológica, debe seguir siendo la "pre-cayetanista", la tradicional, la de los Padres, la de Santo Tomás, la del *Homo-imago Dei,* y la del "apetito natural de la visión".'

Cajetan's role as an innovator was recognized with some little exaggeration more than half a century ago by Dr Sestili: 'Caietanus enim, licet doctissimus et princeps S. Thomae interpres, tamen in hac re videtur apertissime a S. Thoma discedere, et certe primus in quaestionem dubium iniecit . . . .'[33] Similarly, Fr Rousselot, on the subject 'of those who would reduce the whole desire for the intuitive vision according to St Thomas to a secret transformation effected historically in man by grace': this, he said, 'is one of Cajetan's interpretations which many theologians of our times willingly adopt. It is enough to quote against them the elaboration of the system in the *Contra Gentiles*.'[34] Since then more than one historian has pointed it out. To Fr Bainvel, who spoke of progress achieved in Thomistic language and thought by the introduction of the idea of a 'historic nature',[35] Canon Tiberghien replied: 'If it is agreed that it is necessary to state St Thomas' thought with precision, must we not seek to develop it in the same direction that was given to it by St Thomas?'[36] In 1928 Canon N. Balthasar wrote: 'We may wonder how Cajetan could have put forward this exegesis and how it could really have been taken seriously for so long.'[37] In 1933, Fr Motte expressed his satisfaction in the *Bulletin thomiste* at seeing the increasing number of theologians 'who are breaking with the tradition that originated' with Cajetan, because 'fundamentally, Cajetan's exegesis . . . misunderstood the whole point of St Thomas' endeavour'.[38] In 1954 this was still the view of Mgr G. Philips, who observed the great difficulty experienced by Cajetan 'in the face of

[33] 'Quod omnis intellectus naturaliter desiderat divinae substantiae visionem' (in Fr. de Sylvestris Ferrariensis, *Commentaria in libros quattuor contra Gentiles*, vol. 3, Rome, 1900, p. 908). Cf. pp. 954-5: 'In schola autem S. Thomae, non videtur fuisse controversa haec sententia. Sed Caietanus incepit. . . .' Strictly Sestili was only speaking about the question of 'natural desire'; the implications of his remark, however, can be understood. Cajetan, too, like Suarez after him, joined this question with that of the natural end.

[34] *L'intellectualisme de saint Thomas*, 3rd ed. (1936), p. 183 (1st ed., 1908, p. 192). Cajetan's thesis, however, does not appeal merely to this 'secret transformation'.   [35] *Nature et surnaturel*, p. 130.

[36] *La question des rapports du naturel et du surnaturel*, duplicated dissertation, p. 17.   [37] In *Criterion*, IV (1928), p. 473.

[38] Vol. 3 (1933), pp. 660 and 674.

many of the statements of the Angelic Doctor'.[39] And there are others besides.

Now this was already the view of many sixteenth- and seventeenth-century theologians. Opponents of the new idea, like John of Rada,[40] Prudentius,[41] or Macedo,[42] are not alone in telling us so. Suarez, Cajetan's warmest supporter, openly admits it, even emphasizing his part in the matter: 'Caietanus et moderniores theologi tertium consideraverunt statum, quem pure naturalem appellarunt, qui, licet de facto non fuerit, cogitari tamen potest ut possibilis.'[43] Even Báñez, who owed not a little to Cajetan, wrote: '(Dicit Caietanus) quod divus Thomas agit hic de homine sicut theologus, et propterea appellat desiderium naturale illud quod habet homo praesupposita divina ordinatione qua homo ordinatur ad illam beatitudinem supernaturalem: haec, inquam, responsio non satisfacit, quin potius enervat rationem divi Thomae.'[44] Other theologians of the same period were not misled; they did not attribute to St Thomas what was the work of his very personal commentator. This was the case, of course, with Dominic Soto[45] and Francis Toletus,[46] as well as with

[39] *Ephemerides theologicae lovanienses,* 1954, pp. 110-11. It may be supposed that Fr Duval expresses the same opinion, though in paradoxical form, in *RSPT,* 1954, p. 525. Cf. below, p. 188. Cf. Étienne Gilson, in connection with another problem: 'To be unsuccessful, despite all one's good will, in discovering the teaching of the Summa in that of the most celebrated of its commentators does not necessarily prove that one is wrong' ('Note sur le *Revelabile* selon Cajetan' in *Medieval Studies,* XV (1953), p. 206).

[40] *Controversiae theologicae* . . . (Venice, 1614), pp. 2 and 7.

[41] *Opera theologica posthuma in Primam Partem D. Thomae* (Lyon, 1690), p. 46.

[42] *Collationes* . . . , vol. 1, pp. 11-15: 'Scio Caietanum et Iavellum aliter intelligere locum D. Thomae . . . , sed non mihi persuadent suis coniecturis, cum minime fundentur in verbis textus, quae sunt aperta et cum aliis libri contra Gentes concordant.'

[43] *De Gratia,* proleg. IV, c. 1, n. 2 (Vivès, vol. 7, p. 179).

[44] *In Primam Secundae,* qu. 3, art. 8 (*Commentarios ineditos a la prima secundae de santo Tomas,* ed. Vincente Beltran de Heredia, vol. 1, Madrid, 1942, p. 123).

[45] *In IV Sent.* (Douai, 1613, p. 903): 'Hoc plane est mentem D. Thomae detorquere.'

[46] *In Summam sancti Thomae,* vol. 1 (1869), pp. 17-18: 'In nobis inest naturale desiderium et appetitus naturalis videndi Deum. Haec (conclusio) est contra Caietanum, et est sententia Scoti, et indubita sancti Thomae. See other texts below, pp. 152-62.

Estius,[47] but also with Ysambert[48] and Arriaga,[49] who followed him. The ingenuousness of the Carmelites of Salamanca would be required to include Cajetan among those who in all things 'faithfully preserved the deposit' of Thomism.[50]

In their teaching on the last end, the Thomist school of the thirteenth to the sixteenth century contains abundant evidence which openly contradicts the commentaries of the great cardinal. If the attribution of the *Liber propugnatorius* to Thomas of Sutton has been almost impossible to maintain, it is because Thomas of Sutton said quite clearly : 'Per solam visionem Dei est perfecta consecutio Dei, qui est ultimus finis'.[51] And again : 'Beatitudo quam naturaliter desiderat (homo), in visione Dei consistit in speciali.'[52] John Quidort (John of Paris) likewise said : 'In ratione boni habiti proprii immediate per actionem intellectus vel voluntatis (Deus) est finis rationalis creaturae et beatitudo.'[53] The same idea is put forward and established at length by a devious process of thought in the works of Gerard of Bologna, the Carmelite (died 1318), in connection with his examination of the question whether theology was a superfluous science. It is not, Gerard concluded, because the understanding, which is ordered naturally to all being, for this very reason has a natural

[47] *In IV Sent.*, dist. 49, n. 1 (Venice, vol. 4, 1680, p. 551; passage quoted below).

[48] *Disputationes in Primam P. S. Thomae*, vol. 1 (Paris, 1643), p. 90: 'Caietanus et plures alii recentiores ita explicant s. Thomam. . . .'

[49] *Disputationes theologicae in Primam partem*, vol. 1 (Antwerp, 1643), p. 65: '(Argumentum) quod videtur fuisse D. Thomae, desumitur ex appetitu universali. . . . Haec tamen ratio nullo modo convincit. Et ita tandem Caietanus fatetur.'

[50] Salmanticenses, *Cursus theologicus* (vol. 10, Cologne, 1691), Dedicatio (to St Thomas): '. . . eorum qui ex affectu, studio, instituto et fidelitate merito censentur tui indubitanter discipuli, ut Capreolus, Caietanus, etc; hos namque par est credere, quod tuos sensus introspexerint et depositum fideliter custodierint' (Palmé ed., vol. 1, p. 53).

[51] *Quaestiones disputatae* (in Alfaro, *op. cit.*, p. 221).

[52] *In I Sent.*, dist. 3, qu. 1 (*ibid.*, pp. 219-20).

[53] In IV Sent., dist. 49 (ed. Mulla, *Mélanges Pelzer*, p. 500). In his *Tractatus de beatitudine*, Hervé of Nedellec thus summarizes John Quidort's thesis: 'Secundum quod in seipso terminat (Deus) appetitum intellectivum, est finis et beatitudo intellectualis sive rationalis creaturae'. And then he criticizes some of Quidort's conclusions from it, but not his assertions (*ibid.*, p. 504).

desire to see God in his essence, but would be unable to achieve this on its own.[54] The same theory again in John of Naples;[55] in John Tinctor who was the first commentator on St Thomas' *Summa Theologica*;[56] in Clement of Terra Salsa who wrote : 'In visione divinae essentiae consistit tantum intellectus creati vel hominis beatitudo. . . . Ad cognoscendum Deum per essentiam homo habet naturale desiderium.'[57] The 'Prince of Thomists', John Capreolus (died 1444), was no exception : 'Oportet quod ultimus terminus humanae perfectionis sit in intelligendo aliquod perfectissimum intelligibile, quod est essentia divina; in hoc igitur unaquaeque tota rationalis creatura beata est, quod essentiam Dei videt.'[58] There is not a word in his works about 'pure nature'.[59] Nor is there in John Versor (died 1485), who explains the pure doctrine of St Thomas in his commentary on the tenth book of the *Nicomachaean Ethics*,[60] and who, like St Thomas and many

[54] Cf. P. de Vooght, O.S.B., 'Un texte inédit sur le désir naturel de voir Dieu, Gérard de Bologne, Summa, XII, 1 ad 3m' in *Recherches de théologie ancienne et médiévale*, 1953.   [55] *Quodl.* VIII, qu. 18 (Alfaro, p. 230).

[56] Professor in Cologne, died in 1469. *Lectura in Primam Partem*, qu. 12, art. 1 and 4 (Alfaro, pp. 235-6).

[57] *Conclusiones formales super Primam*, in qu. 12, art. 1 (Alfaro, p. 237).

[58] *In II Sent*, dist. 23, qu. 1 (Venice, 1589, p. 403). Capreolus completed his *Liber Defensionum*, in which St Thomas is explained within the framework of a commentary on the *Sentences*, at Rodez, in about 1432. There is another text in Alfaro, p. 241. Capreolus admits on the other hand that man naturally desires this supernatural end 'non sub propria ratione, sed in generali' (*ibid.*, p. 234).

[59] 'I do not know', wrote Fr de Broglie (*RSR*, 1924, p. 196) 'whether . . . before the sixteenth century the attention of Thomists was drawn to this problem (reconciliation of the desire for the supernatural and its gratuity). I found nothing in Capreolus on this natural desire of the intellect. . . . But even this omission is remarkable and it enables one to conjecture that if the Prince of Thomists keeps silence on this explicitly Thomist thesis, it is possibly because he has no solution of a satisfactory nature to offer.' A reservation of this kind for such a motive would be astonishing enough in a Scholastic teacher. And, in fact, Capreolus' silence is not quite so complete. But on the precise point which Fr de Broglie has in view, Capreolus probably saw no difficulty to be overcome : the problem whose terms were gradually to be raised and the solutions offered, numerous at that time, were not fully present to men's minds.

[60] In I. X, qu. 11 : 'Ultima et perfectissima hominis felicitas in visione divinae essentiae consistit. Probatur conclusio. Quia homo non potest esse perfecte felix quamdiu restat sibi aliquid ad desiderandum et quaerendum. Sed homini semper restat tale quaerendum quousque divinam essentiam videat. Ergo. . . . Item. . . .'

others, answers the classical objection thus : 'Nobilioris conditionis est natura potens consequi perfectum bonum cum auxilio, illa quae consequitur bonum quoddam imperfectum sine auxilio.'[61] In his *Quaestiones* on the *Metaphysics* of Aristotle, Dominic of Flanders (died c. 1500) says that the blessedness which forms the consummation of the soul's destiny includes the vision of the divine essence, and he summarizes St Thomas' thought according to the *De Anima,* art. 16, ad 3um : 'Dicit Doctor sanctus quod terminus intellectionis ipsius intellectus possibilis est divina essentia, sed ad hunc terminum non potest pervenire per naturalia, sed per gratiam tantum.'[62]

The spiritual writers of the same period, whether or not they belong to the strict Thomist tradition, have no other teaching. There is for example this passage by John of Schoonhoven, Ruysbroeck's follower and apologist : 'Deus enim omnipotens fecit rationalem spiritum capacem Summae Trinitatis; hinc est quod nullo minus Deo potest spiritus praemiari, nec eius capacitas nec desiderium quietari.'[63] Louis of Blois (Blosius) says the same.[64] Nor does the *Triumphus crucis* by Savonarola (d. 1498) have any other end in view for the rational creature than that to which his desire leads him, that is, the vision of the divine essence; short of that there is no blessedness.[65] It is known that Savonarola was a fervently literal Thomist. His *Triumphus crucis,* a work of apologetics closely resembling the *Contra Gentiles,*[66] which Sestili could still hail as an 'aureum opus',[67] was frequently republished during the sixteenth and seventeenth centuries, and the Propaganda College in Rome was to adopt it as its official manual.

[61] *In lib.* 10, qu. 14 (Alfaro, pp. 237 and 238).
[62] *In Metaphys.,* II, ad 7m. Louis Mahieu, *Dominique de Flandre, sa métaphysique* (1942), pp. 235 and 92.
[63] *Dissertation Venite ascendamus* (c. 1415). Reypens, *RAM,* 1923, p. 264.
[64] Louis de Blois (Ludovicus Blosius), *A Book of Spiritual Instruction* (English trans. by Bertrand Wilberforce, O.P., 1908, pp. 67-71, 108, 161-6).
[65] *De veritate fidei in Dominicae crucis triumphum* (Florence, 1497). bk II, c. 3-6.
[66] Carlo Giacon, S.J., *La Seconda Scolastica,* vol. 1 (1944), p. 28 : 'Il "trionfo della Croce" è come un compendio della Summa contra gentiles di S. Tommaso.'
[67] *Op. cit.,* p. 955.

These circumstances endow its evidence with particular value.[68]

Moreover, although Cajetan and his imitators turned theological speculation in a new direction, they did not construct a system from their innovation, and their point of view remained chiefly noetic.[69] They still represent, therefore, only a stage in the evolution whose main features are here being traced; and in this stage, even within Thomism, they are not followed by all. Thus Diego de Deza (died 1523), a theologian of Salamanca and a great defender of Thomist doctrines, wrote in his *Novae Defensiones*: 'Natura intellectualis naturalem ordinem et aptitudinem habet ex sui creatione ad videndam clare divinam essentiam', and the objection taken from the powerlessness of nature to reach this end does not disturb him.[70] Others, who adopt Cajetan's position on the main point, acknowledge none the less that his interpretation of the *Summa* is not rigorously objective. Even the Carmelites of Salamanca shared this view.[71] Towards the middle of the sixteenth century, at the time of the Council of Trent, the new idea had scarcely made any progress, as the important work of Dominic Soto and that of some others bear witness.

Soto's 'fidelity' and 'acuteness' in the interpretation of St Thomas have been rightly praised.[72] A contemporary of Baius' and his colleague at Trent, Soto (1499-1560) composed his treatise

[68] It is interesting to notice how the word 'supernatural' is itself introduced into the French translation of the work, without changing the author's meaning. *Le triomphe de la croix de J. Savonarole*, translated into French by C. Alix (Paris, 1855), pp. 47 and 221:

Bk 2, preface: 'After having treated of the truths of the natural order, . . . we have now to treat of the supernatural truths.' Latin text: 'Cum superiori libro de iis tractaverimus, quae ratio naturalis per se capere potest . . . , reliquum est, ut ad ea convertamur, quae rationem ipsam naturalem excedunt. . . .'

Bk 4, c. 2: 'They would however be incomplete and of almost no worth in connection with the questions of the supernatural order concerning salvation.' Latin text: 'Primo igitur adversus Philosophos disputantes, probemus quod . . . de iis quae ad salutem pertinent, non sufficienter sed valde parum disseruerint.' [69] Cf. below, chapter six, pp. 184-8.

[70] Bk 4, dist. 49, qu. 4 (Alfaro, p. 241).

[71] *Cursus theologicus* (1878 ed.), vol. 5, p. 378; cf. above, footnote 50, p. 130.

[72] E. Brisbois, S.J.: *NRT*, 63 (1936), p. 984, note 1. He adds that these ideas 'would merit further attention'. See also p. 989.

De natura et gratia during the leisure afforded him by the interval between the sixth and seventh sessions of the Council, only a few years before Baius started work on his *Opuscula*. The book, dedicated to the Fathers of the Council, was published in Venice in 1547.[73] It was to be followed, fifteen years later, by a commentary on the fourth book of the *Sentences,* published at Salamanca in 1561-2, and which Soto wrote right at the end of his life. In both works the teaching is the same and both can be used together for the subject with which we are concerned.[74]

Right at the beginning of the book and before mentioning original justice, Soto speaks in his first treatise of a man 'in puris naturalibis mente concepto'. He wonders what would be the power of this 'natura nuda', that is, what it would be possible for him to know and achieve in the moral order. But he is careful to avoid saying that such a state must be held to be actually realizable. It is a useful fiction, he modestly explains, that there is nothing to prevent our inventing, though there is no warrant for it in scripture or the Fathers.[75] In short he almost excuses himself for introducing it as a mere working hypothesis: 'concipere illum tamen animo et effingere nihil vetat, clarioris disputationis gratia.'[76] It suggests Kant's 'intellectus archetypus' which plays

---

[73] On this work: Vicente Beltran de Heredia, O.P., *Dominico de Soto, Estudio biografico documentado* (Madrid, 1961), pp. 165-8. On Soto, see also J. Stegmüller, 'Zur Gnadenlehre des . . . D. de Soto' in G. Schreiber, *Weltkonzil von Trient,* I (Freiburg i. Br., 1951), pp. 169-230. On Soto, as the follower of Vitoria: Bricio Torres, S.J., *Los Maestros de Salamanca de Siglo XVI ente el Problema del Sobrenatural* (Mexico, 1959), pp. 45-77; Aimé-M. Viel, O.P., *Revue Thomiste,* 1904, pp. 151-66.

[74] It has been said of the dualist theory which is contrary to that of Soto and even of Bellarmine (see below) that it expresses 'the idea of the supernatural order such as it is usually put forward by the theologians of all schools since the Council of Trent' (P. Dumont, 'L'appétit inné de la béatitude surnaturelle chez les auteurs scolastiques' in *Ephemerides theologicae lovanienses,* 1931, p. 206). Even as a mere chronological indication the mention of the Council of Trent here appears to be gratuitous.

[75] *De natura et gratia,* bk 1, c. 3: 'Cum de hoc homine, quem fingimus, nihil vel in sacra pagina vel apud sanctos patres scriptum sit; commodius elucidabitur. . . .' (Antwerp, 1550, p. 8).

[76] *De natura et gratia,* bk 1, c. 3: 'Faciamus itaque imaginando, ut homo hunc in modum naturalis a Deo sit creatus: utpote rationale animal, absque culpa et gratia, et quovis supernaturali dono. De homine huiusmodi, qualem penitus philosophi agnoverunt . . .' (p.6).

134

so great a part in the *Critique of Pure Reason* without its ever being declared possible of realization. Moreover even in the manner in which Soto conceived this man 'in puris naturalibus', what a difference there is from what he was to become in the theological speculation of a later period! This is man as the ancient philosophers pictured him, 'qualem penitus philosophi agnoverunt', a man cut off from his transcendent finality and those higher faculties by which, according to the teaching of scripture and the Fathers, he is made in the image of God. He is a 'homo physicus' who, if we imagine him as real, will have as his sole ideal to live according to reason, that is—for the word 'reason' is equivocal—to contribute his share to the smooth running of the community, without any prospect of a future life. He is therefore, apparently, a mere 'animal politicum'; it is for him that laws and ordinances are made, that the magistracy is established. Fundamentally, if he really existed, he would be a man like us, and able like us to raise himself naturally to a certain knowledge of God, but condemned for want of light to be mistaken about his real end. Soto was well aware that for real man there is only one last end, the end intended by St Augustine when he exclaimed, 'Fecisti nos ad te, Domine!'[77] He knew, also, that there is only one state of blessedness, the blessed vision of God.[78] Among the arguments which he brings forward to establish this a place of importance is given to the argument which was a favourite of St Thomas' on the natural desire which otherwise would be in vain. But the chief argument in his view— 'potissima ratio'—comes from the teaching of the Bible. When

[77] *Ibid.*: 'Cum homo sit rationale animal, finis eius naturalissimus est operari semper secundum rationem, id est, omnia agere propter honestum. . . . Suorum autem finis officiorum in hac vita est pax tranquillusque status reipublicae. Est enim homo politicum animal, natum in societate vivere. . . . Hunc penitus finem philosophi naturales speculati sunt. . . . Est verumtamen finis nobis alter, virtutem viresque naturae nostrae longius exsuperans' (pp. 7-8). 'Neutiquam poterat (noster ille homo) vel naturali acumine intellectus apprehendere, vel suis viribus assequi, summum illum felicissimum finem, ad quem creatus est . . .' (p. 10). Soto frequently quotes the famous passage from St Augustine which his master Vitoria used to quote also (Br. Torres, p. 32).

[78] *In IV Sent.*, d. 49, qu. 2, art. 1 (Salamanca, 1562, p. 584): 'illam veram beatitudinem, quae est videre Deum'; '. . . quae in Dei visione consistit'.

God said, 'Let us make man in our image, after our likeness', it was our very nature that he designated thus; by this he placed in us not only a certain capacity, but by that very reason a 'natural inclination', an 'appetite' and, as St Augustine used to repeat insistently,[79] he who is made in the image of God is made to see God : 'nam simile naturaliter appetit suum simile'.[80]

On the other hand, Soto knew perfectly well that this end is gratuitous and of inaccessible loftiness: 'extra supraque omnem lineam et ordinem naturae conditae, eo quod Deus infinitus sit, omnis autem creatura limitata, ab illaque adeo perfectionis abysso infinitum distans'.[81] And so, not for the purpose of tending to it by virtue of a natural inclination or an 'innate appetite', but to understand it objectively and desire it with an elicited desire, there is need for that supernatural light which was wanting to the ancient philosophers.[82] It is for this reason that more than one theologian—'etiam in schola sancti Thomae'[83]—speaks of it as 'finis supernaturalis'. Soto can understand their point of view. He does not say that their language is at fault; it was the language of his master, Francesco de Vitoria. He himself on several occasions insists on the necessity of revelation if one is to be able to understand and desire 'veram beatitudinem in particulari'; he insists the more, therefore, on the necessity for a supernatural help to be able to reach it, or even to tend effectively to it, to desire it with a desire that is 'pleasing to God'. He is fond of quoting in connection with it the famous texts from Isaiah and St

[79] Soto shows himself here a better historian than some recent writers who endeavour to find the modern idea of 'pure nature' even in St Augustine. It seems difficult to take their writings very seriously, at least for that part relating to the last end.

[80] *In IV Sent.*, dist. 49, qu. 2, art. 1: 'Potissima vero ratio quae me persuasum habet est haec: Quod homo sit imago et similitudo Dei, est naturale; nam quando dixit Deus: "Faciamus hominem ad imaginem et similitudinem nostram", naturam istam nostram designavit. Similitudo autem aut imago Dei certe non solum capacitatem dicit Dei videndi, sed naturalem etiam inclinationem; nam simile naturaliter appetit suum simile . . .' (p. 585). Cf. art. 2 (pp. 591 and 594). [81] *De natura et gratia*, bk 1, c. 4 (p. 10).

[82] *De natura et gratia*, bk 1, c. 4 (p. 10). And *In IV Sent.*, dist. 49, qu. 2, art. 1, quarta conclusio (p. 589).

[83] One theologian was surprised at this 'etiam'; he felt that it ought to be 'praecipue'. I offer him my apologies, but I cannot change Soto's text.

Paul: 'Oculus non vidit, auris non audivit. . . .' But, he observes, many now take the opportunity from this to deny the natural desire. Under cover of a verbal precaution, they transform the teaching. Soto could see the snare and thought it opportune to react against it, and that is why he is particular about using simpler language which he also considers is more traditional:[84] 'Felicitas illa, finis potius dicendus naturalis, quam supernaturalis.' Since the vision of God is the object of a natural desire, since it is for every man, whether he knows it or not, the real end of his nature, it is better, he thinks, to continue to say that it constitutes our 'natural end'. At the same time as being more traditional this terminology also seems to him more rational. The desire is not to be defined by its effect but rather by its cause; therefore it will be called natural not because man could naturally elicit it, but because nature has placed it in him. In like manner, the end will be called natural, not because he could attain to it naturally but only because it is desired by this natural desire. In this precise sense, 'profecto ita censeo, quod finis ille simpliciter sit nobis naturalis'.[85]

[84] In this he was not entirely right. See, for example, Thomas of Strasbourg, *In II Sent*, dist. 23, art. 4: 'Respondeo. . . . Finis naturalis a nulla creatura potest naturaliter obtineri; quia tunc non esset supernaturalis finis, si naturaliter aliqua creatura ipsum posset consequi; sed visio divinae essentiae est finis supernaturalis, maxime loquendo de visione beata, quae est mediante, lumine gloriae . . .' (1345; Venice ed., 1564, vol. 1, fol. 173). Or Capreolus, *Defensiones*, vol 7 (1908), p. 206: 'ordinatum in finem supernaturalem', etc. On the other hand, while rejecting Soto's thesis, Báñez practically adopts his terminology when he writes, *In Primam Secundae*, qu. 3, art. 7: 'illam quaestionem inter theologos agitatam: utrum Deus sit naturalis finis hominis, sive utrum homo naturaliter desideret videre Deum sicuti est'. And qu. 2, art. 8, dubium unicum: 'An speculatio Dei, qua per essentiam ipse videtur, sit finis naturalis hominis.' *Comentarios ineditos a la prima secundae de santo Tomas*, ed. Vicente Beltran de Heredia, vol. 1 (Madrid, 1942), pp. 121-2 and 126-8.

[85] *De natura et gratia*, bk 1, c. 4; and also 'Inquietudo ipsa humani animi . . . fidem abunde facit illum esse finem nostrum naturalem' (pp. 10 and 11). *In IV Sent*, dist. 49: 'Respondetur ergo ad argumenta Caietani, non bene definisse finem naturalem esse illum quem potest homo naturaliter consequi, neque appetitum naturalem illum qui naturaliter potest habere actum elicitum: quoniam appetitus naturalis non debet definiri per effectum, sed per causam. Est ergo appetitus naturalis quem nobis natura inseruit: et eo ipso quod creati sumus ad imaginem Dei, insitum habemus appetitum naturalem ad ipsum videndum. Atque adeo finis naturalis est quem

Soto's terminology here, rather than being St Thomas', is that of Duns Scotus. Soto was well aware of this. It was Scotus who wrote: 'Concedo Deum esse finem naturalem hominis, licet non naturaliter adipiscendum sed supernaturaliter.'[86] St Thomas said, for example: 'Naturale est intellectui humano quod quandoque ad visionem divinam perveniat': he spoke of an end 'quodam modo supra naturam, alio vero modo secundum naturam';[87] or else he said simply 'naturae finis'. Despite this slight difference of terminology he could feel that he was thus expressing the view of both. It was the view of all the old doctors. They did not generally feel the need to add an attributive adjective to the word 'finis'— except to say, like Peter Olivi, for example, 'proprius finis'[88]— because they had no idea of making a distinction between two ends which were both final and transcendent, one of which would have been 'natural' and the other 'supernatural'. The same thing will be found in the works just quoted above of Capreolus, John Quidort or Thomas of Sutton. The practice in the *Summa* of Alexander,[89] and that of St Bonaventure,[90] was of like simplicity. In the same way, only just a few years before Soto, the

naturaliter appetimus: licet consecutio eius et adeptio non sit nobis naturalis' (p. 586). However, when Soto desires to distinguish clearly this final end from the earthly end even he speaks differently. Cf., in the same chapter of the *De natura et gratia*, the passage in which he attacks the opinion of Gregory of Rimini on man's moral powerlessness: 'Hos est hominum haud oculate distinguentium inter finem naturalem et finem supernaturalem hominis.'

[86] *In I Sent.*, Prol., qu. 1, art. 12 (*Opera omnia*, vol. 8, p. 22). On Scotus' theory: Henri Rondet, 'Le problème de la nature pure et la théologie du XVIe siècle' in *RSR*, 25 (1948), pp. 486-7. The whole article is worth consultation and, especially for Soto, it comes to the same conclusions as are to be found here. Already in the twelfth century Isaac of Stella wrote (*Sermo* 25): 'Solum ergo et summum spiritus creati rationalis bonum est, et finis naturalis, rationalis et moralis studii, sive exercitii, id propter quod factus est, contemplari videlicet et delectari in Deo' (*PL*, 194, 1772-3). But 'naturalis' determines 'studii', not 'finis'.

[87] *Tertia*, qu. 9, art 2, ad 3m.

[88] *In II Sent.*, qu. 56: 'non solum secundum fidem, sed etiam secundum rectam rationem constat, quod omnis natura rationalis est per essentiam talis, quod proprius finis non potest per naturam creatam acquiri, sed solum per agens supernaturale.'

[89] *Secunda Pars*, n. 510, ad 6m: 'Finis creaturae rationalis est summum bonum, quod est supra naturam' (Quaracchi, vol. 2, p. 747).

[90] *In II Sent*, dist. 29, art. 1, qu. 2, ad 4m (Quaracchi, vol. 2, p. 699).

Summa of Diego of Deza, speaking of the intellectual creature ordered to the vision of the divine essence, says, 'tanquam ad ultimum finem'.

Yet, ever since the time of Scotus the question had begun to become confused as a result of controversy between the schools of theology. While holding in all essentials the same desire for the vision of God as held by St Thomas, Scotus was wrong perhaps to put it forward too insistently in opposition to a wholly 'elicited' desire, like a 'pondus naturae' analogous to what could be, according to the ideas prevailing at the period, the obscure desire of a brute beast or a stone. Fundamentally, of course, it was only an analogy, but the spiritual element was not sufficiently taken into account. To the former distinction of a natural or necessary desire and an elective or free desire—the one 'physical', the other 'moral'—there now succeeded, from another viewpoint, or there was added, the Scotist distinction of an innate appetite or an 'elicited' act of desire.[91] Consequently, in criticizing this innate appetite, considered as crude appetite, as 'pondus naturae', some Thomist theologians seemed more or less to deny any real natural desire.[92] At least, that is how they were subsequently interpreted.

[91] Cf. Sestili, 'Quod omnis intellectus . . .', *loc. cit.*, p. 955, note: 'Ex mente veterum optimae notae, uti sunt Aquinas, Bonaventura, aliique, appetitus innatus intellectualis naturae non distinguitur contra appetitum sequentem cognitionem, sed contra appetitum liberum, quatenus principium, semen et directio intellectivae apprehensionis et vitalis motus in appetitu innato non est quid acquisitum sed ab ipso summo Bono impressum, valens Ipsum in confuso referre, si principium illud ab intellectu actu accipiatur ut quaedam eius similitudo est, ipsius intellectus aciem informans. Et ideo naturalis, quia inest per modum principii determinantis ad unum, scilicet ad Bonum. Atque hinc, elicitus ab innato distinguitur, per hoc quod sit acquisitus, consequens rationis discretionem, ideoque electivus.'

See also, for example, Durandus, *In IV Sent.*, dist. 49, qu. 8 (Paris, 1550, fol. 362).

[92] Sestili, *op. cit.*, p. 960, note: 'Opportune aestimandum est, manifestam S. Doctoris mentem hac in re, a quibusdam de schola eius forte obscuratam esse, ob systematicam oppositionem Scoti doctrinis. Subtilis enim Doctor cum schola eius acriter sustinet naturale desiderium divinae visionis, quamvis non omnia probanda sint circa modum quo illud explicant atque tuentur. Videntur enim illud admittere tantum per modum cuiusdam ponderis omni cognitione orbati, quod est profecto desiderium vel appetitus lapideus et igneus, non intellectualis.' The over-strict analogy of the *pondus naturae*

With Scotus' 'appetitus innatus' was contrasted an 'appetitus elicitus'—an unsatisfactory expression, not in accordance with former usage,[93] and one which Soto for his part still avoided. Like Durandus of Saint-Pourçain,[94] like Capreolus,[95] he speaks only of an elicited *act*.[96] But soon theologians were no longer so particular.

Now this was not to remain merely a question of terminology nor of point of view. It was a thorough change. With St Thomas, the elicited act of desire was clearly the sign of a genuine natural desire, that is, of an appetite of nature, even when this latter was not mentioned by name; for this reason alone St Thomas could argue from it, as he often did. This is acknowledged not only by good historians but even by theologians who differ widely from his teaching.[97] On the basis of a natural desire that can be observed he sets out to show reflexively what could be called the ontological appetite of intellectual substance, practically identical with its finality.[98] To reduce his thought to the clumsy affirmation of an 'appetitus elicitus' without deep roots in the nature of the soul is to deprive his thought of all its significance. Yet gradually,

had been criticized in advance by St Thomas, *Prima*, qu. 60, art. 1; and qu. 80, art. 1 : 'quamlibet formam sequitur aliqua inclinatio. . . . Forma autem in his quae cognitione participant, altiori modo invenitur quam in his quae cognitione carent.'

[93] Attention has again been drawn to this subject by William R. O'Connor, 'The Natural Desire for God in Saint Thomas' in *New Scholasticism,* 14, 1940, pp. 213-67.

[94] *In IV Sent.,* dist. 49, qu. 8, n. 7 : 'Duplex est appetitus, sc. naturalis et electivus. . . . Actus appetitus naturalis non est aliquis actus elicitus, sed est sola naturalis inclinatio ad illud quod appetitur; actus vero appetitus electivi . . . est quidam actus elicitus qui dicitur velle . . .' (*In Sent.,* Paris, 1550, fol. 362 r).

[95] *Defensiones theologicae D. Thomae,* vol. 7 (1908), pp. 169, 170, 179, 180.

[96] *In IV Sent.,* dist. 49, qu. 2, art. 1 : 'actum elicitum appetendi', 'non solum naturali inclinatione sed etiam actu elicito', 'appetere actu elicito', etc. (pp. 584, 586, 589).

[97] Thus D. Palmieri, *Tractatus de ordine supernaturali,* 2nd ed. (1910), p. 68 : St Thomas 'reapse non de innato appetitu loquitur, sed de elicito; quamvis dici possit sumi ab eo appetitum tanquam signum appetitus innati.'

[98] Cf. *Prima Secundae,* qu. 3, art. 8; *Compendium Theologiae,* c. 104; *Contra Gentiles,* bk 3, c. 50, etc.

under the influences of controversies whose bitterness has hardly appeared here, a section of the Thomist school adopted this course. John of St Thomas sanctioned this impoverished form of exegesis.[99]

Thus, as the Scotist John of Rada (died 1606) was to observe with a mixture of bitterness and irony, whereas the leaders were in agreement, 'discipuli sancti Thomae, ne videantur cum Scoto sentire, Divum Thomam in alienam adducunt sententiam'.[100]

Already this sort of phobia of the 'scotica officina' had probably influenced the position adopted so resolutely by Cajetan, Javelli and Koellin, as well as the more timid explanations of their rare predecessors. At Padua, to a greater degree than elsewhere (as was alluded to above), the dispute between Thomists and Scotists was heated. It was the Scotist theologians of Padua who prepared the first editions of Duns Scotus, while in the small neighbouring city of Vicenza the Dominicans published the *Liber propugnatorius*. At Padua Silvester de Prierio at about the same time wrote his *Malleus in falsas assumptiones Scoti contra sanctum Thomam* which was published in Bologna in 1514.[101] Anti-

---

[99] *In Primam,* qu. 12; *Cursus theologicus,* Disput. XII, *De potentia elevabili ad visionem Dei,* art. 3, n. 7: 'Expresse loquitur de desiderio videndi causam visis effectibus; ergo loquitur de desiderio fundato in cognitione, id est, visis effectibus; qui utique est appetitus elicitus. Absolute autem illum (appetitum innatum) negat' (Solesmes ed., vol. 2, pp. 140-1).

[100] *Controversiae theologicae, Controversia prima,* art. 2 (p. 14), Cf. *ibid,* p. 13: 'Tandem, admisso, quod loquatur de desiderio pro actu elicito, dico ibi necessario subintelligi naturalem inclinationem ad videndum causam: nam ille actus elicitus, quo cupimus videre causam, non dicitur naturalis a D. Thoma, nisi quia consonus et conformis est inclinationi naturae.' P. 11: 'Quarta opinio est Doctoris Subtilis . . . asserentis Deum clare visum esse finem nostrum naturalem quoad inclinationem et propensionem nostrae naturae, quae naturaliter est propensa in visionem Dei; supernaturalem vero quoad assecutionem. Scotum sequitur Sotus. . . . Sanctus Thomas et Doctor Subtilis idem omnino sentiunt.'
See on this subject *Dos Teologos Franciscanos del Siglo XVI (Liquete y Rada), ante el Problema del Sobrenatural;* auctore P. Bernardino ab Armellada, O.F.M. Cap. (Madrid, 1959: thesis at the Gregorian University).

[101] Dedication to Cardinal Nicolas de Flisco: '. . . ut Scoti argotizatiunculas et ruitura fundamenta, quibus in primo volumine Sententiarum adversus divum Thomam Aquinatum, Ecclesia teste, veritatis alumnum abusus est, parvo codice veluti malleolo attriverim.' Details are given in Juan Alfaro, *op. cit.,* pp. 216-17.

Scotist zeal was absorbing energy that could have been used, it might be thought, far more usefully in opposing Averroism; it was very powerful at that time and was victorious in the chairs of the faculty of arts.[102] But it was not in this direction that Cajetan saw the principal danger. He himself had to some extent been influenced by this faculty in which he was, as he says, 'peripatetico lacte educatus'.[103] It has been said of him that 'he struggled with Paduan Aristotelianism'.[104] The remark should be understood of the internal difficulties of his own thought. The chief opponent of his view was Antonio Trombetta, who held the chair of Scotus at Padua, the chair in opposition to his own. Behind Trombetta he saw Scotus himself. His works are an almost continual controversy against Scotus. With the 'scotina officina' he majestically contrasts the 'Theologia'.[105] It has been pointed out that this great mind, who in other matters imitates the calm attitude of its master St Thomas, allows itself to be carried away where Scotus is concerned: 'Non tot verba quod fallacia assumit', he exclaims.[106] And again: 'Taceat ergo praesumptuosa haec vox!' Or: 'Scotus somniavit.'[107] He attributes to his opponent a far more aggressive attitude towards St Thomas

[102] On Averroism in Padua at this period see M. de Wulf, *Histoire de la philosophie médiévale*, 2nd ed. (1905); Ernest Renan, *Averroès et l'averroïsme*, pp. 351-2; Brucker, *Historia philosophiae critica*, vol. 4, pp. 61-9; A. Favaro and R. Cressi, l'Università di Padova (Padua, 1946). See below, chapter seven, *in fine*.

[103] *In Primam*, qu. 1, n. 8.

[104] M. D. Chenu, *Introduction a l'étude de Saint Thomas d'Aquin*, p. 23. Cf. M. M. Gorce, 'Cajetan précurseur de Catharin et Banès' in *Revue Thomiste*, 1934, XVII B, p. 373: 'Cajetan was thoroughly imbued with that rather narrow Aristotelianism which was unable to conceive a spiritual knowledge outside the material conditions in which the mind functions in this world here below. Cajetan's "materialist" tendencies, if one may use the term, are related to "Albertism" as much as to Thomism properly so called. At the Council of the Lateran (1512) at which he sat as master general of his order, Cajetan made a speech to state that the immortality of the soul is not a matter that is to be proved from reason (Mansi, vol. 22, col. 843). But no one was put out. . . .'

[105] *Opuscula*, vol. 3, tract. 4, *De subiecto naturalis philosophiae* (Venice, 1612, p. 157 v).

[106] *In Sententias*, bk 3, dist. 14, qu. 2 (fol. 462 v). Quoted in Alfaro, *op. cit.*, p. 97.

[107] *In Primam*, qu. 12, art. 11, n. 5. Cf. qu. 13, art. 7, n. 8.

142

than it was in fact,[108] as if he required a reason to counter-attack him even more vigorously. If he finds in St Thomas an expression matching one in Scotus, this is sufficient reason for him to reject it.[109] Koellin too seems to fear nothing more than a possible agreement between the two great leaders of their schools,[110] and Javelli regards it as the worst possible form of reproach of Thomist teaching, and the best refutation of it, to be able to say: 'Hoc est incidere in sententiam Scoti.'[111]

Against prejudice of this kind Dominic Soto very rightly reacted. As a strong-minded and cool-headed defender of authentic Thomism he had no wish to see the thought of his master 'watered down' or 'twisted';[112] to restore it in the face of what he regarded as a betrayal, he adopted a contrary terminology to that favoured by his opponents, so that his own bore a slightly Scotist tinge. In its terms, at least, Soto's reaction is more vigorous than that of his colleague and immediate predecessor,

[108] Cf. Étienne Gilson, 'Note sur un texte de Cajetan' in *Antonianum,* vol. 27 (1952), pp. 377-80.

[109] Thus in his commentary *In Primam Secundae,* qu. 113, art. 10, n. 1: 'Primum (dubium) est circa illud: Anima naturaliter capax gratia. Videtur enim secundum praesentem doctrinam, ut in anima sit potentia naturalis ad gratiam. . . . Cuius oppositum in Prima Parte diximus contra Scotum.' Yet St Thomas said quite clearly: 'Naturaliter anima est gratiae capax. Eo enim ipso quod facta est ad imaginem Dei, capax est Dei per gratiam.' Cf. *Tertia,* qu. 9, art. 2: 'Est enim creatura rationalis capax illius beatae cognitionis, in quantum est ad imaginem.'

[110] *In Primam Secundae,* qu. 113, art. 10: 'Potest alicui videri, quia Doctor sanctus vellet, quod anima esset in potentia naturali ad gratiam. Et sic concordaret cum Scoto. . . . Et videri posset, quod Doctor sanctus concordet . . .' (Venice, 1589, p. 964).

[111] *In primum Tractatum Primae Partis Angelici . . . ,* qu. 12, art. 1 (Appendix to Venetian edition of St Thomas, vol. 10, 1695; fol. 21): Javelli first propounds the thesis which he wishes to refute in Scotist terms; he then meets Scotus' arguments and adds that 'some' attribute the same thesis to St Thomas, but he could not have fallen into Scotus' error; he must therefore be understood in a different sense. 'Adverte quod beatus Thomas videtur intendere naturale desiderium inesse creaturae intellectuali videndi divinam essentiam; quod tamen non videtur verum. . . . Praeterea, hoc est incidere in sententiam Scoti, qui vult finem beatificam esse naturalem, licet denominatione extrinseca dicatur supernaturalis. . . .'

[112] *In IV Sent.,* dist. 49, qu. 2, art. 1: 'Respondet autem Caietanus quod intelligit de desiderio cognoscendi causam sub ratione causae, nempe cognoscere quomodo haec efficit, non autem de desiderio videndi essentiam. At vero hoc est plane mentem D. Thomae detorquere.'

Francesco de Vitoria, who also opposed the interpretation initiated by Cajetan but had not thought it necessary all the same to approximate to Scotus' terminology.[113] As an effective rejoinder the course adopted by Soto was none the less almost inevitable, and the history of ideas fully justifies him. But it must be admitted that this series of counter-blows did not favour at the outset the clarity of the discussion.

In any case, no more than Baius or Jansenius, Dominic Soto had no intention of breaking with the fundamental position which was St Augustine's[114] as it was that of St Thomas,[115] Alexander of Hales, St Bonaventure[116] or Duns Scotus. None of them had ever envisaged for man or in general for the 'rationalis creatura', or for any created spirit at all, an end which would be both transcendent and 'purely natural', and which would consist in knowledge of God other than the beatific vision. Nor did Soto himself 'imagine that we could speak of a man ordained to another end;

---

[113] Cf. Bricio Torres, S.J., *Los Maestros de Salamanca* . . . (1959), pp. 26 and 41.

[114] *Contra Iulianum Pelagianum,* bk 3, c. 12; cf. bk 6, c. 10 and 24. As Fr Jacques de Blic very pertinently points out, 'Augustine can see a barrier between the rational creature and the God of its beatitude only in moral downfall; without this downfall there can be no question of excluding the image of God from him for whom it was made' (*art. cit., RSR,* 17, 1927, p. 524). Or Fr Henri Rondet, 'Nature et surnature dans la théologie de saint Thomas' in *RSR,* 23, 1926, p. 61: 'The idea of a distinction between natural end and supernatural end does not even enter his mind.' What Fr Jansen said of Baius, *op. cit.,* p. 85, must also be applied to Augustine: 'The image of God and a purely natural destiny seemed to him mutually exclusive.'

[115] *Quodl.* X, qu. 8, art. 17: 'Et quia anima immediate facta est a Deo, ideo beata esse non potuit, nisi immediate videat Deum.' *De Veritate,* qu. 18, art. 1: 'Homo factus est ad videndum Deum; ad hoc enim fecit Deus rationalem creaturam, ut similitudinis suae particeps esset, quae in eius visone consistit . . .'; ad 7m: 'Ipsa enim humana mens immediate a Deo creatur, et immediate ab ipso sicut in fine beatificabitur'; qu. 8, art. 3, obi. 12: 'Finis propter quem est rationalis creatura, est videre Deum per essentiam' (St Thomas' criticism did not concern this principle). *De virtutibus in communi,* art. 10. *Prima,* qu. 12, art. 1, etc.

[116] *Breviloquium,* Pars VIII, c. 7: 'Nullo minus Deo potest rationalis spiritus praemiari nec impleri, nec eius capacitas terminari' (Quaracchi, vol. 5, p. 289). *In II Sent.,* dist. 16, art. 2, qu. 1: 'Immediate nata est (creatura rationalis) Deo coniungi. Et hic (ordo) est essentialis imagini, et in hoc angelus et anima aequiparantur, quia utriusque mens immediate ab ipsa prima Veritate formatur' (vol. 2, p. 401); dist. 29, art. 1, qu. 2 ad 4m (p. 699), etc.

he merely sought to know what would be the powers of a man who had not at the outset been endowed with supernatural means'.[117] If sometimes he seems to speak differently from St Augustine, if he also gives further information which would be sought in vain in Augustine, it is not that he is unfaithful to him, but his plan, governed by circumstances, is the opposite, for he had to deal not with the Pelagians but with the Lutherans then recently condemned by the Council of Trent at its fifth session.[118] All the same, like his famous predecessors, 'he treats the problems of nature and grace as if he had no idea, within creation, of a natural order distinguished by a natural transcendent end'.[119] And, as a matter of fact, he had none. It could not be said that he passes over the hypothesis in silence; to a greater extent even than these predecessors, he seems quite simply to exclude it in advance. He does not oppose it *ex professo* because it had not yet really taken shape. But he opposed its beginnings. The bluntness with which he undertook to bar the way to the novelties of Cajetan's school leaves no doubt about his position. Against them he repeats, and in exactly the same spirit, the arguments of the earlier Scholastics against the objection taken from Aristotle :

Respondetur (ad Caietanum) quod Aristotles non dixit : si haberent inclinationem, sed : si haberent vim, haberent instrumenta. Nos autem, non dicimus quod natura habet vim, id est potentiam naturalem ad videndum Deum, sed inclinationem dumtaxat.

Praeterea Aristoteles nil de supernaturalibus novit, et ideo non concederet rem aliquam habere naturalem inclinationem ad aliquid, nisi haberet potestatem et naturales vires ad illud assequendum; nos autem concedimus naturam nostram adeo esse sublimem, ut ad illum finem inclinetur quem non nisi per auxilium Dei assequi possumus.[120]

---

[117] H. Rondet, 'Le problème de la nature pure . . .', *art. cit.*, p. 500.

[118] *De natura et gratia,* bk 1, preface (p. 2).

[119] René-Charles Dhont, O.F.M., on St Bonaventure and 'the generality of Scholastics of his times' : *Le problème de la préparation à la grâce, débuts de l'école franciscaine* (1946), p. 211, note 70.

[120] *In IV Sent.,* dist. 41, qu. 2, art. 1.

There was nothing here preventing Soto from affirming, in an unpublished passage, quoted by Fr Bricio Torres,[121] that 'even if God had not decided to grant the beatific vision to the creature, he would not have been unjust to it, because he owed it nothing'. He then launched out into various hypotheses on the subject. All the theologians to whom Soto wished to remain faithful had admitted this before he did, at least implicitly, by saying that the beatific vision is a gratuitous gift. Fénelon said so very explicitly, being very careful to distinguish his hypothesis from that of 'pure nature'. In this way the absolute supernaturality which was destroyed by Baianism was maintained. But here we must note this : no more than Fénelon or the earlier writers, Soto did not imagine another world, the normal world, in which a purely natural knowledge of God would have constituted in eternity the natural and normal end of man.

Even by his invention of a man 'in puris naturalibus mente excogitatum',[122] Soto was still near to the ancients. This man was still Aristotle's man just as he is described, save for the entirely abstract hypothesis of his position in being, described by St Thomas on many occasions. On the other hand, Soto clearly admits, like many before him, that in a certain sense it is a question of a man with a twofold end : one, which is proportionate to his created nature and that he can attain by himself; the other, which is beyond all proportion and consists in eternal life : 'in Dei summe amati per facialem visionem comprehensione'. However, for Soto, as for St Thomas, St Bonaventure and Scotus, this twofold finality which exists in real man does not in the nature of this man constitute the mark of a possible twofold polarity; it is a real and ordered duality. There is no question here of any ambiguity or essential indetermination, previous to a divine choice. Coexisting in man as he actually is, in this being which is made in the image of God, in each of us, the two finalities are both to be made real, the one by the other. The first is determined by the laws of prudence and integrity as they had been explained

[121] *Op. cit.*, pp. 65-6; cf. pp. 84-5.
[122] *De natura et gratia,* bk 1, praefatio (p. 2).

by the 'philosophi naturales'.[123] It is neither removed nor smothered by the other—Soto wishes in no wise to ignore natural values, and the title of humanist could be claimed for him—but it is subordinate to it. Only the second actually deserves the name of last end, and alone it transcends the earthly horizon. In short, in our language no transcendence is to be envisaged without the supernatural.[124]

For information about theological opinions current at the time of Baius there is other evidence than that of Dominic Soto. The works of Baius himself provide a not entirely negligible amount. In his *De caritate* Baius declared that he was scandalized by the teaching of those theologians who allowed in man two different loves of God: a love of God regarded as the author of intellectual nature, and a love of God regarded as making this same nature blessed.[125] Is that not an obvious sign that the distinction made between 'Deus auctor' (or 'principium') and 'Deus beatificator' (or 'beatificans') was still in current use? Now despite Baius' assertions in his *Apologia* to St Pius V (1569), even if this distinction was beginning to be given a meaning different from its original one by certain theologians, it was that used by St Thomas.[126] On the other hand, it did not tally with the distinction required by the theory of 'pure nature' and since then widespread, the distinction between God the 'author of the natural

---

[123] *De natura et gratia,* bk 1, c. 3 (pp. 7-8).

[124] *De natura et gratia,* bk 1, c. 20 (pp. 68-70); c. 4 (p. 9), etc. Soto put Báñez in a difficult position and he made a point of refuting him with the distinctions that we shall see below: *Scolastica commentaria in Primam Partem Angelici Doctoris,* vol. 1 (Venice 1587), col. 448-54.

[125] *De caritate,* c. 4 (vol. 1, p. 93). Proposition 34: 'Distinctio illa, duplicis amoris, naturalis videlicet, quo Deus amatur ut auctor naturae, et gratuiti, quo Deus amatur ut beatificator, vana est et commentitia et ad illudendum sacris Litteris et plurimis veterum testimoniis excogitata' (cf. Le Bachelet, *DTC,* vol. 2, col. 91-2). Cf. St Thomas, *Prima,* qu. 62, art. 2, ad primum, etc.

[126] Cf. *Baiana,* p. 99: 'In hac distinctione nihil aliud improbatur, quam quod quidam contra D. Thomam asserunt, aliquem verum unius veri Dei amorem posse ex solo libero corrupti hominis arbitrio consurgere. . . .' But whether Baius is here criticizing a genuinely Thomist theory or a theory wrongly sheltering under the patronage of St Thomas, makes no difference on the point concerning us here.

order' and God 'the author of the supernatural order'. Of course, these terms, properly explained, could still be used to express the same idea as the distinctions formulated by St Thomas himself. As it is, however, when John of St Thomas, for example, speaks of 'Deus ut auctor naturae' and of 'Deus ut auctor supernaturalis',[127] he included within these two terms a whole idea of the supernatural order which was still foreign, at least roughly speaking, to theology after the middle of the sixteenth century.[128] In the same way, when Báñez and others made a distinction between the 'auctor naturae' and the 'auctor gratiae' they no longer understood this distinction in exact conformity with the teaching of St Thomas.

A document of the first importance reveals the doctrines enjoying particular favour at that time. This is the *Catechismus Romanus*. It had just been published in 1566, in the very year preceding Baius' condemnation, at a time when his theses were much discussed; for some time past they had caused concern. It is well known that this work, without being an official ecclesiastical document—it is wrong to call it the 'Catechism of the Council of Trent'—nevertheless enjoyed great authority. It was drawn up at the request of the Fathers of the Council by Thomist theologians, and on points then the subject of controversy it represents the opinions of their school.[129] It is true that according to certain

---

[127] *Cursus theologicus,* Disputatio XII, art. 3, n. 8 (Solesmes ed., vol. 2, p. 141). In the same way others were to transform the 'Deus auctor naturae' into a 'Deus auctor et finis naturae' or 'finis naturalis': thus Thomas de Lemos, O.P., *Panoplia gratiae,* vol. 1, Isagogicus (1676), 2nd part, tract. 1, c. 6 (p. 14).

[128] Cf. Báñez, *In Primam,* vol. 1, col. 451. In the same way when Baius wrote (proposition 37): 'Cum Pelagio sentit, qui, boni aliquid naturalis, hoc est, quod ex naturae solis viribus ortum ducit, agnoscit', the doctrine that he has in mind must be understood in accordance with the distinction that he attacks in propositions 61 and 62—a distinction which is that of St Thomas between the substance of the act and the mode of performing it, or between the goodness accruing to the act 'ex obiecto et circumstantiis' and that which belongs to it by reason of the internal principle of the agent, 'quod sit a vero Christi membro per spiritum caritatis', and makes it meritorious. This is a distinction which in no way presupposes the idea of a 'pure nature'.

[129] Cf. S. L. Skibniewski, *Geschichte des röm Katechismus* (1903). The draft of the work, first submitted to St Charles Borromeo, was revised in the last place by Cardinal Sirlet.

Protestant theologians the condemnation obtained from St Pius V was the revenge taken by the Jesuits for the publication of the *Catechismus Romanus,* the last manifestation of Augustinianism within the Catholic Church. Harnack asserts this[130] and the Dutch Calvinist Melchior Leydecker (died 1722) stated it as a fact : according to him, between 1566 and 1567 the Church had changed its mind, and it was at this precise date that it became Pelagian.[131] But such a judgment belongs to controversy rather than to history. In addition, it in no way lessens the value of the evidence afforded by the *Catechismus Romanus,* a 'doctrinal explanation capable of completing the theological instruction of priests',[132] on the doctrines then held as traditional. There is no trace in it of any duality, at least not by right, between creation for a natural end and ordering for a supernatural end. Indeed various signs seem to indicate the contrary.

Is it a question, for example, of beatitude? It is twofold : one, essential, which consists in seeing God; the other, accidental, which consists in the possession of accessory goods.[133] Do we want to know why the name of the Father is fitting for God? It is because he has created us in his own image, endowing us, there-fore, with a singular benefit which he granted to no other living being; obviously, what nowadays would be called the super-natural vocation of man (not the infusion of the supernatural gift), his fundamental ordering to a higher destiny (not his present 'raising up') is, for the compilers of the *Catechismus,* already wholly contained in the gift of rational nature made in the like-ness of God.[134] Was revelation necessary? Yes, we are told, and

[130] *Outlines of the History of Dogma* (last English ed., 1957). 'Augus-tinianism achieved its last official monument in the *Catechismus Romanus.* The Jesuits therefore attacked this catechism. In 1567 they were successful in obtaining the condemnation by Pius V of seventy-nine propositions of Baius.'

[131] Leydeckerus, *Disputatio historico-theologica de vario Iansenistarum fato,* thesis XVII. This learned man 'was often lacking in critical sense and moderation'. *Encyclopédie des sciences religieuses,* vol. 8 (1880), p. 200.

[132] E. Mangenot *DTC,* vol. 2, col. 1918. An encyclical of Leo XIII to the clergy of France recommended this 'golden book', one 'remarkable for its doctrinal richness and accuracy'.   [133] Pars prima, art. 12, n. 7.

[134] Pars quarta, *De oratione dominica,* tertia petitio, n. 3.

this answer is not based on a pessimistic theory; the idea of the original fall and the blindness which it must have caused counts for nothing : but in no case would man's reason be sufficient to enlighten him on his last end, since that is above him. Here again, a close relationship is therefore established between the idea of salvation, which is the obtaining of a supernatural end, and the idea of the creature made in the image and likeness of God, that is, endowed with a spiritual nature. The *Catechismus* which makes little use of the word 'supernaturalis' nevertheless here mentions 'supernaturalis revelatio' without relating it to an added 'elevation'.[135] Finally, when the purpose is to describe the 'state of complete nature', terms are used which, it appears, leave room for no doubt on the essential end of man :

> A principio Deus proprii boni appetitionem creatis rebus ingeneravit, ut naturali quadam propensione suum quaererent et expeterent finem, a quo illae numquam, nisi obiecto extrinsecus impedimento, declinant. Haec autem initio fuit in homine expetendi Deum, suae beatitudinis auctorem parentemque, eo praeclarior et praestantior vis, quod is compos esset rationis atque consilii.[136]

This evidence is quite clear. Moreover, it causes no surprise to those acquainted with the teaching of St Thomas Aquinas. Of course we have here the teaching of a catechism which does not go into details about hypotheses nor give subtle explanations.[137] Nevertheless, it offers a body of fairly developed teaching for the use of pastors. And so the traditional simplicity of its formulas gives reason for supposing that its authors remained attached to the simplicity of traditional teaching.

This is further confirmed by examination of the *Lexicon theologicum* of John Altenstaig (died 1525); the edition which is quoted here appeared in 1580, thirteen years after the condemnation of

---

[135] Praefatio, 1 and 2. (It is interesting to compare this passage with the similar passage of the First Vatican Council.)

[136] Pars quarta, *De oratione Dominica,* tertia petitio, n. 3.

[137] Praefatio, 11 : It could hardly intend 'ut omnia christianae fidei dogmata, uno libro comprehensa, subtiliter explicarentur'.

Baius.[138] This lexicon is not so long as Vacant-Mangenot's *Dictionnaire de théologie catholique* of modern times, nor even of Bergier's *Dictionnaire*; for all its brevity, however, it abounds in distinctions and it can be called a technical work. Yet we shall look in vain for the slightest mention of the modern theory of 'pure nature'. There is, it tells us, a twofold end for man, the supernatural end and the natural end; but the latter is defined as 'finis politicus vel civilis'; or else one is 'finis ultimus et principalis', the other being 'minus principalis vel finis sub fine'.[139] The natural can be opposed to the 'violent' to the 'free', to the 'artificial' or lastly to the 'supernatural'; but the explanation given of this last case leaves us very wide of the mark: 'Hoc modo incarnatio non est naturalis sed supernaturalis, quia non fit ab agente naturali naturaliter, sed supernaturaliter, qui a solo Deo potuit fieri.'[140] The article 'status' enumerates three states of man according to the scheme which had for long been classic, with no allusion to that 'status naturae purae' which was shortly to invade all the theological treatises.[141] The article 'appetitus' divides it into natural and free, in the spirit of the old tradition; the first is 'potentia', an 'inclinatio', while the second is an 'actus', a 'velle'.[142] The article 'imago' summarizes in a few words the old teaching about image and likeness.[143] There is no article for 'supernaturalis', but only for 'supermundanus'. The most significant, perhaps, is the article 'beatitudo' because it displays a great profusion of distinctions and subdistinctions, twofold and threefold.[144] Nowhere is there any question of making a distinction between natural and supernatural beatitude; nevertheless, there

---

[138] *Lexicon Theologicum* complectens vocabulorum descriptiones, distinctiones et interpretationes, quae sunt Scholae Theologicae propria, ab ea ad commodiorem doctrinam vel excogitata, vel a profanis auctoribus ad usum suum traducta. Itemque plurima notamina, quae ad intelligenda Theologorum scripta, apprime cum utilia sunt, tum necessaria. Auctore Joanne Altenstaig, Mindelhaimensi, sacrae Theologiae Doctore. The first edition appeared in 1508. The Venice edition (1579) in four columns contains 535 leaves, that of Lyons (1580) contains 670 double-column folio pages.

[139] Pp. 223-4.   [140] Pp. 388-9; cf. *Natura*, p. 386-7.
[141] P. 590.   [142] Pp. 35-6.
[143] Pp. 268-9: 'Imago pertinet ad potentias, scilicet memoriam, intelligentiam et voluntatem. Similitudo vero, ad habitus consequentes, scilicet innocentiam et iustitiam. . . .' Cf. *Similitudo*, p. 571.   [144] Pp. 58-62.

is a 'beatitudo viae' and a 'beatitudo patriae'; or yet again, it is
possible to speak of a threefold beatitude: 'prima, falsa et decep-
toria; secunda, vera et meritoria; tertia, perfecta et praemiatoria:
haec habetur in patria in visione Dei . . .'. When 'beatitudo' is
mentioned by itself it is the last mentioned that is meant; it is
described in terms taken from St Thomas. In this article the
word 'supernaturalis' does not even occur; yet no place would
have been more suitable, it would seem, for a detail of this kind,
if for some reason the modern distinction of two transcendent
beatitudes already habitually occupied theologians' attention.

Altenstaig's *Lexicon* is not one book among many. It is a
representative work. In the second half of the sixteenth century
it was much read. One after another new editions of it were published—Antwerp, 1576; Venice, 1579;[145] Lyon, 1580.[146] It was
to be republished in 1619. From one edition to another it was
corrected, improved. How could it so completely and continu-
ously pass over in silence such precise points of doctrine, which it
would have been easy enough to deal with in a few words, if
these points of doctrine were then really held as traditional, or
if at least the condemnation of Baius had made them obligatory?

The work of Francis Toletus (1532-96), the first Jesuit cardinal,
brings us forward a further twenty years, to nearly the end of
the century.

Like Soto, who was his teacher at Salamanca from 1556 to
1558, Toletus is an important figure in the Church. As professor
of theology at the Roman College for more than thirty years,
preacher in ordinary at the Roman Court, consultor of the Holy
Office, he enjoyed the confidence of three successive popes, the

[145] 'Opus hoc quod vetustate consenuerat, nova hac editione, ab infinitis
pene mendis et erroribus, quibus antae scatebat, repurgavimus.' Venetiis,
apud Haeredes Melchioris Sellae, MDLXXIX.
[146] 'Opus hoc postrema hac editione plurimis in locis maxima est diligentia
emendatum, ac longe melius redditum. Excudebat Ioannes Symonetus Typo-
graphus, Lugdunensis, MDLXXX.'
John Altenstaig is also the author of *Tres libri de felicitate triplici* (1519).
'Una quae dicitur . . . philosophica: humana, falsa et erronea. Altera
christicolarum Deo militantium, terrestris sive viae: vera, recta et meritoria,
vel dispositiva. Tertia caelestis, beatorum sive triumphantium: sempiterna
absoluta et integra.'

last of which, Clement VIII, made him a cardinal; Gregory XIII declared that 'undeniably he was the most learned of all the men of his time'.[147] Montaigne in his turn, speaking of 'Padre Toledo' whom he had just met in Rome, wrote that 'in depth of knowledge, in clearness of exposition, he was a man of rare qualities'.[148] Toletus was very closely involved in the Baianist affair in its second phase. It was he who sent to Gregory XIII an address from the theological faculty at Louvain, asking for the confirmation and renewal of Pius V's bull. Again, it was he whom this same pope in 1580 charged with taking the new bull to Louvain and obtaining Baius' submission. On two occasions he assembled the professors and students of the faculty of theology and exhorted them to active submission; in his presence, after the reading of the bull and the declaration required of Baius, all had to shout out : 'Articulos damnamus, bullam reverenter suscipimus atque obedientiam pollicemur.'[149] No theologian could have been more in touch than he was with the controverted point, better informed of the implications of the condemnation, nor more aware of the requirements of orthodoxy which resulted from it. No one could have felt greater responsibility to take it into account. We now have a work by Toletus, published in 1869 under the editorship of Fr Joseph Paria, in accordance with the autograph manuscript, in which he treats in order and with

[147] Brief of 22 November 1575 to the Duke of Bavaria. Cf. Pastor, *History of the Popes*, English trans., vol. 20, p. 234. Other similar testimony in the Prolegomena of Fr Joseph Paria: *Francisci TOLETI . . . in Summam Theologiae S. Thomae Aquinatis Enarratio ex autographo in Bibliotheca collegii romani asservato* (4 vols, Rome, 1869-70), vol. 1, pp. viii-xv and xxi-xxiv.

[148] *Journal d'un voyage en Italie*, ed. Maurice Rat (Classiques Garnier), p. 122.

[149] Bull *Provisionis nostrae* (29 January 1579). Pastor, *op. cit.*, pp. 234-5. F. Cereceda, art. 'Tolet' in *DTC*, vol. 15, col. 1222. J. Grisar, 'Die Universität Löwen zur Zeit der Gesandschaft des P. Franciscus Toletus (1580)' in *Miscellanea historica in honorem Alberti De Meyer* (1946), vol. 2, pp. 941-68. Documents in connection with Toletus' legation to Louvain and his relations with Baius in Miguel Roca, *loc. cit.* (1953). Cf. L. Ceyssens, *Sources relatives aux débuts du jansénisme et l'antijansénisme* (1957), pp. 257-8, for the address by the three 'seniores' of the theological faculty of Louvain to Urban VIII, and the account of this mission by Toletus. On Toletus' objective and moderate attitude: E. van Eijl, *RHE*, 50 (1955), pp. 539-41.

clarity the problems relating to the nature of man and his last end; nor does he fear to adopt personal positions on these points. The work is a commentary on the *Summa Theologica* of St Thomas, the fruit of repeated teaching, which he must have re-written in its entirety at least twice, if not three times, and which he never ceased to revise right up to the very end of his life. When he died in 1596 he left it in manuscript. Nevertheless, it appears that of all his works it was the one which had his preference; it was the one which he desired most to have published among those which remained in manuscript.[150] Examination of this commentary will therefore prove very interesting for us.

In all essentials the teaching is the very same as Dominic Soto's. Like him, whom he calls his 'very learned master',[151] Francis Toletus follows in general the opinions of St Thomas, readily adding to his arguments, which he terms 'excellent', some arguments which are new, at least in their presentation.[152] Like Soto again, leaving aside certain controversies of the schools, he appeals to the combined authority of Scotus and St Thomas to establish the traditional teaching: 'Quamvis discordia sit inter sanctum Thomam et Scotum, an in actu intellectus an in actu voluntatis circa Deum praecipue beatitudo consistat, tamen in hoc conveniunt, beatitudini esse necessariam Dei intuitivam intellectionem, et hoc sufficit ad vim argumenti huius.'[153] Against the innovating theories he thus sets up all the ancient doctors as a single body. It is the contrary method to Cajetan's, and it is also the contrary teaching. Toletus understood perfectly that henceforth, in this fundamental problem, the fundamental contest is

[150] Paria, *loc. cit.*, pp. xxiv-xxvi. It may be wondered why the work was not published before this and if the difficulty in deciphering the manuscript is sufficient explanation, as Fr Paria alleges. The *Prima Pars* is explained only up to question 64, and the whole of the commentary of the *Prima Secundae* is missing. But the library of the Roman College in 1869 possessed a notebook 'P. Fabii Amodei Lectiones R.P. Francisci Toleti Theologiae Doctoris in Pr. 2ᵉ S. Tho. habitae 20 Octobris 1567' which Fr Paria intended to publish subsequently (*loc. cit.*, p. xvi).

[151] *Enarratio*, vol. 1, pp. 18 and 171.

[152] *Enarratio*, vol. 1, pp. 154 and 155 (*In Primam*, qu. 12, art. 1): 'Ultra rationes S. Thomae, quae egregiae sunt, probatur idem aliis duabus. . . .'

[153] *Op. cit.*, pp. 153-4 (*In Primam*, qu. 12, art. 1).

no longer between the Thomist and Scotist schools, but—for a
far more serious stake—between the old school in its entirety and
a certain modern school which claims Cajetan as its master:
'Haec est (conclusio) contra Caietanem, et est sententia Scoti, et
indubitata sancti Thomae.'[154] One after the other, the great cardinal's positions are attacked, sometimes in rather sharp terms. In
one place Cajetan is not only 'obscure, as usual', he contradicts
himself: 'Caietanus videtur non sibi constare';[155] his explanations
are not always to the point: 'Hinc potest intelligi Caietanum
minime congruenteur esse locutum.'[156] In another place he uses
a flood of words to evade Thomist ideas: 'Caietanus multa
verba consumit; dico tamen quod sanctus Thomas. . . .'[157] St
Thomas' genuine thought must therefore be reinstated, 'quidquid
fingat hic Caitenaus';[158] sometimes it is even the thought of all
the Scholastics that Cajetan's inventions repudiate, only to fall
into novel, false and dangerous opinions.[159] And Toletus makes a
point of re-emphasizing the classical argument of natural desire,
without any of the ambiguous formulas which leave a loophole:
'Dicere quod homo non consequetur suam beatitudinem, aperte
est falsum: tunc enim esset frustra.'[160]

[154] *Op. cit.*, p. 19 (*In Primam*, qu. 1, art. 1).
[155] *Op. cit.*, p. 19 (qu. 1, art. 1); p. 168: 'Ista sententia Caietani non est
consonans.' Cf. p. 160.
[156] *Op. cit.*, cf. p. 149: 'In hac conclusione non fecit munus suum
Caietanus . . . , profecto nullo modo littera aptari potest in tali sensu.'
[157] *Op. cit.*, vol. 2, p. 183 (*In Secundum Secundae*, qu. 26, art. 3, ad 6m).
[158] *Op. cit.*, p. 154 (*In Primam*, qu. 12, art. 1).
[159] Page 79, *In Primam*, qu. 3, art. 3: 'Hec sunt quae docet Caietanus.
Pace tamen ipsius, haec opinio est nova, falsa et periculosa. . . . Haec
responsio peior est. . . . Relinquenda igitur est imaginatio ista Caietani, quae
est contra omnes etiam Scholasticos. . . .' See also pp. 511 and 516 regarding
the sin of the angels: 'Caietanus dixit. . . . Sed omnia ista vides nihil esse';
'Respondet Caietanus. . . . Sed haec responsio est nihil.' Fonseca was no
kinder: about St Thomas' opusculum *De natura generis* he wrote, *In libros
Metaph. Arist.*, vol. 2, col. 968: 'Quae omnia Caietanus videtur aut non
legisse aut non curasse'; c. col. 1021: 'Novam in hac re comminiscitur
distinctionem Caietanus.'
[160] Vol. 1, p. 153 (*In Primam*, qu. 12, art. 1). Cf. p. 20 (qu. 1, art. 1,
secunda conclusio): 'Sanctus Thomas . . . probat hac unica ratione posse
Deum videri a nobis per essentiam, quia aliter desiderium naturale maneret
frustra et otiosum.' See also the passage published by Fr Stegmüller, 'Tolet
et Cajetan' in *Revue Thomiste*, 17 (1935), pp. 358-70.

If it is true, as Fr Charlier recalled fairly recently,[161] quoting Toletus' own admission ('ut prius sanctum Thomam pro viribus explanemus, consequenter Caietanum', that he took Cajetan as his guide in his commentary on the *Summa,* his opposition on the question concerning us is the more significant.

On some points, however, Toletus departs a little from the terminology of St Thomas. He adopts the dubious expression 'appetitus elicitus', which even Soto avoided. In line with the thought of earlier thinkers, however, Toletus understood by this term—like the more traditional term 'appetitus rationalis'—not only a conscious appetite, but an *act,* which can be due to free will, or rather the choice itself of the will; so that he can assert for example : 'Non enim homo absque fide et Dei gratia tendit in Deum fruibilem appetitu elicito'; or again : 'Deus non est finis noster ratione appetitus naturalis, sicut est centrum lapidi, sed ratione appetitus eliciti, eo quod homo ut homo per appetitum rationalem suum in finem tendat.'[162]

That the grace of God is necessary for man to tend freely to God is in that case a very clear truth. And so Toletus hastens to add that this raises no controversy. And it is a grace in the fullest sense of the word. If a twofold 'debitum' is distinguished, the one natural and the other personal, in both cases it must also be asserted : 'Neutra ratione prorsus gratia gratis data confertur ex debito sed ex liberalitate sola Dei.' But the whole difficulty lies in the question of the 'appetitus naturalis', in other words of the 'inclinatio et propensio', of the 'inclinatio et capacitas naturae'.[163] He also prefers not to term the vision of God 'natural end', since it is not due to the nature of man, and man can only attain to it 'sufficiently' and can only be 'disposed' to it by his natural means. He prefers to keep to the language of St Thomas of whom he

---

[161] *Essai sur le problème théologique* (1938), p. 19, n. 10.

[162] Vol. 1, p. 20.

[163] Vol. 1, pp. 17 and 19. Or again : 'capacitas naturalis et appetitus' (p. 19); 'naturaliter instimulatur et instigatur a suo principio et appetitu innato' (p. 20); 'naturaliter inclinatur' (p. 20), etc. *Lectiones ineditae* . . . , folio 269 r.

says in passing 'quam mirabiliter locutus est';[164] at least he makes the distinction, not without a certain subtlety: 'Deus igitur est potentiae finis naturalis, et actus operationis est finis naturalis',[165] which amounts to his returning to the precise language of Soto after evincing some scrupulosity on the matter. But like Soto, Toletus does not hesitate to speak of 'duplex finis' and 'duplex beatitudo'; but it is always in the old meaning, St Thomas' meaning, far different from the one that was to prevail among many theologians. He explains his reasons in connection with the creation of angels. They were created, he says, in a state of natural blessedness, knowing and loving God in so far as he is the natural end of all things. They could not be in possession of natural blessedness from the moment of their creation which alone is the 'finis ultimus',[166] because among other reasons, this blessedness must not only be received from God, but merited; it is given as a reward, as a consequence of an indispensable choice. It is this which enables it to be shown that the vision of God promised in the Bible is not due to nature; it goes beyond nature, it can only be hoped for from divine grace which gives it as a reward to those who are good.[167] The two ends, or the two states of blessedness, however incommensurable they are, both exist

[164] Vol. 1, p. 17: 'Cum igitur Deus excedat appetitum rationalem hominis, non enim rationali appetitu appetitur absque fide et gratia supernaturalibus, inde est quod est dicendus finis supernaturalis. P. 163: 'Non ergo homo per sua naturalia *sufficienter* potest attingere Dei visionem'; p. 166: 'Negatur prorsus quod illud lumen, ut est visionis Dei dispositio proxima, possit alicui ex principio naturae solis inesse . . .' (qu. 12, art. 5). It is always the terminology of St Thomas.

[165] Vol. 1, p. 20 (*In Primam*, qu. 1, art. 1).

[166] Vol. 1, p. 506 (*In Primam*, qu. 63, art. 2): 'Cum duplex sit finis in angelo, naturalis et supernaturalis, dupliciter potuit esse superbia. . . . Posterior, circa finem supernaturalem. . . . Potuit esse inconsideratio in intellectu, scilicet non considerare naturalem non esse ultimum finem, et supernaturalem a Deo esse sperandum.'

[167] Vol. 1, pp. 490-1 (*In Primam*, qu. 62, art. 1). P. 506 (art. 2): 'Posterior (superbia) in hoc erat, scilicet appetere beatitudinem, quam non habebat, velut sibi debitam ob naturam, nec eam sperando ex divina gratia.' P. 163 (qu. 12, art. 4): 'Praeterea, quia visio in Scripturis proponitur ut praemium bonorum: non ergo est debitum naturae', and the continuation which has already been quoted: 'non ergo homo per sua naturalia sufficienter potest attingere Dei visionem'.

within a same concrete order, or rather, a same concrete universe, and a being can no more be content with the first than it can enjoy the second from the outset.

Despite inevitable words like 'desire' or 'beatitude' Toletus' view of things is rather that of the metaphysician (and at first of the theologian) than the psychologist. It is of little importance for his conclusions that, of itself, the natural appetite is not a conscious one. Like many others, he is also put on his guard by the thorny question of the non-baptized child dying in infancy whom, like others, he does not wish to condemn to the pains of hell. This child belongs to the human race, he shares in the same nature as we do, but he has not been able personally to tend towards God 'ut homo', that is, by making use of his 'rational appetite'. He has neither received grace nor made a free choice. This provides a further motive for making a decisive separation between the cause of the natural appetite, which is the actual inclination of nature, and that of the rational appetite, which is an 'elicited' desire. It is enough for Toletus to be able to establish by means of the former the capacity of every spiritual nature in respect of the vision of God.[168] Now this capacity could not be given in vain to nature. Of course, it always remains possible for God to intervene—and he does so, it may well be thought, in favour of the child who has died too young—to arrest the impulse of the elicited desire at a stage earlier than its normal term. Thus suffering can be withdrawn from a being which has not been placed in the necessary conditions to attain this end. Nevertheless, the natural appetite remains beneath, together with the natural capacity. For nature has not been destroyed. In sight of those who discern them they are evidence of the natural end. Thanks to God, the child who cannot see him suffers no 'sadness'. But Toletus' argument is not psychological. If man, placed in the desired conditions, could not attain to God,

[168] 'De naturali enim appetitu loquimur, qui non est actus unus quispiam, at capacitas quaedam naturae ad actum seu finem aliquem' (Stegmüller, loc. cit., p. 360).

his natural appetite would remain 'disturbed' because his capacity would be 'empty'.[169]

Does this mean, in the last analysis, that man, left on earth merely with his reason, would have been able to discern his natural desire clearly enough to arrive at knowledge of his one real end? By no means. As St Thomas very well explained, if God is our supernatural end, it means that he exceeds our power of understanding: 'excedit comprehensionem rationis'.[170] At least this provides us with an indication enabling the two problems to be separated. After giving an affirmative answer to the question: 'utrum beatitudo hominis sit in visione divinae essentiae', one can still ask 'utrum homo per rationem naturalem possit cognoscere finem ultimum esse visionem Dei'.[171] Of course, if man knew his own nature perfectly, he would thereby know his end, and the two problems would form only one, or rather, there would be no problem. But in reality it is not so. Man is very far from knowing himself perfectly.[172] On the other hand, since he does

[169] *Lectiones ineditae in Primam Secundae*, fol. 23 r; qu. 3, art. 8, dubium 1 : 'An per potentiam divinam intellectus humanus possit satiari sine visione divinae essentiae' : 'Notandum prius quod aliud est loqui de appetitu elicito voluntatis, aliud de inclinatione naturali et capacitate. Nunc dico duo. Alterum: posset quidem Deus quoad appetitum elicitum satiare hominem citra sui visionem, *impediendo* desiderium ultra suum actum, puta delectationem aut quid simile; et hoc modo dicunt quidam pueros qui ad limbum descendunt non contristari. Altero modo dico quantum ad appetitum et inclinationem naturalem impossibile est satiari sine visione Dei; id est, quamvis *impediretur* desiderium, tamen non esset impleta undequaque inclinatio et capacitas naturalis. Et ratio est, quia natura est vere capax et idcirco nisi destruatur natura, semper manebit capax et vacua quoad illud quod non habet. Et hoc probatur ex Scriptura, *Psalm*. 15 : "Implebis me laetitia cum vultu tuo", et *Psalm*. 16 : "Satiabor cum apparuerit gloria tua, et implebo illud". Et hoc significat illud Augustini I Confess. c. 1 : "Fecisti nos ad te et inquietum est cor nostrum, donec revertatur ad te." Nam per illud "inquietum" non significat desiderium aut tristitiam, sed vacuitatem.'

[170] Vol. 1, p. 20 (qu. 1, art. 1): 'Ob id S. Thomas egregie dicens Deum esse finem supernaturalem, causam coniunxit, scilicet quia excedit comprehensionem rationis.' And p. 16 : 'Ex eo probat cognitionem revelatam esse homini necessariam, quia finis ipsius supernaturalis est.'

[171] *Lectiones ineditae. . .* , fol. 23 r : 'Non disputo an finis naturalis hominis sit Deus, sed an per rationem naturalem homo possit cognoscere quod factus sit ad visionem Dei.'

[172] *Loc. cit.*: 'Si homo perfecte cognosceret naturam suam, cognosceret finem suum esse visionem divinam.' But (folio 24) 'distinguo illud perfecte. Concedo perfecte in ordine ad causas naturaliter agentes, sed non in ordine

not know the indispensable supernatural means which God desires to procure for him, he would be unable even to suspect that an end so impossible for nature should be his, or at least he would be unable to hope for it.[173] Finally it is a matter of experience that up to the present no one has known this end by the light of nature; for if anyone ought to have been able to know it, it would have been Aristotle or Plato, the great philosophers; but they did not.[174] In addition is it not equally a fact that 'even after the light of faith, many still doubt whether it is possible to see God'?[175] And so Toletus can endeavour to furnish rational arguments, as did St Thomas, and these arguments, after the event, may well have their value: but it is not the arguments, it is revelation which has enlightened him on our fundamental nature. He says so openly. By natural experience alone 'man can only arrive at a negative conclusion; he will know that beatitude consists in no created being, but he will not know positively that it consists in the vision of the divine essence'.[176]

On the other hand, it is worth pointing out that Toletus is by no means pessimistic about human nature, even in its present fallen state. Here is a further point against Lutheran doctrine and against the exaggerated theories of Gregory of Rimini. In a wider sense, both opened the way for the elaboration of a

ad omnes causas et supernaturaliter agentes. Imo dico quod neque angelus hoc secundo modo perfecte cognoscit naturam suam.' And *In Primam*, qu. 1, art. 1, qu. 2 (vol. 1, p. 20): 'Naturali cognitione non potest ita natura animae nostrae cognosci, nec mirum est, cum sit spiritualis, cum angelis magnam habens vicinitatem.'

[173] 'Homo non potest cognoscere naturaliter media ad finem supernaturalem. Ergo non potest cognoscere illum esse suum finem. Probatur consequentia. Quia sicut media habent proportionem ad finem, ita e contra finis ad media, et cum non potest homo cognoscere possibilitatem mediorum, nihil potest suspicari aut sperare de fine' (*Lectiones ineditae*, fol. 24r).

[174] 'Nullus hactenus lumine naturali hoc cognovit. Nam si quis cognoscere debuit, fuerunt philosophi summi ut Aristoteles et Plato. At hi nihil minus,—cum tamen, ut ego non dubito, habuerint nostras Scripturas.'

[175] 'Adde quod multi post lumen fidei dubitant an sit possibile videre Deum.' This last argument, added *ad abundantiam*, takes us back rather to the times of St Thomas.

[176] 'Homo experientia rerum creaturarum non colligere potest nisi unam negativam, quod beatitudo non consistit in bono creato, sed non hanc affirmativam quod in visione essentiae divinae consistat' (fol. 24 v).

natural order, and one of the theses on which they relied in this respect is precisely the Thomist thesis concerning the inclination of created nature to love God more than self—a thesis that Toletus understands at the same time as evidence in favour of the oneness of the last end : 'Natura hominis inclinatur ad diligendum Deum ut finem supernaturalem supra seipsum; hoc est dicere, quod natura inclinatur in dilectionem Dei quae est ex caritate, imo in visionem Dei.'[177] Both share in the humanist tendency that is so strongly pronounced among the theologians of the Society of Jesus. Although they were upholders of tradition they were none the less not pure traditionalists. Their speculations were not marginal to the concerns of their period, and they had no desire for the stagnation of thought. But they did not exaggerate. Nor did they consider that the invention of a purely natural end was indispensable to give nature its proper place and to endow the natural order with consistency and value. Or rather, properly speaking, they did not even think of this fiction, at least with any clarity, for nowhere do they take to its logical conclusion the 'distinction between an order of essences and concrete order'; nowhere do they propound, event to reject it, the hypothesis of a 'dissociation of ends'.[178] For it is actually quite true they do not give explicit and complete criticism of it. They oppose—and very vigorously—its first rough sketches as they encountered them in Cajetan. Their whole teaching is none the less organized without reference to it, and, at least in the form that it was soon commonly to assume, their teaching constitutes an implicit denial of it. It seems that the modern editor of Toletus felt this.[179] The

---

[177] *Lectiones ineditae,* in Ledesma, p. 35, note 95. Also, *In Secundum Secundae,* qu. 26, art. 3 (vol. 2, pp. 180-2) : corresponding, and also optimist, theory in *In Primam,* qu. 1, art. 1 (vol. 1, p. 20): 'Deus auxilio supernaturali praesto est et paratissimus ad iuvandum.'

[178] Henri Rondet, *art. cit., RSR,* vol. 35 (1948), pp. 508 and 510.

[179] Without showing this truth in all its clarity, Fr Paria at least quotes this proposition from his author : 'In nobis inest naturale desiderium et appetitus videndi Deum' (p. 19) as being in danger of shocking the nineteenth-century reader, 'nisi ratio habeatur aetatis, qua scripsit Toletus'. He points out at length that between the writing and publication of the *Enarratio* three centuries elapsed, during which considerable progress was made in theology. It is only right and fair, he says, that account should

least that can be asserted with any show of reason is that they were silent on the subject. Now, chiefly so far as Toletus is concerned, dates and circumstances give to this argument from silence very great weight. After reading Francis Toletus' *Enarratio,* backed by the passages accessible to us in his unpublished lessons, it seems impossible still to maintain that the denial of a possible state of 'pure nature', understood as a state of purely natural finality, was condemned in Baius, or even that the affirmation of such a possible state then appeared as the logical consequence, the necessary consequence, of the condemnation pronounced by St Pius V.

Yet it must also be acknowledged that the position of Toletus at the end of the sixteenth century does seem to be out of date.[180] In his opposition to the new explanations this solid intelligence seemed to lack the necessary breadth either to reconstruct the ancient manner of thought or—in the face of new problems and difficulties—to explain in a new way the arguments justifying the maintenance of the old positions. It stands out even more clearly in his philosophical writings, the commentaries on Aristotle, in which, adopting a rather strange method, he took advantage of the data of revelation for knowledge of our last end, at the same

be taken of times and circumstances in the case of Toletus as in that of other doctors and of St Thomas himself. He also asks that propositions which appear ambiguous should be interpreted in a favourable sense. And he adds finally: 'Fatendum est sententiam de appetitu innato videndi Deum, exortis Baianis et Ianseniis erroribus, quo facilius, ut dictum est, eluderentur cavillationes haereticorum, desitam esse in scholis doceri. Verumtamen non est cur miremur, Toletum in eam sententiam concessisse si animo reputemus: 1. eamdem omnino sententiam professos esse praeter Ioannem Scotum et Dominicum Sotum Toleti magistrum alios benemultos, nec de infimo subsellio theologos; 2. "debitum naturae", quo ex aiente sententia colligunt asseclae Baii et Iansenii, a Toleto prorsus excludi; en ipsa verba. . . : "Visio in Scripturis proponitur ut praemium bonorum, non ergo est debitum naturae" ' (pp. xxviii-xxx).

I shall not insist on the fact that Fr Paria rightly exempts his author from any suspicion of 'demand', nor on the other fact that the *Enarratio* in its final state is much later than the Baius affair and as a result the excuse made is only half an excuse. Where Fr Paria sees a danger of scandal I am inclined to see rather historical evidence, but we agree on the facts.

[180] Cajetan's followers replied to him; cf. the remarks in the margin of the text published by Stegmüller, *loc. cit.,* p. 363, on appetite, power and end, with reference to Aristotle.

time forbidding himself to make use of them for all the rest. As a result, his view appears artificial and at the very least his vocabulary is unacceptable.[181] In itself Toletus' conservatism was legitimate, but it was too exclusively defensive to be effective.[182]

[181] This is why I thought it better not to deal with these philosophical writings.

[182] I know the *Lectiones ineditae* on the *Prima Secundae* only in the quotations given by Fr Joannes M. H. Ledesma, S.J., in his short work *Doctrina Toleti de appetitu naturali visionis beatificae secundum opera eius edita et ineditas lectiones in Primam Secundae* (Compendium dissertationis ad lauream, Pontificia Universitas Gregoriana, 1949). The author seems to minimize the thought of Toletus when he summarizes it in this form: 'Natura pro Toleto, praecise quia intellectualis, eo ipse iam est remote, fundamentaliter inadaequate capax visionis beatificae. Sicuti ergo impossibilis est status hominis in quo eius natura non sit intellectualis, ita impossibilis est status eiusdem in quo haec natura intellectualis non sit remote capax visionis Dei intuitivae. . . .' Beyond the fact that this is not the natural meaning of many of the passages and that many of them are quite incapable of being wrested to bear this meaning, there are two additional reasons against it: 1. Fr Ledesma is obliged to find a radical contradiction between Toletus' theology and philosophy, which is probably going too far. 2. He does not show clearly the grounds for Toletus' very strong opposition to Cajetan, for example, or to Suarez.

Fr Ledesma argues from the fact that Toletus often speaks of the state of pure nature. But the passages to which he refers speak merely: a. of a primitive state of pure nature, preceding the state of justice, which itself can precede the state of grace; there is no question of a state to be defined by a purely natural end; b. or a natural end or beatitude consisting in the purely natural contemplation of God, but which is not the last end and which does not define a state of pure nature in the sense in which the matter is in question. There remains only the passage in which Toletus takes into account the case of infants: these infants go to limbo, where they are not unhappy; but, the fact is that by reason of their special situation God intervenes to 'prevent their desire' being taken to its complete fulfilment, as has been explained. In other words, we have here an exception within our universe, and not the position of a possible universe in which human nature would not have experienced this same desire.

Fr Ledesma solves all the difficulties which could arise in the interpretation of Toletus by a distinction, taken from Fr Lennerz (*De Deo uno*, Rome, 1940, part 1, section 2, p. 120), between an appetite of demand and an appetite of capacity. I accept the distinction and, like him, I apply it to Toletus, but I believe that Toletus understood somewhat differently either the absence of demand or the presence of capacity.

In 1963 in a thesis, also defended at the Gregorian University, Fr Alberto Arenas Silva returned to the subject, considering that his predecessor's point of view 'no le permitio talvez a Ledesma interpretar rectamente algunos puntos de la doctrina de Toledo sobre la vision': *Gratuidad e Immanencia de la Visión Beatífica en los Teólogos Jesuitas*, estudio historico desde mediados del siglo XVI hasta mediados de siglo XVII (Bogota, 1963), p. 11, note 2.

6

Pure Nature and Natural Desire

Even before the Baianist affair, and in the same milieu of Louvain where the stage for it was set, the informed historian can discern the first features taking shape of that theology which, together with that of Cajetan and his school, was to develop towards the end of the century with Molina, Báñez and Suarez.[1] With John Driedo and Ruard Tapper, a trend began to be formed.[2]

Not that they contributed any really new theory. These learned theologians of the erudite faculty of Louvain were not very original minds. But they had a way of recalling certain aspects of traditional truth and leaving others in the shade as if unconsciously they despaired of effecting the synthesis; this method lent itself to misunderstandings and already, by such influence as they enjoyed, was setting theology along a partially new path.

The contribution by Driedo (1480-1535), who intended to oppose both Pelagius and Luther, consisted in showing how the gifts of the supernatural order, being what they are, must necessarily be held to be gratuitous, on any hypothesis, that is, where there is no sin involved. For us in the world today, 'duplicata est gratia'; but already in the state of innocence it was only by an entirely gratuitous gift that 'dignificatur homo in vitam aeter-

[1] It is to the credit of Fr P. Smulders, S.J., that he drew attention to the passages of Driedo and Tapper that I shall quote, in his study 'Der Oorsprong van der Theorie der Zuivere Natuur, vergeten Meesters der Leuvense School' which appeared in *Bijdragen*, vol. 10, pp. 105-27.

[2] On Driedo, Tapper and their theological circle: R. Guelley, 'L'évolution des méthodes théologiques à Louvain d'Erasme à Jansénius' in *RHE*, 37 (1941). Jacques Étienne, *Spiritualisme érasmien et théologiens lovanistes* (1956).

nam'. Grace is not only the mercy by which God frees us from evil; it is every help by which he leads to eternal life even the being who does not need to be freed from sin or wretchedness. For this 'eternal life' is a supernatural good, which is not required for the completeness of human nature and which, in consequence, cannot be owed to this nature ('indebitum naturae humanae beneficium'). God could therefore have refused it without injustice. It would be possible to conceive a still innocent humanity, yet affected like us by arduous work, death and the other difficulties which are our lot; from this mass of men left in their natural condition, God would have taken a certain number to make them the children of his kingdom, and no one would have the right to ask 'Why do you act in this way?'[3]

There is nothing very revolutionary in all this. The reminder of the inherently supernatural character of our divine vocation, involving its entirely gratuitous nature, was very opportune in view of the developments of the Protestant heresy. We have already seen that it was Baius' misfortune to have been unable to recognize this. The hypothesis put forward by Driedo betokens merely a certain lack of thought, and an inability to conceive freedom, even divine freedom except in an arbitrary form. It is true that he does not yet assert as possible and normal for human kind a purely natural finality, but he is certainly not very far from

[3] Ioannis Driedonis a Turnhout, sacrae Theologiae professoris apud Lovanienses, *De Concordia liberi arbitrii et praedestinationis divinae liber unus* (Louvain, 1547; 1st ed., posthumous, 1537), p. 14: 'Etiam si natura humana non esset per Adae peccatum vitiata, ita quod mala, quae nunc patimur, videlicet labor, mors, caeteraeque difficultates, conditiones forent naturae primitus institutae, et ex tali massa Deus aliquos assumeret in filios regni sui, caeteris et innocentibus vel absque culpa exclusis, aut vilioribus usibus deputatis, nec sic tamen iuste esset hominis contra Deum quaerimonia, nec ei posset dicere: "Cur ita facis?" Quia valde multum beneficii praestitit Deus, dans vitam aeternam, quae est supernaturale bonum, ac perinde naturae humanae indebitum, non iniuste negare posset, dare autem non nisi ex gratia. Verum Deus miserator et iustus noluit talem humano generi ordinem instituere, statuens misericorditer hominen ab initio immortalem, purum et mundum. . . .'
Id.: *De gratia et libero arbitrio* (Louvain, 1547, 1st ed., 1537) bk 1, tract. 2, c. 2, prima pars, 'De significatione vocabuli gratiae' (pp. 14-16).
Id.: *De captivitate et redemptione generis humani* (Louvain, 1548, 1st ed., 1534), tract. 6, c. 2, secunda pars (p. 155).

it. But this is only at the cost of complete silence on the problem of finality.

And it is the same with Ruard Tapper whose dominant concern is the same. Nor does Tapper study the question of the end of man in itself; he merely makes a point of showing that the gifts made to the first man, gifts which preserved him from the evils of our present state, were gratuitous gifts, and when he alludes to the 'consortium divinae naturae', it is once again, as with many others, in reference to the primitive state:

> Nam sicut hominem a nativitate caecum (Deus) facere potest, . . . ita et sine gratia gratum faciente et iustitia originali eum creare potuisset, et . . . carentia iustitiae et ad malum pronitas solum defectus fuissent naturales. . . . Non enim hominem creando necessario eum fecit naturae divinae consortem, spiritum suum ad inhabitandum communicando, nec filium et vitae aeternae haeredem. . . .[4]

These statements by Driedo and Tapper are given more precise form twenty years later by Bellarmine.

Robert Bellarmine was only ten years younger than his colleague Toletus,[5] but his training was partially different; he represents another generation, and it does not seem that there was any warmth of intellectual sympathy between the two men. He studied philosophy at the Roman College in 1562-3. Later, in 1567-8, he followed a course in theology not at Salamanca but at Padua, the university where Cajetan had been a student and master. In 1570, with his colleagues Harlemius and Tenerus, he was designated to inaugurate Jesuit teaching at Louvain. Until 1576 he taught the *Summa Theologica* there. He was thus led to concern himself with the teaching of Baius and as he had no fear of

[4] *Explicationes articulorum venerandae Facultatis sacrae theologiae generalis studii Lovaniensis, circa dogmata ecclesiastica ab annis triginta quattuor controversa...*, vol. 1 (Louvain, 1555), p. 126; cf. p. 127 and vol. 2, pp. 7 and 164. It was Tiletanus (Iodocus Ravestein of Tielt, 1506-70), an ardent disciple of Tapper, who collected together the articles for Baius' condemnation: Le Bachelet, *Bellarmin avant son cardinalat*, p. 117.

[5] They were both to be created cardinal, at an interval of several years from each other (1592 and 1597).

tackling burning questions, in his lessons he outlined a refutation of it. This produced the *Sententiae D.M. Baii refutatae*, a work composed of extracts he himself made from his commentary on St Thomas, and published by Fr Le Bachelet.[6] There is something of the spirit of Driedo and Tapper in it, together with a personal note. The discussion remains centred, as with Baius himself, on the question of the primitive state of Adam. The first objection that Bellarmine puts to himself is formulated thus : 'Homo creatus est ad Deum videndum tanquam ad naturalem finem : ergo debebantur ei media; ergo gratia et iustitia non fuerunt homini gratia, sed naturale debitum. . . .' To this the young theologian gives a series of answers set side by side, as if he were inviting the reader to choose :

Poterat Deus creare ad finem aliquem inferiorem, ac proinde non simpliciter debuit ei media ad beatitudinem, sed solum ex suppositione, nimirum supposito, quod Deus hominem creare voluerit ad tam altum finem.

Dico secundo quod hoc non est Deum debuisse aliquid homini, sed solum debuisse suae dispositioni implendae. Homo enim nihil fecerat quo Deum sibi debitorem faceret.

Dico tertio quod istud debitum, qualecumque est, non est naturale, sed supernaturale; voluit enim Deus creare ad tam sublimem finem quo non posset pertingere nisi per media supernaturalia. Est enim observandum Dei visionem non dici finem naturalem hominis, quod homo ad eum naturaliter pervenire possit, sed solum quod natura sit capax visionis Dei, et quod homo naturaliter appetat videre Deum. Sicut lapis quae est in tecto naturaliter appetit esse in centro, et tamen non habet ulla instrumenta naturalia quibus removeat impedimenta ut ad centrum possit penetrare, vel sicut anima separata appetit redire ad corpus et tamen naturaliter non potest.[7]

---

[6] X.-M. Le Bachelet, *Auctarium Bellarminianum* (1913), pp. 314-38; cf. p. 204. By the same author : *Bellarmin avant son cardinalat, Correspondance et documents* (1911), pp. 67-102.

[7] *Loc. cit.*, col. 315A.

As Fr Henri Rondet remarks: 'the third argument brings us back to St Thomas (and to Scotus) by way of Toletus and Soto. But the two first bear the marks of the new age and of the voluntarism initiated by the nominalist school and by Scotus himself.'[8] They do not agree entirely among themselves.

Nevertheless, Bellarmine puts in the mouth of his opponent a new objection whose exact equivalent will be sought in vain in the work of Baius:

> Homo non potuit creari ad finem inferiorem quam sit visio Dei; ergo simpliciter debita erant ei media ad hunc finem. Probatur antecedens: nam intellectus humanus naturaliter est capax visionis Dei et eam naturaliter appetit, nec potest fieri ut non sit eius capax, nisi non sit intellectus sed aliquid inferius.

It is a very interesting objection on two grounds. In the first place it actually shows, as did the preceding one, that the fundamental thesis which Bellarmine is undertaking to refute does not concern the end of man. The opponent whom he sets up before him does not seek to prove that this end is the vision of God; in the preceding objection he took it for granted as accepted by all; in the present objection, he strives in addition to establish it. But here and there he makes use of it merely as an argument to prove what he especially cherished—that the gifts of God were owed to the first man. Consideration of the end is introduced into the discussion, therefore, only indirectly and Bellarmine gives it a place which it does not occupy in Baius' work. But in the second place, remarkably enough, he does not reject purely and simply the statement which he ascribes to his opponent. Still imbued with the Augustinian and Thomist tradition, with his opponent he admits that the human soul, like all spiritual beings, is defined as the capacity for the vision of God, and that in one sense an inferior end cannot be assigned to it without depriving it of its spiritual nature. And so he answers by making a distinction:

[8] 'Le problème de la nature pure et la Théologie du XVIe siècle' in *RSR*, 35 (1948), p. 512.

Respondeo : Quamvis intellectus non potest non esse capax visionis Dei, potuit tamen Deus hominem ordinare, tanquam ad finem, ad cognitionem earum rerum quae naturaliter agnosci possunt, sicut oculus vespertilionis est naturaliter capax visionis solis et posset solem videre si a Deo iuvaretur, interim tamen non est creatus nisi ad videndam tenuissimam lucem nec aliud vidit. Neque frustra est aliqua potentia, quando nullum actum elicere potest; intellectus autem humanus, licet non possit elicere actum visionis Dei, potest tamen multos alios elicere, sicut oculus noctuae licet non possit solem videre, non est frustra, quia multa alia videt.[9]

In his Louvain course, then, Bellarmine was not content with a literal refutation of Baius. He saw that even this refutation *appeared* to compromise the most traditional truths concerning the end of man. So he himself raised the two objections which we have just seen. His answer to the first was at first somewhat groping : it is elaborated in three points which do not all say the same thing and are not imbued with the same spirit. To the second objection which clarifies the first, he answers in a way that is far more coherent and cogent, saving everything that he can of the old teaching. He grants that the soul is capable of God, that this is very true, and it cannot be otherwise; however, God still remains free to actuate or not this natural capacity; thus he could leave man to his own powers, that is to his powerlessness. In the above argument, 'everything, the idea, the comparison with the night bird'—taken from St Thomas—'leaves the impression that Bellarmine has recourse to it only with regret. He would like to be able to grant the assumption of the argument.'[10] But faced with the disastrous consequences that are derived from it he cannot wholly do so.

We have here, then, the idea of our 'pure nature' asserted in principle. For long past and in many ways it had been preparing to emerge. Nevertheless, it can be asserted, with Fr Smulders,

[9] In Le Bachelet, *Auctarium Bellarminianum*, col. 315A-315B.
[10] Henri Rondet, *loc. cit.*, pp. 512-13.

that 'Bellarmine is its creator'.[11] He introduced it, as I said, only indirectly and not without hesitation. But he does not stop there; immediately after admitting it he returns to it, at once encountering Baius in the centre of the discussion which concerned the primitive condition of the human race, and what St Augustine called the state of ignorance and difficulty.[12] It also seems that he was aware that he was putting forward a relatively new opinion, a freshly elaborated theological explanation. He was already a very learned theologian, one of the initiators of our 'positive theology' whose custom it is to proceed by authorities. In the related parts of this work[13] he makes use of authorities in this way, but on this precise point he gives not one reference.

Bellarmine's work is thirty years later than Soto's *De natura et gratia*. Nevertheless, even if it had been more widely known outside the little Baianist party, it would have been very far from obtaining general agreement. The evidence adduced above shows this clearly enough. But, in the form in which the objection was propounded, if its terms and assumptions were accepted, the answer was unavoidable. To save something that was a fundamental point of the Christian faith, the new theory of 'pure nature'—in a form which did not yet sacrifice the 'desiderium

[11] In *Bijdragen*, 1949, p. 126. With the same author I agree, as appears here, that 'the theory of pure nature is not merely a weapon brought against Baianism'; I also agree, but with a little more caution than he, that the system of Baius already appears 'as a reaction against this doctrine which was in process of developing' (p. 127). But however great the interest of these passages of Tapper and Driedo pointed out by Fr Smulders, their doctrinal content should not be exaggerated nor yet their authority and influence.

[12] 'Dicimus concupiscentiam, ignorantiam ac difficultatem quae modo sunt paenae, naturales fuisse futuras, si homo ita creatus fuisset. Homo siquidem non in puris naturalibus sed in magna gloria conditus est. . . .' (Le Bachelet, col. 315B). Cf. *In Primam Secundae*, qu. 109 : 'In sex statibus potest homo considerari : in puris naturalibus, id est sine iustitia et sine peccato originali, in quo statu numquam fuit sed certe esse potuit' (Arenas, p. 51). This aspect of the problem recurs again in chapter eight.

[13] In the same passage Bellarmine writes, for example : 'Altera ratio est, quia gratia facit homines filios Dei, imo et Deum quemdam. Absurdum est autem hominem esse filium Dei aut Deum naturaliter. Ergo gratia non est naturalis. Augustinus, libr. 3 contra Maximinum, c. 15 : 'Ideo, inquit, homo fit gratia filius, quia non est natura' (text appearing in the manuscript and kindly sent to me by Fr Pierre Smulders).

naturae', and which it would probably have been possible to retain subsequently—had become practically a necessity.

For this reason it is hardly surprising to encounter a few years later, in 1586, from the pen of another theologian of Louvain, John of Lens (Lensaeus), a refutation of Baius which almost repeats Bellarmine's view. It occurs in a doctrinal statement drawn up in agreement with the faculty of theology on the invitation of the apostolic nuncio and the archbishop of Malines. John of Lens allows that the raising up of the human nature of Adam can be termed 'natural' in one sense, as with St Leo, provided that in another sense, this time with St Athanasius and St Cyril, it is acknowledged to be 'supernatural', 'humanae naturae longe exsuperans facultatem', and in consequence 'singulari beneficio et virtute Conditoris ei superaddita'; for human nature did not require so great honour and glory, 'quasi videlicet aut non potuerit homo, nisi tam divina esset sapientia praeditus, aut nequiverit esse rectus . . . nisi tam praeclaris esset anima dotibus exornatus'. The last end of man consists 'in Dei clara visione'; now such an end can only be the effect of a goodness of God that is 'plane liberalis', for God would have been able 'servili conditione facere hominem, qui pro suis obsequiis aliam nullam mercedem expectaret'. In this last case, such a man would only have desired a kind of beatitude, that was 'longe minor'. On the nature of this beatitude John of Lens still does not venture to make any precise statement, confining himself to saying that it would have some 'finis vulgaris'.[14]

Bellarmine himself returns to his theory in 1587 during the controversy 'de gratia primi hominis'. There again, as indeed the title of the controversy shows, he deals principally with the primitive state, that is, with original justice and Adam's grace, and it is in this connection that he defines the various meanings of the

---

[14] 'Doctrina eius quam certorum articulorum damnatio postulare visa est, brevis et quoad fieri potuit ordinata et cohaerens explicatio . . .' in Gerberon, *Baiana*, pp. 163-4. This was republished by Fr H. Lennerz, Pontif. Univ. Gregoriana, Textus et documenta, series theologica, 24, *Opuscula duo de doctrina baiana* (1938), pp. 45-6. On John of Lens: R. Guelluy, *RHE, loc. cit.*, pp. 98-105.

words 'naturale' and 'supernaturale'. Then, and much more shortly in chapter 7, he mentions the last end, but he still does so indirectly and always with reference to the first gifts and in the form of an answer to an objection, the thirteenth. It is formulated almost as it is in *Sententiae refutatae* :

> Addi potest obiectio decima tertia in hunc modum : aeterna beatitudo est finis hominis naturalis, ut St Thomas docet in Ia P., q. 12, a. 1. Debuit igitur homo media naturalia habere ad eum finem consequendum; alioqui rebus omnibus esset miserior et abiectior, cum res caeterae fines suos propriis ac naturalibus viribus assequantur. Iustitia ergo, et caeterae virtutes, quae ad hanc beatitudinem adipiscendam necessaria sunt, primo homini naturalia fuerunt.

To this Bellarmine gives the answer :

> Respondeo : non parva quaestio est, sitne sempiterna beatitudo, quae in visione Dei consistit, finis hominis naturalis an supernaturalis. Sed quia non multum facit ad rem nostram illius quaestionis explicatio, admissa parte affirmante, respondeo beatitudinem finem hominis naturalem esse quoad appetitum, non quoad consecutionem. Neque est aut novum aut hominis natura indignum ut naturaliter appetat, quod nonnisi supernaturali auxilio consequi valeat. Non est, inquam, novum, siquidem animae hominum solutae corporibus naturalem habent ordinem et propensionem ad corpora, quorum formae fuerunt, nec tamen iterum coniungi corporibus sine supernaturali auxilio poterunt. Non est natura humana indignum, sed contra potius ad maximam eius pertinet dignitatem, quod ad sublimiorem finem condita sit, quam ut eum solis naturae suae viribus attingere possit.[15]

'A wonderful thought', commented Gratry, quoting these last lines.[16] We might add : a really classical answer, such as every

---

[15] Estius repeated this passage almost word for word : *In II Sent.*, dist. 25, n. 4 (vol. 1, 1672, p. 262).

[16] *De la connaissance de Dieu*, vol. 2 (1854), p. 418.

faithful follower of St Thomas could make, such as is to be found in Capreolus, Soto, Toletus, an answer that the Scotists were particularly fond of making. But then the objection rebounded, requiring a further answer; once again it was the answer of the *Sententiae refutatae* :

> Dicet fortasse quispiam : Esto, egeat homo supernaturali-
> bus mediis, tamen id sequetur, ut non potuerit sine mediis
> illis creari, ac per hoc non potuerit talis creari qualis nunc
> nascitur, neque enim ad finem inferiorem condi potuit, nisi
> natura eius mutaretur; neque negari media potuerunt ad
> finem naturalem obtinendum.
>
> Respondeo : Aequum omnino fuisse ut Deus homini ad
> talem finem tam sublimem ordinato, media necessaria non
> negaret; tamen nihil absurdum secuturum, si negasset. Nam
> tametsi summa illa beatitudo sit finis hominis naturalis,
> tamen est finis improportionatus et praeter eum, habet
> alium finem naturalem sibi omnino proportionatum, qui est
> ratiocinando inquirere veritatem. Quare potuit Deus homi-
> nem per naturalia media ad finem naturae suae proportiona-
> tum perducere; nec altius evehere. Cuius rei exemplum
> habemus in vespertilione qui naturalem habet capacitatem
> et appetitum videndi solem, et tamen credibile est numquam
> futurum ut is videat solem, sed lumen tantum debile ac
> subobscurum, quod est obiectum oculorum non solum
> naturale, sed etiam proportionatum.[17]

In the Roman controversy as in the Louvain refutation, Bellarmine thus shows his concern to remain as faithful as possible to
the teaching of St Thomas; he almost seems to go one better by
adopting without difficulty the Scotist vocabulary in which he
had formulated the objection which he put to himself.[18] On the

---

[17] *De gratia primi hominis,* c. 7 (*Opera,* ed. Vivès, vol. 5, col. 109B-
191A).

[18] Pointed out by, among others, Michel Marcellius, O.E.A., *Institutiones
theologicae,* vol. 3 (1846), pp. 347-8 : 'doctrinam hanc mutuo accepit a Scoto
eiusque schola, in qua sententia de innato intuitivae visionis appetitu
communis est. . . . Et iure quidem ita sentiunt Scotistae. . . .'

other hand, although he was constrained to propound the hypothesis of a man left by the Creator to his proportionate end, he
was very far from transforming this hypothesis into the normal
condition of human nature; he merely says that it would be by
no means absurd, 'nihil absurdum secuturum'. Nor does he have
a high idea of this 'proportionate' end : he does not (like John
of Lens) utter the word 'beatitude'[19] in connection with it; without
explaining to any extent what it could be, he implies that man
would only enjoy very little light, that he would have to continue
to seek the truth by using his reason, as on earth. Although he
alludes to the object illuminated by this light, to the truth attained
by this quest of the reason, it is not to speak of a 'knowledge of
God in any form' (but he does not of course deny it!) but 'of
those things which can be known naturally'; the night bird, he
observes, following St Thomas, does not see the sun, but other
things. Lastly, in both of these two works, Bellarmine shows that
he has certainly felt the weight of the objection put to him : 'nisi
non sit intellectus . . . '; 'nisi natura eius mutaretur'. He is careful
not to exaggerate the point. And thus he is greatly concerned to
say nothing tending in the direction of an unthinkable duality.
For him the soul continued to be determined

by its relationship with God possessed face to face. But since
the supernatural was gratuitous it depended on the divine
will whether the natural virtualities of the soul were completed or not. If God had so willed it we should have
remained half way, away from our real path. Made *essentially* to see God, the soul would have remained existentially
in a possible but unenviable state for one who has known
another destiny. The eyes of the owl are made for the light
of the sun, but they open only on the darkness of the
night.[20]

[19] *In Primam Secundae*, qu. 62: 'Beatitudo simpliciter est visio Dei ad
quam creati sumus; beatitudo secundum aliquid est illud bonum quo vires
naturae pervenire possunt' (Arenas, p. 48).

[20] Henri Rondet, *loc. cit.*, p. 516. The comparison is taken from St Thomas
(e.g. *Contra gentiles*, bk 1, c. 3). who himself found it in Aristotle (*Metaphys.*,
II, 1). In his *De iustificatione* Bellarmine is still concerned with Baius. In bk 5

There is no other reason for surprise therefore that in his spiritual writings Bellarmine disregards so restricted and unattractive an hypothesis. His *Concio Quarta, de beatitudine caelesti* is composed according to an entirely Thomist scheme : philosophers have sought in vain for blessedness in this life; 'maior est cordis humani capacitas ut eam etiam totus orbis possit replere. . . . Tunc igitur et voluntas humana quiescet cum eo bono fruetur in quo caetera bona tanquam in fonte et oceano bonorum omnium continentur.'[21] The short work *De ascensione mentis ad Deum* is possibly more emphatic still. Through his soul, that is through his substantial form itself, through what makes him man, man is an image of God.[22] By this very fact, he is made for God :

> Finis ad quem creatus est homo alius est quam ipse Deus. . . . Homo qui ad finem celsissimum creatus est, tunc finem suum consecutus dici poterit, cum mens eius Deum videbit sicuti est. . . . Essentia huius finalis beatitudinis est visio Dei, per quam imagines Dei, nos inquam ipsi, ad perfectum statum perfectamque similitudinem cum exemplari nostro divino perveniemus. . . . Tu vero, anima, capax a Deo facta es illius doni quod est fons omnium donorum et quod cum Deo summo bono ita coniungit, ut ille in te maneat et tu in eo, luminosae videlicet et speciosissimae caritatis.[23]

(*De meritis operum*) he refutes the theory condemned by Pius V according to which eternal life is due to good works, 'ex eo quod sunt vera legis obedientia, non quia fiunt a persona elevata per gratiam ad statum filiorum Dei'; this leads him to emphasize, like Soto and the earlier writers, the transcendent character of this divine vision to which we are called : 'Visio Dei, in qua proprie vita aeterna consistit, res est non modo supernaturalis, sed usque adeo naturam omnem creatam excedit, ut nec agnosci, nec appeti, nec cogitari possit, nisi Deo revelante : *Oculus non vidit* . . .' (c. 12; vol. 6, 1873, pp. 366-8).

[21] *Opera*, ed. Vivès, vol. 9 (1876), col. 448.

[22] Gradus I, c. 4 : 'Forma igitur hominis substantialis, quae facit illum esse hominem, anima est immortalis, ratione et libero arbitrio praedita, imago Dei, ad exemplar summae divinitatis expressa. . . . Homo igitur imago Dei est . . . ratione spiritus . . .' (*Opera,* vol. 8, col. 242).

[23] *Opera*, vol. 8, col. 244-5; cf. col. 252.

In what was most personal in his ideas regarding the last end, Bellarmine remained, then, faithful to Augustinianism. The distinction that he had been obliged to make occurred only at the level of abstract theory; it did not destroy for him the unity of the spiritual being and it did not affect its movement at the deepest level. Perhaps this is why the Augustinian Henri de Noris, who might have had more than one reason for not liking him, felt able to say this in his praise : 'Bellarminus, grande non Societatis tantum, sed Catholicae etiam Ecclesiae decus.'[24]

In this way we can trace the gradual constitution of the new theory. With Francis Suarez (1548-1617) it took a gigantic new step forward. In short, Suarez was to adopt the hypothesis sketched out by Driedo and Tapper and propounded by Bellarmine and John of Lens, to explain and interpret it according to the principles enunciated in Cajetan's commentaries. He developed a systematic account of it in *De ultimo fine hominis,* a work which he published in 1592, and in *De gratia* which appeared posthumously after 1619.[25] But these works repeat in substance teaching of a much earlier date. As a result it is not always easy to make out which authors of the same period have undergone the influence of Suarez, what others have possibly influenced him and what others, lastly, by a similar process, have arrived at the same result. All these details, however, are hardly to our purpose. It will be

[24] *Vindiciae augustinianae* (1673), p. 28. Fr Le Bachelet has not published the Louvain lectures on the *Summa* from which the *Sententiae Baii refutatae* are taken. He has followed Bellarmine's own advice who stated that they were 'rather imperfect, incomplete and unworthy to be published' (16 April 1617); all the essential material is to be found in the *Controversies.* (Cf. Le Bachelet, *Auctarium Bellarminianum,* p. 11.) Fr A. Arenas Silva, who was able to consult the manuscript, used these lectures in the chapter on Bellarmine in his thesis *Gratuidad e Immanencia de la Visión Beatífica en los Teólogos Jesuitas* . . . (1963), pp. 40-60, to which the reader is referred.

[25] Suarez was born in 1548, became a Jesuit in 1564, theological student at Salamanca from 1566 to 1570 (where among his masters were the Dominican John Mancio and the Augustinian John of Guevara); he taught philosophy at Segovia (1571-4), then theology at Valladolid and elsewhere (1574-80), at the Roman College (1580-5), at Alcala (1585-93), at Salamanca (1593-7), and finally at Coimbra (1597 onwards) where he died in 1617.

sufficient for us to elucidate, both from Suarez and his contemporaries, the principal features of the new system. For it was to spread at that time with extraordinary speed.

Suarez, at least, had no illusions about its antiquity. He regarded it, as his language bears witness, as the result more of personal inference than of assertions handed down.[26] He strained his ingenuity to discover proof of it in St Thomas by the use of interpretative exegesis, but only to find himself bound to declare modestly: 'Assertio, ut opinor, communis est theologorum, licet eam magis supponant quam disputent.' He himself in an endeavour to repair the gap has recourse to a form of argument that appears to be philosophical rather than theological; in it there is usually no question either of the gratuitousness of the supernatural to be safeguarded, or of any document of the magisterium to be complied with. This is certainly significant.

Suarez starts from the idea that man, being a natural being, must normally have an end within the limits of his nature, since according to a principle of Aristotle all natural beings must have an end proportionate to them. 'Necesse est omnem naturalem substantiam habere aliquem finem ultimum connaturalem in quem tendat.' The end of a natural being is always in strict proportion to its means. For Suarez this is an absolute principle, and its application to the case of man is no less absolute, no less undeniable. By virtue of his creation man is therefore made for an essentially natural beatitude. If we suppose that in fact he is called to some higher end, strictly speaking this could only be superadded. The first, by right, was sufficient; alone therefore it remains naturally knowable and alone it can come to a definition of man. If it is objected there is a desire for this higher beatitude, Suarez, before even examining the objection, answers that it is impossible, because, still according to Aristotle, the natural appetite follows the natural power: 'cum appetitus naturalis non

[26] *De ultimo fine hominis,* disputatio XV, sectio 2: to understand our natural condition it is necessary 'praescindere omnia quae supra naturam sunt; quod non solum per intellectum fieri potuit, sed re ipsa potuit fieri a Deo: *quod mihi fere tam certum est,* quam est certum omnia haec supernaturalia bona esse mere gratuita' (*Opera,* Vivès, vol. 4, p. 146).

fundetur nisi in naturali potestate'.[27] It is therefore contradictory
to envisage an end which would be, according to the maxim
adopted by Soto, Bellarmine and Toletus, 'naturalis quoad appe-
titionem, supernaturalis vero quoad assecutionem'.[28] Long before
Fr Garrigou-Lagrange, Suarez decisively rejects this venerable
maxim—although, unlike him, he was unable to attribute the
parentage of this teaching to the Augustinians of the eighteenth
century.[29] As one of his first disciples, Philippe Gamaches of the
Sorbonne, explained it, the natural appetite, which is identical
with nature itself, belongs to the purely natural order: it is
therefore impossible for it to have any bearing on what is supernatural.[30] There is no similar appetite, expect for a form that
is due to nature, an end that nature can attain, either by its own
powers alone or at least with the help of causes of the same order.
'It is quite clear', therefore, that the theory of Suarez excludes
the traditional 'natural desire'.[31]

This was also the view of Vasquez,[32] the rival of Suarez on so
many other matters. It was soon to be the view of Lessius, who
taught theology at Louvain from 1585 to 1601 and emerged as

[27] *De gratia,* prolegom. IV, c. 1, *passim*; and c. 20 again: 'Appetitus autem
naturalis sequitur ex potentia naturali.' Cf. Albert the Great, explaining
Aristotle, *I Ethic.,* tract. III, c. 6: 'Ad haec . . . non est difficile respondere,
supposito hoc scilicet, quod nihil appetitur ab aliquo naturali appetitu et
ordinato, nisi possible obtineri, et quod proportionatum est principiis
naturalibus, quibus appetitus nititur obtinere illud.'
[28] Soto, *De natura et gratia,* bk 1, c. 4; *In Sent.* bk 4, d. 49. qu. 2, art. 1.
Bellarmine, *De gratia primi hominis,* bk 1, c. 7 (vol. 5, p. 191). Toletus, *In
Primam Partem,* qu. 1, art. 1: 'Deus igitur est potentia finis naturalis, at
actus et operationis est finis supernaturalis' (1869, vol. 1, p. 20).
[29] *Angelicum,* 1931, p. 142, note. Cf. Eudes Rigaud, *Quaestiones disputatae
de gratia,* qu. 21 (Auer, p. 223).
[30] *Summa theologica* (Paris 1627), vol. 2, pp. 56-7: 'Nullus est appetitus
naturalis proprie dictus, nec innatus nec elicitus, in homine ad visionem
beatam. Probatur imprimis de naturali innato. Siquidem innatus appetitus
est idem reipsa cum natura appetente, nec nisi sola ratione vel modaliter ab
ea distinguitur; ergo est ordinis pure naturalis; ergo impossibile ut feratur
per se ad aliquid supernaturale, nam . . . modus agendi sequitur modum
essendi; e contrario vero, visio est omnino supernaturalis.'
[31] Blaise Romeyer, for whom this signifies 'rational progress' over the
ideas of St Thomas: *Archives de philosophie,* 18, pp. 50-1.
[32] *In Primam Secundae,* disputatio XXII, c. 2 and 3 (vol. 1, Compluti,
1599, pp. 214-19).

the determined opponent of the Baianist doctrine.[33] It was only in 1615 that Lessius published his favourite work, *De summo bono et aeterna beatitudine hominis,* a book of great spiritual worth. It is interesting to compare it with Bellarmine's *De ascensione mentis,* which was produced in the same year by the same publisher (Plantin of Antwerp); Bellarmine was already decisively outdistanced; the new theory had already gained considerable credit :

> Sicut datur aliqua beatitudo supernaturalis, quam per gratiam Dei consequi possumus, ita etiam statuenda est quaedam beatitudo naturalis quam viribus naturae possimus adipisci. Confirmatur, quia cuilibet rei intra limites naturae respondet sua completa beatitudo, cuius naturaliter est capax, ad quam viribus naturae potest pervenire; alioquin numquam posset intra limites naturae perfici. . . .[34]

This too was the view of the Dominicans John of St Thomas[35] and Peter of Godoy,[36] and it was shared by the Carmelites of Salamanca in their famous *Cursus theologicus,* publication of which began in 1631,[37] the Louvain theologian John Wiggers,[38] the Jesuits Pedro de Arrubal,[39] Antonio Perez,[40] Martinez,[41]

[33] Cf. Lessius to Bellarmine, 29 May and 25 September, 1587, in Le Bachelet, *Bellarmin avant son cardinalat,* pp. 147-53 and 169-72.
[34] *De summo Bono et aeterna beatitudine hominis libri quattuor,* bk 1, c. 9, n. 61: 'Hinc apud doctores illa distinctio beatitudinis et ultimi finis in naturalem et supernaturalem; et duplex illa consideratio Dei, quatenus finis naturalis et supernaturalis hominis. Quae distinctiones etiam locum habent respectu Angelorum' (ed. Hurter, 1869, p. 68).
[35] *Cursus theologicus,* disputatio XII, art. 3, n. 8 (Solesmes ed., vol. 2, p. 141). 1st ed., Alcala, 1637.
[36] Petrus de Godoy, O.P., episcopus Oxonensis, *Opera theologica in divum Thomam,* Disputationes in Primam Partem, vol. 1 (Venice ed., 1686; the approbation is dated 1669), pp. 129-30.
[37] Vol. 5, p. 375 (the publication of this Cursus was spread out over the years from 1631 to 1701; the *De beatitudine* and the *De fine ultimo,* 1644, are by Fr Dominic of St Teresa; the *De Gratia,* 1676, is by Fr John of the Annunciation).
[38] *In Primam Secundae D. Thomae* (2nd ed., Louvain, 1634): 'Naturali appetitus innatus non potest dici aliud esse, quam potentia naturaliter capax alicuius perfectionis aut boni, quod naturae seu naturalis agentis viribus ei potest obtingere . . .' (p. 68).   [39] *In Primam Partem* (1630), pp. 83-8.
[40] *In Primam Partem opus posthumum* (Rome, 1656), pp. 37-42.
[41] *Disputationes theologicae,* vol. 2 (1663), p. 81.

Arriaga,[42] Dominic Viva,[43] J. Navarro,[44] and many others besides. In no other context is Bossuet's dictum more applicable: '. . . Suarez, in whom we can be sure to hear all the others.'[45] Here for example is what is said by 'illustrissimus Godoy',[46] as Noris calls him : 'Appetitus naturalis innatus, solum terminatur ad formam debitam naturae; sed forma supernaturaliter assequibilis non debetur naturae; ergo nequit appetitum innatum terminare'; and again : 'Inclinatio et propensio naturae solum potest terminari ad perfectionem propriis viribus assequibilem.' For Martinez, 'appetitus innatus naturalis non est nisi ad ea quorum potentia est capax per se sola, vel adiuta a concausis naturalis ordinis.' Arriaga is well aware both that St Thomas was of the contrary opinion and that the evidence is against St Thomas. Navarro repeats in a sentence which had become stereotyped since the time of Cajetan : 'Si creatura rationalis secundum se considerata habeat appetitum absolutum innatum beatitudinis . . . , haberet media et instrumenta sufficientia ad acquirendam beatitudinem.' Turned over and over in all its senses, the argument was to be repeated ad nauseam down to our own times without the principle on which it is based ever being submitted to a serious examination. 'Diversimode solet suaderi', wrote Godoy; but we can hardly regard as very original or at all deep the proof of the Jesuit Herice which he reproduces : 'Appetitus naturalis innatus ab obedientiali decet differre. At nullum aliud discrimen inter illos potest constitui, nisi quod naturalis ad formam naturaliter

---

[42] *Disputationes theologicae in Primam Partem,* vol. 1, De Visione Dei, disp. IV, sectio I; disp. VI, sectio 4 (Antwerp 1643, 2nd ed., 1677; pp. 65-6 and 91).

[43] d. 1710. *Cursus theologicus,* pars prima (Padua, 1755): 'Appetitus naturalis non fertur ad terminum naturaliter inassequibilem; sed visio Dei nequit naturae viribus obtineri. . . . Ergo natura non inclinat ad Deum videndum' (p. 29). Pars secunda : 'Implicat dari inclinationem et appetitum naturalem ad actum quoad substantiam supernaturalem. . . . Maior probatur : quia inclinatio naturalis ad terminum naturaliter inassequibilem repugnat' (page 59), etc.

[44] *Cursus theologicus,* vol. 2 (Madrid, 1766), pp. 150-1.

[45] *Instruction sur les états d'oraison* (2nd treatise, c. 71 (ed. Levesque, 1897, p. 185).

[46] *Vindiciae augustinianae,* 1673, p. 131.

assequibilem terminatur, obedientialis vero terminatur ad formam naturae vires superexcedentem.'[47]

It would be wearisome to prolong this list. It may merely be said that the argument, or rather the statement of the principle, is to be found in recent times, unchanged in the writings of Ambroise Gardeil,[48] Garrigou-Lagrange,[49] Joseph de Tonquédec,[50] Blaise Romeyer[51] and Charles Boyer.[52] For the last-named it is a question of a principle 'which forces itself on the mind', just as for Arriaga it was a 'ratio evidens'. It is the same for Fr Pedro Descoqs. 'A desire is natural,' he asserted, 'to the extent that the end to which it aspires is proportionate to nature.'[53] And as Fr de Broglie, whom he had thus thought to refute, refused to endorse this 'false evidence', he replied that 'in scholastic language as universally received, natural desire meant the desire of an object required by an essence as its necessary and legitimate *end*, and was therefore a desire of requirement'; and moreover that this is 'a truth of mere common sense and perfectly

[47] Godoy, *loc. cit.*, p. 130.

[48] 'Le désir naturel de voir Dieu' in *Revue Thomiste,* 1926, pp. 385-6. *La structure de l'âme et l'expérience mystique,* 2nd ed. (1927), vol. 1, p. 282.

[49] 'Le désir naturel du bonheur prouve-t-il l'existence de Dieu?' in *Angelicum,* June 1931, p. 142, note.

[50] *Deux études sur 'la Pensée'* . . . (1936), p. 149 : 'a desire of nature is, essentially, proportionate to the nature. . . .'

[51] 'La théorie suarézienne d'un état de nature pure' in *Archives de philosophie,* vol. 28, pp. 38-9.

[52] 'Nature pure et surnaturel . . .' in *Gregorianum,* 28 (1947), pp. 390-1. On the ground of the evidence Arriaga was frankly critical of St Thomas. On the ground of reason Fr Boyer thought that it was useless to rely on him. Among the witnesses of a slightly earlier period can be quoted Palmieri, S.J., *Tractatus de ordine supernaturali* (2nd ed., 1910), p. 155 : 'Porro quod appetitu innato naturaliter appetitur, dicendum est esse naturae appetentis proportionatum : iste enim appetitus non est nisi ordo quidam necessarius naturae ad certum finem; qui ordo in ipsa natura rationem sui habet; sed hoc existente ordine nequit non esse proportionatum naturae in quod ipsa appetitu innato appetit. . . . Ut recte argumentatur Suarez.' (If supernatural means are necessary to attain the end) 'supernaturalis quoque et nulli appetitui innato respondens dicenda est eadem visio. Non cohaerent sibi videlicet partes huius systematis, et abusus fit verborum.'

[53] *Le mystère de notre élévation surnaturel* (1938), p. 120.

safe to hold', a principle 'derived immediately from the principle of sufficient reason'.[54]

Furthermore, neither Suarez nor the whole army of those who follow him in the assertion of this principle mean to reject from human nature absolutely all 'desire to see God'. This would mean dismissing too obviously a long-standing unanimous tradition. It is merely that the desire which they still admit differs entirely from that of tradition. It could only be a question, they explain, of a purely elicited and conditioned desire, of a certain imperfect desire like some vague willingness. It is a 'velleity', a 'wish' such as arises spontaneously in the mind in connection with all sorts of impossible things which, moreover, are not of essential interest. It is a desire that cannot produce a real uneasiness in relation to its object which, in the natural state, and on the supposition that it can be known, would be acknowledged as a mere vain imagination.[55] If the earlier theologians, they go on to say, appear to teach the contrary, it is only because they use still imprecise and less adequate language.[56]

The question of 'pure nature' which is connected by Suarez with that of natural desire is thus solved, as he says himself, *a priori*. He is not its inventor; we know this from what is said above, and we shall shortly see it in further detail. Nor was it his rival Vasquez, nor Molina who explained the system in 1592 in

---

[54] 'Autour du mystère de notre élévation surnaturel' in *NRT*, 1939, pp. 415-17.

[55] Suarez, *De ultimo fine hominis,* disputatio XVI, sectio 3, n. 7: 'Stando in pura natura, licet homo conciperet aliquale desiderium conditionatum illius visionis, si prudenter se gereret, non esset inquietus, sed esset sua naturali sorte contentus, sicut etiam posset homo illo modo appetere intelligere sine discursu, qui tamen appetitus nec sollicitaret, nec inquietaret animam, quia cognosceret esse de re valde aliena ab humana natura. . . .' 'Appetitum naturalem imperfectum et simplicis cuiusdam complacentiae.' Suarez adds: 'De hoc actu optime intelliguntur loca D. Thomae, quia hic affectus esse potest circa impossibilia . . . , potest in pura natura . . .' (vol. 4, p. 156). It will be noticed that among other things St Thomas insisted on the 'inquietudo'; Suarez, denying it, thinks that he understands St Thomas perfectly. The latter said: 'Nullus tendit in id quod apprehendit ut impossibile' (*De Malo,* qu. 16, art. 3); Suarez concludes that the desire of God does not constitute a real inclination.

[56] Thus Palmieri, *op. cit.,* pp. 71-2.

his commentary on the *Prima Pars,* and who already assumed it in his *Concordia* in 1588. These theologians only strengthen the hypothesis propounded by Bellarmine by basing it on a principle which Bellarmine rejected, a fact which makes it, I consider, far less admissible. Actually, in doing so, not merely do they set up as a system a still modest and unassuming hypothesis, they transform it and falsify it. But they no more invented the principle than the hypothesis. The latter was recent, the former went back a century at least. The first author in whom we find it enunciated forcefully in its application to the soul is Denys the Carthusian.[57] With Denys, far more personal and modern than he is usually thought to be, it was probably the effect of his extensive philosophical reading in the library of his friend Cardinal Nicholas of Cusa.[58] Avicenna especially made a deep impression on him. He returns to the theory on several occasions in two of his works : *De puritate et felicitate animae* (between 1455 and 1465) and the *De lumine christianae theoriae* (c. 1450) which is the 'most important and most systematic' of his writings on dogma :

> Intellectus primae causae agnitionem naturaliter appetit, sed non nisi secundum quod propriae naturae virtus sustinet. . . .
>
> Quemadmodum creati intellectus natura limitata est, sic et intellectuale desiderium ad naturae, a qua fluit, analogiam coarctatum est. . . .
>
> Ostensum est . . . rationes non fore efficaces ad probandum naturali deductione, creatum intellectum in Dei visione felicitari vel etiam eam naturali desiderio appetere, cum

[57] Cf. A. Duval, O.P., *RSPT,* 1954, p. 525 (review of the book by Fr Juan Alfaro) : 'The writer finds no other predecessor to Cajetan than Denys the Carthusian.'

[58] Nicholas of Cusa had brought back from Constantinople in 1437 a fine collection of manuscripts of Greek and Arab authors. These are the philosophers that Denys himself says he has read : 'Plato, Proclus, Aristotle, Avicenna, Al-Gazali, Anaxagoras, Averroes, Alexander, Evempotis (Ibn-Badja), Theophrastus, Themistius and others besides' (*Protestatio ad superiorem*) ; among these others were : 'Alkindi, Albategni, Albumazar Alfragani, Avicebron (Ibn-Gebirol), Anavalpetras (Ibn-el-Bitrodji), Porphyry, Plotinus, Maimonides, Moses of Girone . . .' (Denys' other list). Cf. A. Mougel, *Denys le Chartreux* (1896), pp. 20-1.

naturale desiderium speciem rei sequatur et in id non tendat, in quod naturaliter pertingere nequit. . . .

Naturale desiderium ultra naturalem capacitatem se extendere nequit. . . .

Naturale desiderium in naturalem finem tendit. . . .

Naturalis beatitudinis naturali desiderio . . . cupidus est omnis intellectus. . . .[59]

Padua is some distance from the banks of the Moselle or the Rhine, but the reading of these same philosophers could produce the same effect there. It is unknown whether Cajetan knew the passages just quoted. In any case he had no need to know them any more than he had need to know the *Liber propugnatorius*. But for both him and Denys, the fundamental source is the same : it was the philosophers who applied to man the cosmological principles laid down by Aristotle in his *De caelo*. The three following passages will enable us to judge. The first is by Denys :

Naturale desiderium non se extendit ultra capacitatem naturalem. Naturale enim desiderium secundum ordinem rerum naturalem frustra non potest consistere, cum Deus et natura nihil frustra faciant, secundum Aristotelem, in de Caelo et Mundo. Si igitur naturale desiderium creati intellectus non sistat neque quiescat donec Deum per essentiam contempletur, sequitur quod secundum ordinem rerum naturalem deberetur et corresponderet creato intellectui visio Dei per essentiam : quod falsum est.[60]

The two others are by Cajetan :

Non videtur verum, quod intellectus creatus naturaliter desideret videre Deum : quoniam natura non largitur inclinationem ad aliquid, ad quod tota vis naturae perducere nequit; cuius signum est, quod organa natura dedit cuilibet potentiae quam intus in anima posuit. Et in 2° Caeli dicitur, quod

---

[59] *De lumine Christianae theoriae*, bk 1, art. 51 and 56 (*Opera omnia*, vol. 33, pp. 394-454). *De puritate et felicitate animae,* art. 55, 56, 58 (vol. 45, pp. 431 and 432).

[60] *De lumine Christianae theoriae*, bk 2, art. 56 (*loc. cit.,* p. 454).

si astra haberent vim progressivam, natura dedisset eis organa opportuna. Implicare igitur videtur quod natura det desiderium visionis divinae et quod non possit dare requisita ad visionem illam, puta lumen gloriae. . . .[61]

Certe scimus hanc maiorem, quod nulla naturalis potentia est frustra. Ergo, si scimus hanc minorem, quod in materia vel anima vel quacumque alia re est naturalis potentia ad actum supernaturalem, oportet concedere quod scimus supernaturalia illa debere esse; et sic sciemus resurrectionem mortuorum futuram, et gratiam iustificantem impium, . . . ; quod est ridiculum.[62]

Conrad Koellin (1476-1536) had propounded the same principle as Cajetan.[63] Also Chrysostom Javelli, who professed himself a faithful Thomist against the Scotist Trombetta :

Vanum est arbitrari aliquid naturaliter ordinari in aliquem finem (without the natural means of attaining it.). Unde dicit Philosophus in 2° Caeli : si astra essent mobilia motu progressivo, natura dedisset eis organa ad talem motum. . . . Ex his igitur videtur quod non insit nobis naturale desiderium videndi divinam essentiam. . . .[64]

Similarly there is Francis Silvester (Ferrariensis : 1474-1528), 'the contemporary, rival, admirer and, on occasion, the determined but cautious scorner of Cajetan'.[65] On the point concern-

---

[61] *In Primam*, qu. 12, art. 1. 'Primum dubium (In Leonine ed. of St Thomas' *Opera omnia*, vol. 4, p. 116). Here again it is apparently a matter of refuting Scotus. The passage quoted is the 'dubium'; but the 'solution' did not call the principle in question. Cf. *In Primam Secundae*, qu. 3, art. 8, etc. It is a great pity that Cajetan's commentary on the *Sentences*, which still exists in manuscript, has never found a publisher.

[62] *De potentia neutra*, qu. 2, ad 4, tertio (1496).

[63] *In Primam Secundae*, qu. 3, art. 8 (Venice, 1589, p. 41) (1511).

[64] *In Primum tractatum Primae Partis* (qu. 12, art. 1), fol. 21v. F. Javelli differs from St Thomas on the other points also : cf. N. Balthasar, 'Javellus comme exégète de saint Thomas dans la question de la relation finie' in *Philosophia perennis*, vol. 1, (1930), pp. 151-7.

[65] M. M. Gorce in *DTC*, vol. 14, col. 2086. The first edition of Silvester's commentary on the *Contra Gentiles* appeared posthumously in Paris in 1552.

ing us he begins by contradicting him. He blames him for wrongly interpreting St Thomas.[66] But doctrinally the disagreement is superficial. If we pay particular attention to the main point of the doctrine and the final result, we shall chiefly discover in Silvester the rival of Cajetan, Javelli and Koellin. As these three colleagues had annexed the *Summa* for the new principle, he took over the *Contra Gentiles*. As the matter was by no means obvious, he applied himself to it in a dissertation which he joined to the exegesis of a chapter which, like his colleagues, he wrote 'against the position of Scotus'.[67] He too declared : 'Natura secundum se non habet inclinationem, nisi infra naturae limites', without seeming to realize any more than the others the dangers lurking under this 'secundum se'. He too went in awe of the 'Philosophers' who led him astray; their authority for him was too great for him to dare to understand human nature differently from them. He felt obliged to fashion his language on theirs : 'Potentia tendit ad finem qui naturae proportionatur . . . atque in quem propriis viribus naturae potest pervenire : *sic enim dicitur aliquid naturale apud Philosophos*; nisi abuti vocabulis voluerimus.'[68] How far we are from St Thomas, who, alluding to these same 'Philosophers' and on the same subject, wrote : (In quo satis

[66] *In Contra Gentiles,* bk 3, c. 51, n. 111 (Leonine edition, vol. 14, p. 141A) : 'Respondent quidam (i.e. Cajetan) . . . ; sed hoc non videtur ad mentem sancti Thomae.'

[67] Sestili ed., vol. 1 (1897), pp. 39-41 : 'Si Deus esset finis naturalis, id est, in quem natura inclinat, sed supernaturaliter acquirendus, sequeretur quod natura inclinaret suum subiectum ad aliquid quod esset impossibile ut produceret. Hoc autem in omnibus naturis videtur falsum et etiam repugnat rationi. Tunc enim naturalis appetitus esset frustra in natura, quia nullo modo posset per naturam adimpleri. . . . Est inconveniens quod aliquid appetatur naturali appetitu qui est sola naturae inclinatio, et tamen homo ad illud non possit aliqua virtute naturali pervenire, quia natura secundum se non habet inclinationem, nisi infra naturae limites' (following commentary on bk 1, c. 5; Leonine ed., vol. 13, p. 16).

[68] *In Contra Gentiles,* c. 5, n. 5, para. 4. Compare this with Denys the Carthusian, *De lumine christianae theoriae,* bk 2, art. 56 : 'purum philosophum', 'a philosophante discuti habent', 'a naturali philosopho non queat ostendi' (*Opera*, vol. 33, p. 454); and *De puritate et felicitate animae,* art. 56 : 'secundum philosophos', 'certissima ratione naturalique demonstratione ac philosophica investigatione', 'naturalis philosophica investigatio' (vol. 40, p. 431).

apparet) quantam angustiam patiebantur hinc inde eorum prae-clara ingenia.'[69]

Yet Silvester admits a certain desire, although only elicited and tending to God 'in the common order of beatitude'.[70] In this way he is able to persuade himself that he is not contradicting St Thomas, as he blamed Cajetan for doing. It was this which prompted Fr Rondet to write: 'The dissociation begun by Cajetan is as it were checked by Silvester's explanations. He remains more clearly within the medieval perspective of a sole order. He distinguishes between God known as the first cause and God known as the last end; he does not distinguish between two possible ends.'[71] But, as a matter of fact, his position was much the same as Cajetan's. And Fr Rondet also points out that 'Cajetan probably did not speak of pure nature quite so clearly as is imagined'.[72] New ideas are almost always older in origin than is thought, though their final form is often more recent than a rapid survey seems to reveal. Those who lay the foundations do not yet perceive the consequences which will later appear to be more proximate and obvious. At the beginning of the sixteenth century the complete system of pure nature, therefore, had prob-

---

[69] *Contra Gentiles,* bk 3, c. 48.

[70] *In Contra Gentiles,* bk 3, c. 51, n. 4, 2 (pp. 141-2): 'Si autem secundo modo (i.e., pro actu elicito voluntatis) naturalis appetitus accipiatur, sic non est inconveniens quod appetitus in aliquid naturaliter feratur in quod virtute propriae naturae non potest intellectualis creatura pervenire. . . . Unde sanctus Thomas . . . ait quod, "quamvis homo naturaliter in finem ultimum inclinetur", scilicet sub ratione communi beatitudinis. . . .'

[71] 'Le problème de la nature pure et la théologie du XVIe siècle, *RSR,* 35 (1948), p. 496.

[72] *Loc. cit.,* p. 493. He was particularly anxious to know (and this was for some time in the forefront of the argument) whether or not the possibility of the beatific vision can be demonstrated by reason. He answered in the nega-tive (as in the question of the immortality of the soul). And not to have St Thomas against him, he makes a point of showing that St Thomas was speaking as a theologian and was arguing not with philosophers but with theologians. He wrote, for example, *In Primam,* qu. 12, art. 1, n. 4: 'Adverte hic quod haec opinio (intellectum creatum non posse videre Dei essentiam), iudicio meo, non est Avicennae aut philosophorum (quoniam saltem prima Intelligentia creata cognoscit quid est Deus, apud Avicennam quoniam ipse est illius proximum principium); sed haec opinio fuit aliquorum Christiano-rum, ut puto. Et ideo contra eam ex his quae fidei sunt disputat, ut patebit.'

ably not yet emerged; but the 'divorce' which it was to sanction had already begun.

'When Cajetan rejected all natural desire,' writes Fr Duval, 'he carries to the extreme limit a point of view shared by all those who before him upheld the possibility of such a desire, namely, that this desire could not be efficacious.'[73] I would agree, if it is understood that 'carry to the extreme limit' is a euphemism meaning 'contradict'. Henceforward there was a Thomist trend, there was a Thomist school to maintain, in opposition to St Thomas, that 'rational nature is an enclosed whole in which active tendencies and capacities rigorously correspond'.[74] There was a Thomist school to propagate this new principle from which the new system was to emerge. In his commentary on the *Prima Secundae,* published at Salamanca in 1577, Bartholomew of Medina (1528-80) restates the principle with the same reference to the *De caelo* :

Caelum non est in potentia naturali ad calorem, quoniam per agens naturale non potest ad actum reduci; sed in natura non est agens naturale ad visionem Dei; ergo non est potentia naturalis. . . . Et dicit Aristoteles in 2° *De Coalo*. . . .[75]

Seven years later, in 1584 in his commentary on the *Prima,* which also appeared at Salamanca, Dominic Báñez (1528-1604)

---

[73] A. Duval, O.P., in *RSPT,* 1954, p. 525. For the same author Cajetan's originality is 'rather to have developed what was said before his time more or less implicitly, and to have asserted as universally possible a state envisaged by the earlier theologians concerning the fate of children dying without baptism' (*ibid.*). Actually, that is one of the more easily discernible antecedents of Cajetan's theory. But the theory itself is perhaps not quite so explicit. It is one thing to assert a certain state, in our concrete universe, for beings who have been unable to attain to their human maturity; it is quite another to affirm a possible universe where this state would be the normal state of humanity. This, it seems to me, constitutes, not a passing from the lesser to the greater, but a real change.

[74] *Ibid.*

[75] *In Primam Secundae,* qu. 3, art. 8 (Venice ed., 1590, p. 46); cf. *ibid.,* propr. 2a : 'Illa sententia, quae asserit nos inclinari ad Deum videndum pondere naturae, sine cognitione et appetitu elicito, falsa est et improbabilis. Imprimis est aperte contra doctrinam sancti Thomae, qui locis adductis manifeste loquitur de desiderio procedente ex effectuum cognitione.'

adopts both the principle and the reference. 'Ut patet inductive', he states.[76] The Dominican Thomist school therefore was in advance of the theologians of the new Society of Jesus. It was only in 1588 that Molina's *Concordia* was to appear. At the time when Báñez published his commentary, Suarez, it is true, already enjoyed a certain reputation, but Báñez was hardly inclined to take him for his master; and the *De fine ultimo* of Suarez only appeared in 1592. Marcelli, the Augustinian, greatly exaggerates when he appears to attribute to the *Loiolitae Theologi* the entire paternity of the new system which is rejected by his own school.[77] But it may well be thought that no one did more to spread it than Suarez.

Whoever was first in the field, the principal argument—actually the only one, for it is always this which recurs in forms that scarcely vary—at the basis of this new system would certainly have astonished, not to mention Scotus, St Augustine and St Thomas himself. For does not the whole of Augustinianism, in the widest sense of the term and therefore including the whole of ancient tradition, consist in emphasizing the essential difference that there is on this question between the beings of nature, and the soul which is open to the infinite? Following Cajetan, Medina, Báñez, Suarez and Vasquez,[78] a whole crowd of theologians were to quote as unanswerable Aristotle's remark in the second book of *De caelo*: 'Si natura dedisset caelis inclinationem ad motum progressivum, dedisset etiam instrumenta ad talem motum.' If in nature there is no agent capable of procuring the vision of God—

---

[76] *Scolastica commentaria in Primam partem,* qu. 12, art. 1 (Venice ed., 1587, col. 449). Cf. *In Primam Secundae,* qu. 3, art. 7 and 8 (*Commentarios ineditos,* ed. V. B. de Heredia, vol. 1, 1942, pp. 120-32).

[77] *Institutiones theologicae,* vol. 3 (Foligno, 1846), p. 344: 'Omnes ferme Loiolitae Theologi, quibus hac in re adhaeserunt etiam Thomistae praeclarissimi plures.'

[78] *In Primam Secundae,* disputatio 22, c. 3: 'Quoties est inclinatio naturalis ad aliquam formam, per quam potentia patiens perficitur, necesse est etiam instrumenta et principium efficiens naturale, quod possit potentiam coniungere cum illa forma, sive principium sit in eo quod perfici debet, sive in alio. . . . Si astra natura sua haberent propensionem ad motum progressivum. . . .'

and how could there be?—it is absurd, it is 'ridiculous' to suppose in it a desire for this vision. It is by virtue of the same argument, or by the same kind of 'induction', that the position was reached of maintaining that the natural perfection of the angels must make them unable to sin, since the most perfect of bodies, namely the heavenly bodies, are undeviating in their courses as they are incorruptible in their essence. But where Aristotle could see an analogy,[79] Christian philosophy saw principally a contrast. In its view the spirit, 'mens', was not subject to the same laws as the bodies, and the image of God could not be likened to unreasoning beings. In the classical distinction between the 'naturalia' and the 'divina', the soul counted among the 'divina' and had for long been studied within the framework of 'theology' and not in that of 'physics'. Such was the teaching of Boethius,[80] Cassiodorus,[81] handed down to the Middle Ages by Isidore of Seville,[82] and adopted by Hugh of St Victor in his *Didascalion*.[83] This teaching was merely the expression of one of the aspects of the anthropology of the Fathers of the Church. Although inserted in nature, man was nevertheless not simply a natural being.[84] By all that was best in him he dominated it. 'A great world within a small world', Origen and Gregory of Nazianzus had said paradoxically in order to define this paradoxical being.[85] For St Augustine, who

[79] Actually, rather than Aristotle, it was his commentators; less the 'Philosophus' than the 'Philosophi', on whom these theologians do not always provide us with much information. The celebrated passage of the *Nichomachean Ethics* in which Aristotle gives us a glimpse of a destiny for man 'surpassing man' is well known. But it is a passage in which it would be wrong to see, *simpliciter,* an anticipation of the Christian idea.

[80] *In Porphyrium dialogus,* I (*PL,* 64, 11 B-C); cf. *De Trinitate,* c. 11 (col. 1250).

[81] *De artibus* . . . , c. 3 (*PL,* 70, 1168D).

[82] *Etymologiae,* bk 2, c. 24, n. 13 (*PL,* 82, 142B).

[83] *Eruditio didascalica,* bk 2, c. 3 (*PL,* 176, 752-3). *Ysagoge in Theologiam* (ed. Landgraf, pp. 63-4).

[84] For the contrast between mind and nature: St Gregory of Nyssa, *On the Creation of Man* (French trans. by Jean Laplace, *SC,* 6, 1944, pp. 131-2 and 150).

[85] Origen, *In Leviticum,* hom. V, n. 2 (ed. Baehrens, p. 449). Gregory, *Orations,* 38, c. 11 (*P.G.,* 36, 321-4); Andrew of Crete (*PG,* 97, 1069B). Cf. Bossuet, *Sermon on the annunciation,* 1662 (*Œuvres oratoires,* vol. 4, 1921, p. 295).

divided the whole of creation into heaven and earth, following the first verse of Genesis: 'In principio fecit Deus caelum et terram', every spiritual creature—the human soul as well as the angels—was included in the 'caelum' and shared in its unity.[86]

This mystical view, expressed in language that was sometimes excessively Platonic, was nevertheless not entirely inherited from Platonism. It had taken shape in a doctrine of the created spirit, which itself was not, as had been asserted somewhat too airily, without metaphysical implications. After the patristic period it had dominated the whole of the Middle Ages.[87] It was unable to hold its own in its entirety when, with the advent of autonomous philosophical speculation, the rational and inductive method was introduced into anthropology. For at that point the primary interest turned to the soul, not as it appeared to itself in the processes of the spiritual life or as it could know itself reflected in the glass of scripture, but as it appeared objectively to 'scientific' observation. Yet this new doctrine and this new viewpoint did not result in the abandonment of the essentials of the old doctrine. With St Thomas as with St Bonaventure and all the great Scholastics, the human soul always remained the 'image of God'. St Thomas, especially, rediscovered by philosophy many of the affirmations of mystical thought. Although he was the enemy of a paradox when it was merely witticism, he never failed to recognize it in the very nature of things and so to speak in the stuff of being. Thus, as the worthy heir of St Augustine he declared: 'Creatura rationalis in hoc praeeminet omni craeturae, quod capax est summi boni per divinam visionem et fruitionem, licet ad hoc indigeat auxilio divino gratiae.'[88] And again: 'Eo ipso quod facta est ad imaginem Dei, capax est Dei per gratiam, ut Augustinus dicit.'[89] And also:

---

[86] *De Genesi ad litteram,* bk 1, c. 1-4 (*PL,* 34, 247-50).
[87] Cf. Hugh of St Victor, *De sacramentis,* bk 1, pars 6, c. 1 (*PL,* 176, 263-4); *De sacramentis legis naturalis et scriptae* (col. 22).
[88] *De malo,* qu. 1, c. 5. Cf. *Contra Gentiles,* bk 3, c. 147.
[89] *Prima Secundae,* qu. 113, art. 10.

Sicut homo suam primam perfectionem, scilicet animam, acquirit ex actione Dei, ita et ultimam suam perfectionem, quae est perfecta hominis felicitas, immediate habet a Deo, et in ipso quiescit; quod quidem ex hoc patet, quod naturale hominis desiderium in nullo alio quietari potest, nisi in solo Deo. . . . Oportet igitur quod, sicut prima perfectio hominis, quae est anima rationalis, excedit facultatem materiae corporalis, ita ultima perfectio ad quam homo potest pervenire, quae est beatitudo vitae aeternae, excedat facultatem totius humanae naturae.[90]

And again: 'Est enim creatura rationalis capax illius beatae cognitionis, inquantum est ad imaginem Dei.'[91] Also: 'Ultimus finis creaturae rationalis facultatem naturae ipsius excedit.'[92] And also: 'Finis propter quem est rationalis creatura, est videre Deum per essentiam. . . . Homo factus est ad videndum Deum: ad hoc enim fecit Deus rationalem creaturam, ut similitudinis suae particeps esset, quae in eius visione consistit.'[93] And there are many other passages besides. They explain one another fairly clearly and so discourage the efforts often made to deaden their effect.

St Thomas, it should be noticed, was well aware of the principle which, starting with Cajetan, was to enjoy a brilliant career in modern Scholasticism. In certain sections it even happened that he made use of it; he did so to establish the necessity of the infused virtue of charity, which causes us to love God as he should be loved. In other words, he knew perfectly well that our 'natural desire' by itself is by no means efficacious, and that in no way is it enough to lead us to our end; in short he did not confuse

---

[90] *De virtutibus in communi,* art. 10.

[91] *Tertia,* qu. 9, art. 2; and ad 3m: 'Visio beata est quodammodo supra naturam animae rationalis, in quantum scilicet ad eam propria virtute pervenire non potest; alio modo est secundum naturam ipsius, in quantum scilicet secundum naturam suam est capax eius, prout est ad imaginem Dei facta.'

[92] *Compendium Theologiae,* c. 144.

[93] *De Veritate,* qu. 8, art. 3, obi. 12 (principle assumed in the answer) and qu. 18, art. 1.

effective desire with efficient desire.[94] He had recourse to it again
—fundamentally in the same sense—in the case of an objective
desire, due to a love of friendship.[95] But he did not turn it into
a universal principle. He refused to apply it mechanically to the
case of the created spirit in its relation with its last end. If it was
quoted to him in this context, he rejected the deceptive analogy
as unworthy : 'Creaturae irrationales non ordinantur ad altiorem
finem quam sit finis qui est proportionatus naturali virtuti ipsarum.
Et ideo non est similis ratio'.[96] To spare his interpreters any suspicion of incoherence on the matter, he took care to distinguish
the two meanings in which the word 'natural' can be used :

> Aliquod dicitur naturale dupliciter : uno modo, cuius
> principium sufficiens habetur ex quo de necessitate illud
> consequitur, nisi aliquid impediat. . . . Alio modo dicitur
> aliquid alicui naturale, quia habet naturalem inclinationem
> in illud, quamvis in se non habeat sufficiens illius principium
> ex quo necessario consequitur.[97]

But he did not add, nor does he say anwhere else, that this second
kind of natural inclination is only a sort of 'velleity'.

Having thus established the full Augustinian principle, St
Thomas then endeavoured to discover a kind of peripatetic
orthodoxy, by appealing to some other principles of the Philosopher, such as : 'What we are able to do by our friends is as if
we could do it by ourselves.'[98] Or the other maxim : 'It is better
to be able to do more with external help than to be able to do

---

[94] *De Spe,* qu. 1, art. 8; *Prima Secundae,* qu. 62, art. 3; *De virtutibus in
communi,* art. 10, etc.
[95] *In III Sent.,* dist. 27, qu. 2, art. 2 ('Utrum caritas sit virtus') ad 4m :
'Desiderium autem naturale non potest esse nisi rei quae naturaliter haberi
potest.'
[96] *Prima Secundae,* qu. 91, art. 4, ad 3m.
[97] *De Veritate,* qu. 24, art. 10, ad 1m.
[98] *Prima Secundae,* qu. 109, art. 4, ad 2m : 'Illud quod possumus cum
auxilio divino, non est nobis omnino impossibile, secundum illud Philosophi
in 3 Ethic., quae per amicos possumus, aliqualiter per nos possumus.' This
was in answer to those who objected that man cannot accomplish all the
precepts of the natural law. Cf. Capreolus, *In II Sent.,* dist. 28, qu. 1, art.
3 (*Defensiones,* vol. 4, col. 304B).

less by ourselves',[99] and he adduced health as an example.[100] He thus set aside the objections of those who did not understand the nobility of the spirit. He brought the sublime exception back within the common rule: the case of the spirit became a simple one of species, and logical appearances were not in danger. It is an innocent artifice and too obvious to deceive anyone. Further, the two principles invoked were scarcely comparable with the axioms of metaphysics, for God was not a friend like any other nor is his grace a mere external help. Explanations of this kind, however, are typical of St Thomas, who can still find the means to quote Aristotle at the very moment when he deviates from his teaching, and who appears always to apply a general law by means of ingenious comparisons. Remarkably enough, he succeeds, without sacrificing the cogency of his thought or the clarity of its expression. His conciliatory frame of mind involves no doctrinal concession.[101]

His concern to be accommodating to some extent—and here we should see guilelessness rather than cunning—did not cause St Thomas to yield on the fundamental principle. We can see it in a passage of the *De veritate* which still invokes Aristotle but no longer appeals to his familiar comparisons:

Dicendum quod, sicut dicit Philosophus in 2° Caeli et Mundi, in rebus invenitur multiplex gradus perfectionis. . . . Creaturae igitur irrationales, nullo modo ad perfectam bonitatem, quae est beatitudo, pertingere possunt; sed pertingunt

[99] *De Malo,* qu. 5, art. 1: 'Multo enim melius est quod est capax magni boni, quamvis ad illud obtinendum indigeat multis auxiliis, quam illud quo non est capax nisi parvi boni, quod tamen absque exteriori auxilio vel cum pauco auxilio consequi potest; sicut melius dispositum dicimus esse corpus alicuius hominis si possit consequi perfectam sanitatem, licet multis auxiliis medicinae, quam si possit consequi solum sanitatem quandam imperfectam, absque auxilio medicinae.'
[100] *Prima Secundae,* qu. 5, art. 5, ad 2m: 'Nobilioris conditionis est natura, quae potest consequi perfectum bonum, licet indigeat exteriori auxilio ad hoc consequendum, quam natura quae non potest consequi perfectum.'
[101] For an analogous example see *Prima Secundae,* qu. 111, art. 1, in connection with Denys' hierarchical principle. Cf. Étienne Gilson's perceptive remarks in his *L'esprit de la philosophie médiévale,* vol. 1, p. 244; Eng. trans. *The Spirit of Medieval Philosophy* (1936), p. 218.

ad aliquam bonitatem imperfectam, quae est eorum finis naturalis, quam ex vi naturae suae consequuntur. Sed creaturae rationalis possunt consequi perfectam bonitatem, id est, beatitudinem. Tamen, ad consequendum indigent pluribus quam naturae inferiores ad consequendos fines suos. Et ideo, quamvis sint nobiliores, non tamen sequitur quod ex propriis naturalibus possint attingere ad finem suum, sicut naturae inferiores. Quod vero ad beatitudinem aliquis contingat per seipsum, solius Dei est.[102]

The inborn grandeur and wretchedness of the spiritual creature! It is wrong to see practically only a succession of sins in our concrete humanity; it is also wrong to ascribe a keen perception of it only to such thinkers as Augustine or Pascal. Unlike them, St Thomas does not explain to us in moving terms this inner contrariety of the spiritual creature, but he examines it as a metaphysician. He 'greatly esteems this theme and often returns to it'.[103] he is fond of showing in 'intellectual nature', beneath an apparent opposition which at first sight is repugnant to 'common sense' and causes the same objection to recur again and again, the close union of dependence and nobility. For him, since this 'intellectual nature' is not a 'creatura naturalis', a 'res naturalis', a 'forma materialis' or an 'ens naturale',[104] it cannot be merely that 'animal of a higher species', which, following the Greeks, Taine was to mention.[105] In it he discerned the activity of an 'appetitus superior'.[106] Beyond the 'dynamism of natural forms' he pointed to a 'dynamism belonging to the spirit': 'a deeper dynamism, which not only aims at the completeness of an essence

---

[102] *De Veritate*, qu. 8, art. 3, ad 12m. The objection was 'Natura non deficit in necessariis. Sed attingere finem, maxime est de necessariis naturae. Ergo unicuique naturae provisum est ut possit pertingere ad finem suum. Sed finis propter quem est rationalis creatura, est videre Deum per essentiam. Ergo rationalis creatura ex naturalibus puris potest ad hanc visionem pervenire.'

[103] Henri Rondet, in *RSR*, 1946, p. 72, n. 3 (and references).

[104] *Prima Secundae*, qu. 110, art. 2. *Secunda Secundae*, qu. 2, art. 3. *De Veritate*, qu. 3, art. 2. *In II Sent.*, dist. 25, qu. 1, art. 1, etc.

[105] *Philosophie de l'art*, vol. 2 (5th ed., 1890), p. 185.

[106] *Der Veritate*, qu. 25, art. 1.

and the manifestation of its powers, but also tends to make up for the lack of the essence with regard to the totality of the being'.[107] Without failing to acknowledge its nature, he could recognize in the human spirit something else than a totality closed in upon itself or upon this world;[108] something else than a special kind of being seeking the way of perfection in accordance with its degree, its order, its natural dignity in the scheme of things;[109] something else than a determined and determinate essence pursuing its stability, development and propagation : an impulse, a 'desire' by which man is led at least to understand that 'it is no longer a question of fulfilling nature, but of transcending it'.[110] And so he could see no contradiction in saying in so many words in his commentary on Boethius on the Trinity : 'Quamvis homo naturaliter inclinetur in finem ultimum, non tamen potest naturaliter illum consequi, sed solum per gratiam.' For he could clearly see the reason for it : 'et hoc est propter eminentiam illius finis'.[111]

'The highest glory of man is to be predisposed to an end which exceeds his own power.'[112] A modern Thomist thus faithfully summarizes the teaching of his master. It may be wondered, then, by what mistaken point of view another Thomist could talk in this connection of a 'so-called Christian conception' belonging to 'the prehistory of Catholic theology' to which 'Thomist teaching' is in opposition.[113] I know of only one 'prehistory of Catholic theology', that which preceded the coming of our Saviour. As for the conception just mentioned, it is both 'Christian' and 'Thomist', and if St Thomas had taught another he would have placed him-

---

[107] Joseph de Finance, Être et agir dans la philosophie de saint Thomas, pp. 339-40.

[108] See Le Mystère de Surnaturel (1965), chapter six : English trans. The Mystery of the Supernatural (1967), pp. 131ff.

[109] It was restricted to this by Denys the Carthusian, De puritate et felicitate animae, art. 55 : 'Naturale, ergo, intellectualis substantiae desiderium in eam intellectus perfectionem proficiscitur, quae ei secundum propriae speciei naturalem dignitatem, gradum, ordinem atque capacitatem competit' (Opera, vol. 40, p. 431).

[110] J. de Finance, loc. cit.

[111] In Boetium de Trinitate, in fine (qu. 6, art. 4, ad 15m). Cf. the other texts quoted above.

[112] J. de Finance, op. cit., p. 341.

[113] A. Gardeil, in Revue Thomiste, 1926, pp. 384-90.

self outside the great traditional stream.[114] But this is not the case. Thomist doctrine is authentically Christian.

In the sixteenth century Silvester Ferrariensis cavilled at the text, which is clear enough, of the *In Boetium,* in order to destroy its effect.[115] He did not want St Thomas to have thought as he did, because in his view Duns Scotus would have been in agreement with him. 'Videtur Sanctus Thomas sentire cum Scoto.' This dispute was not the whole of the matter but it played its part. Nowadays there is a strong tendency to denounce concordant interpretations in the history of theology—and it is right to do so. On the other hand, who can tell the damage done by the concern to set schools in opposition? Scotus, like St Thomas, made a distinction for the mind between an 'obiectum inclinationis' and an 'obiectum attingentiae'.[116] Like St Thomas, too, he declared, perhaps in more striking terms, but with equal conviction, the fundamental inequality existing between the end of the spiritual creature and the natural means at its disposal to attain to it; this he saw as the characteristic mark of its dignity : 'non vilificatur, sed dignificatur'.[117] All the Scotists repeated it : 'quo maior creatura, eo amplius eget Deo'.[118] All admitted in man and angel the same dignity as images of God, and as a consequence assigned

[114] Among the witnesses of a former age there is, for example, Pseudo-Hugh, *Miscellanae,* bk 1, tit. 7 : *De dignitate et libertate rationalis creaturae*: 'Sola rationalis creatura ita condita est, ut ipsa bonum suum non esset, sed ille a quo facta est. Magna ergo dignitas, ut nullum ei bonum praeter summum sufficeret, et item magna libertas, ut ad bonum suum cogi non possit' (*PL,* 177, 482-3).

[115] *In Contra Gentiles,* bk 3, c. 51, n. 4, 2 (Leonine ed., vol. 14, col. 141-2). Cf. bk 1, c. 5 (Sestili, vol. 1, pp. 39-40).

[116] Cf. Ephrem Longpré, *La philosophie du Bienheureux Duns Scot* (1924), pp. 184-6.

[117] Cf. *In IV Sent.,* d. 49, qu. 2, art. 24: 'Quicumque alius appetitus appetit extrinsecum propter naturam cuius est; ideo non coniungit simpliciter appetibiliori quam sit esse naturae cuius est. Voluntas autem amat aliquid nobilius se, et plus quam naturam illius cuius est; ideo coniungit appetibiliori et in se et sibi quam sit natura cuius est.' See also *In I Sent.,* dist. 4, qu. 1, art. 3 : 'Voluntas inclinatur ad omne ens sicut ad per se obiecta; ergo non quietatur in aliquo uno ente nisi illud includat omnia entia quantum possunt includi in aliquo uno; possunt autem tantum perfectissime includi in uno ente infinito; ergo potentia potest tantum quietari in summo.'

[118] This is a principle which is continually recalled in the Scotist tradition; see, for example, B. Mastruis de Medulla, *In I Sent.,* disput. 6, qu. 2 (Venice, 1675, p. 383).

to them the same end. The Thomists, for their part, did not differ on this fundamental point. It will suffice to quote here two great figures in the Franciscan tradition, Peter Olivi and Raymund Lull. This is how the first puts it :

> Non solum secundum finem sed etiam secundum rectam rationem constat quod omnis natura rationalis est per essentiam talis quod proprius et ultimus finis eius non potest per naturam creatam acquiri, sed solum per agens supernaturale; nec potest esse in aliqua forma mere naturali, immo oportet quod sit in forma virtuali et gratifica et modo ineffabili unita et uniente cum supernaturalissimo Deo. . . . Unde et quando naturaliter appetit summam beatitudinem, secundum rem appetit illam quae est supernaturalis, quia in nulla alia potest salvari ratio summae beatitudinis, nec ratio summi boni.[119]

The second is no less clear with his mixture of dialectic and geometrical imagination :

> Et quando natura fuit creata, in illo instanti creato in quo creata fuit, incepit tendere per medium concreatum ad suum finem secundum cursum naturalem. Et hoc fecit per suum actum naturalem sibi coessentialem, qui est de sua essentia, ut non sit otiosa, et quod suus appetitus sit de sua essentia; sed per suum actum, suum finem ultimum attingere non potest, quoniam finis attingitur per supremam naturam, quae dat naturae naturatae principium et esse. . . . Idcirco sequitur circulus et triangulus, inquantum principium et finis nostrae naturae se invicem respiciunt et sibi invicem correspondent supra cursum naturalem, et nostra natura est in medio illorum duorum terminorum supradictorum secundum cursum naturalem. . . .[120]

---

[119] *In II Sent.*, qu. 56 (ed. Jansen, Quaracchi, 1924, pp. 300-1). None the less, he says at the same time : 'Et tamen haereticum esset et erroneum, dicere quin omnis natura rationalis ex sua essentia et natura exigat talem perfectionem et finem, unde et pro tanto est ei naturalis.'

[120] *Declaratio per modum dialogi edita,* c. 17 (ed. Otto Keicher, *Beiträge* . . . , vol. 7, f. 4-5, Münster, 1909, pp. 121-2). Cf. c. 19 (pp. 123-4) and c. 135 (p. 189).

In the middle of the sixteenth century Soto, as we saw, remained faithful to the common tradition, anxious as he was to combine in his teaching the leading ideas which St Thomas and Scotus had also held. These ideas, it must be repeated, were specifically neither Thomist nor Scotist, but Christian. In answer to the objection which had just appeared insuperable to Silvester Ferrariensis and to Cajetan, and which was soon to appear so to Medina, and then to Báñez and Suarez, he wrote:

Facile respondetur, magis exinde effulgere celsitudinem humanae naturae, quod, cum nulla possit esse natura creata, quae ulla sit proportione ad assequendum felicitatem illam quae exsuperat omnem sensum, nihilosecius angelica et humana, ad imaginem Dei conditae, illum haberent pro fine ultimo.[121]

In the following generation the two first Jesuit cardinals said the same. This principle, said Bellarmine, is no novelty, and far from stating anything unworthy of human nature, it really exalts its peculiar dignity.[122] And Toletus on a more frankly Scotist note says: 'In hoc potius magnificatur homo, quod sit ad tam altam finem, ut Deo tanquam supernaturali agente indigeat ad ipsius consecutionem.'[123]

In the following century, even when the theory of pure nature was triumphant, there were several who on this point thought the same. Through their teaching the traditional idea of the dignity

[121] *De natura et gratia,* bk 1, c. 4.
[122] *De gratia primi hominis,* bk 1, c. 7 (*Opera omnia,* vol. 5, p. 191). See above, chapter six, pp. 170-1.
[123] *In Summam S. Thomae,* vol. 1, In Primam (1869), pp. 19-20. But not content to reproduce with St Thomas the principle taken from the third book of the *Ethics,* Toletus quieted the scruples of those who did not understand how a 'natural power' could be 'indigea et inops' with a reason which shows perhaps that the feeling which was formerly so acute of the opposition between the image of God and beings of lower nature had diminished: 'Non est novum hoc in natura: nam multis dat appetitum sufficientem, tamen actus cum adiutorio. Lapidi dedit gravitatem, sed non brachia quibus auferret impedimenta, quominus descendat in locum suum. Imo hominibus dedit voluntatem ad multa, et negavit vires ipsa per se exsequendi. Ita dedit homini appetitum naturalem videndi Deum, tamen actus cum auxilio alterius.'

of human nature was to remain in existence. Thus we find in Estius: 'Sane pertinere id videtur ad hominis dignitatem, quod finis eius ultimus tantae sit excellentiae, ut quamvis eum appetat naturaliter, ad eum tamen solis naturae viribus nequeat pertingere, sed opus sit ipsiusmet finis, id est Dei operatione supernaturali.'[124]

On the other hand Estius clearly admits that the Creator is by no means bound to grant to man supernatural beatitude. But when he refers to the idea of a natural beatitude he has it explicitly in view within the confines of earthly life. He raises the following objection: a man, left by God 'in puris naturalibus', ought to be able to attain to some form of natural beatitude as to his last end; but this is impossible: how could he live in happiness when he has always to fear the hour of death, with no hope of finding happiness in an after-life since his soul, separated from the body for which it longs and to which it cannot be reunited by its own powers, will always be imperfect and unsatisfied? To which he answers, not without implying that as a matter of fact he has nothing very satisfactory to put forward concerning this concept of natural beatitude: 'Videtur dicendum quod hominis beatitudo mere naturalis non potuisset esse perfecta, et proinde nihil esse absurdi, si coniunctas haberet cum certa expectatione mortis multas alias huius vitae miserias. . . .'[125]

The Servite, John Prudentius, in the wake of Bellarmine, Estius and Toletus, restates this important principle and makes a point of showing that it is the teaching of St Thomas. He sees in it the mark of unique excellence of the spiritual being, for it is the sign that it transcends the whole sphere of created activities or those which could be created:

> . . . excellentiam et dignitatem, qua rationalis natura caeteras irrationales antecellit, repositam esse in eo quod ita naturaliter assequantur finem quem naturaliter praeoptant, at rationalis, finem in quem naturaliter inhiat minime naturaliter lucratur. Ratio huius differentiae ex diversitate finium, ad

[124] *In II Sent.*, dist. 25, n. 4 (Paris, 1680, p. 262).
[125] *Ibid.*, dist. 19, n. 10 (pp. 173-4).

quos praedictae creaturae ordinantur, est poscenda. Equidem, finis ultimus irrationalium est perfecta operatio tendens in bonum aliquod particulare, quod essentialiter finitum et limitatum est, qua propter facultatem naturalem illarum minime superans. . . . (On the contrary, for the spiritual being) praescribitur operatio perfecta, tendens in bonum universale infinitum et aeternum, adeo eminens, ut totam sphaeram activitatum naturalium creatarum et craebilium longo intervallo superexcedat. . . .

Creatura vero rationalis, ob dignitatem qua prae caeteris pollet, tendit in finem altiorem, naturalem sphaeram suae activitatis excedentem, atque ideo propria naturali facultate inassequibilem, et solum per gratiam sui Creatoris comparabilem.[126]

Yet these reminders become increasingly rare among professional theologians. Even among the Scotists the principle was soon only maintained in a diminished sense. The mystics alone, because their teaching was not taken very seriously, were allowed to remember it.[127]

It will have been noticed that Suarez, no more than any of his predecessors, in his argument does not introduce any motive of doctrinal security. Yet actually it is for the purpose of being in a better position to establish the possibility of a natural end, other than the vision of God, that denies to nature any desire for the supernatural. If there were no natural beatitude, he explains, the supernatural end would be owed to man : this is an inadmissible conclusion, but how is it to be avoided? Of course there are those who deny this : 'quibus autem modis discursum factum subterfugerent, nec satis video, nec tempus est hic examinandi.'[128] It is

---

[126] *Opera theologica posthuma in Primam Partem* (Lyon, 1690), pp. 43-53.

[127] See, for example, the devotional books by Bérulle, the works of the Capuchin, François d'Argentan : *Grandeur de Dieu and Grandeur de Jésus-Christ.* See also the teaching, which is close to that of Bellarmine and Soto, in St Francis de Sales, *Traité de l'amour de Dieu,* bk 1, c. 16 (several English translations, the latest *The Love of God,* 1963). Bossuet criticized this teaching in his pastoral instruction given at Cambrai on 15 September 1697. Cf. below, pp. 270-2.

[128] *De ultimo fine hominis,* disput. XVI, sect. 2 (vol. 4, pp. 153-4).

a pity that Suarez, who did not usually take short cuts, did not
here take the time to explain for us both sides of the argument;
but at least his thought is clear. What it does show is how one
innovation leads to another. A second decisive step had been
taken on the way separating modern theology from the old. To
refute Baius, Bellarmine propounded, but still within narrow
limits, the possibility of a purely natural end. Suarez indeed went
further, very much further than Bellarmine who designated this
purely natural end only as 'alius finis naturalis', 'aliquis finis
inferior' and did not define it by a knowledge of God, but, and
on any hypothesis this point is of capital importance, continued to
see in the vision of God the intrinsic end and the perfection of
human nature, at the same time as the object of its desire.[129] He
goes further than Gregory of Valencia, who invoked against
Cajetan the authority of St Thomas and who at least, like Bellarmine, did not discard the Thomist terminology and acknowledged only one 'beatitude', strictly speaking.[130] As has plainly
appeared, he went further than Toletus who energetically maintained the teaching of his master Soto, showing that it was the
traditional teaching and that, whatever Cajetan might say, it was
held in common by the two great Scholastic leaders, Duns Scotus
and St Thomas. He goes further than Estius (died 1613), who
also, in declared opposition to Cajetan, thought it at least prob-
able that man tends by an innate natural desire to the vision of
God, this being the 'end' of every spiritual being, the 'natural
centre', outside which he is doomed to remain in a constant state

[129] Bellarmine, *De gratia primi hominis,* bk 1, c. 7: 'Tametsi summa illa
beatitudo sit finis hominis naturalis, tamen est finis improportionatus, et
praeter eum, habet homo alium finem naturalem sibi omnino proportionatum' (p. 191). *Sententiae Baii refutatae*: 'Poterat Deus creare ad finem
aliquem inferiorem, . . . hominem ordinare tanquam ad finem, ad cognitionem
earum rerum quae naturaliter cognosci possunt' (*Auctarium,* p. 315).
[130] Gregory of Valencia, *Commentaria theologica,* vol. 2 (3rd ed., 1603),
col. 98-9: 'beatitudinem sub ratione sua propria et particulari, nimirum, ut
est visio et fruitio Dei' (col. 100-1). Cf. Bellarmine, *De ascensione mentis in
Deum per scalas rerum creatarum,* gradus 1, c (Avignon, 1823, pp. 31-2).
Fr E. Elter, *De naturali hominis beatitudine ad mentem scholae antiquioris*
quotes in the same sense several other authors of the seventeenth century:
Becanus, Coninck, Pallavicini (*Gregorianum,* 1928, pp. 303-6).

of unrest.[131] Suarez goes further, in one sense, than even Molina, who at least openly conceded that the maxim 'finis naturalis quoad appetitum' still in his day was the expression not only of the Scotist theory, but the commonest opinion of the Scholastics.[132] Vasquez, who on this point shares the opinion of Báñez,[133] Molina and Suarez, makes no mystery of its novelty: he calls it 'opinio recentiorum';[134] yet far more than his great rival, like Bellarmine and Gregory of Valencia, he retains the idea of only one 'beatitude'. And Arriaga, for example, is perfectly well aware that in upholding the new opinion he is taking the opposite view to St Thomas.[135]

All theologians are not wholly committed to this 'opinio recentiorum' or, as A. Verrièle says, to this 'new systematiza-

---

[131] *In IV Sent.*, d. 49, n. 1 (Venice, vol. 4, 1680, p. 551). Estius produces three other arguments in favour of his theory. Like Soto and Toletus, he considers that it is the teaching not only of St Augustine, but of St Thomas and Duns Scotus as well: 'Sic enim sentiunt sanctus Thomas et Scotus in prologo I Sententiarum, ac rursum Scotus et Durandus in hanc distinctionem, et post eos Dominicus ibidem, refragante licet Caietano. Probatur autem ex Augustino. . . .' See also dist. 4, n. 1 (p. 36), etc.

[132] *Commentarius in Primam Partem,* qu. 12, art. 1, disput. 2: 'Communior Scolasticorum sententia asserit in nobis inesse appetitum naturalem ad beatitudinem in particulari, atque, ea de causa, illam dicendam esse finem nostrum naturalem, non quoad assecutionem ac simpliciter,—ea enim ratione omnes fatentur dicendum esse simpliciter finem nostrum supernaturalem—sed quoad appetitum et potentiam passivam' (Lyon, 1593, p. 98). In 1639 the Scotist A. Hickey, *In IV Sent. Scoti,* was to say once more of this thesis: 'Theologorum communior'. And Sylvius, *In Primam Partem,* qu. 95, art. 1, although he changed the emphasis: 'Quamvis . . . beatitudo consistens in clara Dei visione, possit quadam ratione dici finis naturalis hominis, nimirum quoad aliqualem appetitum seu desiderium; quoad assecutionem tamen, et simpliciter loquendo, est finis supernaturalis' (*Opera,* vol. 1, 1714, pp. 564-5).

[133] *In Primam Secundae,* disput. XII, c. 3, n. 11 and 12.

[134] *In Primam Secundae,* qu. 5, art. 8; disput. XXII: 'An insit creaturae rationali naturalis appetitus suae beatitudinis. C. 1: Quattuor sunt opiniones Scolasticorum. . . . Quarta est opinio Recentiorum, qui docent nullum esse appetitum naturalem ad beatitudinem in singulari, sed solum capacitatem et potentiam quam vocant obedientialem' (vol. 1, 1599, p. 214). In those days they did not mind labelling an opinion 'recentior' or propounding theses 'against St Thomas and many others' (Toletus, *In Primam,* qu. 23, art. 6; cf. Le Bachelet, *Prédestination et grâce efficace,* vol. 2, pp. 4-5).

[135] *Disputationes theologicae in Primam Partem,* vol. 1 (Antwerp, 1643), pp. 65 and 66: 'Argumentum quod videtur fuisse D. Thomae. Haec tamen ratio nullo modo convincit. Secundo probatur a D. Thoma. . . . Respondeo. . . .' This unabashed frankness was at least a sign of vitality.

tion'.[136] Certain defaulters have already been mentioned, like Prudentius and Macedo. And there are others like Didacus Ruys de Montoya (died 1632), Caesar Recupito (died 1647)[137] or John Baptist Rossi (died 1646), all three Jesuits, still holding in a more or less mitigated form, after the example of Toletus, Bellarmine and Estius the doctrine of natural desire. Rossi states clearly that he holds it 'contra Caietanum, Ferrariensem et aliquot alios Thomistas'. And above all there is the unanimous Scotist School whose leader in the seventeenth century was the brilliant controversialist John of Rada.[138] But objectors or not on the question of natural desire, all were to agree henceforward on the point of 'pure nature'. All, or almost all, were to come to an understanding to promote, or to assume as established, the idea of 'pure nature' in the sense that the term had just been given. In this, despite their numbers, they did not form a separate school : the new-style Thomists and Scotists were to speak about the subject exactly like Molinists or the followers of Suarez. 'There were even Thomists to be found,' the Jansenist Hugot remarked with some surprise, 'who in part accepted this system, although it was of no use to them, nor did they need it in defending and upholding the teaching of St Thomas.'[139] Indeed, at the end of the fifteenth century some such were to be found to prepare the way for it and in the sixteenth century to inaugurate it, and even before the publication of the *Augustinus* there were many to propagate it.

From the time of the Congregations *de Auxiliis* Thomists as a body were won over to the new theology. The author of the controversial *In Divi Thomae et eius scholae defensionem,* Navarrete, is one of those who went further still. With a certain malicious

[136] 'La doctrine de saint Thomas sur Dieu' in *Revue apologétique,* 1929, p. 428. Fr Elter, *loc. cit.,* has clearly shown that there was a conflict here between the old school and the new.

[137] *De Veritate,* VI, qu. 2.

[138] *Controversiae Theologicae inter sanctum Thomam et Scotum,* vol. I (Venice, 1614), controversia prima : 'An Deus clare visus sit finis naturalis hominis?' Also Hickey (1639) : cf. Doucet, *loc. cit.,* p. 196.

[139] *Instruction sur les vérités de la grâce et de la prédestination* (new ed., Avignon, 1752), p. 115. This question of 'pure nature' is, we know, one of the points on which the Jansenists were to declare that there was 'a great likeness between Pelagianism and Molinism' (*ibid.,* p. 111).

cunning he even turned against traditionalists like Soto the argument derived from the excellence of the spiritual being;[140] as a result he in his turn had to meet the objections and answers of St Thomas.[141] At the same time that great opponent of Molinism, the stormy Thomas de Lemos, in his *Panoplia gratiae,* came out as a staunch upholder of pure nature.[142] To cut short the objections of the Baianist party, he, like Bellarmine, conceded to this nature all the 'natural' helps desirable, thus reducing to some extent the scandal provoked in the Thomist camp by Molina's teaching, but only to cause other difficulties. These were to lead to further hypotheses : thus Godoy, after adducing a number of instances, put forward the hypothesis that in an order of pure nature God would not have been able to oblige man to love him.[143] The systematization, the complexity was to increase. But with the *de auxiliis* controversy, everything happened as if the two great rival schools, personified in some sort by the two great orders, had decided to form an alliance in this particular field, thus disposing, they thought, of the Baianist question, so that they could contend with greater ease on another field, with increas-

---

[140] *Controversia 33, De inclinatione hominis ad beatitudinem.* Navarrete thus sums up Soto's sixth argument : 'Quaelibet res mundi habet suum determinatum finem, in quem naturaliter tendit; ergo etiam homo; sed talis finis non est extra Deum.' To which he answers as follows : 'Respondeo quod in hoc manifestatur excellentia hominis super omnes alias res corporeas, quia in istis est iam secundum ordinem naturalem finis earum praefixus, homo tamen est ordinatus ex gratia Dei ad finem quem secundum se et ex viribus propriis non potest velle' (vol. 1, Vallisoleti, 1605, pp. 200-2).

[141] Cf. *Prima Secundae,* qu. 109, art. 5, ad 3m; but the content is now quite different.

[142] *Panoplia gratiae,* vol. 1, *Isagogicus* (1676), 2nd part, tract. 1, c. 4 : 'Si Deus crearet hominem in puris naturalibus ipsi naturae debitis absque ordine aliquo ad supernaturalem finem, cum solo ordine ad finem naturalem (quem posse ita Deum creare nec est vertendum in dubium). . . .' 'Quis enim neget posse Deum hominem illum, si ipsum conderet in ordine ad solum finem naturalem, auxiliis specialibus illius ordinis illi naturali fini proportionatis ita iuvare, ut illum naturalem finem consequi valeret?' (pp. 7 and 8).

[143] P. de Godoy, *Disputationes theologicae in Primam Secundae,* vol. 1, tract. 5, disput. 42, n. 3 (Venice, 1686, p. 324). The Molinists did not find the same difficulty here in admitting that man could without the help of any grace have 'aliqualem Dei amorem propter se'. Cf. Moranias, *Antijansenius* (1652, p. 201); but on the other hand they had to contend with tradition.

ingly was absorbing their attention and demanding their energies. This was the controversy on the mode of efficacy of grace and predestination.[144] At all events, it is pertinent to observe, as Fr Théodore de Régnon[145] has already pointed out, that consideration of the 'state of pure nature', a latecomer in the history of theology, was only acclimatized in the theological schools after Baius. 'We must not try to find this question before its time.'[146]

---

[144] Since then, most of the Thomists made considerable progress in this direction, especially after John of St Thomas, and among the theses on the *bonitas moralis* and on the *status purae naturae* which they wished to have condemned in Molina's works, there is more than one that they have become the first to defend. Cf. Serrey, *Historia Congregationum de auxiliis* (1740), p. 166; Portalié, in *DTC,* art. 'Augustinisme', vol. 1, col. 2554.

[145] *Études historiques sur la Trinité*, vol. 3, p. 373.

[146] F.-G. Desjardins, S.J., 'De l'ordre surnaturel' (extract from the *Revue des Sciences Écclésiastiques*, 1872, p. 31): 'What man would be, in a state of pure nature . . . is a question of importance, no doubt, but one which derived from Scholasticism. The arguments which it provoked were extremely useful in throwing light on the philosophical notions of nature and grace; but we must not try to find this question before its time.'

7

The Problem of Beatitude

The two preceding chapters will have been enough to show in part, at least, that the system known as 'pure nature', however simple the term may now appear, is complex in its origins, and that many different factors were necessary to give it birth. Thus, as so often happens in the history of ideas, it is to be explained by a series of imperceptible transformations rather than by conscious innovation.[1] It will not be without interest to examine, as it were under a microscope, the two principal transformations which gave the patent of nobility to 'pure nature', enabling it to be discovered in the ancient writers and especially in St Thomas.

The first concerns the problem of beatitude and of the last end; the second concerns the arguments about original justice. By these two indirect means of approach we can observe the introduction of the new system. In the first place the commentators on St Thomas were its principal vehicle, and then there were the explanations of the primitive state of man, explanations which had more connection with the commentaries on the *Sentences*. In both cases, the new system benefited also by certain ancient formulas, non-suspect because of their age, which were endowed with a new meaning.

St Thomas' commentators, while sincerely regarding him as an authority and wishing to be his faithful disciples, were yet prompted by certain preoccupations which were entirely unhistorical. They interpreted his thought with the mentality prevailing at their own times and in relation to the arguments in which they had to take part. It happened thus with the passages of the

[1] Although Denys the Carthusian, for example, as we have seen, was clearly conscious of being in opposition to St Thomas.

207

Summa and those from others works dealing with the questions of salvation, the last end and beatitude. The distinctions added, although unknown to St Thomas, were nevertheless framed in authentic Thomistic formulas.

St Thomas, speaking of human acts, produced the axiom that every agent acts with an end in view, and that this end must be in conformity with his nature; whence he concluded that the end of man, a rational creature, must be to act 'secundum rationem'. Recognizing that 'many infidels' acted according to reason by the practice of the moral virtues, he therefore acknowledged that they had realized the end of man; that end at least, he stated, 'that is not beyond the natural power of man', what he called 'finis ultimus in aliquo genere' to distinguish it from the 'finis naturalis' or the 'finis ultimus simpliciter'.[2] On the other hand, reading the 'Philosophers', he found quite different ideas on beatitude from those for which Christianity had given him the hope. Thus Avicenna spoke of the union of the soul with the Active Intelligence,[3] and despite the opposition that this doctrine encountered among Christians, it continued to consititute a certain danger.[4] In the ancient Greek writers St Thomas encountered the description of a perfect and blissful life to be found wholly within the city or at least in temporal life. Now in his 'wonderful good-will and kindness for the masters'[5] it was his constant method to cling to whatever was in some degree compatible with his own

[2] *Prima Secundae,* qu. 65, art. 2: 'Virtutes morales, prout sunt operativae boni in ordine ad finem qui non excedit facultatem naturalem hominis, possunt per opera humana acquiri; et sic acquisitae sine caritate esse possunt, sicut fuerunt in multis gentibus. Secundum autem quod sunt operativae boni in ordine ad ultimum finem supernaturalem. . . . Patet igitur ex dictis quod solae virtutes infusae sunt perfectae et simpliciter dicendae virtutes, qui bene ordinant hominem ad finem ultimum simpliciter; aliae vero virtutes, sc. acquisitae, sunt secundum quid virtutes, non autem simpliciter: ordinant enim hominem bene respectu finis ultimi in aliquo genere, non autem respectu finis ultimi simpliciter.'

[3] *De anima,* p.v. 5, c. 6 (fol. 26v.), etc.

[4] William of Auvergne, *De anima,* bk 2 (p. 112b). Cf. Gundissalinus, *De anima.* René de Vaux, O.P., *Notes et textes sur l'avicennisme latin,* pp. 78-80. A.-M. Goichon, *La philosophie d'Avicenne et son influence en Europe médiévale* (Paris, 1951).

[5] A. D. Sertillanges, *Dieu,* vol. 2, p. 350 (*Somme théologique,* edition de la Revue des Jeunes).

faith and he took great pains not so much to correct them when it seemed necessary as to explain and complete what they said.

That was his usual attitude to Aristotle, the 'Philosopher' in the highest sense of the term, an attitude that we find shared to a very great extent, at least during his first period, by St Bonaventure.[6] In extreme cases, when impeded by the text before him, St Thomas would go so far as to say, 'Aristoteles loquitur inquirendo', and we are then, as Fr Chenu observes, 'almost past the bounds of fidelity'; or else, he 'justifies the deficiencies of the Philosopher by his respect for the proper objectives and limitations peculiar to one discipline: the solution of the problems concerning the soul is no concern of the philosophy of nature'.[7] Whenever he can, even down to the use of words, he takes care to justify him and follow him.[8] We have already had an example of this above. So it is not surprising that very largely he accepts Aristotle's views on contemplation of the cosmos, the exercise of prudence and wisdom, or on the perfection of human nature. He is glad to find in him, thanks to a process of implicit transposition,

[6] Bonaventure, *In II Sent.*, dist. 19, art. 1, qu. 1, ad 3m: 'Ad illud quod obicitur de Philosopho, quod intellectus corrumpitur, etc., dicendum quod illum verbum pium debet habere intellectum.' Also *In Hexaemeron*, VII, 2-3: 'De aeternitate mundi excusari potest, quod intellexit hoc ut philosophus, loquens ut naturalis, sc. quod per naturam non potuit incipere. . . . Item quod posuit felicitatem in hac vita, quia forte non erat de consideratione sua.' Of course, speaking of ancient philosophers in general St Bonaventure adds: 'Sed adhuc isti in tenebris fuerunt, quia non habuerunt lumen fidei', but St Thomas did just the same. In *Magnanimité* (1951), p. 481, n. 1, Fr Gauthier gives, it seems to me, a somewhat forced commentary on this passage; Fr Gillon says with a greater show of reason, *Angelicum*, 1949, p. 138: 'kindly forbearance'. On the saint's courtesy and reverence for Aristotle, 'ille excellentior inter philosophos' (*II Sent.*, dist. 1, p. 1, art. 1, qu. 2), cf. Patrice Robert, O.F.M., 'Le problème de la philosophie bonaventurienne' in *Laval philosophique et théologique*, 1950, pp. 152-6. In the question *Utrum anima rationalis sit immortalis* (ed. Glorieux, 1950, pp. 72-3), Bonaventure goes so far as to maintain that the error of the mortality of the soul 'improbatur per sententiam Philosophi dicentis: intellectus separatur. . . .'

[7] *Introduction a l'ètude de saint Thomas d'Aquin* (1950), p. 180. Cf. Étienne Gilson, *L'esprit de la philosophie mediévale* (1932), vol. 1, p. 244. See above, pp. 193-4.

[8] Thus *Secunda Secundae*, qu. 123, art. 5: 'Utrum fortitudo proprie consistat circa pericula mortis quae sunt in bello' (cf. Aristotle, *3 Ethics*, VI, 10). St Thomas answers affirmatively to agree with Aristotle, for in this category all perils 'quae imminent in particulari impugnatione, quae communi nomine bellum dici potest . . .' can be included.

especially on the subject of the act of contemplation, 'such full agreement with the teaching of the saints and so rich a store of proofs for its service'.[9] Of course, this process is not entirely unconscious. He was well aware that there had been progress from the views of Aristotle to those of the 'saints';[10] nevertheless he could not make up his mind to declare that there had been a 'break'.[11] A kind of 'modesty' held him back. He would never agree to say, as very shortly Henry of Ghent was to do: 'Philosophus . . . circa ipsum finem vitae humanae in multis errabat.'[12] It was enough for him to explain that the Philosopher had in view only happiness in general, or that he was only speaking of that to be obtained in this life and by the principles of philosophy.[13] Aristotle, he believed, does not deny that there can be another happiness,[14] but he had not to mention it since that was not his object; in his *Ethics* there was no reason to deal with what concerns the state of another life.[15] Having made this point St Thomas could refer to a passage of the *Nicomachean Ethics* in

[9] R. A. Gauthier, O.P., 'Trois commentaires "averroïstes" . . .' in *Archives d'histoire littéraire et doctrinale du Moyen Age*, vol. 16, (1948), pp. 265-6.

[10] J. de Finance, S.J., *op. cit.*, p. 339, note 1: 'It seems to me that in St Thomas, here as elsewhere, there is a certain tension between the demands of his metaphysic (and I should add: and also of Christian tradition) and his respect for the Philosopher who, having apparently exhausted the resources of reason, was yet unable to discover the conditions of true beatitude. St Thomas is well aware of the progress which the Christian revelation has enabled reason to make, . . . but he experiences a sort of shame in outdoing Aristotle on his own ground.'

[11] R. A. Gauthier, *loc. cit.*, p. 252: 'We are launched at once right into Christianity, but far from Aristotle and his dream of a well-balanced man. . . . But it does not appear that St Thomas is aware of this great break arising from the very depths of his conscience as a Christian; in any case, he has after all pointed out the Philosopher's mistake, and rectified it without appearing to deal with it.'   [12] *Quodl.*, XII, qu. 13.

[13] *In Ethic.*, bk 1, lectio XV, 180: 'Est notandum quod Philosophus non loquitur hic de felicitate futurae vitae, sed de felicitate praesentis vitae.'

[14] *In IV Sent.* d. XLIX, art. 1, sol. 4: 'De hac felicitate (imperfecta) philosophus . . . determinat, aliam quae est post hanc vitam nec asserans, nec negans. . . .'

[15] *In Ethic.*, bk 1, lectio XVII, 212: 'Quaerere autem utrum homines post mortem aliqualiter vivant secundum animam, et utrum cognoscant ea quae his aguntur, aut ex his aliquo modo immutantur, non pertinet ad propositum, cum Philosophus hic agat de felicitate presentis vitae.' And bk 3, lectio XVIII, 590: 'Neque ad Philosophum pertinebat de his, quae ad statum alterius vitae pertinent, in praesenti opere loqui.'

connection with the promises of the Gospel[16] and maintain that there is no analogy more suitable to give a glimpse of eternal life than this description of earthly contemplation.[17] Was it not wonderful to be able thus to give a commentary on the Beatitudes, or the discourse after the Last Supper, or Jesus' words to Martha and Mary by the teaching of the ancient Philosophers 'who could not have had full knowledge of the final happiness'?[18]

All the same it was necessary on occasion to measure the gap between their teaching and Christian doctrine. St Thomas did so again in the same spirit, making use of a distinction which avoided his condemning anyone. He said that things are not to be considered in the same way and according to the same principles by the 'philosopher' and the 'faithful'. The philosopher considers man as he is in himself, according to his species, leaving out of account his last end, while Christian revelation teaches us what man is, what all things are in relation to God, their author and their end. On the one hand the immanent causes or internal principles of beings are studied, on the other, our eyes are fixed on the first and supreme cause. There follow from this two series of complementary, but not contradictory, truths.[19] Instead of one being set

[16] *Contra Gentiles*, bk 3, c. 25, *in fine*: 'Hinc est quod dicitur: "Beati mundo corde, quoniam ipse Deum videbunt" (Matt. 5:8) et: "Haec est vita aeterna, ut cognoscant te solum Deum verum" (John 18:3). Huic etiam sententiae Aristoteles (*Ethic.*, X, 10) concordat, ubi ultimam hominis felicitatem dicit esse speculativam quantum ad speculationem optimi speculabilis.'

[17] *Ibid.*, c. 63: 'Huius autem perfectae et ultimae felicitatis in hac vita nihil est adeo simile sicut vita contemplantium veritatem, secundum quod est possible in hac vita. Et ideo Philosophi, qui de illa felicitate ultima plenam notitiam habere non potuerunt, in contemplatione quae est possibilis in hac vita ultimam felicitatem hominis posuerunt (*Ethic.*, X, 8). The parallel with Martha and Mary follows.

[18] Cf. the more detailed analysis by Anton C. Pegis, 'St Thomas and the Nicomachean Ethics' in *Medieval Studies*, 25 (1963), pp. 1-25: St Thomas' attitude is that of a theologian 'who openly recreated the truth of the past in the light of revelation in order to save the present'.

[19] *Contra Gentiles*, bk 2, c. 4: 'Quod aliter considerat de creaturis philosophus, et aliter theologus.' This distinction is not peculiar to St Thomas. Cf. Gauthier of Bruges, *In I Sent.*, d. 18: 'Theologus considerat res ut a Deo sunt vel ut ordinantur ad ipsum. . . .' Gauthier distinguishes three points of view: those of the *logicus*, the *metaphysicus* and the *theologus*. See *Études d'histoire littéraire et doctrinale du XIII⁰ siècle*, II, p. 18 (E. Longpré).

against the other, both must be accepted, two ultimate goods, as we saw above.[20] The second, which consists in the vision of God, is 'perfect beatitude', 'true beatitude' or more simply 'beatitude'. St Thomas was careful never to apply the word 'beatitude' to that earthly and limited happiness, 'that happiness that dwells in man'. He was careful, too, to remind us that in the present state of life there cannot be perfect beatitude but only 'some participation in beatitude'.[21] Nor would he agree to use this fine term to designate the knowledge that the 'separated souls' could have, or the contemplation of the 'separated intellects' envisaged by the Arabian philosophers. The latter were at that time numbered among Thomas' principal opponents and so could not enjoy the same leniency as Aristotle; while he was interpreted and continued, the Arabs were openly opposed. But in both cases St Thomas always made a point of teaching that in the fullest sense of the term there is only one beatitude, that which is 'laid up for us in heaven', and it is the possibility of this one beatitude, attested by faith, which he endeavours to establish by philosophy.[22]

This teaching influenced, and is reflected in, the formulas of the three commentators whom we have already encountered. Thus Cajetan: 'Creatura rationalis potest dupliciter considerari: uno modo absolute, alio modo ut ordinata est ad felicitatem', and: 'Auctor tractat de homine ut theologus, cuius est considerare

[20] *De Veritate*, qu. 14, art. 2: 'Est autem duplex hominis bonum ultimum . . . ; quorum unum est proportionatum naturae humanae . . . , et haec est felicitas de qua philosphi locuti sunt: vel contemplativa, quae consistit in actu sapientiae; vel activa, quae consistit primo in actu prudentiae, et consequenter in actibus aliarum virutum moralium. Aliud est bonum hominis naturae humanae proportionem excedens. . . .' Cf. qu. 27, art. 2.

[21] *Prima Secundae*, qu. 3, art. 2, ad 4m; *In IV Sent.*, d. XLIX, qu. 1, art. 1, 2, etc. Cf. *Contra Gentiles*, bk 3, c. 48.

[22] *In IV Sent.*, d. XLIX, qu. 1, art. 1, sol. 4 (against Aristotle's position); *ibid.*, art. 2, etc. On the beatitude and supernatural end of human nature according to St Thomas, see Henri Bouillard, *Conversion et grâce chez saint Thomas d'Aquin*, pp. 77-80. Cf. R. A. Gauthier, *loc. cit.*, p. 263 (on supernatural beatitude): 'In addition to *beatitudo imperfecta*, which is the happiness of this life, it is the only beatitude of which St Thomas ever speaks.' Melchior de Saint-Marie, O.C.D., in *Ephemerides carmeliticae*, 2 (1948), p. 296: 'St Thomas knows but one last end for man: heavenly beatitude which consists in the intuitive vision and enjoyment of God.'

creaturas non secundum proprias naturas, sed ut ad Deum sunt relatae.'[23] There is the same explanation at greater length given by Javelli: 'Ipsa natura intellectualis alio modo consideratur a philosopho, alio modo a theologo: nam a philosopho consideratur ut est talis naturae, habet tales proprietates consequentes naturam, ut potest operari, et tantum operari ex principiis activis suis intrinsecis; a theologo consideratur ut creata est a Deo ad ipsum Deum, ut obiectum beatificum.'[24] Like the two others, Koellin at first faithfully follows his text when, commenting on the third question of the *Prima Secundae,* he makes the distinction between perfect and imperfect beatitude, or philosophical and theological beatitude, placing the first among the many 'operationes viaticae', but the second in the one 'operatio sempiterna patriae'.[25] Nor is there anything remarkable, at least from the Thomist point of view, in the similar assertion by Báñez: 'Homo, si tantum secundum perfectionem naturalem suae speciei consideretur, habet quidem finem determinatum a natura, scilicet rationalem vitam agere secundum legem naturae.'[26] So far, it is still St Thomas speaking through the mouth of his commentators. But immediately afterwards the interpolation begins, and once the thought of the latter is made explicit, it takes a different direction from that of the author they are explaining.

St Thomas said that man may be considered in his nature independently of his relationship with God. The commentators, after repeating his statement, explain that this man can be considered in his essential relationship with God, the author and end of nature. St Thomas, after distinguishing the two viewpoints of

---

[23] *In Primam,* qu. 12, art. 1 (In St Thomas, Venice ed., vol. 10, 1595, p. 38v). Cf. *In Primam Secundae,* qu. XII, art. 8.

[24] *In primum tractatum Primae Partis (op. cit.,* appendix, p. 21v).

[25] *In Primam Secundae,* qu. 3, art 2: 'Beatitudo imperfecta, quae est operatio circa Deum in via. . . . Operationes viaticae, et etiam in quibus consistit imperfecta beatitudo viae. . . . Beatitudo perfecta non est operatio viae, nec contingit hominem in via esse simpliciter beatum, sed ut hominem, ut habet Philosophus. . . . Ex quibus patet, quomodo philosophica quidem beatitudo non est perpetua, sed theologica.' Cf. art. 1 and 7, and qu. 2, art. 8; this is an objective commentary by St Thomas on the one beatitude (Venice, 1589).

[26] *In Primam Partem,* qu. 12, art. 1 (Venice, 1587, col. 453).

the philosopher and the theologian, not only because this distinction is valid in itself, but also, as we have already seen, to avoid placing Aristotle in formal contradiction with the Christian faith, applied himself to establishing a bridge between these two points of view by means of his doctrine of 'natural desire'. His interpreters, on the other hand, make a point of completing the break by confining philosophy for ever to the narrow point of view of the 'Philosopher', who knew nothing of creation. They will have nothing to do with 'natural desire', except that which springs from divine revelation and the contemplation of the effects of grace.[27] How marvellous, no longer to find any desire to see God in a being who at the outset has been purposely cut off from all relationship with God! But this initial abstraction was forgotten and only the consequence deriving from it retained. The earliest followers of St Thomas, when they did not use their master's cautious language, after explaining his teaching, stated: 'Alio modo iudicabant Philosophi de beatitudine, *sed male.*'[28] Now, following their example, this man of the philosophers is made real by hypothesis and becomes the man ordained by God for natural

[27] Thus Javelli, *loc. cit.*: 'Tota haec quaestio est mere theologica, et conatur B. Thomas procedere ex revelatis et acceptatis a fidelibus, etc. Considerato autem homine ut ordinatur in Deum ut in obiectum beatificum sicut sibi in Scriptura revelatum est, dicet Theologus quod naturaliter desiderat illam speculationem, quoniam, cum credat se esse creatum ad illum finem, nulla alia cognitio quam habeat de Deo quietat eum.' Or Cajetan, *loc. cit.*: If the rational creature is envisaged as ordered to happiness, 'sic naturaliter desiderat visionem Dei, quia ut sic, novit quosdam effectus, puta gratiae et gloriae, quorum causa est Deus ut Deus est in se absolute.' Or also Koellin, *In Primam Secundae*, qu. 3, art. 8: 'Nota pro fundamento dicendorum, quod homo dupliciter consideratur: uno modo praecise naturaliter; et sic naturaliter appetit beatitudinem secundum communem rationem, et sic etiam cognoscit effectus Dei naturales, qui dependent a Deo ut est prima causa modo naturali, et sic desiderat cognoscere Deum ut est causa prima universalis; quae cognitio, habetur per scientias physicas. Sed alio modo consideratur homo . . . , ut est ordinatus ad beatitudinem supernaturalem, inquantum ex revelatione divina intelligit aliquid de beatitudine supernaturali et ut ex revelatione divina cognoscit effectus Dei, qui sunt gratia et huiusmodi, ut est praedestinator ad beatitudinem supernaturalem: et hoc secundo modo, scilicet ex suppositione cognitionis talium effectuum, homo naturaliter appetit cognitionem Dei, ut est causa talium effectuum' (p. 41).

[28] Hugh Ripelin of Strasbourg, *Compendium Theologicae veritatis*, bk 7, c. 23 (Lyon, 1649, p. 548; under the name of Albert the Great).

beatitude—though this beatitude is, of course, conceived differently from theirs. 'Finis ultimus creaturae rationalis,' says Cajetan, 'ut sic, est Deus dupliciter : primo ut obiectum beatitudinis possibilis naturaliter, secundo ut obiectum beatitudinis revelatae.'[29] And also : 'Si non superadditus esset a Deo ordo ille supernaturalis, quaelibet intelligentia ultimum naturale absque peccato haberet pro beatitudine ultima : hoc enim modo philosophi posuerunt entia illa pro beata.'[30] For St Thomas, Aristotle's man was man 'absolute consideratus'; Cajetan repeats this, but interprets its thus : 'Philosophus . . . hominem bonum constituit in ordine ad finem naturalem.'[31]

We can now see the implications of Cajetan's statement that St Thomas envisaged the problem of beatitude 'ut Theologus'. In Cajetan's view that did not mean merely that St Thomas considered the last end with which the Philosophers were not concerned. It meant also that this last end which engaged St Thomas' attention was no longer the 'natural end' with which he had been concerned as a philosopher. The man whose beatitude was defined by St Thomas was therefore merely the man who by a kind of miracle had actually received a supernatural finality and who had complied with certain supernatural conditions. Studying this man, later to be termed 'historical', St Thomas, still according to Cajetan, reasoned only in accordance with revealed principles and always for the benefit of theologians who, like him, held these principles. For the better grounding of his interpretation, Cajetan was concerned to eliminate from his interpretation of St Thomas all consideration of philosophers like Avicenna.[32] Javelli did the

[29] In Primam Secundae, qu. 71, art. 6, n. 9.
[30] In Primam, qu. 63, art. 3, n. 13.
[31] In Secundam Secundae, qu. 23, art. 7, n. 1. Cf. In Primam Secundae, qu. 114, art. 1, n. 1 : 'non de homine adoptato in filium Dei, non de homine in statu peccati vel gratiae sed absolute; or qu. 3, art, 8, n. 1 : 'licet homini absolute non insit naturaliter huiusmodi desiderium'; or qu. 109, art. 2, n. 1 : 'de homine in puris naturalibus, quomodo consideratur a philosophis', etc.
[32] In Primam, qu. 12, art. 1, n. 4 : 'Adverte hic quod haec opinio (intellectum creatum non posse videre Dei essentiam), iudicio meo, non est Avicennae, aut philosophorum, quoniam saltem prima intelligentia creata cognoscit quid est Deus, apud Avicennam, quoniam est illius proximum principium; sed haec opinio fuit aliquorum Christianorum, ut puto. Et ideo contra eam ex his quae fidei sunt disputat, ut patebit.'

same, with equal lack of reason.[33] And Koellin repeated in the same sense the phrase which, he thought, explained everything: 'Loquitur (Thomas) ut Theologus.'[34] Macedo had no difficulty in refuting this theory.[35] Already in his commentary on the *Sentences,* St Thomas had compared, side by side, the views on this subject of 'certain philosophers' and 'certain theologians' and he quoted in particular 'Alpharabius'.[36] But if we could believe, as the three commentators assert, that St Thomas never envisaged in his argument any but 'certain Christians' who dared not believe in the beatific vision, the gradual change of emphasis effected by their commentary would be less perceptible.

But once this change of emphasis had been effected, the idea of a normal end, at once natural and transcendent, was raised. There was no longer any question, as Koellin observed above, of that imperfect happiness obtained by the 'operationes viaticae'. But the novelty of the idea is revealed by its difficulty in achieving a settled form, that is, by the hesitancy regarding the object of this new form of beatitude.

In the first place 'imperfect beatitude' could be conceived after the pattern of the beatitude devised by Avicenna and his imitators, that is, by contrasting it with 'perfect beatitude', like the knowledge of a created being in contrast with the knowledge of the uncreated being. Dominic of Flanders (d. 1481), a Thomist, did this:

> Duplex est felicitas seu beatitudo hominis. Quaedam est perfecta, et illa consistit in eo quod est perfectio intellectus

---

[33] *In Primam,* qu. 12, art. 1: 'Ergo B. Thomas, ut bene dicit Expositor, non intendit arguere contra Avicennam; neque enim Avicenna erat fidelis. . . .'

[34] *In Primam Secundae,* qu. 3, art. 8 (p. 41).

[35] Macedo, *Collationes* . . . , vol. 1, p. 20, refuted this thesis. He showed that St Thomas, especially in *Prima,* qu. 12, art. 1, had Avicenna in mind, although he did not name him (Av., 9 *Metaph.,* c. 5), as does also St Bonaventure in several corresponding passages, and as Scotus pointed out, *ibid.,* pp. 13-14, Macedo says that Cajetan's exegesis of the Thomist 'natural desire' has no foundation in the texts; in putting it forward Cajetan shows a certain shrewdness, but principally 'guile'.: 'Non ergo nego subtilem esse Caietanum, novi hominis acumen; sed illo tamen haud paulo subtilior est Scotus! Astutior fuit Caietanus' (p. 72).

[36] *In IV Sent.,* dist. 49, qu. 12, art. 1, solutio.

secundum essentiam et non secundum alicuius participationem. Cum ergo verum sit obiectum et perfectio intellectus, praedicta felicitas non consistit in cognitione *veri creati*, quia tale non est verum per essentiam, sed in cognitione *primi veri*, scilicet ipsius Dei. Et sic loquitur Doctor Sanctus de felicitate in Contra Gent. et in Prima Secundae. . . . Alia est felicitas imperfecta, et talis bene consistit in contemplatione *substantiarum separatarum*.[37]

This was the way followed principally by Denys the Carthusian who at least recognized that St Thomas, and Giles of Rome, had rejected it.[38] In accordance with the 'ordo hierarchiae'[39] Denys laid down that the 'separated soul' would be naturally satisfied, 'felix et quieta', by its contemplative union with the 'intelligentia imi ordinis' placed immediately above it.[40]

Secondly, this imperfect beatitude could be based on the case of children dying unbaptized being extended to the hypothetical case of good 'pagans' who were to enjoy in the next life a natural happiness inferior to supernatural beatitude; to obtain an idea of this happiness it was sufficient to extend to life beyond the tomb

[37] *In XII Libros Metaphys. Aristot.*, bk 1, qu. 2, art. 1 (quoted by J. Alfaro, *op. cit.*, p. 238). When Dominic wrote that the end of man consists 'essentialiter' in the vision of the divine essence (Dominic of Flanders, VI, qu. 5, art. 1), there is nothing there to our purpose, for he simply means to oppose the Scotist thesis which places beatitude 'essentialiter in operatione voluntatis'. Cf. Louis Mahieu, *Dominique de Flandre, sa métaphysique* (1942), pp. 325 and 355-6.
[38] Thus *De lumine christianae theoriae*, bk 1, art. 51 (*Opera omnia*, vol. 33, p. 293). Cf. St Thomas, *In IV Sent.*, dist. 49, qu. 2, art 1.
[39] Bk 2, art 65: 'Ordo namque hierarchiae est, ut superiores purgent, illuminent et perficiant inferiores' (p. 465).
[40] Bk 1, art. 47: 'Quoniam igitur rationalis anima in umbra ultimae intelligentiae creata est . . . , manifestum est quod per contemplationem intelligentiae imi ordinis ac unionem ad eius intellectuale lumen sit naturalis beatitudo separatae statuenda' (pp. 289-90). *De puritate et felicitate animae*, c. 16 and 58 (pp. 40, 406 and 433). Cf. the text *Homo cum in honore* (end of twelfth century), influenced by Arab neo-Platonism: 'Omnis beatitudo et felicitas animae rationalis est tantum a superioribus essentiis, et in existentia sua cum illis' (M.-Th. d'Alverny, *Archives d'hist. doctr. et litt. du moyen âge*, 13, p. 291). Cf. Martin Beer, *Dionysius der Kartäusers Lehre vom desiderium naturale des Menschen nach der Gottesschau* (Munich, 1933), who endeavours to prove that if Denys criticized St Thomas it was because he misunderstood him (pp. 117-18).

the contemplation described by the ancient philosophers. It was only necessary to make use of the passages in this sense to be found, not in St Thomas himself, who did not yet in such cases mention either 'natural end' or 'natural beatitude', but in a Thomist tradition which had grown up just after the first generation. Thus in Thomas of Strasbourg this occurs:

> Illi qui descendunt in peccato originali solo, non sunt frustra; quia, quamvis non consequantur finem supernaturalem, consequuntur tamen finem naturalem. Possunt enim habere evidentiorem contemplationem, quam quicumque philosophus umquam habere potuit in hac vita; quae quidem contemplatio est naturalis finis hominis virtuosi.[41]

And there is this in Peter de Palude (d. 1342):

> Beatitudo supernaturalis est perfectior realiter naturali. Alioquin manifeste vana facta est spes nostra et inanis fides nostra, si aeque realiter obtinent perfectam beatitudinem pagani vel saltem pueri non baptizati qui habent naturalem, sicut baptizati habent supernaturalem.—Item, naturalis comprehensibilis (est) et demonstrata a philosophis. Supernaturalis autem in cor hominis non ascendit.[42]

Lastly, there was the example once again of Denys the Carthusian who, starting with his denial of any natural desire of the vision of God, used the very form of St Thomas' argument to come to a different conclusion. There is in man, said Denys, a natural desire to know God by a knowledge that is natural but perfect in its own order. Now such knowledge is impossible here below. It must therefore be enjoyed in the other life, for a natural desire cannot be in vain:

[41] *In IV Sent.*, bk 2, dist. 33, qu. 1, art. 3, concl. 2, ad 1m (Alfaro, p. 382). It will be noticed that Thomas of Strasbourg is speaking of things which, according to him, are within our universe, and not of a possible and generalized hypothesis concerning another universe.

[42] *In IV Sent.*, d. 49, art. 3 (Alfaro, p. 275). For St Thomas, his predecessors and successors, cf. the clear but somewhat concordist thesis by B. Gaullier, *L'état des enfants morts sans baptême d'après saint Thomas d'Aquin* (1961).

Facile est ostendere quod in hac vita non sit animae naturalis beatitudo statuenda. . . . Ostensum est in nulla divinorum agnitione huic vitae possibili contentari seu sistere intellectuale desiderium. Ob hoc igitur non est in hac vita perfecta ac ultimata felicitas, quam omnis utique natura, virtus et species secundum propriae perfectionis subsistentiam desiderat. Neque inane est tale entis desiderium, neque potest humanus intellectus felicitate ea frustrari ad quam naturalem inclinationem habet. . . . Quemadmodum autem separatae animae status deiformior est atque liberior, sic prorsus eius operatio purior est atque desiderabilior. . . . Necesse itaque est ut in illius intelligibilis contemplatione consistat naturalis beatitudo animae separatae, per cuius unionem optime secundum naturae suae proprietatem vivit ac convenientius agit. . . .[43]

Yet Bellarmine showed a greater respect for tradition at the very time when the needs of controversy caused him to propound the new hypothesis; he only assigned to the inferior end, whose hypothesis he was putting forward, a contemplation of 'created things' or 'natural things'.[44] In this at least he was following very closely on St Thomas, who wrote for example in *De veritate*: 'Unde est ultima perfectio ad quam anima potest pervenire, secundum Philosophos, ut in ea describatur totus ordo universi et causarum eius; in quo etiam finem ultimum hominis posuerunt qui secundum nos erit in visione Dei.'[45] In his turn Báñez, after speaking first in genuinely Thomist language of the natural end, as was mentioned above, goes on, again like St Thomas: 'At in nulla operatione perfecte quiescit (homo) in hac vita'; but at once he adds, and this is not entirely Thomist: 'Si autem quaeras de fine naturali post hanc vitam, respondeo quod ad

[43] *De lumine christianae theoriae*, bk 1, art. 46-51. Cf. *De puritate et felicitate animae*, art. 58: 'Naturalis beatitudinis naturali desiderio . . . cupidus est omnis intellectus. . . . Naturaliter ergo loquendo illa Dei cognitio perfecta est . . .' (*Opera*, vol. 33, pp. 288-93 and vol. 40, p. 433). Cf. J. Alfaro, *op. cit.*, p. 293.
[44] Cf. above, chapter six, p. 173.
[45] *De veritate*, qu. 2, art. 2.

auctorem naturae pertinebat, ut animae immortali aliquod praemium esset paratum, quod certe consisteret in cognitione et contemplatione rerum naturalium, non autem in Deo clare viso; et tunc fateor animam non esse perfecte beatam.'[46] Báñez did not try to justify the new hypothesis by the passage in the *Summa* on which he was commenting. But especially with Báñez and Bellarmine, the fact that the evolution was still in progress is indicated by the twofold reservation and the timidity accompanying the new hypothesis : on the one hand, the definition of the transcendent natural end by contemplation, not of God, but of 'res naturales', and on the other, the admission that this contemplation does not fully satisfy the desire.[47] But such reservations were not to last for long. They were overwhelmed by the boldness of the new principle propounded by Denys the Carthusian and by Cajetan.

Yet despite this there was always to be a certain indecision. Some theologians confined themselves to cautious formulas. They would say, for example, with the Jesuit Jean Martinon (1586-1662; 'Antoine Moraines'), a faithful disciple of Suarez and a strong opponent of the Jansenists, that the natural end consists principally 'in adhaesione ad Deum per cognitionem et amorem

---

[46] *Loc. cit.*

[47] In his commentary on the *Prima Secundae*, qu. 3, art. 8, dubium, Báñez makes use of formulas on both points that are already less 'archaic' : 'Possumus assignare homini finem naturalem in quo naturaliter quiesceret, nec amplius ultra desideraret, videlicet, ut anima eius . . . frueretur contemplatione Dei secundum quod illa poterat haberi ex cognitione perfecta totius universi, maxime substantiarum separatarum a materia.' Báñez saw clearly the objection that could be raised by those who followed St Thomas. And so he added : 'Et si dicas, quod tunc excitabitur appetitus ad cognitionem Dei sicut in se est : respondetur, quod illud desiderium *suspenderetur*; quoniam esset inutile, et non secundum prudentiam; siquidem aperte iudicaret anima non esse possibilem huiusmodi cognitionem Dei.' It must be said that the answer is rather weak. The word *suspenderetur* will be noticed coming close to Toletus' 'impediretur desiderium' (*Lectiones ineditae in Primam Secundae*; cf. above, p. 159, note 169). But Toletus was concerned only with the case of infants; with Báñez it included the whole of humanity in the hypothesis of a natural end. With Toletus it was a question of a divine intervention and of an exceptional case; with Báñez it was, so to say, an automatic action of nature in a universal order. *Toto caelo differunt.*

viribus naturae possibilem';[48] or else, with the Augustinian of Louvain, Michael Paludanus (d. 1652), also an anti-Jansenist, they would explain that it is impossible to have a distinct idea of this natural end. Among all the others, it is possible to discern a twofold inclination : on the one hand, the natural end consists in a knowledge of God that is still abstract and known by its effects : this to some extent recalls contemplation of 'natural things'; on the other hand, it is a question of an intuitive knowledge, or one at least by 'infused ideas', to which the term 'possession' applies. In addition there are mixed formulas. But on all sides it is finally admitted that this natural knowledge of God would gratify to the full the desire of human nature. It should be noticed also that the second form, substituting intuition for abstraction, possession for induction, tended increasingly to prevail over the first. In this evolution there is a profoundly immanent logic.

Suarez, for example, believes that the knowledge of God in the separated and 'unexalted' soul would be, as it is here below, 'abstractiva et per effectus'; but his is by no means the rather pessimistic idea that was Bellarmine's : it would be, he thinks, a very real beatitude since it would consist 'in perfectissima naturali coniunctione cum Deo per intellectum et voluntatem, quantum ex creaturis naturali lumine intellectus cognosci potest'.[49] Molina, on the other hand, showed some reserve, though he admitted, in a rather more agreeable sense, that the vision of the essence of God was alone capable of satisfying the natural desire.[50] In the same way in 1623 his opponent Thomas de Lemos wrote : 'Certum est non posse esse finem naturalem perfectum . . . , sed esset beatitudo quaedam naturalis extra Deum, qua proinde perfecta non esset, etiam in ratione beatitudinis naturalis.'[51] The Carmelites of Salamanca said almost that the

---

[48] *Anti-Jansenius* (Paris, 1652), p. 196. Moraines acknowledges that the 'antiquiores theologi' do not speak of 'a state of pure nature'; but is it only, as he seems to say, because they treat 'brevissime' of a matter which the 'recentiores' developed 'fusius' (p. 191)?

[49] *De fine ultimo*, disput. 15, sect. 1, n. 6 and n. 3.

[50] *In Primam* (Lyon, 1953), qu. 12, art. 1, disp. 2.

[51] *Panoplia gratiae*, vol. 1, *Isagogicus* (posthumous, 1676), vol. 2, tract. 1, c. 4, p. 7.

final form within the limits of nature does not merit the name of beatitude save 'diminute et valde imperfecte'.[52] For Becanus, in 1639, the natural intellect cannot be gratified by any natural knowledge.[53] In 1646, Oviedo said that all natural beatitude can only be 'valde imperfecta et secundum quid'.[54] John of St Thomas, in 1637, spoke only of a 'contemplatio Dei per suos effectus'.[55] 'Contemplatio abstractiva Dei', said John Martinez de Ripalda in 1648,[56] as did Francesco Amici in 1650.[57] But in 1685 Esparza's *Cursus theologicus* speaks of a 'perfecta Dei cognitio ex creaturis'[58] and in 1687 Silvester Maurus accentuates the optimism when he writes: 'Cognitio Dei per creaturas quietaret naturale desiderium.'[59]

Simonnet's *Institutiones theologicae* in 1723 says: 'perfectissima quaedam contemplatio Dei abstractiva'.[60] In 1765 Rupp's *Praelectiones theologicae* intensifies the formula: 'Beatitudo illa naturalis esset cognitio Dei abstractiva . . . sed in termino esset perfecta, absque omni miseria et imperfectione.'[61]

Going a step further, certain theologians left out the words 'ex creaturis'.[62] After speaking of 'abstractive knowledge', there was mention of 'abstractive intuition' and 'abstractive vision'[63] and

---

[52] *Cursus theologicus*, vol. 5, tract. 9, disp. 6, dub. 1.

[53] *Summa theologiae scholasticae*, vol. 2 (Lyon, 1639), p. 42.

[54] *Tractatus theologici* (Lyon, 1646), tract. 1, n. 130.

[55] *Cursus theologicus*, vol. 2, (1st ed., Alcala, 1637), disp. 12, art. 3, n. 23.

[56] *De ente supernaturali*, vol. 3, disp. 8, sect. 7, n. 71.

[57] *Cursus theologicus*, vol. 3 (Antwerp, 1650), p. 295.

[58] *Cursus theologicus*, (Lyon), vol. 1, p. 30.

[59] *Opus theologicum*, bk 6, tract. 7, qu. 47, n. 21.

[60] Vol. 4, *De gratia,* p. 87. 'Cognitio abstractiva Dei clara,' said Dominic Viva (d. 1710; *Cursus theologicus*, 1755 ed., p. 29).

[61] Vol. 2 (Heidelberg, 1765), p. 133; p. 138: 'Quod beatitudinem status purae naturae . . . attinet, dici potest, eam ponendam fuisse in cognitione Dei abstractiva, quidem, sed perfecta. . . .'

[62] They reappear, however, in a good theologian like A. Verrièle, *Le surnaturel en nous* (1932), p. 34. But cf. Palmieri, *op. cit.*, 2nd ed., p. 110: 'Potest vero cognitio abstractiva Dei in possessione finis perfectior esse, quatenus perfectiore modo sit determinata. . . . Ceterum advertendum est, in beatitudine spectandum esse non tantum cognitionem et amorem Dei, sed cetera quoque bona naturae convenientia.' And previously Rupp, in the passage quoted in the previous footnote.

[63] Henri Keller, *De gratia*: 'visio solum abstractiva et naturalis' (*Theologia Wiceburgensis*, 1880 ed., vol. 7, p. 144; c. 1, art. 2).

the protests of Macedo (d. 1681) against these false concepts were ineffectual in the face of the evolution in course.[64] The adjective 'abstractive' came to be omitted just as the determinative phrase 'ex creaturis' had been. From the idea of a possession by man of his natural end, almost imperceptibly there emerged the idea of a natural possession of God in the attainment of this end. Thus in 1763 Gotti wrote: 'Cum enim in eo statu (homo) esset ordinatus in Deum ut auctorem naturae, ex possessione illius in tali ordine capacitas eius positiva expleretur.'[65] In the present century Fr E. Peillaube mingles prudence with daring, reserve and generosity, when he writes: 'Reason does not tell us in what the natural possession of God could consist; to gratify our desires God would probably make himself known by other ways than abstraction and reasoning, for example, by means of infused ideas.'[66] For Fr V. Cathrein, natural beatitude is not only a 'perfect beatitude' but it is so thanks to 'a very perfect knowledge of God', a 'very perfect union with God'.[67] One of the last authors to treat of this question proves to be one of the most intrepid: 'Is it absurd', wrote Fr Pedro Descoqs in 1938, 'to conceive a real vision of God, the author of nature, which would not reveal him in accordance with the interior perfections of the transcendent supernatural order, but which, while remaining in some way proportionate to our nature, would go beyond the order of abstract concepts or infused species?' Such an explanation, he considers, 'would be capable of providing a very simple and very neat solution' to the many difficulties in interpreting the passages of St Thomas about the natural desire for the vision of God.[68] As a matter of fact, it is

[64] Macedo, *Collationes* . . . , vol. 2 (1673), p. 399: 'Si esset visio, esset intuitiva, per quam videretur Deus in se prout videtur hodie a beatis; ergo supernaturalis. . . .' (Si esset cognitio abstractiva) 'non esset satis ad praemium; et monstraret Deum imperfecto modo cognosci, et excitaret desiderium videndi intuitive.'

[65] *Theologia scolastico-dogmatica* (1763), vol. 2, 1, qu. 2, dubium 1.

[66] *La destinée humaine* (1930), p. 56.

[67] 'De naturali hominis beatitudine' in *Gregorianum*, 1930, pp. 406-8.

[68] *Le mystère de notre élévation surnaturelle* (1938), p. 126. With the same intrepidity the author states: 'This distinction was certainly familiar to the old Scholastics.' To prove it he quotes Cajetan, who seems to me to say exactly the opposite. Returning to the same idea in *NRT* (1939) Fr

'very simple and very neat' to reduce to the natural level what St Thomas, and with him all the Fathers, not to mention Christian tradition itself, said of the supernatural. A direct vision of God obtained by natural man : the clear evidence of the historical error as well as the doctrinal deviation does not prevent this strange explanation from being in the line of reasoning of this movement whose final stage it marks. But this way of understanding, on a last analysis, the natural object of the desire as equal to the beatific vision itself, shows clearly the dissatisfaction in which this doctrine of natural satisfaction leaves its proponents.

In any case, in this new system the only remaining link of the created spirit with the end which God has promised us will be no more henceforward than that of a sheer 'obediential power'; in other words, the idea that the Fathers and the early Scholastics had worked out to account for miracles, will in future be applied to the problem of the last end. As well say that every link will be broken since this 'obediential power' is something not only purely passive—in the problem concerning us the ancients mentioned no other power than a passive one—but purely negative : a mere word to denote the 'non-repugnance', the non-resistance of every creature to divine Omnipotence : 'aliquid negativum, scilicet, quamdam non repugnantiam ad potentiam divinam';[69] 'capacitas et possibilitas, seu non repugnantia ad videndum Deum'.[70] The supernatural and the miraculous will no longer be only analogous

---

Descoqs goes a step further : 'This solution is strictly inspired by Cajetan, Silvester Ferrariensis, and followed by a whole host of old Scholastic authors' (p. 410). Rather than speak of a 'whole host' it would have been better to mention one or two by name. Of course, there is room for difference of opinion on what is meant by 'old'. The writer grants afterwards that he has not made 'a sufficiently thorough study to take a decided stand on the subject' (*ibid.*). He then asks us to read in the text of his pamphlet 'immediate vision' for 'intuitive vision', which was, he says, 'a pure slip of the pen' (p. 411). I must say that I find it difficult to understand this contrast between an intuitive vision which can only be supernatural and an immediate vision which would be purely natural.

[69] Balthazar Navarrete, O.P., *In D. Thomae et eius scholae defensionem,* vol. 1 (1605), p. 192 : 'Quidquid pertinet ad ordinem naturalem consideratur ut in potentia obedientiali respectu ordinis supernaturalis', and p. 194.

[70] John of St Thomas, *In Primam*, qu. 12, art. 3, n. 13 (*Opera*, vol. 2, 1934, p. 142).

in certain features and are interdependent in their existence. The miraculous will no longer be a simple sign of the former : it is the former which will become simply a special case of the latter.

There again, superficially at least, these commentators follow in the path traced by their master, for no innovation ever appears to have an absolute beginning. Of course, St Thomas far from confusing what we call the supernatural with the miraculous, in search of analogy derived from the heavenly bodies sought it rather in the normal action that the higher bodies exert on the sublunary bodies; thus in one passage he quotes the phenomenon of the tides.[71] Far from speaking habitually of obediential power in connection with aptitude for the supernatural, beatitude and the vision of God, on the contrary he more than once declared in a very general formula that 'the soul is naturally capable of grace'.[72] He answered certain objections in advance, noting that there are two ways for a thing to be natural.[73] Nevertheless, although he acknowledged in the soul a twofold passive power, one natural and the other obediential, as in every other creature, he did so, for example, to explain the miracle of the infused knowledge in Christ's soul.[74] But in a very general sense he none the less recognized in the creature, as such, a certain power of obeying God to receive in itself all that God willed : 'In tota creatura est quaedam obedientialis potentia, prout tota creatura obedit Deo

[71] *Secunda Secundae*, qu. 2, art. 3. From a certain point of view, he says the spiritual nature is like the others; two things combine for its perfection: an active intrinsic principle and an impulse received from the higher nature; but in the case of the spiritual nature this impulse can only come from God and its end consists likewise in participation in the divine goodness and in the vision of the divine essence. In other passages St Thomas reduces even miracles to this general pattern, but without assimilating them to the case of God's action on the soul: *Prima*, qu. 105, art. 6, ad 1m.

[72] *Prima secundae*, qu. 113, art. 10; *Tertia*, qu. 9, art. 2, ad 3m. Cf. *In II Sent.*, dist. 30, qu. 1, art. 1, ad 5m; *In IV Sent.*, dist. 17, qu. 1, art. 5, ad 1m. *De Malo*, qu. 2, art. 11, ad 14m, on the *habilitas* of human nature to the vision of God and to grace.

See P. Charlier, O.P., 'Puissance passive et désir naturel selon saint Thomas' in *Ephemerides theologicae lovanienses*, 1930. Henri Bouillard, *op. cit.*, pp. 80-1.

[73] *Prima Secundae,* qu. 6, art. 3, ad 2m; *De Veritate*, qu. 24, art. 10, ad 1m.

[74] *Tertia,* qu. 11, art. 1. Cf. Gilson, in *Arch. d'hist. doctr. . .* , 31, pp. 82-6.

ad suscipiendum in se quidquid Deus voluerit.'[75] If therefore it was certain that the created spirit could not of itself see God, and if nevertheless we are sure, whatever the explanation, that it can see him, we must still in this connection speak of the 'potentia obedientialis', the stamp of every creature, the sign of its 'naturalis subiectio ad Creatorem',[76] what St Bonaventure called 'naturalis obedientia creaturae'.[77] This did not allow one to speak of a 'potentia obedientiae *tantum*', especially since the characteristic of this obediential capacity or power was, St Thomas pointed out, the inability ever to be gratified to the full: 'talis capacitas non potest impleri, quia quidquid Deus de creatura faciat, adhuc remanet in potentia recipiendi a Deo'.[78] Lastly, in a sense that is no less general, St Thomas still allowed the term 'miraculous' to be applied to any work that God alone was able to carry out.[79]

Without denying, any more than St Thomas did, the soul's natural inclination and capacity, and the image of God, in regard to its natural end, St Thomas' followers had copied their master's language. For example, after proving that in the intellect there is a natural appetite for the vision of God, Gerard of Bologna had allowed that one could call 'obediential power' that power which in us tends naturally to its object without being able to attain it by natural means.[80] With a similar intention, and perhaps also with the secret plan of accentuating the difference from Scotus' language,[81] Capreolus had made a distinction between

---

[75] *De virtutibus in communi*, art. 10, ad 13m. *Tertia*, qu. 1, art. 3, ad 3m; qu. 11, art. 1; qu. 44, art. 2 ('Utrum convenienter facta fuerint miracula per Christum circa caelestia corpora'), ad 1m: 'Naturale est cuilibet creaturae ut transmutetur a Deo secundum eius voluntatem.'

[76] *De malo*, qu. 5, art. 5, ad 4m: 'Inest cuilibet rei creatae naturalis subiectio ad creatorem, multo magis quam corporibus inferioribus ad corpora caelestia.' Cf. *In IV Sent.*, dist. 8, qu. 2, art. 3, ad 4m.

[77] *De mysterio SS. Trinitatis*, qu. 1, 2, ad 7m (Quaracchi, vol. 5, p. 57b).

[78] *De veritate*, qu. 29, art. 3, ad 3m. Cf. qu. 12, art. 3, ad 18m.

[79] *Prima Secundae*, qu. 113, art. 10; *Tertia*; qu. 9, art. 2, ad 3m. Cf. *De potentia*, qu. 1, art. 3, ad 3m; qu. 6, art. 1, ad 18m.

[80] *Loc. cit.*

[81] As a matter of fact his explanation occurs in the course of an argument aimed at Scotus. It seems that it is the desire to differ from the latter in the question of the possibility of natural knowledge of the supernatural end which directly inspired Capreolus' language on the subject, and this remains still quite close to that of St Thomas.

226

natural power properly so called and natural power improperly
so called, comparing the latter with obediential power.[82] By this,
however, he did not, any more than Gerard of Bologna, mean to
deny a real natural capacity in the sense of a real natural inclination.[83]

Yet another problem, closely bound up with that of finality or
natural desire, was that of knowing how to explain the insertion
in the faculties of rational nature thus 'inclined', of the actual
disposition making it capable, if God willed, effectively to attain
this end—since its natural desire or its natural capacity to receive
it did not qualify it to attain it by its own resources.[84] It is in this
connection that among other solutions it is possible to introduce
that of an 'obediential power' to grace and the infused 'habitus' in
this life, and then to the light of glory. Fr Gillon has discovered
an unpublished work of Bernard of Auvergne (between 1290 and
1300) which mentions the obediential power of the will to receive
charity or the other supernatural 'habitus'.[85] An anonymous
Quaestio of the beginning of the fourteenth century, edited by
Dom Lottin, distinguishes likewise natural power and obediential
power as corresponding to acquired 'habitus' and infused
'habitus'.[86] In about 1314 Peter Paludanus in his commentary
on the fourth book of *Sentences* wrote : 'De eductione beatitudinis
sunt tres opiniones', and he explained the second opinion in the
following terms :

Secunda, quod aliud est dicere formam praeexistere in
potentia, aliud educi de potentia. . . . Visio igitur beatifica

[82] *In Prolog.*, qu. 1 : 'Conceditur ergo quod ad illum finem homo naturaliter
ordinatur, loquendo de ordine naturali illo modo quo dictum est potentiam
obedientialem esse naturalem. Negatur tamen quod ad illum finem homo
naturaliter ordinetur, sic quod habeat ordinem proprie naturalem aut
potentiam naturalem.' Cf. E. Elter, 'De naturali hominis beatitudine ad
mentem Scholae antiquioris' in *Gregorianum*, 1928, p. 286.

[83] Fr Victorin Doucet, O.F.M., felt able to remark on this subject: 'Tali
autem distinctione, ut patet, non negat Capreolus vere naturalem capacitatem
et inclinationem seu ordinationem naturae ad supernaturalia' ('De naturali
seu innato supernaturalis beatitudinis desiderio iuxta Theologos a saeculo
XIII usque ad XX' in *Antonianum*, 1929, pp. 188-9).

[84] See for confirmation St Thomas, *In IV Sent.*, dist. 49, qu. 2, art. 6.

[85] *Revue thomiste*, 47 (1947), pp. 308-9.

[86] *Psychologie et morale aux XII* et XIII* siècles,* vol. 4, 2, p. 754.

et omnis forma supernaturalis accidentalis praeexistit in potentia passiva subiecti, quia non potest esse sine illo sine miraculo. Item educitur per consequens de illa potentia non naturali sed obedientiali, et praeexistit in potentia supernaturali, non naturali.[87]

It will not be necessary to remember here that Peter Paludanus had no hesitation on occasion in differing from St Thomas, even on important matters.[88] The appeal to a 'supernatural' or 'obediential' power in his work, as in Bernard of Auvergne or in the anonymous *Quaestio,* is entirely in agreement, not only with the thought, but also with the language of St Thomas. In his Question *De virtutibus in communi* St Thomas had actually written :

In tota creatura est quaedam obedientialis potentia, prout tota creatura obedit Deo ad suscipiendum in se quidquid Deus voluerit. Sic igitur et in anima est aliquid in potentia, quod natum est reduci in actum ab agente connaturali, et hoc modo sunt in potentia in ipsa virtute acquisitae; alio modo aliquid est in potentia in anima quod non est natum educi in actum nisi per virtutem divinam : et sic sunt in potentia in anima virtutes infusae.[89]

But it is clear that neither in the authors quoted above nor in St Thomas himself, does this recourse to a 'supernatural' or 'obediential' power concern the finality of the spiritual creature. It concerns the means of achieving it. It is merely a logical application of the traditional axiom : 'Visio Dei, . . . supernaturalis quoad assecutionem' or 'attingentiam'.

Later, with Denys the Carthusian, it was to be otherwise. The

---

[87] *In IV. Sent.*, dist. 49, qu. 8 (Venice, 1493, fol. 238 r, 1-2). Cf. Gillon, *loc. cit.*, p. 310, note; the older edition that I am using differs in two details from the text given at this point.

[88] On the nature of original sin, for example. Cf. Raymond M. Martin, O.P., *La controverse sur le péché originel au début du XIV⁰ siècle* (1930), p. 236.

[89] *Utrum sint aliquae virtutes homini ex infusione* (art. 10, ad 3m). Cf. Eudes Rigaud, *In II Sent.* : 'Deus . . . non solum gratificat ipsam substantiam animae per gratiam, sed etiam ipsas potentias per virtutes' (Bouvy, *Recherches de théologie ancienne et médiévale*, 27, p. 336).

following passage from *De puritate et felicitate animae* appears somewhat hesitant :

> Deus namque sanctus et superadorandus liberrimus est auctor omnemque universi naturam ac ordinem libere sapientialiterque instituit. Nullatenus ergo ad nunc institutum inditumque rebus ordinem limitatus est, sed eius voluntati omnia parent, quippe quae universorum mensura est et prima causa. Unde quidam theologi non mediocris ingenii omni aiunt naturae creatae obedientialem quamdam innatam esse virtutem, qua, in his quae supra naturam sunt, Omnipotentissimi queat conditoris parere imperio. Ita quoque in mente creata intelligere par est. Ipsa enim natura animae ad supernaturalem Dei munificentiam absolutamque potentiam relata appetitum ac capacitatem supernaturalis beatitudinis sortita est; estque eorum ad quae supernaturaliter instituta est et ordinata, capax ac cupida.[90]

The difficulty seems obvious, particularly in the last sentence where the first part affirms that in the soul's very nature there is a desire and a capacity for supernatural beatitude, while the second part declares this same soul to be 'capable and desirous' of this same supernatural beatitude only when it has been ordered to it by an ordination which it did not possess by the mere fact of its nature. We see here Denys' tendency, in agreement with what we have already observed of him, to subject the 'mens creata', in its relationship with God, to the rules governing inferior natures.

It is this same tendency which finally leads Cajetan continually to contrast natural power and obediential power in the human soul, stating that the power of the soul not only in relation to grace, but to supernatural acts and the happiness of the beatific vision, 'non est naturalis, sed obedientialis'.[91] Toletus, who held the

---

[90] *De puritate et felicitate animae*, art. 59 (*Opera*, vol. 40, p. 433).
[91] *In Primam Secundae*, qu. 113, art. 10. *In Primam*, qu. 12, art. 1. *De potentia neutra*, qu. 2 (*Opuscula*, vol. 3, 1612, pp. 156-7). H. Rondet, *art. cit.*, pp. 490-3. Alfaro, *op. cit.*, pp. 131-41.

contrary view, points this out.[92] Conrad Koellin, adopting Cajetan's thesis and his terminology, tries in vain to establish in the
face of the evidence that this new language goes back to St
Thomas himself.[93] To get rid of the passage which, using his
own words, he is contradicting, he quotes inopportunely other
passages dealing with different matters, and he can only feel
authorized to do so because, with no justification, he assimilates
the case of miracles and prophecy to that of the last end.[94] We
have here a further indication of that 'naturalization' or 'materialization' of the soul which we have already seen at work. It is a
further application of the principle according to which every being
must find its end, corresponding to its natural appetite and
natural power, within the limitations of its own nature. The case
of the soul has to be included as a whole in the more general case
of the natural being.

Soon Bartholomew of Medina (1527-81), having reproduced
Cajetan's teaching and arguments—including the celebrated
argument taken from the *De caelo*—in opposition to the 'natural
desire to see God', unashamedly concludes: 'Ex hac doctrina
sequitur aperte quod non est potentia naturalis ad videndum
Deum sicuti est: nullus enim ex viribus naturae potest consequi
istum finem; ergo non est potentia naturalis; *potestas enim
miraculorum* ea de causa non est naturalis, quia non possumus
eam habere ex viribus naturae.'[95] Yet he feels himself to be on
shaky ground and so he is willing to concede a probability to the

[92] *In Primam sancti Thomae*, qu. 1, art. 1: 'Dicit igitur Caietanus Deum
esse finem supernaturalem, et potentiam in nobis ad divinam visionem esse
non naturalem, nec violentam, sed obedientialem' (1869, vol. 1, p. 18).

[93] *In Primam Secundae*, qu. 113, art. 10 (p. 964).

[94] Koellin argues from two passages: *De veritate*, qu. 12, art. 3, and *De
virtutibus in communi*, art. 10. But this second passage does not here mention
the end; it contains only a general remark about every creature. In the first
passage it is a question of prophecy. In it St Thomas distinguishes between
natural prophecy and miraculous prophecy; there is, he said, in connection
with the latter in human nature a passive power, which is 'potentia, non
naturalis, sed tantum potentia obedientiae, sicut est in natura corporali ad
ea quae mirabiliter fiunt'. It may be seen if Koellin has good grounds for
concluding as he does: 'Unde Doctor sanctus per capacitatem naturalem
intelligit potentiam obedientialem naturae insertam.'

[95] *Expositio in Primam Secundae*, qu. 3, art. 8 (Venice, 1590, p. 45, 2).

contrary opinion in view of the acknowledged authority of its
adherents and the reasons with which they support it. Medina
follows Cajetan also in his method, which consists in getting
away from the text of the *Summa* in some degree to argue directly
against Scotus, whose simpler formula of 'finis naturalis' standing
alone could lend itself more easily to equivocation;[96] but he does
not dare to invoke the authority of St Thomas for his conclusions,
and even admits, practically speaking, that he is in contradiction
with him, observing that 'rationes D. Thomae aliquando sunt
probabiles, non necessario concludentes'.[97]

These precautions and reservations are not often to be found
subsequently. The theologians who in after years opposed the
doctrine of 'natural desire' also, but far more decisively, fell back
on 'obediential power'; and in an effort to re-establish some link
with the earlier Scholastics across the gap opened towards the
end of the fifteenth century, they appealed to medieval texts
about miracles.[98] The contrast seems at first somewhat lessened

[96] Right at the beginning of the *Explicatio articuli* he raises the problem
in tendentious terms: 'In hoc articulo est quaestio gravissima: utrum
beatitudo hominis naturalis sit in visione divinae essentiae?' And in the first
place he examines Scotus' answer.

[97] *Ibid.*, p. 47, 1: 'vel dicatur, rationes D. Thomae optime demonstrare,
desiderium humani pectoris non posse perfecte satiari usque ad Dei visionem
et fruitionem . . .'.

[98] Certain writers, employing a similar method, endeavour to make use of
the Augustinian theory of 'rationes seminales'. M. A. Darmet, *Les notions de
raison séminale et de puissance obédientielle chez saint Augustin et saint
Thomas d'Aquin* (Belley, 1934), has shown clearly that this was not the
genuine meaning.
As a matter of fact the Franciscan school for long past had applied the
Augustinian teaching about 'seminal reasons' to the problem of the relationship between nature and grace. Thus Gauthier of Bruges, *Quaestiones
disputatae,* qu. 9 (Longpré, p. 89): 'Ad tertium dicendum secundum Augustinum 6 super Genesim, quod duplex est potentia passiva: una quae habet
etiam rationales seminales, et alia quae non habet, et haec est pure receptiva,
Primae respondet activa naturalis; secundae respondet activa supernaturalis, et talis potentia passiva est in natura respectu fidei, gloriae, gratiae
et infallibilitatis ad malum; haec enim non habent rationes seminales.' But
these explanations were not meant to reduce the aptitude of the soul for the
supernatural to a purely obediential potentiality; they were meant to
emphasize the complete independence of the supernatural agent, the complete gratuitousness of his gifts, but without prejudice either to the supernatural finality of human nature or to the desire which is its expression
(*ibid.*, p. 90).

when, instead of texts about material miracles, they adduce those concerning either the hypostatic union[99] or the conversion of sinners.[100] But fundamentally this changes nothing. When this theory of the obediential power is adopted in strict and exclusive form we are at once very far from St Thomas,[101] very far, obviously, from Scotus, and very far indeed from the old Scholastic tradition.

A certain number of Scotist theologians have not failed to point this out. In 1614 John of Rada, author of the *Controversiae inter sanctum Thomam et Scotum,* did so.[102] His example was followed

[99] Thus Báñez, *In Primam Secundae,* qu. 5, art. 1 : 'In nulla definitione creaturae intellectualis includitur tanquam propria differentia vel propria passio, quod possit videre Deum per essentiam; sed solum est in illa potentia obedientialis in ordine ad Deum supernaturaliter operantem, quae nulli cognita est ad quantum sese extendat, nisi ipsi Deo, qui cognoscit suam omnipotentiam supra totam naturam : quemadmodum naturaliter nemo potest cognoscere potentiam obedientialem quam habet humanitas ut assumatur a Verbo; quemadmodum etiam in naturalibus nemo potest cognoscere potentiam obedientialem ligni ad figuras artificiales, nisi quatenus cognoscit potentiam artificis per artem' (*loc. cit.,* p. 167). And also Vasquez, *In Primam Secundae,* disput. 23, c. 2 : '(Potentia ad visionem est) obedientialis tantum capacitas, quoniam potentia passiva dici solum potest naturalis ex forma quam recipere potest. . . .' (Scotus wants the desire to be called natural not by reason of its end, but 'quia oritur ex principiis naturae'): 'Hoc tamen responsum nullius momenti est : nam si hoc sufficeret, ut appetitus ille innatus est diceretur naturalis, eadem ratione capacitas, quae est in natura humana ad dona gratiae supernaturalia, et ad ipsam unionem hypostaticam, dici potest naturalis appetitus, quod tamen nullus hactenus dixit.'

[100] There are references also to be found in St Augustine. Cf. Darmet, *op. cit.,* and P. de Vooght, 'Le miracle chez saint Augustin' in *Recherches de théologie ancienne et médiévale,* 1938, p. 330.

[101] Cf. M.C. (Dom Cappuyns), *Bulletin de théologie ancienne et médiévale,* vol. 3 (1938), p. 261 : the idea of obediential power 'does not seem to be applicable in his teaching on natural desire. The only distinction in St Thomas that must serve to resolve the contradiction between the natural character of the desire and the supernatural character of its object is that of the two orders of finality and realization.'
Fr Roland Gosselin, 'Béatitude et désir naturel' in *RSPT,* 1929, saw clearly that for St Thomas the relationship of the reasonable creature with the supernatural order is 'a unique relationship and that any comparison can only throw light on it in a very defective way'; although he persisted in wanting to apply to this relationship the idea of obediential power, and ascribed to St Thomas a distinction between specific finality and obediential finality, he admitted different values of obediential power (pp. 212 and 217).

[102] John of Rada shows that Scotus and St Thomas are here in agreement against Cajetan and his successors. *Controversiae,* pars prima, art. 1 : 'Potentia receptiva actuum supernaturalium est naturalis in ordine ad eosdem

in 1655 by Bartholomew Mastrius. Endeavouring to wean the Scholastics of his day from quarrels about words, Mastrius wanted to show that there is a certain relationship of man to the vision of God which is 'more intrinsic, more essential and more con-natural' than is stated by Suarez and the other modern theologians when they speak of obediential power; therefore, it is legitimate to speak of 'really natural power', that is 'quae fluit a principiis naturae', while being obediential by the fact that it is 'super-naturalis quoad attingentiam'.[103] And a few years later, it was a Capuchin, Marc de Bauduen, who more simply and less timidly sought to restore the separated brethren to unity by bringing them back to the 'theological paradise' (1661), that is, to the old doc-trine of the natural desire, under the leadership of the Angelic, the Seraphic and the Subtle Doctors, those 'three great lumina-ries shining in the sky of sacred theology'.[104]

But it is not quite so easy to return to the paradise of unity. John of Rada, Mastrius and Bauduen were crying in the desert. And in the Thomist school itself the commentators on St Thomas were arguing with one another.

As it happened, the transformations that had occurred could not fail to provoke at least a few scruples, the more so since the theologians always had before them in their function of inter-preters and 'lectors' the actual text of St Thomas. Despite their disregard for history and their slender critical sense,[105] they could not help noticing that certain very clear formulas still remained.

actus; non solum naturalis subiective, sed etiam formaliter, quia naturaliter est propensa et inclinata in eos. Conclusio est D. Thomae, *Prima Secundae,* qu. 113, art. 10, ubi aperte hanc nostram tenet conclusionem, quidquid eius discipuli in contrarium fateantur. Est etiam haec conclusio Doctoris Subtilis' (Venice, 1614, p. 7).

[103] *In I Sent.* (2nd ed., Venice, 1675), vol. 1, pp. 382-428 (Disput. sexta, De visione beata): 'Non video quo spiritu ductus Caietanus Scotum repre-hendit.'

[104] Marcus a Baudunio, *Paradisus theologicus,* vol. 1, pp. 77-8, tract. 1, qu. 12, dubium: 'An nobis sit naturale desiderium videndi Deum intuitive' (2nd ed., Lyon, 1667). Cf. Julien Eymard d'Angers, in *Antonianum,* 1954, pp. 51-6.

[105] M.-B. Lavaud, O.P., *Revue thomiste,* vol. 10 (1927), p. 315; 'Exegesis and history concerned them far less than the fundamental nature of things' (on the Thomists of the sixteenth and seventeenth centuries).

Hence there developed among them a 'bad conscience' which found open expression in their many attempts at explanation. Not only did these attempts vary from one author to another, as John of St Thomas could not help pointing out,[106] but often the same writer would put forward several, which were contradictory, without troubling to choose among them, for the sole purpose of getting out of the difficulty at all costs. The attempts provide evidence of a resourceful and fertile ingenuity which was exercised most of the time in opposition to mere objectivity. Roughly speaking, it can be said that there were three types. When St Thomas speaks of 'a natural desire to see God', sometimes it is thought that he envisaged nature already raised up by grace and instructed by revelation, sometimes this desire is diminished even to the point of depriving it of all metaphysical meaning, and sometimes, lastly, it is decided that the vision of God in question could only be an external knowledge, attaining to God as the author of natural creation.[107] Here were three kinds of explanation, three ways of sketching out a doctrine which held danger of scandal, three misleading developments whose tangled fortunes pursued their course uninterruptedly from the time of Cajetan until our own days.[108]

For the first type of explanation, which is Cajetan's own, we can see, for example, what the Dominican de Godoy has to say. Having raised the objection that, according to St Thomas, only

[106] *In Primam,* qu. 12, art. 3, n. 6: 'Valde dividuntur (discipuli et commentatores D. Thomae) in explicando quomodo iste appetitus sit naturalis' (*Opera,* vol. 2, 1934, p. 140).

[107] This is near enough the picture drawn by Victorin Doucet in *Antonianum,* 4 (1927), pp. 193-5.

[108] A very simple observation would be the primary condition for agreement, namely, that 'capacitas naturalis' does not mean merely 'capacitas obedientialis' and that 'desiderium naturae' does not mean merely 'non repugnantia'. In addition, it is clear, surely, that these 'effugia' lead to the transformation of a doctrine which obviously holds for St Thomas a very high place and to which he attaches great importance, into a truism of little interest. Cf. John of St Thomas, *loc. cit.,* pp. 9 and 13; cf. n. 14: 'Si rationalis creatura non haberet capacitatem, sed repugnantiam ad videndum ipsum Deum in se, tale desiderium volendi videre causam illorum effectuum esset inane et non conforme ipsi naturae' (p. 143). Of course. And again, n. 8: 'Solum supponit ratio (D. Thomae) quod possit (homo) videre effectus supernaturales, et quod illis visis, non erit contra eius naturam, sed valde illi conforme, velle videre eorum causam.'

supernatural beatitude satisfies the desire of the human spirit, he answers :

> D. Thomam ibi loqui de homine elevato per gratiam, qui, appetitu innato connaturali gratiae, et appetitu inefficaci naturali elicito supposita cognitione per fidem de possibilitate visionis beatificae, desiderat quidditativam Dei cognitionem, et de isto loquendo, verum est quod D. Thomas asserit, non satiari omnem appetitum illius per cognitionem Dei quoad an est; nec hoc exigitur a beatitudine naturali, de cuius ratione non est, nisi quietare omnem appetitum hominis considerati intra limites purae naturae. Si autem homo in illo statu constitueretur, cum de supernaturalibus nihil cognosceret, nullatenus Dei quidditativam cognitionem appeteret, sed omnis appetitus illius sisteret in cognitione Dei quae ex effectibus creatis posset haberi.[109]

Báñez offers us an example of the second type, in his commentary on the *Prima Pars,* qu. 12, art. 1 : 'In creatura spirituali est quaedam velleitas, et quoddam desiderium imperfectum videndi Deum; ex quo colligit D. Thomas probabiliter, quod visio beatifica sit possibilis, nec frustretur tale desiderium naturale.'[110] It is left to the reader to judge whether here Báñez emasculates St Thomas' thought less than he blames Cajetan for doing.[111] Indeed, there is a certain vacillation here in Báñez' thought; in the case of the angel he approves the explanation which he rejected for the case of man : 'Quod autem divus Thomas dicit, l. 3 C.G., c. 50, quod angeli non quiescunt in cognitione naturali, loquitur de facto, quoniam creati sunt cum fide beatitudinis supernaturalis.'[112]

[109] *In Primam Secundae,* vol. 1 (Venice, 1686), p. 3.
[110] *In Primam* (1584 ed., p. 447). Cf. *In Primam Secundae,* qu. 3, art. 8, dubium : 'Divus Thomas in suis rationibus non intendit ostendere demonstrative possibilem esse nobis beatitudinem, quae in Dei visione consistit; sed solum intendit ostendere quantum consonet atque conveniat supernaturalis hominis beatitudo cum ipsa hominis natura; siquidem sola illa beatitudo potest omnem appetitum creaturae rationalis, etiam conditionalem, implere' (vol. 1, 1942, p. 131).
[111] *In Primam Secundae,* vol. 1, p. 123.
[112] *Loc. cit.,* p. 131.

According to the third type of explanation in St Thomas, it is a question only of natural beatitude. This was the explanation of Silvester Ferrariensis, which was also adopted by Ysambert. Having stated an objection to what is the only possible meaning of St Thomas, he answers:

> Respondetur, causam aliquam posse duobus modis cognosci: primo, eo perfecto modo quo ipsa est in se cognoscibilis; secundo, quatenus est cognoscibilis per eos effectus, per quos excitatur in nobis desiderium videndi illam.
>
> Iam in homine considerato secundum sua naturalia, nullum est absolutum desiderium videndi Deum primo modo: nec proinde clare et intuitive; quia tale desiderium est semper rei alicuius tanquam possibilis apprehensae et cognitae. At homo iuxta sua naturalia tantum consideratues, non cognoscit naturaliter aut apprehendit cognitionem intuitivam divinae essentiae, ut possibilem; cognoscit enim solummodo Deum ex effectibus constitutis intra ordinem naturae, intra quem clara visio Dei non continetur, vel aliquid habens naturalem ordinem.

Having said this, Ysambert does not refuse to entertain the second explanation; the desire for natural beatitude does not exclude a certain velleity for supernatural beatitude. But Ysambert no longer thinks of inquiring whether the text of St Thomas which he is explaining mentions one or the other (actually it mentions neither, but only the one thing which Ysambert and others wished to avoid):

> Adde, quod si desiderium quoddam videndi Deum sicuti est, fingatur in tali homine, tunc non tam fore desiderium loquendo proprie, quam velleitatem quandam: cum tunc cognosceret se pro tali statu posse ea tantum cognoscere de Deo quae possunt deduci ex rebus creatis.[113]

The Jesuit Navarro with his eclecticism adopts solutions one and three; quoting St Thomas, *Prima Pars*, qu. 12, he writes:

[113] *Disputationes in Primam Partem S. Thomae*, vol. 1 (Paris, 1643), p. 90. Cf., for example, St Thomas, *Prima Secundae*, qu. 3, art. 8.

THE PROBLEM OF BEATITUDE

'His, et similibus, solum probatur vel appetitus elicitus supposita fide, vel innatus ad aliquam cognitionem naturalem Dei.'[114]

The Dominican Medina, whose attachment to 'obediential power' we have already seen, was even more eclectic since he offered his readers a choice of the three solutions:

Ad argumenta ex D. Thoma respondetur:
In primis, quod rationes D. Thomae sunt probabiles, non necessario concludentes, maxime cum in expositione divinorum mysteriorum . . . versantur;
vel dicatur, quod loquitur de homine illustrato lumine fidei;
vel dicatur, rationes D. Thomae optime demonstrare, desiderium humani pectoris non posse perfecte satiari usque ad Dei visionem; caeterum, satiatur ex cognitione rerum divinarum, quae per naturam haberi potest.[115]

In short, one after the other, concurrently, or one at choice, all the hypotheses are envisaged to evade a doctrine which St Thomas stated in very clear terms, and which he rightly regarded as fundamental. The men who did this were not his opponents or indifferent to him; they were his disciples, those who declared themselves to be the sole genuine heirs of the master. The paradox was the greater in that they did it at the very time when they were claiming to defend his teaching against Scotus and his school. And the best representatives of the Scotists, as we have seen, realized this. In defending the Scotist tradition they were, by the same token, conscious of defending the principles of Thomism against its unfaithful representatives. Rada, in speaking of the natural inclination to beatitude, expresses himself in the following terms: 'Conclusio est D. Thomae. . . . Aperte hanc nostram tenet conclusionem, quidquid eius discipuli in contrarium fateantur. . . . Eius discipuli in varias secantur opiniones

---

[114] *Cursus theologicus,* vol. 2 (Madrid, 1766), p. 152.
[115] *In Primam Secundae,* qu. 3, art. 8 (Venice ed., 1590, p. 47). The thesis is apparently aimed against Scotus; but the followers of Scotus, says Medina, produce, in addition to Scotus' own arguments which are repeated by Durandus and Soto, five other arguments which they claim to have been taken from St Thomas, and Medina refutes them.

(whereas) in hac quaestione . . . Sanctus Thomas et Doctor subtilis idem omnino sentiunt.'[116] An independent, John Prudentius,
a Mercedarian, also remarks on this in his treatise on the vision
of God : 'Mirum est, quot obiectiones et scrupulos machinati non
sit auctores contra efficaciam praedicti sanctissimi discursus. . . .
Nec minoris est admirationis, diversitas viarum in quas dispersi
Thomistae mentem sui angelici magistri exprimere praetendunt,
ut obiectionibus in eius discursum iniectis satisfaciant. . . .'[117]

This scattered body of disciples, trying, each in his own way,
to destroy the principles of their master, should not surprise us.
The very refusal of objectivity in their exegesis was bound to beget
this state of affairs. In attempts to evade the issue each was
thrown back upon the fantasy of his own subjective inventions.
But what is to be wondered at is the reason for such a refusal.
Did it arise from a greater concern for the supernatural character of our destiny, a supernatural character which St Thomas'
text did not in their view fully safeguard? I believe that the profound, and unnoticed,[118] reason is rather the reverse. Towards the
end of the fifteenth century, in the first period of the Renaissance,
a feverish enthusiasm for philosophy infected certain minds. A
large number of Christian thinkers were won over at that time
by the renascent naturalism. In its 'Avicennian' or 'Averroist'
form, the theory which represented the great temptation for the
thirteenth century was opposed most effectively by St Thomas
with his continuation of St Augustine and his Christianization of
Aristotle. It was this which reappeared with increased vigour in
certain theological circles; or at the very least it frightened them.
Denys the Carthusian, in the name of Avicenna, was in opposition

---

[116] *Controversiae theologicae inter S. Thomam et Scotum,* pars prima
(Venice, 1614), p. 11.

[117] *Opera theologica posthuma in Primam Partem D. Thomae* (Lyon, 1690),
De visione Dei, dubium IV : An ratione naturali possibilitas visionis demon-
strabilis sit? (p. 46).

[118] 'When you are criticizing the philosophy of an epoch, do not chiefly
direct your attention to those intellectual positions which its exponents feel
it necessary explicitly to defend. There will be some fundamental assumptions which adherents of all the various systems within the epoch unconsciously presuppose' (A. N. Whitehead, *Science in the Modern World*, 1925,
p. 71, quoted by W. K. C. Guthrie, *The Greeks and their Gods*, 1950, p. 138).

to St Thomas. Shortly afterwards Cajetan reflected the training which he had received at Padua.[119] As a sincere believer he did not of course reject the supernatural. But he relegated it to the class of things termed miraculous, that is, he placed it among the arbitrary exceptions with which the philosopher had not to concern himself, even within the boundaries of faith, in his reasoning.[120] And so we have the attenuated, corrected and sincere form of the celebrated theory known as that of the 'twofold truth'. Theology thus became a special branch studied side by side with philosophy. There was no longer a Christian idea of man. 'The living image of the living God' was forgotten.[121]

[119] Cf. P. Mandonnet, in *DTC,* vol. 2, col. 1313: His time in Padua 'left a deep impression on Cajetan'; 'this university was at that time a famous centre of humanism and philosophism'. And col. 1326: Cajetan in 1512 published a commentary on the *De anima* of Aristotle: 'the commentator is of the opinion that Aristotle actually professed the doctrine that Averroes attributed to him: the unity of one intellectual soul for humanity and the mortality of the individual soul'.

[120] Cf. Pomponazzi, *De Fato, libero arbitrio et de praedestinatione* (Basle, 1567, Petri Pomponatii philosophi et theologi doctrina et ingenio praestantissimi Opera). Bk 5, c. 4: 'Homini autem Deus duos dedit fines, unum naturalem, alium vero supranaturalem. Naturalis autem finis hominis est Dei intellectio, quae per naturalia haberi potest. Supernaturalis autem est eiusdem Dei intellectio. Sed longe excellentior prima, ad quam perveniri non potest, nisi per supernaturalia et per Dei gratiam, secundum particularem influxum.' And pp. 980-1: 'Quanquam sic sit quod Deus voluerit ab aeterno homines esse beatos, intelligendum tantum est de beatitudine quae debetur hominibus ex puris naturalibus, ad quam per naturalia pervenire possunt.' Pontus de Tayard, bishop of Chalons, *Discours philosophiques* (1587): 'Anaxagoras, when asked for what end he thought he was born, answered, "To see heaven and the sun"; and my opinion will not be condemned by the holiest of judgments if I add that man is born to contemplate the world.' Cf. Abel Jeandet, *Pontus de Tyard* (Paris, 1860). See on the other hand Petau's protest, representing the Christian tradition: *De opificio sex dierum,* Proemium, I (*Dogmata theologica,* vol. 4, 1868, p. 226).

[121] Cf. P. Noël, O.P., *Œuvres de Tauler,* vol. 3 (1911), pp. 255-6, note.

8

The Problem of the Primitive State

Obviously, in this new way of explaining St Thomas there could have been no question originally of finding a device for the refutation of Baius. Nor does it appear, as some have thought, that concern to oppose Lutheranism played a leading part in the development of this exegesis.[1] For the latter, although not historical, was not consciously tendentious. Nor can any special purpose, any determinate intention, be discerned here. The phenomenon is something impersonal; it is the expression less of the thought of an author than of a situation. It formed one of the signs of that break in unity characteristic of the end of the Middle Ages and the coming of a new world. In its own way, at the intellectual level, it betokens the manifold disintegration of Christendom which, despite certain more favourable trends, forms so sombre an introduction to the modern period. Theology had reigned as queen of the sciences, and on occasion it had possibly taken unfair advantage of its title. Now it was beginning to lose its position; after dominating the whole of knowledge it was tending to become merely a separate branch.[2] The supernatural

[1] This is one of the motives discerned by Fr Doucet, *loc. cit.* Cajetan and his followers achieved distinction in the controversies of the early stage of the Reformation. The dates of the teaching seem nevertheless to show that their position had been adopted in advance. In any case it was made possible at least by the general state of mind prevailing in the Schools. (Cajetan's commentary on the *Prima* was completed in 1507.)

[2] From the sixteenth century onwards 'the Scholastics took no interest in contemporary philosophy, both as regards the reproaches that it addressed to them and the new systems which opposed them. . . . Far from contending with these new systems, the Scholastics of this period—save for rare exceptions—wished to have nothing to do with them. Treating their rivals with disdain, they sufficed unto themselves, and voluntarily cut themselves off,

end which is, so to say, the keystone of the arch, was no longer that of philosophy. The study of man was cut in two parts, the second of which no longer had roots in the first, and in this way an essentially good movement was dangerously perverted towards differentiation in the analysis of reality, and towards the recognition of an increasing autonomy at the various levels of human activity.

Of course, the new teaching did not make its way without encountering opposition in theological circles and its originators themselves were still far from building a whole system on it. The first controversies provoked by the Reformation, although they obtained some adherents for the new teaching, injected no new elements into it. But at this juncture, with the coming of Baius and the raising of the question of 'pure nature' with a certain acuteness in the sphere of human origins, there was a natural joining of forces, a fact which was to give shape to a whole new theology and greatly increase the power of its advance.

In what state, in relation to sanctifying grace, did Adam—or the angel—come from the Creator's hands? Was there at least a first interval of time during which he did not yet possess this grace? Had he even received it before his ordeal? In short, was he created 'in gratuitis', or only 'in naturalibus'? The question had for long been classic. For the first time at the beginning of the thirteenth century Prevostin of Cremona had spoken of a creation in grace, taking this term in its exact sense; but although he appealed, in the case of the angel, to St Gregory's authority and in that of man to St Anselm's,[3] William of Auxerre felt able to reproach him for departing from the usual view.[4] As a matter of fact all parties claimed to follow St Augustine, but this could not fail to seem ambiguous since it was not couched in the

shut up within a circle which grew continually narrower' (Maurice de Wulf, *Histoire de philosophie médiévale,* 2nd ed. (1905), pp. 519-20). But this picture requires some qualification.

[3] *Summa* (Todi, ms 71, fol. 89 and 92). On the whole question see J. B. Kors, O.P., *La justice primitive et le péché originel d'après saint Thomas; les sources, la doctrine* (Kain, 1922). Cf. J. Bittremieux, 'La justice originelle et la grâce sanctifiante' in *Revue Thomiste,* 1921, pp. 121-40.

[4] *Summa aurea,* bk 2, tract. 1 (fol. 35).

categories in which people were now called on to provide an answer. The twelfth-century theologians were still much nearer to the problems faced by Augustine and even to their terms;[5] but already a twofold line of interpretation was beginning to take shape among them : according to one party, with St Anselm at their head, Adam had first and foremost to preserve the justice in which he had been created; according to others, who in this were following Hugh of St Victor and Peter Lombard, he had principally to acquire justice, the absolutely primitive state being regarded as a neutral one, symbolized by the 'terra inanis et vacua' mentioned by the book of Genesis. On the one hand, therefore, a state of justice that was already positive, on the other an innocence that was still negative.[6] St Albert the Great, less decided than Prevostin of Cremona, wavered between the two theories.[7] The Franciscan authors, drawing their inspiration from William of Auxerre,[8] endeavoured to reconcile the differing testimony of the 'saints' by adopting, at least so far as man was concerned, a middle solution which discerned two phases in the state of innocence. It was the same with the Dominican Peter of Tarentaise (c. 1264-7), for whom man was by nature 'informabilis ad gratiam'; Adam did not possess this grace from the time of his creation, but he received it subsequently, before the time of his trial.[9] This was the view of the *Summa* of Alexander of Hales,[10] and of St Bonaventure, who adopted it as 'communior et

[5] The expression 'iustitia originalis', however, is due to St Anselm.
[6] See for example Arnaud de Bonneval, *Hexaemeron* (PL, 189, 1518-19).
[7] In his commentary on the *Sentences* he does not follow Lombard's opinion for the case of the angel, and in the case of man only so far as to fulfil his office of commentator and not without a formal reservation : 'quod tamen ego non credo, licet sustineam propter Magistrum' (*In II Sent.*, dist. 3, art. 12; dist. 24, art. 1). In his *Summa theologica*, where the conservative tendency prevails, there is no reservation at all (*Secunda Pars*, tract. 14, qu. 90): 'In hac (gratia) non fuit creatus Adam, ut dicit Augustinus.'
[8] *Summa aurea*, bk 2, tract. 10, c. 3, qu. 2 (fol. 61).
[9] *In II Sent.*, dist. 29, qu. 1, art. 2. On this work: H. D. Simonin, in *Beatus Innocentius PP. V, studia et documenta* (Rome, 1943), pp. 163-213.
[10] *Secunda pars*, qu. 91, m. 1, art. 1 : 'Alii ponunt ipsum (Adam) fuisse conditum solummodo in naturalibus, non in gratuitis gratum facientibus. Hoc magis sustinendum est, quia magis est rationi consonum et auctoritatibus probatum et divinae excellentiae declarativum.'

probabilior', saw it as 'required' by a 'multiplex ordo', and to
justify it had recourse to the general principle 'Necesse est quod
omne quod Deus facit, sit perfectum *vel perfectibile*',[11] and to
express it made use of the classical distinction between image and
likeness.[12] Eudes Rigaud, who also made a point of distinguishing
two successive 'states', 'ante gratiam' and 'in gratia', endeavoured
to explain certain opposing 'authorities' by assuming that for the
primitive state they only meant to speak of 'gratiae gratis datae'.[13]
The same view is to be found in William de la Mare who considered it in accordance with 'the order of wisdom' that the 'esse
naturale' and the 'esse gratuitum' were spaced out in time.[14] St
Thomas, at first undecided,[15] finally unreservedly adopted—we
shall shortly see why—Prevostin's view.[16] In the *Summa* there
is scarcely a trace of the old view when St Thomas says that
Adam was created outside paradise, and subsequently admitted

[11] *In II Sent.*, dist. 29, art. 2, qu. 2: 'Est alia opinio communior et probabilior, quod homo prius tempore habuit naturalia, quam haberet
gratuita. . . . Multiplex ordo hoc exigebat, ut homo prius fieret in naturalibus, quam in donis gratuitis ornaretur' (dist. 3, pars 2, art. 1, qu. 1; also
for the angel, dist. 4, art. 1, qu. 2, ad 4m: 'Ideo, secundum ordinem
sapientiae, non statim debuit dare (gratiam), sed expectare motum liberi
arbitrii: quod et fecit; unde ad se conversis sine mora dedit gratiam.' *Sermo I
in dom. 12 post pent.*: 'Non fuit concreata gratia homini, sed dilata fuit
quousque homo quodammodo per actum rationis se disponeret ad suscipien-
dam gratiam' (Quaracchi, vol. 9, p. 399).

[12] *In II Sent.*, dist. 29, art. 2, qu. 2, ad 1m: 'Alterum dedit (Deus
homini), scilicet imaginem, et ad alterum habilem fecit, videlicet ad similitudinem, quam postmodum pro loco et tempore ei dedit.'

[13] II, 29, qu. 1: 'Adam in primo statu fuit quando non haberet gratiam
gratum facientem, et iterum fuit quando haberet. Unde distinguitur in illo
statu duplex status, scilicet, ante gratiam et in gratia. Illae autem auctori-
tates, quae dicunt, quod non fuit in gratuitis, concedendae sunt de gratuitis
gratum facientibus. Sed illae quae dicunt, quod creatus fuit in gratuitis,
intelliguntur de gratis datis' (ed. J. Bouvy, *Recherches de théologie ancienne
et médiévale*, 28, 1961, pp. 90-1).

[14] II, 29, qu. 3: 'Est alia opinio, quae dicit quod non habuit; quae communior est secundum sanctorum attestationem, et propter ordinem Sapientiae
quae hoc requirebat ut sicut aliud est esse naturale et aliud esse gratuitum,
et (conferantur?) diversis temporibus.'

[15] *In II Sent.*, dist. 4, qu. 1, art. 3; dist. 20, qu. 2, art. 4; dist. 29, qu. 1,
art. 2. Also *De veritate*, qu. 28, art. 2, ad 4m et 5m.

[16] *Prima*, qu. 95, art. 1.

AUGUSTINIANISM AND MODERN THEOLOGY

to it.[17] Scotus, on the other hand, followed Hugh, Bonaventure and the others.[18] Matthew of Aquasparta did so too.[19]

From then onwards the Thomist and Scotist solutions shared the schools of theology between them. As we know, the fathers of Trent in their decree on original sin took care that their language should not appear to take sides on the question.[20]

But by this state 'tam sine gratia quam sine culpa' rather different things could be understood. In the 'naturalia' or 'pura naturalia', frequently mentioned in medieval texts, it was possible to introduce 'original justice' with its gifts of completeness and immortality, or else, taking the expression 'pura naturalia' in its strictest sense, to apply this only to the properties owing to nature and deriving from its principles.[21] And in line with this thought, it was then wondered whether it was possible to envisage— although actually we know that it did not happen in this way— a creation of man 'in puris naturalibus' in the strictest sense, that is, not only without sanctifying grace, but without even the gifts of justice, completeness, immortality, and with none of the 'gratiae gratis datae'. Could man have come from the hands of the Creator with only the constituent elements of his nature as man?

---

[17] *Prima*, qu. 102, art. 4.

[18] *In II Sent.*, dist. 5, qu. 1, art. 5: 'In prima mora fuerunt omnes in naturalibus'; qu. 2: 'Potest probabiliter sustineri quod in primo instanti fuerunt uniformes in statu naturae, creati sine gratia'; dist. 28, qu. unica: 'Potuit aliquis esse in puris naturalibis tam sine gratia quam sine culpa.'

[19] *In II Sent.*, dist. 29, art. 1, qu. 2 (J. Auer, *Die Entwicklung der Gnadenlehre in der Hochscholastik*, 1, 1943, p. 73).

[20] Estius points it out, *In II Sent.*, dist. 25, n. 1: 'Unde satis liquet . . . , dum ita circumspecte locuti sunt . . . studio voluisse abstinere a definienda quaestione inter Catholicos disputata' (Paris, 1680, p. 255). Tauler follows Bonaventure's and Scotus' view, but understands it in accordance with his own teaching about the 'state of pure nature' in which he believes that Adam was in paradise: *Third Sermon for the Blessed Sacrament*, n. 4 (ed. Hugueny, vol. 2, p. 106).

[21] This was observed, for example, by Thomas of Lemos, *Panoplia gratiae*, vol. 1, *Isagogicus*, vol. 2 (1676), pp. 11-12: 'Ne autem in aequivoquo disputatio procedat, explicandum est diligentius, quid per has voces homo in puris vel solis naturalibus, tam sanctus Thomas quam Doctores caeteri intelligant. Nec enim semper idem omnino per illas voces significant.' There follows an analysis of the principal passages of St Thomas in which the expression occurs, sometimes in one sense and sometimes in another. See also Bellarmine, *De gratia primi hominis*, c. 3.

In this new question it was no longer a matter of knowing whether original justice was independent or not of sanctifying grace— itself a question much debated through the scholastic period—and whether Adam enjoyed the former before the latter was conferred upon him; but could original justice have been refused to him before any sin on his part, as it was actually taken away from him after his sin?

Here again there were different answers. Some writers, heedful of the Creator's sovereign freedom, did not believe that they could reject the hypothesis; like Richard of Middleton, they admitted that the first man could have been subject to a certain 'labour', a certain 'angustia' by nature and not as a punishment.[22] Others, struck rather by the eminent dignity that accrued to man from his end, sought to reconcile, as far as they could, the gratuity of the 'superadded' gifts with the pressing need that, it seemed to them, human nature in all its complexity had of these gifts. Giles of Rome, to whom a whole school of thought looked as an authority,[23] was one of the most positive in this sense:

> Cogimur dicere fuisse quamdam opportunitatem et quamdam necessitatem et quoddam debitum, quod natura humana in sui institutione fuerit cum quodam dono supernaturali et gratuito. . . .
>
> Licet Deus potuisset facere naturam sibi secundum suum cursum derelictam, voluit, secundum decentiam suae sapientiae et bonitatis, producere naturam humanam cum quodam dono gratuito, quod vocabatur originalis iustitia. . . .[24]

[22] *In II Sent.*, dist. 30, art. 2, qu. 1 : 'Natura humana ante peccatum, sicut instituta fuit cum iustitia originali, nulli potuit subiacere paenae. Sicut vero potuit a liberrimo. . . . Dei institui, non repugnasset certe alicui subesse paenalitati, quae tamen ei non punitio sed labor quidem et angustia fuisset' (p. 375).

[23] See below, chapter nine.

[24] *In II Sent.*, dist. 30, qu. 1, art. 1; dist. 37, qu. 2, art. 1. Cf. dist. 31, qu. 1, art. 1, where the question of the end is raised directly (Venice ed., 1581, pp. 408, 442-3, 467). Cf. Hervé Noël, *Quaestio de peccato originali*, and *In II Sent.*, dist. 30 (in R. Martin, *La controverse sur le péché originel au XIV* *siècle*, Louvain, 1930, pp. 28-31, 56-7, 102-3).

St Thomas Aquinas had encountered the question right at the beginning of his career. He had then envisaged on one occasion, in the abstract, without connecting the problem with that of the last end, the possibility of 'another man'—'alium hominem'—left by God in the state of being liable to suffering and death.[25] But whenever subsequently he considered either the finality of the rational soul[26] or the righteousness in which scripture teaches that this soul was created[27] or lastly the noble state in which it was born—he goes so far as to assert, at least according to certain manuscripts,[28] its divinity, and that is the reading adopted by the older editions—he concluded that grace must have been granted to him in the act of creation itself because there was no other means of ensuring for him, 'ratione suae compositionis',[29] this original justice, this twofold righteousness of soul without which he was unable to conceive the soul. Such a solution must have satisfied him the more in that in it he was uniting both the Augustinian teaching on the primitive state and Aristotle's principles on the human composite. This was the solution adopted by, among others, John of Paris.[30] Yet all, even in the Thomist school, did not go so far. Thomas of Strasbourg, the Augustinian, for

[25] *In II Sent.*, d. 31, qu. 1, art. 2, ad 3m: 'Poterat Deus in principio, quando hominem condidit, etiam alium hominem ex limo terrae formare, quem in conditione naturae suae relinqueret, ut scilicet mortalis et passibilis esset, et pugnam concupiscentiae ad rationem sentiens; in quo nihil humanae naturae derogaretur, quia hoc ex principiis naturae consequitur.' If St Thomas had envisaged the end of such a being, probably he would have attributed to it, if he had thought of it as without grace until the end, an earthly happiness. But more probably it is a question here only of a being 'in quo potest salvari ratio entis' (cf. *Prima,* qu. 25, art. 5 ad 1m).

[26] *In II Sent.,* dist. 30, qu. 1, art. 1. *De Malo,* qu. 5, art. 1.

[27] *Prima,* qu. 95, art. 1; cf. qu. 100, art. 1, ad 2m.

[28] *In epistulam ad Romanos,* c. 5, lect. 3: 'Natura humana dupliciter potest considerari. Uno modo secundum principia intrinseca, et sic mors est ei naturalis. . . . Alio modo potest considerari natura hominis secundum quod per divinam providentiam fuit ei per iustitiam originalem provisum. . . . Hoc autem providentia divina disposuit propter divinitatem (*or* dignitatem) animae rationalis, quae, cum naturaliter sit incorruptibilis, debebatur sibi incorruptibile corpus. Sed quia corpus . . . secundum naturam suam incorruptibile esse non potest, supplevit potentia divina quod deerat naturae humanae, dans animae virtutem continendi corpus incorruptibiliter.' Cf. editions of the Commentaries on the Epistles, Paris, 1563 (21r) and 1636 (p. 47). [29] *De Malo,* qu. 5, art. 1, etc.

[30] *In II Sent.,* dist. 20, qu. 6 (ed. J. P. Muller, 1964, p. 159).

example, like Giles of Rome, occupies here an intermeditate position; according to him, before his sin man did not have sanctifying
grace; but Giles would not have agreed that divine goodness left
man, at the first instant of his creation, endowed only with the
perfections of his nature without original justice; that would have
meant inflicting a punishment on him before he had committed
any sin.[31]

Such was the question which until the sixteenth century was
continually under discussion, the one which the Baianist controversy was to make more actual and vital until in the end it
changed its whole aspect. Baius appealed to St Augustine and to
St Thomas against an opinion which he wrongly asserted was
new and which he pronounced absurd. Man, he said, could not
have been created without the gifts of the Holy Spirit which were
indispensable to his moral rectitude.[32] But we know what was the
general climate of thought to which this thesis of his belonged.
In opposition to him, despite the apparently contrary authority of
St Augustine and despite the Thomist principles on the role of
original justice, some effort was made to bring into favour the
thesis of 'pura naturalia'. As in the case of Richard of Middleton, but with more assurance and without the scruples that had
made him still speak of 'paenalitas', it was held that man could
well have experienced, not as a punishment for sin, but by the
very fact of his nature, mortality, concupiscence and the whole
series of ills to which Adam's heirs are subject. In his course of
lectures at Louvain Bellarmine insisted: 'Dicimus concupiscen-

---

[31] *In II Sent.*, dist. 28-29, qu. 1: 'Homo antequam peccavit, habuit
gratiam gratis datam, non solum quantum ad naturales perfectiones, quae
sibi a Deo perfectissime fuerunt collatae sine suis meritis, et per consequens
totaliter gratis: sed etiam habuit gratiam gratis datam quantum ad donum
gratuitum supernaturale, scilicet originalem iustitiam, qua potuit immortaliter
semper vivere, et immaculatus corporaliter et spiritualiter perpetuo perma-
nere. Et istud decuit divinam bonitatem, quia *alias homo prius sustinuisset
paenam, quam commisisset culpam.*' To the objection arising from the fact
that neither the angels nor the animals have need of such gifts, he answers
that the situation of human nature is not like theirs. And then: 'Sccundo
dico, quod primus homo antequam peccavit non habuit gratiam gratum
facientem.'
[32] *De prima hominis iustitia,* bk 1, c. 4 (p. 55); cf. c. 6 (pp. 57-8).

tiam, ignorantiam ac difficultatem, quae modo sunt paenae, naturales fuisse futuras, si homo ita creatus fuisset. Homo siquidem non in puris naturalibus, sed in magna gloria et honore conditus est.'³³ The majority of theologians were to imitate Bellarmine, and what some medieval writers regarded merely as 'not repugnant' came increasingly to be held as the normal condition.

It was traditional to reckon a certain number of successive 'states' in the unfolding of the history of salvation, from the creation of human nature in Adam until its fulfilment in glory. The first of these states was that of 'natura humana bene condita', according to St Gregory the Great's phrase,³⁴ or 'ordinate instituta'.³⁵ A *Summa* of the school of Laon in the twelfth century called it 'status bonae naturae'. It is also termed 'status naturae conditae, institutae, integrae. . .'. But this state itself could be divided in two, and in two ways. The first way was that adopted in another treatise of the school of Laon, which distinguishes the state in which the first man was before his sin, and the state in which he would have been subsequently if he had not sinned: 'unum quidem ante delictum, in quo tametsi mors aberat ab eo nec adhuc ullo modo peccaverat, poterat tamen in eo voluntas esse peccandi. Alter vero, in quo mutari potuisset, si firmiter in Dei praeceptis manere voluisset; tunc etiam id adeptum foret, ut non modo non peccare vellet, sed ne posset quidem aut peccare aut velle delinquere.'³⁶ The second way was the one we have seen above, that of the Franciscan school; the *Summa* of Alexander of Hales gives expression to it by speaking of a 'status naturae simpliciter', or a 'status pure naturalis' or 'status conditionis' and a 'status gratiae' which came shortly afterwards but did not last.³⁷ In their list all the authors mention next the 'status culpae', or the

³³ *Sententiae Michaelis Baii* (Le Bachelet, *Auctarium Bellarminianum*, p. 315). The influence of the language of the Fathers can be felt here, but it is certainly no longer their teaching.
³⁴ *Moralia in Iob,* bk 20, n. 28: 'Natura igitur humana bene condita, sed ad infirmitatem vitio propriae voluntatis lapsa' (*PL*, 76, 154 A).
³⁵ Cf. St Thomas, *Compendium theologiae*, c. 187.
³⁶ Quoted by Landgraf in *Scholastik*, vol. 13, p. 371. (Cod. Bamberg, can. 10, fol. 23).
³⁷ II, p. 1, inq. 4, tract. 3, tit. 1, c. 1, ad 1m (Quaracchi, vol. 2, p. 730).

'status post lapsum', or 'status praesentis naturae sui mutabilitate turpiter vitiatae',[38] 'status corruptionis' and 'status naturae lapsae'. There then came, in the third or fourth position, according to whether or not account was taken of the duplication of the first state, the 'status naturae reparatae', which could itself be divided into 'status gratiae' and 'status gloriae' (or 'paenae aeternae').[39] And so Alexander of Hales could well remark : 'Multiplex est status hominis'.[40]

Nevertheless, the fundamental scheme remained threefold. If, like the pre-Scholastics, attention was paid principally to man's situation in relation to evil and to good, that is, to his freedom, three distinct states were discerned in order—innocence, wretchedness and glory; for even after the work of redemption and even after the reception of grace, human nature here below remains affected by concupiscence, the consequence of sin; it is still in a state of wretchedness.[41] If, with the Scholastics, man's situation in relation to the gifts of God was envisaged, there were discerned, also in order, completed nature, fallen nature and redeemed nature.

In none of these older lists, in any case, was there room for a certain sort of 'pure nature', which had not yet been thought of. Cajetan himself, in distinguishing five 'status' or 'modi' of rational nature, seems not to have thought of it.[42] Even the expression 'state of pure nature' in the sense that was one day to prevail, would have appeared contradictory, for a 'pure nature' could only be a nature considered according to its specific principles alone, in its essence, abstractly, whereas a 'status' presupposed a realization, qualified in some manner.[43] But after the sixteenth century

---

[38] Summa 'Origo et principium', School of Laon (O. Lottin, *Mélanges Pelzer*, p. 84).

[39] Alexander of Hales, *Summa, loc. cit.*   [40] *Ibid.*

[41] This is why the Summa 'Origo et principium', which does not mention glory, knows only two states; and the other text of the Laon school, which duplicates the primitive state (or adds to it the state which would have followed for Adam if he had chosen the good), knows only three, the third being : 'Tertius status est post delictum, in quo mors illum necessario secuta est et peccatum ipsum et voluntas peccandi' (Landgraf, *loc. cit.*).

[42] *In Primam Secundae,* qu. 109, art. 2.

[43] Cf. J. B. Kors, *op. cit.*, pp. 115-36.

this contradiction was no longer felt. The exact meaning of the word 'status' became blurred. By a mixture of the two abstract and concrete points of view, this 'state of pure nature' was to be added to the old lists. Like them the new lists were often fluid; on occasion they became complicated : thus Gregory of Valencia and Thomas of Lemos, the two famous opponents in confrontation on the *de auxiliis* congregations, both differentiated between six states of human nature, which they counted in somewhat different ways.[44] Nevertheless, just as the old scheme was fundamentally threefold, the new scheme which was obtained in this way was essentially fourfold.[45] The first of the four states in this series, which was henceforward no longer homogeneous, was the state of pure nature : a state that was not real like the three others, neither historical nor concrete, but simply possible, or more exactly 'futurable', whose position was intended to guarantee the gratuitous character of the prerogatives adorning innocent humanity in paradise.[46]

The renewed discussion on 'natura pura', or, as was still to be said for some time, on 'pura naturalia', concerned, properly speaking, only two things : on the one hand, bodily suffering and death; on the other, concupiscence, or to use St Augustine's language, acclimatized by the *Sentences* of Peter Lombard, the state of ignorance and difficulty.[47] The problem is always posed, therefore, within the context of human nature, that is, of a mixed nature, compounded of body and mind, sensuality and reason, paradoxically enough made up of an immortal soul and a corruptible body. But it was here that the

[44] *Valentia, Commentaria,* vol. 1 (1603), 1216. Lemos, *op. cit.,* p. 9.

[45] The number four possessed the advantage of being traditional in itself, as St Augustine had enumerated four states of free will in man : 'ante peccatum', 'sub peccato', 'sub gratia', 'in gloria'.

[46] Cf. Antoine Moraines, S.J., *Anti-Jansenius* (Paris, 1652), p. 191 : 'Fusius de his statibus tractant recentiores eius (S. Thomae) interpres . . . licet humana natura hos solum status habuerit reipsa . . . plures tamen esse et concipi possunt, quos accurate distinguunt recentiores theologi : nimirum, status naturae purae. . . .'

[47] For an exact understanding of St Augustine's views on this subject, see Yves de Montcheuil, 'L'hypothèse de l'état originel d'ignorance et de difficulté, d'après le De libero arbitrio de saint Augustin' in *RSR*, 1933.

change of meaning crept in whence 'pure nature' in its new acceptation emerged. Each of the four states that are distinguished is defined statically, according to the logical meaning of the word,[48] by it own characterstics, without any connection or passage from one to the other, and without any thought at first of its bearing on finality. Yet these problems were to be solved without even having been propounded, and while for St Thomas 'in the sense in which the word "ordo" designates a relationship of finality' there was 'only one *ordo,* that which joins the spirit to its one and only final end',[49] the *state* of pure nature, henceforward undisputed, was also to become a purely natural *order.*

Some time had elapsed since the golden age of Thomism. The idea of a finality intrinsic to being was now, if not absent or opposed, at least generally inoperative. Thus, in fact, it was no longer seen that there was an essential difference between the old idea of Adam created without grace or even without preternatural gifts, and the idea of man destined for a natural end was taking shape and becoming more pronounced every day. The change from one thesis to the other occccurred without it being suspected that there was any occasion to justify it.[50] The explanation of the first, which alone relied on explicit reasons, was accompanied by a formula which assumed the adoption of the second. Commented on, twisted, interpolated in this way—and in complete good faith—the old texts were easily made to furnish authority

[48] Cf. St Thomas *Secunda Secundae,* qu. 183, art. 1 : 'Status significat, proprie loquendo quamdam positionis differentiam, secundum modum suae naturae, quasi in quadam immobilitate.'

[49] Schütz, *Thomas-Lexicon,* p. 555. H. Bouillard, *op. cit.,* p. 80.

[50] Thus Thomas of Lemos, *op. cit.,* p. 11 : 'Aliquando per voces istas (in puris naturalibus) intelligunt . . . naturam cum iustitia originali, sicut ab aliquibus sine gratia iustificante condita ponebatur; in qua significantur et alia supernaturalia dona elevantia hominem in finem supernaturalem.' Readers will notice the equivocal nature of the words in this passage where Thomas of Lemos wants precisely to get rid of equivocation. According to him, would St Bonaventure, for example, have believed that Adam in his first state was destined to a purely natural end? One of the colleagues of Thomas of Lemos, Joseph Gallien, wrote also in 1745 : 'In the days of St Thomas no one doubted the possibility of the state of pure nature; since even most theologians held that this state had existed in the first condition of man and the angels' (*Lettres théologiques touchant l'État de Pure Nature,* 2nd letter, p. 14; cf. p. 4).

for the new doctrines. The argument about nature in its first state[51] was applied without effort, absolutely, to the angel and to every spirit that could be created. There was to be continual confusion, a few examples of which we shall see below. But we can observe at this point how the second stage operated as already we have done for the first. Molina and Suarez provide us with an example just like that given by Cajetan and his two followers.

The *Concordia* of Molina (1588) is the first real work of Scholastic theology published by a Jesuit. It is also one of the first in which the theory of the four states appears. This theory occurs at the beginning of the book, a mere matter, says Molina, of convenience of arrangement. But what thus appears to be done only for ease of explanation is in reality pregnant with doctrinal consequences. The viewpoint adopted by the author is in the first place strictly that of free will in relation to grace in conformity with the actual title of the work.[52] In this way the new theory was inserted in some way in the Augustinian tradition, and this brings to mind the famous description of the four successive states of human nature which St Augustine had defined in connection with the 'posse peccare'. In the same way the description of the first state is in entire agreement with Scholasticism : it is the state of man 'in puris naturalibus', that is, 'sine peccato et sine gratia, ac sine ullo dono supernaturali'. An early Scholastic would have been able to accept it, not suspecting that it as good as called in question the supernatural finality of the human soul.[53]

[51] There is a very clear definition of the opposing positions in, for example, Giles of Rome, *In II Sent.*, dist. 31, qu. 1, art. 1 (pp. 442-3).

[52] 'While neither Baius nor the censors of Louvain and Douai in 1586 took any interest in the problems of psychology, in Molina's *Concordia,* in 1588, a statement on the nature of human freedom precedes a theory of the works of grace' (Anthony Levi, *loc. cit.,* p. 294).

[53] Just as the way in which Gregory of Valencia defines the state of pure nature in no way prejudices the question of finality. *Commentaria,* vol. 1 (1603), cl. 1216 : 'Primus (status) est hominis in puris naturalibus, scilicet, neque ullo dono gratuito, neque ullo peccato obstricti. . . . Fuit tamen possibilis hic hominis status, et potest etiam in illo considerari homo, quatenus ordine quodam rationis prior est natura, quam supernaturalia dona gratuita.'

In this state, Molina continues, nature is to be left in the duality with which it was born, and so a contest ensues as between two contrary natures, and at every moment man can deviate from the natural end peculiar to him according to his higher part, that is, from working in accordance with right reason. There again, there is nothing but what is harmlessly traditional; we can recognize the language used by St Thomas in his treatise on human acts. Yet we must be on our guard: the term 'finis naturalis' which has slipped into Molina's sentence is a transitional formula which, imperceptibly, will take us very much further. And now we are at the second state, that in which our first father was actually established. It comprises certain privileges, since in Adam God created the whole of human kind with a supernatural end in view.[54] This way of connecting the preternatural gifts enjoyed by innocent humanity with its supernatural vocation can also find authority in Thomism. But in the process, without saying so expressly, and above all without the slightest proof, Molina gradually accustoms us to the idea that the normal last end of man, his essential end, that which now belongs fundamentally to his nature and directs its whole activity, is not the vision of God but some 'natural beatitude' of an inferior order. The hypothesis, thus prepared for by imperceptible stages, is finally explicitly formulated in the course of the description of the third state, which is that of man after sin; but it is done as if it were an idea already accepted, a truth already established: as a consequence of his sin, Adam lost the preternatural gifts, but his natural powers remained to him, 'quales illas essemus habituri, si in puris naturalibus ad finem tantum naturalem a principio conditi fuissemus'.[55]

[54] *Concordia*: 'Primus est status naturae humanae in puris naturalibus, sine peccato et sine gratia, ac sine ullo dono supernaturali. Hunc statum numquam homo habuit, neque unquam habebit; philosophi tamen naturales in eo crediderunt hominem fuisse conditum. Haec omnia in causa sunt, ut solus homo, qui quasi duabus naturis inter se contrariis constat, a fine naturali secundum portionem superiorem sibi proprio, hoc est ab operatione secundum rectam rationem, quam saepissime deviat. . . . Secundus status est, in quo reipsa primus parens fuit constitutus. . . . Cum enim Deus in Adamo totum genus humanum in finem supernaturalem condiderit . . .' (1876, pp. 16 and 17). [55] *Concordia*, qu. 14, disput. 3.

Suarez too takes as his starting-point the old idea of man made 'in puris naturalibus'. He uses a phrase which shows clearly how from this idea the passage to the modern idea of 'natura pura' occurred. It is to be found in the Prolegomena of his treatise *De gratia*. Having recalled that man could have been created without the enjoyment of the supernatural gifts, he adds: 'Amplianda est quaestio ad totum tempus.' For why should not what is possible at a given moment not remain possible indefinitely? In other terms, why could not what constituted the first state (real or possible, concrete or abstract) of human nature be envisaged as itself forming a complete cycle? Why should not the *state* of pure nature be prolonged in this way into a natural *order,* fitted to find its fulfilment in a natural end? Despite the 'quaestio' which he uses, Suarez does not—any more than Molina—really ask himself the question. For him, it is already solved, for the reason we saw in the last chapter. After all, if it is only a matter of duration, we can grant him the point: 'plus vel minus temporis non mutat speciem'. A purely natural order was therefore possible, not only, as many had allowed for long past, at different degrees among their numberless hypotheses 'ex potentia Dei absoluta', but 'ex potentia ordinata' : 'naturalis (finis) sufficit'.[56]

Among Suarez' contemporaries, and much later still, the same process can be observed. Everywhere the terminology used bears traces of the old problem which concerned merely the creation of man and his original state. The new idea appeared clearly as an additional problem. It is so in the short work that one of Vasquez' disciples, Isidore de Torrès, actually devoted to the various states of human nature. He explains that the state of pure nature, which is a state mentioned by theologians as an addition

---

[56] *De gratia,* Prolegomenon 4, c. 1 : 'An possit homo in statu purae naturae creari.' Suarez himself observes, *ibid.,* n. 16 : 'Homo potuit in puris condi naturalibus. . . . Assertio, ut opinor, communis est Theologorum, licet eam magis supponant quam disputent.' The proof that he then undertakes to furnish looks very much like a *petitio principii* : 'Probatur ratione, quia, cum finis ultimus hominis duplex sit, potuit Deus creare hominem ad solam beatitudinem naturalem. . . . Quamvis enim necessario (Deus) creet (naturam humanam) propter aliquem ultimum finem . . . nihilominus oportet ut ille finis sit supernaturalis, quia naturalis sufficit' (n. 17).

to those formerly listed, is that in which man would have been
created without grace or sin, and he holds it as certain that such
a creation could have taken place. And he adds : 'Potest *etiam*
Deus ita condere naturam, ut nollet eam ordinare ad beatitudinem supernaturalem.'[57] The addition had been made, but Torrès
does not seem to have perceived it any more than Suarez and
Molina did. Moreover, as many have pointed out, St Thomas did
not speculate on the question of knowing what man 'conditus in
puris naturalibus' was capable of, as he speculated on the 'natural
desire' of beatitude. And so each theologian could endeavour to
have the great doctor on his side by providing some subtle reason
for his silence.[58] The innovation crept in more easily in this field
of the primitive state than it did in that of the last end; it had
no need of an involved exegesis for its justification. As it arrived
just at the right moment to stave off the peril of Baianism, it
could hardly be unwelcome. Before the end of the sixteenth century this innovation, in combination with that going back to the
time of Denys the Carthusian and Cajetan—and it was this
which formed the real danger—had drawn away in its powerful
current an important number of theologians.

For some time still many an argument 'de statu purae naturae'
was to be confined within the context of origins. Jansenius, and
following him Arnauld, were highly critical of a last end which
was anything but the vision of God; but in other passages they

[57] Luisius Turrianus, *Tractatus de gratia,* opusculum 1, disputatio 2
(Lyon, 1632), p. 5.
[58] Cf. Didacus Alvarez Metinensis, O.P., *Responsiones ad obiectiones
adversus concordiam liberi arbitrii cum divina praescientia . . . prout a S.
Thoma et Thomistis defenditur,* bk 5, c. 5 : according to Suarez: 'Sanctus
Doctor in tractatu de gratia nihil dixit de homine in puris naturalibus,
signum ergo est, illum sub homine lapso comprehendere, secundum rationis
paritatem : neque enim credendum est, vel illum statum hominis ignorasse,
vel incompletam tradidisse. . . . Ergo . . . idem sensisse videtur do homine in
puris naturalibus quod de homine lapso.' To this Alvarez replied that this
induction was false. Nevertheless, 'non sequitur quod S. Thomas illum statum
purae naturae ignoraverit, vel diminutam doctrinam tradiderit; nam, cum
medium aliquo participet utroque extremo, tradendo doctrinam exactam
utriusque extremi, censetur sufficienter explicasse ea quae pertinent ad
statum medium' (vol. 2, 1624, pp. 63 and 70-1). Cf. *Prima Secundae,* q.
109, art. 2 and 3.

were led to oppose the idea of a first and purely natural state.[59] Against it they quoted passages like the following from St Augustine : 'Grave iugum super filios Adam . . . non fuisset, nisi originalis delicti meritum praecessisset';[60] or this from St Prosper : 'Quod est humanae miseriae, non de institutione Creatoris, se de retributione Iudicis.'[61] Fr François Annat answered this in 1652 in the fifth book of his weighty work *Augustinus a Baianis vindicatus*. The eleventh chapter is entitled 'Bonum naturae conveniens posse differri ad tempus, salva providentiae aequitate'. In it we can read the following :

> Ut dicatur possibilis status purae naturae, *necesse non est supponi perpetuum*; neque modo negotium ei facessimus, cui placeat illa sententia quae diceret, sicuti supposita rationalis animae immortalitate consentaneum est ut Deus tali homines regat providentia, quae impediat ne sit aeternus separationis illius status : sic, supposita beatitudinis capacitate, consentaneum esse providentiam quae non patiatur, in creatura rationali nullo peccato impedita, perpetuam esse impotentiam aspirandi ad bonum cuius capax est. Non dico hoc esse necessarium aut verum, sed, dato, non concesso, dico nihilominus stare quod intendimus. Nec similiter negamus, quin pura natura sibi relicta brevi tempore labi possit in statum peccati, unde puta esse desineat. *Non ergo pugnamus pro perpetuitate status pure naturalis*; hoc postulamus, ut saltem pro aliquo tempore concedatur possibilis. Erit autem, si aliqua possit esse boni etiam debiti dilatio. Nam hoc quoque modo mortalem fuisse Christum absolute dicimus, etiamsi debita illi esset, et statuto tempore concedenda immortalitas.[62]

[59] *Augustinus, De haeresi pelagiana,* bk 6, c. 11 (vol. 1, pp. 147-8). Cf. *De statu purae naturae,* bk 2, c. 19 : 'Pelagianos, purae naturae architectos.' Arnauld, *Seconde Apologie pour Monsieur Jansénius* . . . (1645), bk 2, c. 11 (*Œuvres,* vol. 17, p. 140). But the two points of view are sometimes combined. See below, chapter nine.

[60] *Contra Iulianum,* bk 4, c. 16 (quoted by Arnauld, *Œuvres,* vol. 17, p. 143 and vol. 41, pp. 298-9).

[61] *Contra Collect.,* c. 21 (quoted by Arnauld, vol. 17, p. 142).

[62] Bk 5, c. 11, n. 1 (p. 517). Cf. c. 12 (p. 532): 'Ipsi quoque putatis esse Augustinianum, et a vobis atque a nobis non incommode intelligitur et expli-

This does not mean that Fr Annat is ready to agree with Jansenius and Arnauld in the rejection of any idea of a natural beatitude; but he distinguishes two problems, and in dealing with the problem of pure nature, he is satisfied here with asserting the initial possibility; he does not transform it into a cycle or complete order which would be included in an appropriate last end.

Traces of this origin of the theory, which is closely related to the theory of origins, could be found at a later date.[63] Nevertheless, passages like Fr Annat's at this period were already exceptional. The deviations that we have observed in Molina, Suarez or Isidore de Torrès prevailed. Indeed they were almost inevitable, since the system of which they were the preparatory stage was already virtually preformed in the philosophical tendencies of the period. The distinction between Thomists, Scotists and Nominalists was no longer at work here. The time when it governed intellectual life was over. Another age was in the process of being born, an age when minds were governed by quite other considerations. 'Pure nature' in its new acceptation was not therefore the invention or the special property of any of the old schools. It figured among the principles of none of them, but it was to become the common portion of what henceforward was to make up the 'School'. In view of the general ideas which in some sort formed the intellectual atmosphere then being breathed by the theologians of all parties without distinction, it had become practically impossible to refute Baius in any other way without the danger of making concessions in greater or lesser degree to his error.

catur, dari auxilium innocenti naturae debitum, eoque sensu naturale, quo possit amari Deus et coli in imperfecta quadam et decolorata beatitudine; hoc acceptamus, atque inde argumenta vestra contra possibilitatem status purae naturalis irrita reddimus.' This 'imperfecta quaedam et decolorata beatitudo' may mean here a last end which is not earthly, but it is not very clear.

[63] It is so in B. de Rubeis, *De peccato originali* (1757), a work directed against Jansenius, c. 52-3; the hypothesis is introduced in connection with the primitive state, but it is much more a question of concupiscence, of the possibility of observing the natural law, and so on, than of the last end (ed. of 1857, pp. 302-9).

Despite the little foundation for it in tradition, 'pure nature', understood as a complete order, had thus become a quasi-necessity. If it was to be safely avoided, what was probably needed was a more definite philosophy and a deeper level of religious thought than this unhappy period usually possessed, despite the greatness of its concrete religious achievements. For all the brilliance of its development, the theological movement originating in the Council of Trent remained—and it is hardly surprising—inadequate to the gigantic task confronting it. It did not equal in power the religious movement that it was intended to buttress, and the whole extent of the Catholic movement for reform was thereby seriously restricted. The evolution which had previously begun to take shape continued to progress. In the field of anthropology as in others, a twofold separation became more pronounced, exaggerating or falsifying entirely legitimate differentiations, and began to bear its fruits—the separation of independent philosophy and traditional theology, and, within the latter, the separation of Scholastics from spirituals. The second was already old; the first had been taking shape for some time; in practice it was realized with Montaigne, until the process was complete doctrinally with Descartes.[64] Both figure in some sort in the constitution of the new system.

It is clear, moreover, that after the dialectical abuses, after Luther, Calvin and Baius, a recasting of the theology of the supernatural was necessary. Minds had evolved, ideas and problems had changed, the words themselves had more or less altered in meaning. From now on a preciseness of statement and a caution were required with which the older writers had not to be burdened. The distinction between the various 'orders' required a more complete technical equipment than St Augustine or even

---

[64] 'In everything that (Montaigne) says, he leaves the faith out of account' (Pascal, *Entretien avec M. de Sacy*). Descartes was to write 'etiam pro Turcis'; he had no opinion about grace, he always took 'great care to confine his curiosity to natural things' (Baillet). Cf. Louis Bouyer, *Autour d'Erasme* (1955), p. 188 : From the sixteenth century 'the ascent from the human to the divine is made as from one stage to another. The contact between these two worlds, henceforth closed in on themselves, each complete in itself, remains purely external' (English trans. *Erasmus and the Humanist Experiment*, London, 1959, p. 211).

St Thomas had at his disposal. It is certainly a pity that there was not to be found a great mind to carry out this recasting with full awareness of the task in hand, preserving at the same time the sense of tradition in the new system. Less daring and more given to innovation though they were, the theologians who improvised the defence of orthodoxy are yet not to be blamed. They did what they could, as quickly as possible with the means at their disposal. They were perhaps more logical, in any case they were more clear-sighted, and when all is said and done, they rendered the Church a far greater service than those who, no less incapable of reviving genuine Augustinianism, could only take their stand on equivocal or over-subtle positions which at the time of Jansenism were to facilitate the revival of Baianism.

But perhaps we are better equipped nowadays to rediscover in its first vigour, and without falling into archaism, the genuine Augustinian spirit—or rather the whole of ancient tradition. Perhaps, too, the system which we have observed emerging in Javelli and Cajetan, and which took shape at the time of Baius in a form that was still moderate and became systematized already in Medina, Molina and Suarez, and was soon to triumph with the Carmelites of Salamanca, John of St Thomas and many others, has since then sufficiently shown its consequences, both doctrinally and in practice, for us to be in a position to discern its weak points. Of course, it is not the 'pernicious system' that the Jansenist party, right to the end, made a point of denouncing in caricature.[65] Against Baius' ideas on original corruption, which recalled Luther's theology when he railed against nature as a hot-bed of pestilence, and reason as the 'devil's prostitute', it helped to maintain the rights of a sound humanism.[66] In this way,

[65] Thus the *Lettres d'un théologien à M. sur la distinction de Religion naturelle et de Religion révelée* (by Abbé Rivière, alias Pelvert, c. 1768), pp. 34 and 6: 'I distinguish . . . the teaching of the Jesuits and their followers on the state of pure nature from that of the more accurate theologians who consider this state as impossible, or at least as non-existent.'

[66] Even when defined by its 'natural end', 'pure nature' seems to have been postulated in the first place not so much in favour of the gratuity of the supernatural as in favour of nature itself in reaction against Baianist pessimism. It was intended principally to show that man, even fallen man,

psychologically it appears bound up with one of the most wonderful successes shown us by the history of the Church : the Jesuit missionary movement of the end of the sixteenth and the beginning of the seventeenth century. Another connection, more paradoxical perhaps but attested none the less by the facts, conspired to endow it with a certain nobility. In reaction against an excessive and unilateral eudemonism which, erroneously claiming the authority of St Augustine, was in danger of injuring the very essence of Christianity, the theocentric trend originating with St Francis de Sales often made use of the same theology. The 'new mystics' were naturally to seek the assistance of the new theologians. To the great discomfort of Bossuet and of poor Noailles, Fénelon in his own way brought Molinism into the controversy over pure or disinterested love. It is true that he refused to allow his hypothesis, taken from the 'tradition of the saints', to be confused with that of pure nature, the result of debates in the schools; it is true also that immortality appeared to him, as to the old theologians, bound up with 'Christian beatitude', a natural beatitude being in his view only something passing.[67] Nevertheless, by insisting as he did on the obligation on every man to love God even to the extent of sacrificing himself to his glory, should God refuse him that blessed vision which always depends on a free and gratuitous will,[68] Fénelon moved, if one may say so, in a theological climate which was ensured by the partisans of 'pure nature'. It was no chance encounter nor an arbitrary alliance if many Jesuits so warmly embraced the Archbishop of Cambrai's cause. Nor yet was it the result of chance or of purely individual combinations of thought if Noailles and even Bossuet, whose

retains at least a little real freedom; that children who die unbaptized are not condemned to the pains of hell; that the actions of good pagans are not sins, and so on.

[67] *Troisième lettre à M. l'Archevêque de Paris sur son Instruction pastorale* (*Œuvres,* Paris, vol. 2, p. 495). *Responsio D. Camerensis ad epistolam D. Parisiensis* (*ibid.,* p. 553). *Troisième lettre en réponse à celle de Mgr l'évêque de Meaux* (p. 654).

[68] *Première lettre à M. l'Archevêque de Paris* (pp. 470-5); *Première lettre à M. de Chartres* (vol. 3, pp. 128-9). We should notice, moreover, that such a case practically belongs to those 'impossible suppositions' of which the mystics of his school were fond.

theology tended towards that of the 'disciples of St Augustine', were led in spite of themselves to falsify the idea of charity in their controversy with Fénelon.

The new system therefore did render distinguished services. Everything that it desired to ensure was to continue to be. None the less, its technique was insufficient and even its inspiration was not always enough. And on a last analysis some of its results proved unfortunate. For after all, it effected a separation between nature and the supernatural which was finally to be fatal. Was not the relative autonomy which it granted to nature, as it defined it, a temptation to independence? Did it not encourage in this way the 'secularization' let loose at the Renaissance and already anticipated in the preceding centuries by the Averroist movement?[69] Was the dualism which it tended to establish even conceivable? Is it really certain that it at least succeeded in maintaining in all its completeness the idea of the supernatural? Was it not too wide a concession to opponents to admit the hypothesis of a state— and as a result to acknowledge in us a whole sphere of activity— in which it was not the principles of sovereign charity and unconditional submission that reigned, but those of commutative justice? In the last place, were the anti-Baianist theologians always able to distinguish fully between the two orders made separate by their own zeal? And does not this fact lead to the reflection that the trend which they originated led in the following century to the assured success of the theory of 'natura creata supernaturalis' which, though not condemned of course, remains more than suspect? Some held that the supernatural is only gratuitous in relation to us sinners, others that it already was so in relation to Adam. But both Baius' opponents and supporters only too often agreed on a purely extrinsic and relative definition of the supernatural in accordance with its inaccessible and gratui-

[69] Speaking of the apologetic engendered by this new system Fr Richard Defrennes once wrote : 'We have the right to be sorry about this secularization of thought . . . , and we can wonder what was its responsibility for the present confusion of thought and morality' : 'Essai de synthèse de la théologie dans la Charité' (Congrès des lecteurs des Provinces franciscaines de langue française, Brives, 1932), p. 18, note 3.

tous character, without going back to the final reason for this gratuitousness which, on any hypothesis, makes it inaccessible for any nature whatever, that is, without going back to its intrinsically divine character. Why, therefore, could not a created being have been imagined, one superior to man and the angel, for whom whatever is supernatural for the angel or for man, and even the beatific vision, would have been natural? This hypothesis was systematized—though not propounded for the first time, for it was an old Nominalist fancy—and in some sort taken to its final point of perfection by Martinez de Ripalda, one of the most voluminous of Baius' adversaries and, so to say, his official refuter.[70] The fact is that, together with those theologians who adopted the new system in its entirety in so far as it was exclusive, Ripalda, cut off from tradition, lost sight of the whole object of the Christian revelation in its concrete fulness. In the supernatural he could no longer see anything but a 'super-nature', 'a sort of second storey carefully placed on top of lower nature by the heavenly Architect',[71] without discerning in it at the outset what is above all nature.[72]

---

[70] *Adversus Baium et Baianos* (1648). Last century it had a vigorous opponent in Fr Jovene, *De vita deiformi,* duplicated course of lectures given at the Institut Catholique in Paris, pp. 357-87.

[71] Cf. Karl Rahner, *Mission and Grace,* vol. 1 (London, 1963), p. 63.

[72] Although he did so more decidedly than others, Baius was not alone in misunderstanding the supernatural. From the end of the Middle Ages onwards there had been a general lowering of the spiritual standard among the theological speculators of late Scholasticism. Then, as Thomassin observed, in the sixteenth century, and still in the seventeenth, many of those who contributed to the controversy on grace were as if hypnotized by the twofold problem then raised by *gratia actualis*: either they wished to determine the degree of wretchedness to which sin had reduced nature, or else they endeavoured to find a way of reconciling grace and freedom in the work of salvation. Of course, the idea of our 'elevation' was not absent—the word was used more than ever—but understanding of it was sometimes inadequate. Thomassin, *Consensus Scholae de gratia*: 'Frequentius etiam et evidentius de gratia actuali sermonem habere, quam prius. . . . Accuratius incumbere in defensionem auxiliorum generalium ad tuitionem libertatis nostrae et possibilitatis mandatorum, ne impiis quidem exceptis, adversus Lutherum' (Vivès, vol. 6, pp. 357-8). And on the theologians of the following century: they have, he said, paid too much attention to the *auxilia actualia,* although they did not expressly separate them from sanctifying grace, and it was this conduct which made additional difficulties in the controversy with the Protestants and rendered the Jansenist deviation easier (pp. 473-4).

9

From Jansenius to the Present Day

With Ripalda we come to that generation of theologians who refute Baius through Jansenius. Not seldom the victims of the same narrowness of method as their forbears, and far less aware of the novelty of their theories, these theologians were no more successful in re-establishing Augustinian thought in its true light. Thus, in opposition to the new heresy, they did not confine themselves to rejecting its final conclusions as they were set out in the five condemned propositions,[1] or to emphasizing, sometimes to excess, its kinship with Protestant teaching;[2] then, too, they would discuss the passages of Augustine which seemed to favour it,[3] or else, on the model of Annat[4] and Moraines,[5] would just drop the Doctor of Grace on those points on which he seemed to them to go too far, and they would appeal from his exclusive authority, as Jacques Pereyret did,[6] to the compensating authority of the

[1] Such, for example, were François Bonal and the group of Franciscans studied by Henri Bremond, *Histoire littéraire du sentiment religieux en France*, vol. 1, 3rd part, c. 1. English translation, *A Literary History of Religious Thought in France* (1928), Vol. 1, pp. 305ff.

[2] Thus Dechamps, *Defensio censurae sacrae Facultatis theologiae parisiensis* (1646). It was the 3rd ed. of this work which, with additions, was published in 1654 under the title: *De haeresi iansensiana ab apostolica Sede merito proscripta libri tres ad SS. Papam Innocentium X*. Cf. A. de Meyer, *Les premières controverses jansénistes en France*, pp. 199-202.

[3] This was the case with Dechamps again. Fr Daniel complained of this method which was confined to setting one text against another, a method which was too common for his liking among both Catholics and heretics: *Défense de Saint Augustin* (*Œuvres*, vol. 2, pp. 329-30).

[4] *Op. cit*. See Noris, *Vindiciae Augustinianae* (Padua, 1673), pp. 21-6. Noris also says of him (p. 125): 'Uti caeteris recentioribus eruditione inferior est, ita universos in censura adversus Augustinum ferenda facile superavit.'

[5] *Anti-jansenius* (Paris, 1652), pp. 680-2. Cf. Noris, *loc. cit*.

[6] *Traité de la grâce*, dictated at the Collège de Navarre at the Sorbonne in 1650. It was opposed by M. de Barcos: *Augustini . . . auctoritas in Ecclesia*. Cf. the proposition condemned by Alexander VIII.

263

Greek Fathers and of a wider tradition; in general, they came to use the same tactics as had come to be used in the end against Baius. Without seeking from Augustinianism a deeper and more certain understanding of the question as a whole, they developed their refutations on the basis of the idea of 'pure nature' which henceforward was solidly established. Jansenius, however, had not been condemned for this: this was undeniable as was often pointed out, and on this Macedo[7] and Berti[8] insisted, as Fernand Litt reminds us.[9] It was none the less after Jansenius, and in reaction against him, that in the schools there came to be established the idea of two beatitudes determining two last ends and of a natural 'perfect' beatitude.[10] It was then, too, that the Scotist school watered down its formulas, retreating in the face of the new Thomism, against which it had at first protested: its 'appetitus innatus' became an 'appetitus naturae valde consentaneum', its 'capacitas' became a 'mere capacitas' and so on. The two parties continued the argument as to whether the desire was 'innate' or 'elicited', but the debate had no longer any fundamental interest. Whereas the new Thomists had only recently been saying as against Scotus that there was no 'innate' desire, but only an 'elicited' desire, from which nothing conclusive could be deduced, it was now the Scotists who, against the rare Thomists faithful to 'natural desire', maintained that there is no elicited desire but only an innate desire, from which nothing can be proved.[11] Thus,

[7] *De statu naturae purae* (1673).

[8] *August. systema . . . vindicatum,* dissert. 2, preface: Jansenius had upheld the impossibility of pure nature as Baius had done, and he was not blamed for it by the Church. Gerdil was to say the same thing in about 1770: 'Notes on the theological theses of an Augustinian' (*Œuvres*, Naples ed., vol. 5, pp. 472-5).

[9] *Op. cit.*, p. 78; cf. p. 151.

[10] E. Elter, S.J., 'De naturali hominis beatitudine ad mentem scholae antiquioris' in *Gregorianum*, vol. 9 (1928), pp. 269 and 284-5. Before Jansenius' time even those who were prepared to accept the idea of 'natural beatitude' often said: 'beatitudo tantum imperfecta', 'quodammodo felicitas dici potest,' 'valde imperfecta', 'aliqua beatitudo', 'beatitudo secundum quid', etc. Afterwards these restrictions disappeared almost completely. See above, chapter seven.

[11] Claudius Frassen, *Scotus Academicus* (1st ed., 1673).

with an equal rejection of the old tradition a new conformism was established and was soon triumphant.

Besides the advantages that it offered in the anti-Jansenist controversy, the new idea provided a convenient framework for the explanation of the doctrine. A Thomist theologian explained it in the following century: 'The theologians,' he remarked, 'have no other interest than to maintain the possibility of the state of pure nature, since it provides them with an easy and convenient means of making the distinction and preventing confusion between the natural and the supernatural.'[12] In addition, of course, both schools encountered it as the final result of one of their own tendencies. In Thomism it marked the extreme point of that consolidation of creatures in their own being which had, so to say, provided the backbone for the translucent and fluid world of Augustinianism. In Scotism it helped to express the keen sense of the sovereignty of God which could not be limited by the laws of any being whatever. Molinism, on the other hand, embodied in it its high regard for human freedom, which it looked on, perhaps too easily, when it yielded to its propensity, as a kind of independence in respect to grace. Here in brief, then, lies the explanation of how so recent an idea became not only common among theologians of every school, but occupied an increasingly important place in their synthesis.[13]

The first of the theses which the Jesuits published in Louvain on 12 March 1641, in opposition to the passages of the *Augustinus*, which reproduced the teaching of Baius' fifty-fifth propo-

[12] Joseph Gallien, O.P., *Lettres théologiques touchant l'État de Pure Nature* (Avignon), 1st letter, p. 110.

[13] Belleli, *Mens Augustini de statu creaturae rationalis ante peccatum* (Antwerp, iuxta exemplar Lucernae impressum, 1711), bk 3, p. 199: 'Controversia de possibilitate status purae naturae celeberrima, hac nostra aetate facta est. (Those who follow St Augustine exclusively assert that such a state is impossible.) E contra vero quamplures ex universo scholasticorum coetu possibilitatem illius status adstruere nituntur. Quoniam autem Baius et Iansenius Augustini mentem tueri et explicare conati sunt, sed infelici labore—Augustini enim veritatibus varios ipsorum errores miscuere,— inde factum est, ut quamplurimi ab Augustini casta sententia desciverent.' Also Berti, *Systema augustinianum de gratia . . . vindicatum* (*De theologicis disciplinis*, 1792, vol. 8, p. 388), and de Carboneano, *De propositionibis ab Ecclesia damnatis* (Migne, *Theologiae cursus completus*, vol. 6, col. 680-1).

sition, declared : 'Tam angelica quam humana natura potuit condi sine ullo dono supernaturalis gratiae, in puris naturalibus : gratiam enim naturae indebitam esse ex ipsis terminis est manifestum.' The fourth of the eight propositions, drawn up by Isaac Habert in 1644 to be submitted for censure to the Sorbonne and then to Rome, is a passage from the *Augustinus* which denies this possibility. Thus as the attack by Jansenius was more detailed and far more severe than that by Baius, so the rejoinder was now more immediate and showed greater awareness of the means at hand. The defensive weapon with ready in advance.

The Louvain theses, of course, were said to be 'in accordance with St Augustine and tradition'. But they could not be called just 'doctrina catholica' or even 'doctrina communis', but more modestly 'doctrina theologorum societatis Jesu'.[14] Isaac Habert's proposition was not accepted in Rome.[15] Moreover, neither Habert, nor the Jesuits of Louvain, distinguished in the formula the question of concupiscence from that of natural end; in this they were only following Jansenius himself and the great Arnauld who more than once went from one to the other.[16] In the *Augus-*

---

[14] *Theses theologicae de gratia . . . in quibus doctrina theologorum societatis Iesu contra Corn. Iansenii Augustinum defenditur* (Paris, Chastellain, 1641). As we know, the future bishop of Apt, 1695 (d. 1736 at Marseilles), a very zealous anti-Jansenist, had an edition published at his own expense; at that time his name was Abbé Joseph-Ignace de Foresta de Cologne.

[15] *La défense de la foy de l'Église et de l'ancienne doctrine de Sorbonne touchant les principaux points de la grâce.* Habert there lists 'twelve deceptions' by Jansenius in his enumeration of the Louvain theses. It is in the attached letter, sent to Rome, that he formulates the eight propositions, the fourth of which is in the following terms : 'It is obvious that another nature endowed with reason could not be given existence without receiving the gift of supernatural grace', with reference to the *Augustinus*, vol. 2, bk 2, c. 4 (Cf. A. de Meyer, *op cit.*, pp. 183-6).

[16] *Seconde Apologie de Jansénius*, bk 2, c. 11. At the beginning of the chapter, Arnauld sets out a description of the state of pure nature without alluding to the last end : it is a question only of the old meaning. Then, a little further on, comes a second description in which is added the trait regarding the end : 'There would have to have been powerlessness or injustice in God if, without any sin on the part of the rational creature, he allowed it to groan in the dreadful and wretched state in which we see all languishing; in this darkness of the mind, in the intense darkness in which all men are buried when they are born and for long after their birth; in this powerlessness to do good or in seeing it and being unable to do it in their wretched weakness; in this shameful rebellion that they feel within

tinus, the question of the 'pura naturalia' in the old sense of the term, remained predominant as having a direct relationship with the central question of sin and its consequences. In this connection Jansenius formulated fairly accurately St Augustine's theory of the desire for beatitude and also drew his inspiration from him in the criticism which he made of the idea of natural beatitude : to follow certain philosophies concerning the idea of such a beatitude was, he declared, to show uncommon pride, for it amounted to attributing happiness to the powers of nature alone. Yet, although it was explained and backed up by a commentary on passages from St Thomas, the impossibility of a purely natural end arose in the *Augustinus* more particularly as a subsidiary argument, to establish that God could not create an intellectual nature without at once bestowing grace on it.[17] In the preceding chapter, we saw in connection with Fr François Annat that Jansenius' opponents often remained on this ground. Actually, in general they did not raise even the question of finality and, in the terms in which they expressed it, their thesis is incontestable even in the view of those who would not admit the idea of a purely natural end. This persistent confusion ensured for the idea the additional advantage of more numerous and, especially, older authorities. Lastly, the way in which the primitive 'natural' state, by the introduction of more or less natural helps, was brought closer to the state of 'complete nature', as it was called, contributed to the admission of the new thesis without apparent difficulty.[18]

themselves and which obliges them to blush even for their legitimate actions; and lastly, in their entire impossibility to become happy, although they feel naturally drawn to happiness, because it can only be found in the enjoyment of God, which cannot be acquired by the powers of nature alone, and yet without it it is impossible for a creature, made in the image of God, to be anything but wretched' (*Œuvres*, vol. 17, pp. 141-2); and c. 12 (pp. 147-8). Cf. *Quaestio theologica quod est nomen Dei, thesis tertia* (vol. 10, p. 34). See also the *Catéchisme de la grâce* by Feydeau, c. 1. Hugot, *op. cit.*, pp. 110-11, was able to distinguish the two meanings far better, but without seeming to understand that they could be dissociated.

[17] *Augustinus*, bk 2, 'De statu purae naturae'.

[18] As a result of these helps there was a tendency to reduce the subjection to concupiscence. In addition, as was seen above, the old state of complete nature was often defined formerly by the expression *Pura naturalia*, a factor

However, as was shown in connection with the Baianist controversy, the system of pure nature, since for the majority of its upholders it consisted in the denial of the old teaching on the 'desire to see God', was not really traditional, and it offered no adequate basis for refutation. No doubt it seemed very convenient. It enabled the error to be opposed by something more than mere denial—a positive explanation whose apparent clarity and logic satisfied the controversial needs of the times. Thus for a time orthodoxy was preserved. But fundamentally, rather than cutting off the evil at its roots, the new system was merely a clearing of the ground. To ensure that over one region of human activity grace should prevail, it exposed another whole region to the danger of secularization. In opposition to the pessimistic exaggerations concerning the present corruption of nature, there was claimed for fallen man the power of performing certain morally good actions at least, for the reason that since free will was not destroyed by original sin there was no need for a special help to take its place or to restore it. After all, it was a little excessive to agree with the Jansenists, as formerly with the Baianists, on an idea of grace which, to say the least, was very incomplete. For what was thus set up as an ideal was human action performed solely by man's powers—whatever was said about 'assistance' or 'natural graces' acknowledge as necessary in other respects—and, as a result, freedom as its own master independently of God. A certain level of human sufficiency was first established. Only in the next place was an entirely contingent and wholly extrinsic supernatural order conceived which was placed above the natural order regarded in advance and in its very fulfilment as the normal

contributing to increase the confusion. Hence the possibility of assertions like the following from J. Gallien, *op. cit.*, second letter, pp. 17-18: 'Discussion on this state has changed. Formerly, everyone agreed about its possibility and it was only a question of knowing whether it had or had not existed. Nowadays, everyone agrees that it never existed, but the discussion is about whether it could have been possible. Jansenius and his disciples hold that it was impossible. . . . The remainder of theologians think otherwise, and consider the possibility of the state of pure nature as a truth which it is not allowed to doubt. . . . This discussion . . . arises from the fact that the Jansenists have reversed the true idea that was always held about this state' (cf. p. 15).

and properly human order. In this way something was added to the naturalist conception, which was neutralized by being completed with a supernatural theory, but it was not corrected or changed in itself. What was maintained, or made more explicit, was more than a necessary duality; a dualism was established according to which in practice positions could be held which were radically opposed to the conclusions that the Jansenists derived from their principles. But rather than refutation, the dualism stood out on analysis principally as a compromise.[19] It was too weak a weapon to make victory certain.

The Baianist controversy did not, any more than did the Jansenist trouble, which lasted more than a century, result in making this compromise obligatory. Whatever its usefulness at the time the thesis of 'pure nature' could not entirely lay aside its character as a system or obtain any other standing than that of an opinion of the Schools. This is shown in many of the ways of speaking of it. Joseph Saenz de Aguirre, the author of a *Theologia Sancti Anselmi,* mentions three different positions regarding it: some call it impossible, others absolutely possible, others really possible. Now among the first, in addition to Protestants, Baius and Jansenius, he places a certain number of orthodox theologians, and among them he quotes neither St Thomas nor his first disciples, but merely some of his commentators, the first of whom is Cajetan.[20] It is, says Saenz de Aguirre again, a question discussed by the 'theologi recentiores'. Right at the end of the eighteenth century the Jesuits of Paris, who, like their colleagues of Louvain, were the most ardent promoters of

[19] This stands out particularly in the great work by Ripalda (mentioned above). He never quotes Jansenius, but the work is directed against him from one end to the other, as the principal Baianist.

[20] *Theologia S. Anselmi,* vol. 3 (new ed., Rome, 1685), p. 64: 'An sit possibilis status naturae humanae purae, seu carentis omni dono superaddito ad colendum et diligendum Deum. . . . Huic quaestioni, a Theologis praecedentis saeculi tractatae fere obiter, sed nunc in Belgio celeberrimae, occasionem praestare videtur Anselmus. *Theologi recentiores,* in Prolegomenis ad Tractatum de gratia, communiter distinguunt varios status naturae humanae, in quibus illa fuit, aut esse potuit. . . .' Like many another, De Aguirre confuses the two kinds of 'pure nature'. P. 68: 'In qua re triplicem invenio sententiam. . . .'

the theory, frankly acknowledged this. In a series of theses defended on 26 February 1692, after summarizing the teaching of St Augustine and mentioning the points on which all Catholics agree concerning the subject of the state of innocence, they added: 'Sed *Scholastici quaerunt* utrum homo creari potuerit in statu purae naturae, hoc est, cum mediis mere naturalibus, ad beatitudinem mere naturalem consequendam; vere quidem potuisse affirmant. At Augustinus hac de quaestione contra Pelagianos nihil habuit dicere; quaedam tamen ex ipso attulimus, quae huic *Scholae opinioni* favent.'[21]

This was to go too far. As a matter of fact there are many authors throughout the seventeenth century who do not mention such an opinion or who expressly reject it.

The new idea of 'pure nature' finds no place in Bérulle's views. In many passages of his *Opuscules de piété* Bérulle distinguished clearly the order of nature and that of grace,[22] but none the less he did not maintain the paradox of human nature as it is seen to emerge from ancient tradition.[23] 'One of our differences from other creatures,' he wrote, 'is that they were created perfect in their state and without the expectation of a further new degree which they lack; but man's nature was not created to remain in the limitations of nature; it was made for grace, and destined for a state raised above its power'. This expectation, he considered, is essential for us, for man's 'spirit emanated from God, with a relationship to God, as bearing his image and likeness, and was created to enter into communication with God's own essence: 'divinae consortes naturae'.

And it was the same with many spiritual writers, less open than the controversialists to the fluctuations of theological opinions,

[21] In Aug. Le Blanc (i.e. Serry), *Historia Congregationum de auxiliis,* Appendix, col. 474. In 1761, the *Dictionnaire théologique portatif* (by Alletz) stated: 'Pure nature, according to certain theologians, is a state . . .' (p. 332).

[22] For example, *Opusculum* 160, 1: 'The world of nature and the world of grace are two states, two orders and two such different worlds and so clearly separated and yet one exists and is to be found in the other' (G. Rotureau, Cardinal de Bérulle, *Opuscules de piété,* p. 454).

[23] *Opuscula* 132, 3 and 27, 3 (Rotureau, pp. 389 and 130).

FROM JANSENIUS TO THE PRESENT DAY

but whose doctrinal worth was as a rule by no means negligible. 'Who is not aware,' asked François Bonal, for example, 'that if grace and nature are separated none is more wretched than the rational animal?'[24] Bonal was none the less strongly opposed to Jansenism.[25] The Capuchin François d'Argentan in his turn in quite classical terms contrasted 'natural beings, created for natural ends' with man, made by God 'in his image for a supernatural end'.[26] 'Why,' he asked again, 'did God make the soul rational? Is it not obvious that it was so that it could possess him for eternity?'[27] Another Capuchin whom we have already encountered, Marc de Bauduen, conveyed the same teaching in its ancient simplicity in his Scholastic treatise called *Paradisus theologicus*: in his view, the object of our beatitude could only be God, our formal beatitude could only be the vision of its essence[28] and so, according to him, it was necessary to continue to say with Scotus: 'Deum clare visum esse finem naturalem hominis ratione appetitus naturalis et eliciti, sed esse in finem supernaturalem ratione mediorum quibus acquiritur.'[29] For the Dominican Vincent Contenson, too, the rational creature has only one really possible last

[24] *Le Chrestien du temps* (1655), p. 18.
[25] *Op. cit.*, 2nd part, pp. 4-5, etc. Cf. p. 150: 'There are two sorts of creation, to which we have contributed nothing. . . . Our first birth, and our second generation, says St Augustine, are two purely gratuitous favours.'
[26] *Les grandeurs de Jésus-Christ* (1674). New ed., 1837, p. 247.
[27] *Op. cit.*, vol. 3, pp. 65-6. Similar passages in the works of the Capuchins Sebastien de Senlis (*Les entretiens du sage*, 1637), Yves de Paris (*Des miséricordes de Dieu en la conduite de l'homme*, 1645) and Léandre de Dijon (*Les vérités de l'Évangile ou l'idée parfaite de l'amour divin imprimée dans l'intelligence cachée du Cantique des cantiques*, 1661); cf. Julien Eymard d'Angers, 'Le désir naturel du surnaturel' in *Études franciscaines*, 1950, vol. 1, pp. 211-23.
[28] 2nd ed., vol. 2 (Lyon, 1607), pp. 14, 23 and 32: 'Obiicies: beatitudo est supernaturalis; et homo est in ordine naturae; ergo non potest consequi beatitudinem. Respondeo verum esse quod homo non potest viribus naturae consequi beatitudinem, quae est ordinis supernaturalis; sed illam potest consequi adiutus lumine gloriae, quod est supernaturale lumen. Ex dictis colligitur, quod homo est capax beatitudinis, et habet inclinationem naturalem ad videndum Deum; et talis inclinatio est potentiae passivae ad formam, qua subiectum perficitur, et in ea quiescit; tamen beatitudinis consecutio est supernaturalis, quia obiectum beatitudinis est supernaturale.'
[29] *Paradisus theologicus*, vol. 1; cf. Julien Eymard d'Angers, 'De beatificae visionis naturali desiderio apud Bonaventuram lingonensem et Marcum a Baudunio' in *Antonianum*, vol. 29 (1954), pp. 45-62.

end: the vision of God, face to face; and, basing his thesis on St Augustine and St Thomas, he is able to explain and defend it, in agreement with a certain number of his colleagues and other theologians, against the opinions of the *recentiores*.[30] Concerning the Thomists, his contemporaries, who preferred to follow the new ways, he remarks: 'Mirum est quot subterfugiis tam aperta angelici nostri doctoris sententia, tot rationum longe praestantissimarum momentis stabilita, eludatur.'[31]

Contenson, of course, was suspected of Jansenist sympathies. But Bérulle certainly was not. If Port-Royal, through Saint-Cyran, had inherited only his spirit, Port-Royal would not have been Jansenist. Nor was it possible to suspect Bonal of Jansenism. Henri Bremond included him among his group of devout humanists; the same applies to François d'Argentan who opposed Jansenius with some ferocity, to Marc de Bauduen, for whom it was enough to be traditional, uncontroversially and without excessive subtlety. Nor did the former Jesuit Francesco Macedo, who out of his love for Scotus received permission to join the Cordeliers, spare Jansenius. While he refused to admit that its raising up to the supernatural creates any right in nature, this 'strenuus insectator Iansenii' makes no secret of it that he regards a purely natural order as impossible, and does not fail to protest against those who, on the authority of the Bulls of Pius V and

---

[30] *Theologia mentis et cordis* (1668), bk 7, dissertatio 3, c. 1, speculatio 2 (Vivès, vol. 2, pp. 277-91).

[31] *Op. cit.*, pp. 288 and 291: 'Quidquid obiiciunt recentiores, probat solum . . . statum naturae purae esse de potentia Dei absoluta possibilem.' Several theologians, Contenson's colleagues, endeavoured in vain to include him among the upholders of the new view by explaining that he understood the 'ordinary power of God' in a purely consequent sense, as 'that which governs or leads creatures according to the laws that he has himself established'; thus Gallien, *op. cit.* (1745), second letter, p. 82; or G. M. Albertinus, *Acroases de Deo . . . Creatore* (Venice, 1800, p. 223), refuting the writer of the annotation to Estius who had accused Contenson of maintaining a Jansenist thesis: 'Non haec Contensonii est opinio, qui eatenus non potuisse hominem de potentia ordinata in puris naturalibus fieri docet, quia de hac potentia ordinata ad id quod perfectum est Deus semper respicit: minime vero quod distortum aliquid aut malum fecisset, si in pura natura hominem condere voluisset. Adde Theologos potentiam Dei ordinatum, non antecedenter ex eo quod faciendum esset, sed consequenter ex eo quod factum est metiri.' Something of this explanation is certainly worth remembering.

Gregory XIII, condemn this opinion.[32] John Prudentius, the Servite, who in his day was a great authority,[33] held a similar view. Like Macedo and Contenson, he denounced the treachery of modern Thomists who, following Cajetan, Medina and John of St Thomas, 'squander', as he puts it, and 'destroy' the words of the master whom they claim to explain in their determination not to recognize in human nature any absolute and really natural desire regarding the vision of God. St Thomas, observes Prudentius, admitted such a desire and drew from it conclusions with the help of arguments that were clearer than daylight. It is extraordinary to see the tricks that were resorted to by these so-called disciples of St Thomas to weaken the efficacy of the arguments.[34]

The Augustinian school *par excellence*, or at least properly so called—that formed by the Hermits of St Augustine—is more categorical still. Made famous by Frederico Gavardi, Henri de Noris, Fulgentius Lafosse, Fulgentius Belleli and Giovanni Lorenzo Berti, amid all the controversy and objections, it maintained its doctrine unchanged. It was a school of theologians in a somewhat narrow sense of the word. They had no intention of setting themselves up as apologists nor did they endeavour to construct a complete system; like Giles of Rome[35] before them, they based their conclusions on scripture and hardly sought to know what could or could not be demonstrated by reason. When they dealt with this last point they were deliberately restrictive: 'Sententia nostra sit ista: possibilitas visionis beatificae non potest probari demonstrative solo lumine naturali.'[36] But on the

---

[32] *Collationes*, vol. 2, pp. 396-400: 'De statibus naturae humanae', 'De statu purae naturae'. Cf. Berti, *Augustinianum systema* (1747), p. 163.

[33] His *Opera theologica posthuma super Q. XII, XIV et XIX Primae Partis* appeared in Lyon in 1690 with a long dedication by F. J. Linas, the master general, to Cardinal Peter de Salazar; it is an extravagant eulogy of Prudentius. There are also fulsome praises by the censors.

[34] *Op cit.*, pp. 45-53.

[35] Thus *In II Sent.*, dist. 31, qu. 1, art. 1 (Venice, 1581, p. 443).

[36] Lafosse, *Augustinus theologus* (4 vols, 1676-83), vol. 3, p. 139; cf. p. 184: 'Cum igitur haec elevatio non possit naturaliter cognosci, nec consequenter appetitus innatus ad visionem beatificam. Quare argumenta, quae nos ad probandum huiusmodi appetitum, non sunt argumenta pure physica, et naturalia, sed theologica et radicaliter supernaturalia, in quantum fundantur supra revelationem et fidem, qua credimus hominem esse elevatum a Deo

issues at stake they made no concession, and their way of expressing them was not calculated to win over to their position those
who at that time were concerned with the consequences of the
Baianist and Jansenist affairs. Possibly to distinguish them from
the Jansenist school, there was usually attributed to them the idea
of a metaphysical possibility of pure nature and a merely 'moral'
necessity of the supernatural by reason of the wisdom and goodness of the Creator.[37] It is certainly true that many of their expressions seem to signify this kind of extenuated necessity : 'ex quadam
decentia', 'ex decentia divinae bonitatis', 'secundum aliquam
iustitiam decentiae et congruitatis',[38] or again 'titulo Providentiae',[39] 'lege iustissima Providentiae', 'attenta Dei Providentia',
the first group recalling those of Giles of Rome,[40] and the second
those of St Thomas in the *Contra Gentiles*.[41] But in most cases the
context shows that the moral necessity in question is not so much
the finality as the means to achieve it; the help of grace—'supernaturalia gratiae auxilia'[42]—and the light of glory, not the destiny
itself; or, if you like, the effective gift of beatitude to the individual, not the ordering of human nature in general to this
beatitude.[43] The rational creature, says Gavardi, for example, can

ad ordinem supernaturalem et gradum gratiae et gloriae. Sunt tamen ex
parte physica et naturalia : quatenus probabili ratione ostenditur hominem
debuisse elevari ad finem supernaturalem, et consequenter ipsum appetere
naturaliter.'

[37] Thus Palmieri, *Tractatus de ordine supernaturali,* 2nd ed. (1910), th. IX,
p. 59.

[38] Lafosse, vol. 3, p. 133; cf. p. 51: 'ex aliqua iustitia decentiae et
congruitatis'.

[39] Berti, *Augustinianum systema . . . vindicatum,* dissertatio II, c. 1, n. 8:
'. . . supernaturalis gratiae auxilia conferenda fuisse, ut posset finem suum
adipisci; non quod huiusmodi auxilia sint naturalia, pertineantque ad
naturae constitutionem; sed potius quia ad finem verum consequendum,
rationales creaturae egent adminiculis naturae ordinem excedentibus, et
quae propterea ipsis quodammodo debeantur, sive titulo Providentiae, quae
nulli denegat media necessaria ad finem assequendum, ut docuit Norisius.'

[40] *In II Sent.,* dist. 31, qu. 1, art 1 (Venice, 1581, p. 443).

[41] Bk 4, c. 52: 'divina Providentia supposita', 'considerando divinam
Providentiam'.   [42] Berti, *op. cit., ibid.*

[43] I said 'in most cases', for it is not entirely true for Lafosse. In addition
the formulas of Lafosse and Noris are not so strong as Belleli's. The last,
who is far more insistent, refuses to 'descend', as he puts it, to their explanations. *Mens Augustini de statu creaturae rationalis ante peccatum,* bk 3, c.
12: 'Scio doctissimos viros Norisium et post ipsum Fulgentium Lafosse, in

have no other last end than the possession of God; this is his
principal basis for establishing that it is created 'in gratia'.[44]
According to Noris it would be morally impossible that, in the
state of innocence, the sentient desire was not subject to reason.[45]
According to Belleli and Berti, God in his wisdom and goodness
must grant man the grace, that is, the only means which enable
him to attain his end; for given that man is made in the image of
God, that is, endowed with reason, he is ordained to see God.
Belleli, therefore, distinguishes a twofold 'raising up'; 'Nam
elevatio alia est ad finem nobilissimum, alia autem ad media
quibus est comparandus', and he says of the first: 'Illa ad
naturam ipsam pertinet, quae imago Dei est, et in nullo nisi in
Dei possessione potest esse quieta'.[46] In his explanation of his
colleague's thought he brings out this distinction very clearly, and
concludes from it: 'Consequens est deberi, spectata Providentia,
quae singulis rebus media ad finem assequendum necessaria sup-
peditat, ipsi creaturae rationali donum gratiae, sine quo numquam posset ad beatitudinem pervenire.'[47]

And so these Augustinians are in no doubt that the end of the
spiritual being, and consequently of man, is normally and on any
hypothesis beatitude, as defined by St Thomas, which is what
they and we term the supernatural end.[48] So sure are they of

eas responsiones descendisse ut assererent Deum debuisse rationali creaturae
dona gratiae suae elargiri, non debito rigoroso sed ex pura puta decentia'; the
expression is equivocal, Noris only used it to exclude the 'debitum ex intimis
naturae natum praecise, et secundum se, et non prout stat sub Providentia
iustissima Conditoris' (p. 468; cf. p. 472).

[44] *Schola aegidiana*, vol. 4 (Naples, 1690), p. 365.

[45] *Vindiciae augustinianae*, c. 3, n. 2 (Padua, 1673), pp. 26-38.

[46] *Mens Augustini. . . , loc. cit.*, pp. 415-16; he continues: 'Quapropter,
ad illum finem elevata dicitur eo ipso quod excellentioris ordinis supra
corpora et infra Deum ad ipsius imaginem et similitudinem conditus est.'

[47] *Augustinianum systema* . . . , dissertatio II, c. 1, par. 6, n. 5 (p. 390); n. 1:
'Propterea quod theologus noster doctissimus ac praestantissimus propugnaverit
creaturam rationalem, quae ad Dei imaginem condita est, debuisse ordinari
in visionem Dei intuitivam, ideoque mediis ad hanc obtinendam necessariis
fulciendam ornandamque fuisse, attenta Dei providentia, quae nulli creaturae
denegat quidquid necessarium illi est ad finis sui consecutionem' (p. 388).
Cf. n. 8.

[48] Even on the subject of the end, however, they add a distinction, which
is set out below in the quotation from Marcelli. See below, footnote 50.

tradition, so clear and satisfying do they find the teaching of St Augustine and St Thomas, that this, for them, is more an axiom than a truth to be established. They think it enough to recall that God had freely desired this end for his creature before creating him in his own image. And so in their thought, the discussion on the subject of 'pure nature' is usually directed towards 'the first state of the rational creature' far more than towards his destiny. They are well able to distinguish these two meanings of 'pure nature' and the two controversies which they have occasioned while observing at the same time that there is a 'connection' between them.[49]

Nothing is clearer in their thought, which only differs from one to the other by a few details. Marcelli, a later author, summarizes them all very clearly, recalling like them the teaching of St Augustine :

> Persuasum fuit Augustino, divinam non decere bonitatem atque iustitiam, ut rationali creaturae ad Dei imaginem factae, adeoque naturaliter ipsius visionem appetenti, gratiae denegetur auxilium ad illam consequendam necessariam. Atque idcirco, ex quo Deus, ad imaginem suam condendo illum, ad suipsius ordinaverit visionem, tanquam ad ultimum finem, sequitur impossibilem esse statum purae naturae.[50]

[49] Lafosse, vol. 3, pp. 42-3 : 'Status naturae purae duo importat : alterum essentialiter, alterum vero accidentaliter. Essentialiter importat carentiam ordinationis et elevationis ad finem supernaturalem, seu visionem beatificam; accidentaliter vero importat concupiscentiam.' And pp. 50-1 : 'Nolumus tamen in eo quaestionem nostram immorari, utrum videlicet Deus potuerit creare hominem in puris naturalibus quantum ad hoc, quod esset mortalis, dominanti concupiscentiae subditus, aut aliis infirmitatibus circumdatus : sed scopus propositae difficultatis est, num homo debuerit creari cum ordine ad finem supernaturalem, quanquam sit connexio inter hanc duplicem controversiam.'

[50] *Institutiones theologicae*, vol. 3 (1846), p. 346. Also p. 344 : 'Supposito nempe quod hominem ad imaginem ac similitudinem suam condiderit, cum ratio imaginis ordinationem importet ad Deum ipsum intuitive videndum tanquam ad ultimum finem, quem absque gratiae auxilio assequi non valet, tenebatur Deus aliquo titulo supernaturalis gratiae ornamento illum fulcire.' And p. 345 : 'Dedecet summam Creatoris bonitatem, ut homini ad imaginem et similitudinem suam, nimirum propter suiipsius intuitivam visionem condito, necessaria desint media ad illam obtinendam.' The distinction established by Marcelli, in the same paragraph, between absolute power and ordinary power, seems to correspond exactly to Berti's, referred to above.

To the classic objection, 'Si Deus naturalem appetitum homini ad intuitivam sui visionem indidisset, naturalia media ad illum explendum debuisset ei suppeditare', Marcelli gives the same answer as de Soto, thus emphasizing the continuity of tradition. With regard to those who raise a similar objection, the upholders of the possible state of pure nature in the modern sense, he still calls them, right in the middle of the nineteenth century, 'neoterici quidam Theologi'.[51] A theologian of later date, though he is not so firm on the general positions of the school, is no less clear in his explanations. In his treatise *De homine lapso et reparato,* Nicolas Le Clerc de Beauberon treats the question of 'pura natura' at length in connection with the primitive state. On this point he differs from his master Noris, whose thesis he regards as too like that of Jansenius. It is then that in his refutation of the latter he undertakes to prove that a state of pure nature is possible 'quoad viam', as the popes had laid down; but he reserves wholly the question of knowing whether it is so 'quoad terminum'.[52] The whole discussion, therefore, for him as more often than not for his predecessors, deals not with the last end but the conditions of the present life.[53]

This was the traditional way of raising the problem, so long as the idea of 'the image of God' kept something of its force and the idea of 'natural beatitude', the final development of an order of pure nature, had not been invented. And so it would be wrong,

[51] *Op. cit.,* p. 358.
[52] *Tractatus theologico-dogmaticus de homine lapso et reparato* (Luxemburg, 1777). 'Nonnulli theologi, status purae naturae possibilitati quoad viam, ut a summis pontificibus statutum est, addicti, illum quoad terminum per accidens possibile non existimant, quia naturalis beatitudo ipsis non videtur vera beatitudo. Haec opinio, quam, pro nostro instituto, intactam relinquemus' (Migne, *Cursus theologiae completus,* vol. 10, col. 822).
[53] Some theologians who opposed the thesis of the Augustinian school at first recognized its exact purport. One of them was P. M. Gazzaniga, O.P., *Praelectiones theologicae,* vol. 4 (2nd ed., Bologna, 1797), pp. 582-3: 'Aliqui insigniter docti Theologi omnino contendunt, statum naturae purae esse impossibilem. . . . (Dicunt hominem) ordinari necessario debuisse ad finem supernaturalem, . . . et, quoniam innatum ei tributum est perfectae beatitudinis desiderium, ad divinam bonitatem pertinuisse, ut etiam illa media supernaturalia ordinis ei suppenditarentur, quibus hunc finem assequi posset, attenta nimirium benefica Dei providentia.'

even if the solution of these Augustinians is rejected, to regard it as a new solution, intended as an attenuation, at least verbally, of Jansenism. Their orthodoxy, however precarious it may be thought to have been, has nothing in common with what Mgr Duchesne called 'an orthodoxy of converts'. As the heirs of an ancient tradition, excessively turned in on their inheritance, given to a far too pessimistic estimate of the consequences of sin, in the precise question concerning us they owed nothing either to Jansenius or to Baius. In this they differed from other 'Augustinians' of their period, from those like the celebrated Dom Robert Desgabets, a Benedictine of the Congregation of Saint Vanne, the author of an unpublished treatise *De l'état de pure nature selon les sentiments de saint Augustin*.[54] Noris, their leader, was an able historian and although he shared too largely the exclusive Augustinianism of Jansenius, at least he did not need to have recourse to the modern *Augustinus* to obtain information on Pelagius or St Augustine. It is in all sincerity and, it can be said, with entire objectivity—even if on occasion they are obliged to emphasize the fact to allay the suspicions of their opponents—that they criticize Baius and reject 'the Jansenist heresy'.[55] They hold resolutely to the teaching of their patriarch, Giles of Rome, who had explained the whole matter at length in his commentary on the second book of the *Sentences*.[56] Even if they sometimes men-

---

[54] Cf. René Taveneaux, *Le Jansénisme en Lorraine*, 1640-1789 (Paris, 1960), pp. 129-30.

[55] Berti does so at length, *De theologicis disciplinis*, vol. 3, bk 17. On Baius, see Belleli, *Mens Augustini*, bk 3, c. 21. Noris gave a commentary on the bull of St Pius V at Rome 'under the eyes of the Inquisition and of the Roman court' (Ilharat de la Chambre, *Traité historique et dogmatique sur la doctrine de Baius et sur l'autorité des Bulles des Papes qui l'ont condamnée*, Paris, 1731, vol. 1, pp. 214-15).

[56] Giles of Rome, *In II Sent.*, dist. 30, qu. 1, art. 1 (Venice 1581, pp. 408 and 409): 'Cogimur dicere fuisse quamdam opportunitatem et quamdam necessitatem et quoddam debitum, quo natura humana in sui institutione fuerit cum quodam dono supernaturali et gratuito sui: videlicet, quod anima humana de sui natura incorruptibilis, corpori incorruptibili per originalem iustitiam uniretur; quod Deus, sine culpa animae, non infunderet animam humanam incorruptibilem corpori de necessitate corruptibili. . . . Sed huiusmodi debitum et huiusmodi necessitas, non potuit esse absolute et simpliciter, quia tunc gratia non esset gratia, et illud donum gratuitum, videlicet originalis iustitia, per quam poterat anima se praeservare sine peccato, et

tion grace in a context in which Giles spoke rather of 'original justice', because he was thinking more especially of Adam's first state, it is no less true that Giles, and this is the essential point, like them, thought of no other last end than rest in God, as it had been described by his master St Augustine.

Whenever they can find some precedent in Giles or St Thomas, the terminology used by these Augustinians is apt to be close to that of the moderns and thus they had no difficulty in saying that the vision of God is our 'supernatural' end, or again, as it had always been said in the Schools, that grace is 'superadded' to nature.[57] If, to deny the possibility of a last end that is purely natural and regarded as normal, they find themselves in agreement with Jansenius, it is, as they all point out,[58] by virtue of another principle and in another spirit. Such an observation on their part is by no means pure opportunism; it arises from a sincere

per quam corpus poterat praeservari sine corruptione, fuisset simpliciter debita, non gratia data: cum non poterat dici illa originalis iustitia esse debita simpliciter et absolute, sed secundum quamdam decentiam divinae bonitatis.'

'Tertia via ad hoc idem, sumi potest ex ipso fine, ad quem homo est ordinatus et factus. Nam factus est ad habendum Deum et ad quiescendum in ipso, iuxta illud Augustini: Fecisti nos ad te. . . . Quod ergo homo in sui primordio factus fuerit talis, quod de necessitate stare non posset, sed opporteret ipsum averti a Deo et carere fine sibi debito ad quem est effectus et ordinatus, non decebat divinam bonitatem. Et quia hoc esse non poterat aliquo supernaturali dono, quod communiter ponitur fuisse originalem iustitiam, per cuius carentiam incurrimus peccatum originale. . . .'

See also dist. 22, qu. 2, art. 1; dist. 31, qu. 1, art. 1; dist. 32, qu. 2, art. 1; dist. 38, qu. 1, art. 2; dist. 41, qu. 1, art. 1.

[57] Thus Berti, vol. 8, pp. 374 and 386, etc. Cf. Giles of Rome, In II Sent., dist. 16, qu. 1, art. 3: 'quando in potentiis animae, in quibus consistit imago Dei, superadduntur habitus vel actus tendentes in Deum' (p. 14).

[58] Belleli, Mens Augustini, pp. 122-4. Berti, loc cit., p. 388, etc. Also the Franciscan De Carboneano, De propositionibus ab Ecclesia damnatis. Some authors accuse as Baianist or Jansenist anyone who denies the possibility of pure nature; nevertheless the Baianists are guided in this matter by principles that have been declared heretical by the Church: 'si ergo theologi sint, qui principia illa improbent ac alia via instruere conentur, vel Deum hominem concupiscentiae rationi rebelli subiectum condere initio non potuisse, vel debuisse etiam illum supernaturali gratia donare, cur damnati errores contra Apostolicae Sedis sententiam arguuntur? Sunt vero quam plures, qui hominem fieri potuisse, qualis nunc nascitur, negent, ac nonnulli etiam qui, attenta divina providentia nequidem sine gratia condi posse propugnent. Ex iis autem nemo cum Iansenianis convenit in damnatis erroribus. . . . Opinio haec novatorum haeresim detestatur' (Migne, vol. 6, pp. 680-1).

and reasonable conviction. I should not dare to say that their 'obscure ideas' of semi-need, of pseudo-necessity or quasi-gratuity denote in them 'a sorry poverty of thought'. Nor does it appear, if at least we confine ourselves to the problem of finality, that these ideas are really 'the soul of the Augustinian system'.[59] It is generally in assuming the supernatural finality of human nature that these theologians then say, as Giles of Rome had said before them : 'Cum dicimus necessarium fuisse hominem in sui institutione produci cum quodam dono supernaturali . . . , non est intelligendum talem necessitatem fuisse absolute et simpliciter, sed secundum decentiam divinae benignitatis.'[60] And in their thinking, such a kind of necessity did not create in man either a semi-need or a complete one.

Yet it must be admited that the difference here noted between means and end, that is between finality and its realization, tends on occasion to disappear. Actually these Augustinians formulated two other distinctions which also concern finality. Moreover these distinctions can help us to see better the support for their ideas that they considered they could find in tradition. If they had investigated them even more thoroughly, especially the first of them, they would probably have encountered this tradition itself in its living inspiration and by its means dispelled the scruples of many theologians and obtained their support. But for this more than knowledge was required; a power of spiritual re-invention would have been necessary of a kind that is hardly to be thought

[59] Cf. Guy de Broglie, 'De la place du surnaturel dans la philosophie de saint Thomas' in *RSR*, 14 (1924), pp. 202-3. The writer has changed his view somewhat on the subject of the Augustinian school. In 1924 he was wondering whether, fundamentally, 'the Augustinians have ever been able to defend their position in any other way than by giving up the attempt to understand themselves'. Yet in 1948 in his *De fine ultimo humanae vitae* he seemed to think that its representatives of the seventeenth and eighteenth centuries were the authentic continuators of the tradition of Giles of Rome (p. 261). In an article which was published a few months later (*Gregorianum*, 29 (1948), pp. 445-6), he regarded their teaching as a 'neo-Augustinianism' of an erroneous sort which could claim the authority of neither Giles of Rome nor any of his disciples right up to the middle of the seventeenth century. (Cf. *Gregorianum*, 1948, p. 451, on the 'cavillationes' of Noris and Belleli.)

[60] Giles, *In II Sent.*, dist. 30, qu. 1, art. 1 (p. 409); or dist. 31, qu. 1, art. 1 (p. 443).

of at their time. They were merely preservers of the tradition, and that is not the best way to be traditional. Their Augustinianism was not exactly false, but it was incomplete and somewhat arid. Of the two distinctions that they offer us, the first is made from the point of view of man and the second from the point of view of God.

For the formulation of the first they took their inspiration from the account of the creation as explained by St Augustine.[61] If we consider man, they tell us, 'according to his species', there is nothing in him demanding a supernatural end; but God, having wished to make him 'in his own image', had by that very fact made him with a view to his own likeness—which is only another name, when it comes to its end, for the vision of God.[62] It would be a complete misunderstanding to take this 'image of God', or 'this dignity according to which man is the image of God',[63] for some reality superadded to the spiritual soul. For Lafosse, Belleli and Berti, as it was for St Augustine and for all the Fathers and also for St Thomas, it is principally the soul itself considered in its higher part, with its natural powers of reason and free will : 'Cum (anima) sit imago Dei, est etiam naturaliter gratiae capax.'[64] If the idea of the 'image' adds something to the idea of the 'species' it is only in the sense that it is a fuller and more concrete view of the same reality; in the Christian view it no longer appears only in its 'specific' constituents, as it does to the abstract view of the philosopher—or in its phenomenological activity, as it does to the far more abstract view of the scholar—but it is grasped

[61] *Confessions*, bk 13, c. 22, n. 32: 'Neque enim dixisti: fiat homo secundum genus; sed: faciamus hominem ad imaginem et similitudinem nostram.'

[62] Cf. Berti, *De theologicis disciplinis*, bk 12, c. 3: 'Nihilo tamen minus, considerata ut imago Dei et relate ad finem ultimum, oportebat. . . .'

[63] Lafosse, *Augustinus theologus*, vol. 3, p. 95: 'natura humana secundum se praecise considerata, sive secundum quod exigit ex propriis principibus... ; humana tamen natura si consideretur ut est imago Dei ...'; p. 92: 'quatenus natura humana consideratur secundum se. . . . Si tamen natura humana consideretur secundum dignitatem partis superioris, in qua imago Dei effulget ...'; p. 93: 'illius dignitatis, secundum quam est imago Dei ...'.

[64] *Loc. cit.*, p. 96, with a quotation from St Thomas, *Prima Secundae*, qu. 113, art. 10.

in the depth of its being and its dynamic aspect. In this way we are informed that the soul is something other than a mere 'nature', that it exceeds the confines of 'Nature' and enjoys with the Creator a relationship of 'belonging', that is, both of dependence and kinship which have no analogy in the rest of creation. 'Rationalis natura, eo ipso quod imago Dei est, excellentissimum finem habet, qui eiusdem viribus longo intervallo superstat.'[65] From this point it may just be seen—but through the works of these Augustinians it could only be a glimpse—that another idea than that of 'pure nature' could account for, and even more thoroughly, divine independence in connection with it.

It was this that the second distinction, they thought, could succeed in showing. This distinction, to which Marcelli had recourse,[66] is nothing else than the classic one between absolute power and power ordained by God. He has no thought of contesting, he says in the name of his whole school, that by his absolute power God could designate for man any other end he pleased; this suffices for man not to have the right to demand anything, for, if the introduction of the idea of 'ordained power' reduces the objectively realizable hypotheses, it none the less confers on the creature no new right that it can exercise. Nicolas Le Clerc says similarly that, regarded in his absolute power, God is always free to refuse eternal life even to him whose works are good, but the case is different if he is regarded as the just judge who, according to his ordained power, is faithful to his promises.[67]

[65] Belleli, *De statu creaturae rationalis ante peccatum*, bk 3, c. 12.
[66] *Op. cit.*, col. 1126: 'Deus, ut Dominus absolutus, creaturarum bonis operibus affluentem, de potentia absoluta sine iniustitia vita aeterna destituere potest, eam in nihilum reducendo; secus ut iustus iudex, et de potentia ordinaria, et suis promissis subdita.'
[67] *Institutiones theologicae*, vol. 3, p. 345. There is a similar distinction made in Bernenc, *Systema augustinianum de divina gratia, excerptum ex operibus RR. PP. Belleli et L. Berti* (2 vols, Lyon, 1768). Vol. 1. p. 10: 'Statum naturae purae plurimi scholastici possibilem affirmant, tametsi de facto exsistentem negent. Contendimus nos impossibilem esse non quidem absolute in se, ex ratione omnipotentiae divinae, sed ex quadam decentia, quatenus infinitae Dei bonitati, iustitiae et sapientiae munus.' But it will be noticed that here the *status naturae purae* essentially concerns the primitive state, in any case the condition of man without grace and supernatural

By adopting this position the Augustinians intended to hold themselves at an equal distance from two extremes—from 'requirement' or 'necessity' on the one hand and on the other from 'pure suitability'. It has also been pointed out that they only applied to the destiny of man a theological scheme that was fairly widespread and applied without scruple to other problems which arose in analogous terms, such as those of the immortality of the soul, the resurrection of the body, or the immaculate conception of the Virgin Mary.[68] It remains difficult to be certain, if not for the heart of the matter, at least in the manner in which it is expressed, that their system provides complete satisfaction for the mind. There is always a certain disquiet provoked by hearing that the highest benefit of all, the one which includes all the others and thus realizes the very fulness of gratuitousness, is given to us 'iuxta exigentiam naturae', even when the statement is followed at once by 'prout stat sub iustissima Dei providentia'; it will always be tempting to see as an attenuation the assertion that 'non omnis ratio debiti excludit gratuitatem gratiae'.[69] Although it can hardly be accepted just as it is, the Augustinian system at least had the merit of showing better than others how man is the 'grande profundum' according to Christian tradition.[70]

As a matter of fact it was not wholly a group apart. Earlier even than Giles of Rome its fundamental distinction could claim the authority of St Augustine, often quoted and explained in early Scholasticism.[71] But without going back so far, it certainly appears that Estius in the seventeenth century thought almost

means, whereas he is made for a supernatural end that he cannot attain naturally. It is for this reason that God, *ex quadam decentia*, will without any possible doubt give him these supernatural means, and will not leave him to his 'pure nature'. For some of Noris' Augustinian predecessors see Winfried Boexe, O.E.S.A., *Introduction to the Teaching of the Italian Augustinians of the 18th century on the Nature of Actual Grace* (Héverlé-Louvain, 1958), pp.14-25.

[68] P. Augustinus Trapè, 'De gratuitate ordinis supernaturalis apud Theologos Augustinenses litteris encyclicis "Humani generis" praelucentibus' (*Ex Analectis Augustinianis*, vol. 21, n. 3, typis polyglottis vaticanis, 1951), pp. 250 and 262.

[69] Bernenc, *op. cit.*, vol. 1, pp. 342 and 344.

[70] A. Trapè, *loc. cit.*, p. IV.

[71] Cf. A. Trapè, *loc. cit.*, p. 255.

the same. In connection with absolute power, Estius said, concerning the gift of immortality, it is certain that without injustice God would have been able, as master of the whole world, so to institute human nature that the body would be subject to all sorts of afflictions which are the lot of animal nature, and therefore to death: 'cum enim creaturae suae Deus nihil debeat nisi quantum promittendo se obligat, iniustitiae argui non potest, si eam quando et quo modo vult, destruat'. Then, further on, dealing with the last end, he also states: 'It cannot be denied that God would have been able to hold man in a servile state, without the latter being able to expect any reward for his services.'[72] It was in his power not to call man to heavenly glory. In this way, it should be noticed, the gratuitousness of the supernatural order was not only asserted, but once again the sovereign independence of the Creator in relation to his creature and the absolute gratuity of his gifts in all circumstances were also asserted: for the idea was also excluded for a 'natural order' defined as the order in which man would have needs and rights. Estius is one of the theologians most remarkable for his extensive knowledge of the traditional sources and by his solid interpretation of them: 'doctor fundatissimus'. He was accused of Baianist tendencies and yet it has been possible to take from his works a refutation of Baius. His opinion thus assumes a certain significance. That this was, moreover, the very spirit of the original Augustinianism has already been observed at the beginning of this book.

More paradoxically still, Fénelon here adds his voice. This 'out and out Molinist'[73] is astonishingly close to those who, to many a Molinist, passed for Jansenists in disguise. He believed, of course, that is was possible for the supernatural end not to have existed, without distinguishing in relation to it absolute power and ordained power. He blames Bossuet and Noailles for compromising this truth at the very least, and drew upon himself

---

[72] *In II Sent.*, dist. 19, n. 2 and 10; dist. 25, n. 4 (Paris 1680, pp. 167, 172-4, 261). I think that these various passages are all to be understood in accordance with the clause expressly formulated in the first of them: 'si de absoluta Dei potentia loquamur'. But this absolute power is not simply bare power. [73] *Nouvelles ecclésiastiques*, for the year 1745, p. 109.

reproaches from Gerberon who approved his doctrine of pure
love; Gerberon considered that he had compromised it by wishing
to defend it 'by certain principles contrary to St Augustine'.[74]
But, as we saw in the last chapter, he refused nevertheless to allow
what was his dearest hypothesis to be confused with that of 'pure
nature'. Outside supernatural beatitude in this connection he did
not envisage any transcendent and eternal beatitude. God, he said,
'does not strictly speaking owe us any eternal beatitude'.[75] Without any change in the 'order' in which creation was established,
God could, he thought, decide to annihilate me in death, and
knowing it in advance, I would none the less be obliged to serve
him and love him. It is therefore within our own world—as with
every other possible or conceivable world—that the Creator, if
he does not bind himself by promises, is free to give or not to
give his creature access to beatitude. Fénelon held that there was
no ambiguity here. This is how he puts it in answering the Archbishop of Paris' criticisms :

> You take it very ill that I have proposed hypotheses of
> different states from those in which it has pleased God to
> place us. . . . My hypotheses are founded on God's freedom.
> Do you deny it? You say that I can suppose that he would
> have reduced men to the state of pure nature. No, Monseig-
> neur, my hypothesis has nothing in common with this state.
> What is to be thought of an argument in which almost
> always you attack me by putting words into my mouth which
> I never said? Deny to your heart's content the possibility of

[74] Gerberon, letter (unsigned) to Fénelon, 1698 (Fénelon, *Œuvres*, vol. 9,
p. 428): 'Your Grace assumes it as a truth that God can, without impairing
his wisdom, goodness and justice, create an intelligent nature which has no
relation with grace and glory. Nothing is more contrary to the principle
with which St Augustine attacked the Pelagians. . . . The rank held by
your grace in the Church does not allow him to excuse himself from learning
thoroughly about these matters at a time when they are the subject of so
much argument. . . .' On the relations between Gerberon and Fénelon, see
the learned and penetrating study by Jean Orcibal, 'La spiritualité de Dom
Gabriel Gerberon, champion de Jansénius et de Fénelon' in *Revue d'histoire
de l'Église de France,* 43 (1957), pp. 151-222.
[75] *Troisième lettre à M. l'archevêque de Paris sur son Instruction pastorale*
(vol. 2, p. 495).

the state of pure nature. For my part, I take care not to be imposed upon and to leave the precise case I have stated for the consideration of others foreign to it. It is a question only of the case in which man loves God supernaturally by the help of grace, and in which God, free in the distribution of his supernatural gifts, does not give him the intuitive vision. This hypothesis is put forward by a great number of holy writers. . . . Is it fanciful to say, following the Catechism of the Council of Trent, that God could have subjected us to his glory without any reward?[76]

We cannot here go into all the finer points of this controversy which is not sufficiently known to the historians of theology. Whatever may be the case with its more tortuous aspects, on the central point just mentioned Fénelon's teaching, which is metaphysically different from Berti's, is here religiously like it. Actually, Fénelon does not tie this contingency of the supernatural end to the sole idea of a superadded order, a superadded finality, and what others call a purely natural end does not appear to him to be due in any way. He cannot admit any order of things in which the relationship of man to God would be governed by a 'debitum naturae', or any order in which the 'vires naturae', with or without 'natural' helps, would suffice for everything. If, for other theologians, pure love and pure nature appear to be in opposition, for him, on the contrary, in a certain sense, they coincide. It is the disinterestedness necessary for pure love which causes him to

[76] *Troisième lettre* . . . (vol. 2, pp. 654 and 664). Noailles wrote, in *Réponse de M. de Paris aux quatre lettres de M. de Cambrai*: 'I admire the fertility of your imagination. Your draw up schemes, systems of love for a possible state, like that of pure nature. . . .' Fénelon answered: 'Naturae purae status possibilitatem me adstruere dicis, ut systemati labanti succuram. Num cernis, illustrissime praesul, hunc statum maxime distare a statu purae naturae?' (vol. 2, pp. 534 and 553-4). Cf. *Dissertatio de amore puro*, prima pars, c. 2, n. 1: 'Illud non est essentiale caritatis motivum, . . . quo sublato, remaneret integra caritas. Atqui sublata beatitudine supernaturali, seu visione intuitiva, . . . remaneret integra caritas. Ergo. . . .' And a little further on, to prove his thesis, Fénelon quotes the *Catechismus Romanus*, pars secunda, in Decal., proemium, n. 18: 'Neque id quidem silentio praetereundum est, vel in hoc maxime suam in nos Deum clementiam . . . ostendisse, quod, cum sine ullo praemio nos potuisset, ut suae gloriae serviremus, cogere, voluit tamen suam gloriam cum utilitate nostra coniungere.' See above pp. 149-50.

introduce, so to say, tests, a series of hypotheses one of which seems to be similar to that of pure nature. But whichever of these hypotheses is in question, with him all are so different from the 'pure nature' propounded in ordinary theology that equally well it can be said, as he asks us to say, that in reality he excludes this hypothesis.[77] Thus the positions are reversed and in both camps true Augustinians are to be found.[78]

Whatever may be thought of these antecedents and analogies the existence of the Augustinian school shows at all events that 'pure nature' did not find support everywhere. Its most determined upholders did not, however, dare to lay it down as equal to a dogma. Berti was able to point out that the French bishops, in their pastoral instruction on the acceptance of the Bull *Unigenitus* in 1714, had been careful not to allude to it at all: 'dogmata Ecclesiae a placitis Scholasticorum scite, considerate et sollertissime discernentes'.[79] Abbé Ilharat de la Chambre in 1739 published the two volumes of his *Traité historique et dogmatique sur la doctrine de Baius et sur l'autorité des papes qui l'ont condemnée*, which is severe towards Baius but moderate in its interpretations and conclusions. In it he protested against certain intemperate writers who endow mere opinions with the status of Catholic dogma, even if these opinions are 'certainly true', thus claiming to remove 'from theologians that freedom which is so natural to man and so useful to the pursuit of truth'.[80] Berti himself could observe that towards the middle of the century many Catholic authors still held the opinion contrary to the new

---

[77] See again *Dissertatio de amore puro*, pars tertia, in fine, after quoting the African martyr Victorianus: 'Mercedem quidem inter martyria sperabat, sed ita ut haec spes imperaretur a caritate praeveniente, et idem tormentum perferre voluisset, etiamsi nulla esset speranda beatitudo in altera vita.'

[78] We have here an example of those passages of the same writer that are revealed by a fairly thorough examination of the doctrines, contrary to the conventional schemes. Fénelon seems to go one better on the subject of pure nature while Berti denies it; both emphasize an aspect of the truth, an aspect of the thought of St Augustine, and these two aspects are bound up with each other although they appear to be in opposition. Both, but Fénelon better than Berti, opposed the Jansenist deviations.

[79] *De theologicis disciplinis*, vol. 8, p. 374.

[80] Vol. 1, pp. 3 and 215.

'pure nature'. His evidence is confirmed shortly afterwards by that of an opponent, the Dominican Bernard de Rubeis. While main taining the new doctrine the latter wrote concerning it 1757, in the preface to his work *De peccato originali* : 'Lis agitur inter theologos.' It was a famous controversy in which he took part not without a certain heat regarding questions which he never-theless acknowledged to be intricate and open to free discussion : 'Subtiliores accedunt, quae agitantur in scholis, quaestiones de possibili natura pura.'[81]

Yet despite the moderation of the bishops more than one theo-logian had already overstepped the mark. By no means all the Jesuits maintained the reserve of their Parisian colleagues and the most daring among them did not fail to find imitators and sup-porters. As Abbé d'Etemare,[82] who was often unreasonable, com-plained, they wanted 'pure nature' to be canonized, in all possible senses, by the condemnation of Baius. In 1719, without the name of author or publisher, appeared a book whose authorship was claimed at a later date by Saléon, the stubborn and unfortunate opponent of the Augustinians who died archbishop of Vienne. It was called *Le système entier de Jansénius et des Jansénistes renouvelé par Quesnel*. When he came to comment on Quesnel's

---

[81] *De peccato originali* (1757), preface. The author adds that the solution he adopts himself is only 'frequentior'. Further, it is true this modest state-ment gives way to formulas like 'frequentissima Theologorum ratio', then 'frequentissimus gravissimorum Theologorum chorus'; as he proceeds the controversialist becomes more heated. It is interesting to observe how B. de Rubeis interpolates 'clarifications' into the text of St Thomas to make it agree completely with the new doctrine: *op. cit.*, c. 37, quotation from *Prima Secundae*, qu. 5, art. 5 (the words in brackets are additions by de Rubeis): 'Beatitudo imperfecta, quae in hac vita haberi potest (quaeve unica ut homini praestituta a Deo foret, nulla est repugnantia), potest ab homine acquiri per sua naturalia (sive insitas vires consideres, sive necessarium Dei creatoris adiutorium inter dona naturalia computandum), eo modo quo (potest ab homine acquiri per sua naturalia) et virtus, in cuius operatione consistit (beatitudo naturalis). Sed beatitudo hominis perfecta (ad quam gratuito Dei favore sublimatam credimus naturam humanam) consistit in visione divinae essentiae. . . .'

[82] *Lettre à l'auteur du Catéchisme historique et dogmatique* (*Catéchisme* . . . , vol. 111, beginning): 'When Molinist theologians maintain the possibility of the state of pure nature, a possibility that they want to pass off in the shadow of the bulls against Baius, for an article of faith. . . .'

thirty-fifth proposition, which was couched in these terms:
'Gratia Adami est sequela creationis, et erat debita naturae sanae
et integrae', Saléon—or the writer to whom he lent his name[83]—
not only laid it down that 'all orthodox theologians state on the
contrary that God could have created man without destining him
to enjoy happiness in heaven; that consequently he could have
created him without giving him sanctifying grace'. With the same
assurance he added: 'It is the opinion of St Thomas, whose
authority we have already quoted, as well as the decision of St
Pius V against Baius, who dared to teach the contrary.'[84] Yet if
we look at the passage of the book to which Saléon refers us we
read there merely that 'St Thomas was so convinced that God
could have created man in a purely natural state that he does not
condescend to put forward this question in his *Summa*; he takes
it as certain, and on this supposition he asks whether Adam
received sanctifying grace at the moment of his creation, or
whether he only received it some time afterwards, and although
he decided that Adam received the grace at the moment of his
creation, he always supposes that God could have created him
without this grace.'[85] Obviously we are here right outside the
question. In stating, contrary to St Thomas, that Adam did not
receive sanctifying grace at once, was St Bonaventure here teaching that God at first only assigned to him a purely natural end?[86]

Despite his episcopal dignity and the praises of him to be found
in the *Dictionaire des livres jansénistes,*[87] here Saléon is scarcely
more than a pamphleteer of the kind produced by both camps in

[83] According to *Nouvelles ecclésiastiques* (1728) the work was by the
Jesuit Talota, and Saléon had propagated it directly it appeared when he
was vicar general of Aix (*Table des Nouvelles*, vol. 2, 1767, p. 806).

[84] *Op. cit.*, 3rd part, c. 10 (p. 284).

[85] *Op. cit.*, 2nd part, c. 7 (p. 274), with reference to *Prima*, qu. 95, art. 1.

[86] Saléon was also the author of a *Baianismus redivivus in scriptis PP. FF.
Belleli et Berti . . .*, and of a *Iansenismus redivivus* (1744-5). See below, p.
300.

[87] 1755 ed., vol. 2, p. 58. As we know, this Dictionary was placed on the
index on 11 March 1754, as the *Bibliothèque janséniste* had been on 20
September 1749.

these wretched controversies.[88] There was no more moderation to be found, for example, in the pastoral instruction of a bishop on the other side, Charles-Jean Colbert de Croissy (d. 1738), bishop of Montpellier, condemning the *Histoire du peuple de Dieu* by Fr Berryer. Not content with asserting that speculations on the state of pure nature are 'vain imaginations of the new theologians' and that tradition is unfavourable to their system, the polemical prelate claims that this system amounts, more or less, to the Pelagian heresy and that it everywhere introduces confusion into religion.[89] Less moderate still were the *Lettres d'un théologien à M. XXX sur la distinction de Religion naturelle et de Religion révélée et sur les opinions théologiques*. The anonymous author, who was Abbé Rivière, alias Pelvert, an ardent Jansenist, could not tolerate the 'system of the Jesuits', to which he opposed the teaching of 'more correct theologians'; it was, he said, 'only after the Jesuits had infected most of the schools with this pernicious system that this distinction of natural religion and revealed religion was introduced' to the greatest detriment of religion.[90] These excesses do not detract from the soundness of certain critical remarks. Although they exaggerate the danger in ordinary life, Pelvert and the Bishop of Montpellier are both right when they

---

[88] Saléon, in company with Languet, archbishop of Sens, was one of those who 'in their zeal, more ardent than enlightened, for the Bull *Unigenitus*' (Gratry, *De la connaissance de Dieu*, vol. 2, 1854, p. 416) denounced Belleli and Berti to Benedict XIV (see below). They also denounced them to the Assembly of the French clergy in 1747 and to the University of Vienne (see below).

[89] *Ordonnance et Instruction pastorale de Mgr l'évêque de Montpellier, portant condemnation de deux ouvrages, dont l'un pour titre*: 'Histoire du peuple de Dieu . . .', *par le P. Isaac Joseph Berruyer de la Cie de Jésus . . .* (1731): 'The Pelagians admitted the reality of the state of pure nature, . . . the defenders of the new opinions admit its possibility. But you have only to follow them a little to see that they defend its possibility in such a way that they make it as real as they can' (p. 11). Cf. *Lettres théologiques* by Abbé Gauthier, vol. 3 (1756), p. 67, on the theology of the Jesuits, 'this rehash of Pelagius'.

[90] There is no date or place of publication. For the account of the 'system of the Jesuits' the author refers to the great *Hexaples* (17—) and the *Denonciation de la doctrine des ci-devant soi-disans Jésuites, tant sur le dogme que sur la morale, à Nosseigneurs les Archvêques et Évêques de France* (1767).

point out the general duality, or rather the dualism, which results from the duality of ends.[91]

Gradually however, and despite these protests, a habit was formed. The very attachment of the Augustinian school to the old tradition concerning the one finality was really too narrow and too incomplete;[92] in addition, it was too bound up with the pessimistic theories propagated by the Jansenist movement. Thus by its denial it could only strengthen among the general body of theologians the contrary attachment to the idea of 'pure nature'. Once again this idea was so simple and so convenient. It seemed to make everything so clear. As Fr Le Vaillant de la Bassardries, a Jesuit, put it in his poem in twelve strophes, it explained so well God's freedom :[93]

> He could have confined Adam his creature
> To those gifts alone belonging to pure nature,
> And without lavishing on him his rarer blessings
> Could have limited his bounty to less perfect gifts.
> How could Adam have blamed him for this
> Without putting forward a rash and unjust complaint?
> Although for ever shut out from eternal happiness,
> Could he have accused God of being lacking in love?[94]

In addition, an unwarranted interpretation of the condemnations of Baius and Quesnel seemed to endow this idea with a sort of consecration. In the struggle against the encroachments of

[91] *Ordonnance*, pp. 23-5; *Lettres*, pp. 43-4.

[92] However, in addition to certain passages in Lafosse, there was at least the beginning of an explanation on gratuitousness in Belleli, *Mens Augustini* . . . , bk 3, c. 21 and c. 62. In c. 21, occurred the classic assertion : 'Si autem ita homo sine gratia condi non potest, non sequitur gratiam esse naturam, quinimmo consequens est finem hominis nobilissimum esse, ut nec ad diligendum ipsum, nec possidendum natura sola sufficiat.' The criticism of Baius follows.

[93] *L'accord de la grâce et de la liberté, poème, accompagné de remarques critiques et historiques* (Tournai, 1740).

[94] Hymn II, verses 69-76. The doctrine here is better than the verse, but it cannot do without some explanation. Not everything in this poem is so peaceful in tone. At the end, the author writes a hymn to the virtues of Louis XV, saying that he deserved immmortal honour for exterminating Jansenism.

naturalism, whose influence the modern theologians unwittingly underwent, they naturally had recourse to the idea without looking further, using tactics or following an instinct analogous to those of their predecessors. In this way there grew up, right in the foreground of theology, a whole body of doctrine which, having developed wholly in the field of the controversies of the schools, in the end came to appear as the indispensable bulwark of the faith and the very groundwork of Catholic teaching.

Ripalda's war-cry, 'Exterminandus est appetitus innatus!',[95] was then to be echoed further and further afield. This *Delenda est Carthago* had in view far more than just a Scholastic thesis. Without being intended to, it destroyed the whole of the ancient anthropology. The 'desire to see God' or, in the language usual nowadays, 'the desire for the supernatural', which for so long, both for the Fathers and the Scholastics, had been the primary explanatory principle of man, and with man, of the whole of nature, this king-pin of Christian philosophy could not withstand the blows that fell upon it.[96] The theologians who attacked it did so with all the greater ferocity in that they were as if hypnotized by the peril that the Baianist doctrines had caused to the faith, then by the increasing unbelief on all sides and finally by the rising tide of immanentism in its many forms. They imagined that in this way they were waging a holy war in the name of Christian orthodoxy, thus preventing the salt of doctrine from losing its savour. Actually, without their realizing it, they were losing valuable ground, in some degree yielding to the prevalent naturalism and making the most dangerous of concessions to a world entirely unconcerned about its higher destiny.

But the more they conceded, the more they were obliged to

[95] *De ente supernaturali,* bk 1, disput. VIII, sect. 4, n. 2. Cf. disput. IX, sect. 4, n. 23: 'Hinc vero tandem absolute appetitum exterminandum a natura.'
[96] The editor of the commentary on the *Summa theologica* by Toletus, J. Paria, S.J., made the observation in 1869, in his Prolegomena, n. 25 (p. 29): 'Fatendum est sententiam de appetitu innato videndi Deum, exortis Bainis et Iansenianis erroribus, quo facilius eluderentur cavillationes haereticorum, desitam esse in scholis doceri.' But not perhaps so quickly nor so generally as he appears to state.

continue to do so. The idea of 'pure nature', when seen in isolation, became ever more demanding. The more they adopted this idea, the more they found themselves led to consider this nature as complete, consistent, sufficient and of itself independent of any superior 'order'. And as a result, they were obliged all the more to reject everything that could have been interpreted—quite wrongly—as even a remote 'demand' in respect to the supernatural. They were thus condemned, by the very logic of their first step, in some way to bid continually higher. Their system became increasingly top-heavy and closed in upon itself. By this new sword of Solomon man 'was cut into two parts'.[97] Obviously, the supporters of a separate philosophy were to find an advantage in this. What had been established by the theologians as a doctrinal safeguard was made by these philosophers into a fundamental objection. The journalists of Trévoux had already complained of a 'subterfuge on the part of the Deists' who, they said, 'did not even wish to find out whether there was a divine revelation'; a line of 'conduct', they added, which 'was opposed to sound reason and dangerous in itself',[98] but it was difficult for a theology which carefully put on one side the whole supernatural order to dislodge these 'Deists' from their position.[99] Later on we find Moehler concerning himself with the criticisms of Catholic dogma made by Baur. This dogma, said Baur, endows the whole of Christianity with the appearance of a vast 'opus supererogationis'. This was true of a certain school of theology, but Moehler had no time even to seek to remedy it.[100] In 1861 Canon F. Duilhé de Saint-Projet, on the subject of the philosophers of his time, repeated the observation of the journalists of Trévoux: 'Directly it is a question of the divine, of the origin of the Church,

[97] Cardinal Pie, *Deuxième Instruction synodale sur les principales erreurs du temps présent* (*Œuvres*, vol. 3, 6th ed., 1879, p. 166).

[98] *L'esprit des Journalistes de Trévoux*, vol. 4, Paris, 1771, p. 240.

[99] Others were to take on the task fairly soon. 'This God of natural religion will have the right only to a short existence. . . . The God of Light is dead, if ever he was wholly alive': Pierre Burgelin, 'Réflexions sur la religion naturelle' in *L'Homme devant Dieu* (1964), vol. 2, p. 316.

[100] Cf. E. Vermeil, *Jean-Adam Moehler et l'école catholique de Tubingue*, p. 184.

they fall back on a polite refusal.'[101] Cardinal Pie encountered this obstacle without realizing that he himself had helped to construct it or at least to consolidate it. In his well-known *Instructions pastorales* in which he commented on the decrees of the provincial council of Bordeaux and those of Pius IX regarding the 'supernatural order', he protested against those who 'confuse' and those who 'separate' the two orders. At the same time, however, he 'distinguished' them in such a way that he was in considerable difficulty in answering the objections of the spokesmen for 'philosophism' and 'natural religion', so much so that his continual protests against the 'secularization' of a society dominated by an 'essentially secular spirit' remained unavailing.[102] In his *Tractatus de ordine supernaturali,* Fr Palmieri encountered the preliminary objection of certain rationalists :

> Contradictio videtur esse in hac sententia de ordine supernaturali. Nam gratuitus asseritur eo quod indebitus naturae, et simul necessarius, ideoque debitus si actu existat, ut necesse sit homini ad eum pertinere, si felix esse velit; cum e contrario haec sit privilegiorum indoles, cuiusmodi est ordo supernaturalis, ut possint recusari.

The answer could not be otherwise than weak :

> Respondemus, nullam esse contradictionem. Haec enim duo optime concilientur, et quod ordo sit gratuitus indebitusque naturae, et quod homines teneantur ad illum pertinere. Deus enim Dominus naturae potest profecto decernere ad maiorem suae gloriae manifestationem, ut homines ordinentur in finem naturae quidem indebitum sed possibilem et perfectiorem, in eumque tendant mediis proportionatis, quae ipse opportune confert. In qua hypothesi, necessitas ordinis supernaturalis oritur ex institutione seu lege Dei, cui omnes subsunt, quin ille desinat esse gratuitus et

---

[101] *Les études religieuses en France,* p. 396.
[102] *Op. cit., passim*; vol. 4, p. 327; vol. 7, p. 375.

indebitus. Talis enim dicitur comparatus cum natura, quae per se illum nequit exigere.[103]

Moreover, it was all very well to talk of a historical and actual supernatural order; the futurable that had been imagined at first was to be found whole and entire, without essential modification within this order. It alone became the legitimate subject of thought. Nature and 'supernature' (the term that was increasingly used) were paired off in such a way that the second came to seem to jealous reason only a vain shadow, a sham adornment.[104] In proportion as the one became a complete system, the other seemed to the thinker to become superfluous. Despite the apologists, man settled into 'natural religion'. The whole Christian institution seemed thus to assume, as Baur had said, an artificial character and the bread of doctrine was proffered as a stone. But the theologians were caught in their own trap. By some of them, as much indeed as by the philosophers, the supernatural was to be rejected, exiled or hunted down.[105] In these rational speculations it was necessary that nothing should allow it, its presence or its very possibility, to be even suspected, in the way a void suggests the idea that it could be filled. All philosophical reflection which might possibly allow the mind to glimpse something of the mystery of the supernatural was forbidden. The slightest of its signs was to be rooted out; the smallest of its appeals in nature

[103] *Tractatus de ordine supernaturali*, 2nd ed. (1910), pp. 38-40. From works like these we can see emerging the problem which lay behind the work of Maurice Blondel.

[104] Scheeben introduced the word (*Übernatur*), in a technical sense, making a distinction between it and 'supernatural'. Although this refinement does not seem really necessary, Scheeben should not be held entirely responsible for the actual widespread use of the term (a wrong use) instead of 'supernatural'. Cf. M. J. Scheeben, *Die Herrlichkeiten der göttlichten Gnade,* pp. 21-3. *Nature et grâce*, introduction, French trans and notes by Bernard Fraigneau-Julien, P.S.S. (1957). Joseph Milla, S.A.C., *Die Lehre vom Übernatürlichen bei Matthaeus Joseph Scheeben* (Rome, 1961). Fr Louis Bouyer has shown very clearly one of the doctrinal drawbacks inherent in the term: *Introduction à la vie spirituelle* (1964), p. 155: Eng. trans. *Introduction to Spirituality* (London, 1961).

[105] Cf. M. Matter, reflecting the attitude of the thinkers of his own century: 'the supernatural, which we relegate . . . to the ends of the world together with the god of Epicurus' (*Le mysticisme en France au temps de Fénelon* (1865), p. 282).

was to be quelled. And so it was that Christians in a kind of sacred frenzy destroyed with their own hands the magnificent edifice whose preservation the centuries of faith had handed down to them. It seems, as Jacques Maritain remarked, that

> at the time of Guillaume du Vair and Charron, and then of Descartes, it all happened as if thinkers who were still Christians had imagined a man of 'pure nature' entrusted with philosophizing to whom was superadded a man with the theological virtues charged with meriting heaven. Later the non-Christian rationalists, more logical in maintaining the same error, were to reject as a superfluous duplication this man with the theological virtues.[106]

This is a view which is not far wrong. But to apportion the blame equally—if we can talk of blame in an evolution of ideas and doctrines which goes beyond individual cases—it is only right to complete this view by Adolphe Franck's judgement on the matter: 'Some of the ideas for which reason and philosophy are reproached with the greatest bitterness and which are usually regarded as an invention of the philosophers of the eighteenth century'—and even also of the seventeenth and sixteenth centuries —were 'at first maintained and propagated by theologians'.[107] The separate philosophies, which had themselves become secularized theologies, owe much to 'separate theology'.

In this separatist movement, almost all the theological schools were caught up, and it can be said the Thomists, who since Cajetan had opened the way for innovations, on this fundamental issue subsequently eagerly became Molinists, Suarezians and Ripaldists. The teaching and even the terminology of their master came to be regarded with suspicion among them. Several of them, still continuing to swear by his name, became the apostles

---

[106] 'La notion de philosophie chrétienne' in *Bulletin de la société française de philosophie*, session of 21 March 1921, p. 62.

[107] *Réformateurs et publicistes de l'Europe, XVII° siècle* (1881), pp. 5-6. On Charron, cf. J. Vianey, in *Histoire de la littérature française illustrée* (1923), vol. 1, p. 216; J. B. Sabrié, *De l'humanisme au rationalisme, Pierre Charron* (1913); Henri Busson, *La pensée religieuse française de Charron à Pascal* (1933).

of a hermetically closed 'natural philosophy'. They adopted what Cardinal Dechamps was to call 'the doctrine of the mere juxtaposition of nature and grace',[108] and, the better to avoid immanentism, which was only too threatening, they burned what their ancestors, to whose authority they continued to appeal, had worshipped for so long.[109]

Yet the Church by no means yielded to this panic.[110] Not only did her leaders refuse to choose between the upholders and opponents of the 'natural desire' or 'innate appetite' of the vision, not only did they discourage those who wished to obtain from them condemnations in the affair, but the very idea of 'pure nature', understood as forcefully as the most excessive of its proponents desired, was never sanctioned by an act of the supreme authority. The Augustinians of the eighteenth century, despite the weakness of their defence and in spite of being compromised to some extent with the Jansenist position, were at least tolerated. Noris was denounced more than once and the examination of his works, ordered by Innocent XII in 1695, was concluded in his favour.[111] Belleli, who was twice delated to the Holy Office, was also never censured. When Berti was attacked in 1744 and 1745 by Saléon, then Bishop of Rodez, for the 'perversity of his opinions' and his 'attachment to heretical novelties' as shown in his treatise De theologicis disciplinis, the two theologians entrusted by high authority with the presentation of a report on

---

[108] Lettres philosophiques sur la démonstration de la foi, letter 13 (Œuvres, vol. 16, pp. 295-6).

[109] Cf. P. Noël, O.P.: The commentators on St Thomas 'had to react against the excesses of emerging subjectivism, and since the sixteenth century the reaction has increased continually under the influence of Cartesianism, ontologism, Kantianism, all of which it was necessary to oppose. So far was this true that the theologians, guided by the best of intentions, fell into the opposite extreme. . . . The divine spark shining in our souls . . . was no longer regarded as the image, the reflection of the image of the living God' (Œuvres de Tauler, vol. 3 (1911), pp. 255-6, note).

[110] If only people had managed, like Fr Le Bachelet, 'to give its proper emphasis to the censure of certain propositions and not go further than the Holy See' (DTC, vol. 2, col. 62).

[111] In 1731, Abbe Ilharat de la Chambre singled out 'the work of the learned Cardinal Noris' to delimit the work of Baius and state clearly the meaning of his condemnation: op. cit., vol. 1, pp. 212-15.

this work could only praise its learning and teaching.[112] Berti was authorized to answer Saléon. He did so in his *Augustinianum systema de gratia, ab iniqua Baiani et Ianseniani erroris insimulatione vindicatum* (1747; published in 1749), which bore laudatory appreciations from the two censors, the Dominican Ricchinius and the Franciscan Philip Lipperi de Carboneano.[113] Benedict XIV himself came energetically to his defence.[114] This pope, who reigned from 1740 to 1758, was personally a great admirer of Noris whom he called in a brief 'Romanae Ecclessiae splendidissimum lumen'.[115] On 31 July 1748 he sent an admonition to the Grand Inquisitor of Spain, Francisco Pérez de Prado, who at the instigation of Causani had just condemned the Cardinal's works. On three occasions the pontifical brief declared that these works were free from all suspicion of Baianism or Jansenism, that there was nothing in them worthy of the slightest censure and that their author had moreover 'dispelled, uprooted, torn out even to their smallest strands' the scruples that his opponents wanted to provoke. After complaining that the Spanish Inquisitor had accepted the accusations which had been rejected by the solemn and reiterated judgments of the Roman pontiffs, Benedict XIV recalled in the last place that the Holy See was accustomed to favour the freedom of the theological schools and that it could not

---

[112] On this incident and on all the controversy in connection with the Augustinians, see Émile Appolis, *Entre Jansénistes et Zelanti, le 'Tiers Parti' catholique au XVIIIᵉ siècle* (1960). On 'the difference that the Church has always made between the condemned theories of Baius and the orthodox theories of the Augustinians', see F. Litt, *op. cit.*, pp. 95-102.

[113] Cf. Berti's work in the edition by Bassani, vol. 13 (1792), pp. 279-80: 'Opus hoc, non solum utile, sed etiam necessarium esse censeo, ut ex eo facile discere queant omnes, . . . et ne amplius orthodoxas opiniones cum damnatis erroribus confundant, et misceant, . . .' Unfortunately such wishes are always powerless.

[114] *Correspondance de Benoît XIV avec le cardinal de Tencin* (ed. Émile de Heeckeren, 2 vols, 1912), vol. 1, pp. 216, 230, 259-60, 281-2, 313, 316, 324.

[115] Brief *Inter maximas*, 31 March 1745. Cf. the letter sent by Riballier, syndic of the faculty of theology in Paris, to Le Clerc de Beauberon, who was then vice-dean of the faculty of Caen: 'After Benedict XIV has praised Cardinal Noris so highly in several places of his learned works, it would be both ridiculous and unjust to blame a theologian because he thought that he could follow the example of so learned a pope' (14 December 1775: Migne, vol. 10, col. 919).

allow others in the Church to be more exacting.[116] Writing in the following year to Cardinal de Tencin he once more insisted on the fact that Noris' works had been 'approved four times in Rome' after solemn examination; that their author had subsequently been made 'consultor of the Holy Office and cardinal' and that the recent measures taken in Spain should be regarded as capricious.[117] 'In matters not decided by the Church,' he went on, 'everyone can follow the guidance of his reason.'[118] He constantly returned to the need for a multiplicity of schools within the Church : 'We love them all,' he said, 'although they differ among themselves in their opinions; we leave to each its freedom, and if one unjustly accuses another of heresy and the latter defends itself "mordicus" with sound arguments . . . , we shall never abandon this latter even if, in return, the accused becomes the accuser, as happens on many occasions.' This is why in 1749 he approved the condemnation of the *Bibliothèque janséniste,* an 'impudent work which dubs as Jansenist so many men of standing by reason of their dignity, piety and knowledge'.[119] But Benedict XIV was

[116] *Bref de N.S.P. le Pape Benoît XIV au Grand Inquisiteur d'Espagne* : 'cum ea Baianismi aut Iansenismi nota careant et carere constet, post multiplicatum super eis examen, in hac suprema Inquisitione romana. . . . Celeberrimus Author universis adversariorum petitionibus occurrit, scrupulos iniectos exturbat, evellit, eradicat. . . . Colligere poteris Baianismi et Iansenismi notam Norisio impositam, novam non esse, eam repetitis solemnibus Romanis iudiciis fuisse penitus eliminatam, nec licuisse Hispanae Inquisitioni eam iterum in controversiam vocare' (the Brief is quoted in full in Le Clerc, *op. cit.,* Migne, vol. 10, col. 1131-5). On 19 February 1749 another letter from the pope required the Inquisitor to remove from his Index the *Historia pelagiana.*
[117] 14 May 1749 (Heeckeren, vol. 1, pp. 484-5); cf. 25 June and 6 August (pp. 495-6 and 507). The details of this affair can be read in Émile Appolis, pp. 155-74.
[118] A. Tencin, 7 September 1742; also: 16 March 1746; 14 May and 2 July 1749; 21 January 1750 (cf. Appolis, *op. cit.,* pp. 161-2 and 280).
[119] This is also why the Pope would not allow an accusation to be accepted in Rome without the accused being allowed to put forward his defence. To Cardinal de Tencin, 21 January 1750 (vol. 2, p. 5); to the same, 22 September 1745 (vol. 1, p. 211); 16 November 1746 (pp. 281-2); 22 March 1747 (p. 313); 4 April (p. 316); 2 July and 10 September 1749 (pp. 501 and 515); 17 September (p. 517). The learned Jesuit Francesco Antonio Zaccaria, Muratori's successor as librarian at Modena, did not hesitate to speak of the 'very proper decree prohibiting the *Bibliothèque janséniste*' (Appolis, *op. cit.,* p. 216).

himself very firm in his opposition to Jansenism and his resistance
to the 'appellants' against the Bull *Unigenitus*;[120] he did not allow
himself to be led into confusing what was really quite distinct.

In 1750 and 1751 Benedict XIV was once more obliged to
reject the pressing requests by Languet de Gergy, archbishop of
Sens, who wanted him to approve a further censure against
Belleli and Berti. The prelate was left with the only resource, that
of publishing his censure himself, together with his two letters to the
Pope, in his collected works.[121] A similar misadventure happened
to Saléon whose successive efforts, together with Languet's, with
the assembly of the French clergy in 1747, then with the university
of Vienne, and finally with the Holy See, were in each instance
fruitless. Neither his *Baianismus redivivus,* nor his *Jansenismus redivivus,* both addressed to Rome, had obtained the condemnation
asked for, and his pastoral instruction of 1750,[122] followed by
the publication of a *Iudicium* in 1753, forming the last attacks by
the old warrior, had no more success. In 1756 a commission of
theologians once more cleared Berti who had just answered
Languet in a further *Apologia.* Meanwhile, with considerable
energy, Berti in his *Systema augustinianum vindicatum,* composed
at the Pope's invitation and printed at the Vatican in 1749, had
managed to draw up a whole list of study houses and universities
in which the impossibility of 'pure nature' was publicly taught.[123]

[120] To Cardinal de Tencin, 14 May 1749 (vol. 1, pp. 485-6). Cf. *ibid.*,
pp. 23-4, 55-6, 169, 312, 435, 511 etc.; vol. 2, pp. 368, 376-7, 481, 495.
[121] On this incident see *Nouvelles ecclésiastiques,* 1753 and 1755 (*Tables,*
vol. 2, 1767, p. 103). Their ardent partiality must be taken into account.
In this year 1755, the fourth edition of the *Dictionnaire des livres jansénistes*
once more violently accused Belleli and Berti. The latter is termed 'determined
heretic', writing with 'duplicity and bad faith' and teaching Jansenism
'without modification or restriction' (vol. 1, p. 445 and vol. 3, pp. 107-10).
[122] Cf. his *Instruction pastorale . . . au sujet d'une prétendue apologie
intitulée: Augustinianum systema . . . , que le P. Berti, religieux augustin
d'Italie, a fait imprimer et distribuer* (Vienne, 1750).
[123] *Systema augustinianum,* diss. 2, c. 1, par. 9, n. 12: 'In celeberrima
Universitate lovaniensi, etiam postquam omnes Theologi quinque propositionum damnationi et celebri "Formulario" subscripserunt, Theologi nostri ad
hunc usque diem docuerunt, status purae naturae impossibilitatem; testorque
ulterius, ne ullum insignium Theologorum nostrorum ex Italis audivisse, qui
eamdem impossibilitatem non tradiderit, ac in praesentia non tradat.' And

Benedict XIV was grieved at these continually recurring quarrels. 'We fear,' he wrote, 'that a great conflagration will be lighted; these things pierce our heart; we would willingly give our blood for the peace of the Church.' He was pained to see 'so many persons, commendable for their talents and their education, who waste their time in scandalous argument when they ought to devote all their efforts in fighting the atheism which, coming from England, is penetrating into those parts where Catholicism is most flourishing'.[124] After his death, however, and until the end of the century, controversy over 'pure nature' continued.[125] On 23 December 1779, the general of the Augustinians published an encyclical letter, revised by the pope, in which could be read: 'If opponents continue to call us Jansenists, remember that it was always the lot of the defenders of the teaching of the Church thus to be treated by their adversaries. The best Catholics found themselves accused of Sabellianism by the Arians, Apollinarianism by the Eutychians, of Manicheism by the Pelagians. So distrust this vain spectre of Jansenism. . . . It is a phantom from which the popes themselves, the custodians of truth, have exonerated many famous Augustinian theologians.'[126] On 1 August 1780 the *Nouvelles ecclésiastiques* reviewed the theses defended two years previously at the house of the Conventual Franciscans in Naples:

> Among other strange assertions, these religious claim that since original justice, sanctifying grace, immortality and so on, are not due to innocent man, it must be concluded that

c. 2, par. 6, n. 2: the universities of Vienne and Toulouse, several schools in Germany, teach the same doctrine (vol. 8, pp. 403 and 409). De Carboneano, *op. cit.*, col. 681, quotes a list of other names.

[124] Letters to Tencin, 11 February 1750 and 1 May 1752; cf. 3 May 1752 (Correspondence, ed. Heeckeren, 1912, vol. 2, pp. 10, 173 and 184).

[125] In 1759 the general of the Augustinians explained to Clement XIII the theses of his school and concluded that 'nonnisi per summam iniuriam (eam) traduci posse, tanquam infecti Baii, Iansenii ac Quesnelli erroribus iure merito damnatis'; in a petition to the same on 6 August 1765, he again complained of the 'calumnia heterodoxiae' (W. Boexe, pp. 58 and 63).

[126] Cf. *Nouvelles ecclésiastiques,* 26 June 1780. This issue for 24 July announced the French translation of this 'Circular Letter' (Paris, in Latin and French, 57 pages, 41 of which are devoted to an 'Introduction').

the state of pure nature is possible. The conclusion is not correct. . . .

Moreover, to establish the possibility of this state it would be necessary to prove not only that God owes nothing to man, but also that man, by his nature, owes nothing to God; according to this system man supposedly in this state of pure nature would not be obliged to love God as his last end since he is not called to possess him; and to be without guilt he needs to have only the natural virtues to fulfil the duties of the natural order, to limit himself to a natural end with no relationship with God.[127]

In 1781 there appeared the second volume of the posthumous treatise on grace by Gourlin (1775).[128] In it a whole dissertation was devoted to 'pure nature'. If the possibility of this state is admitted, said Gourlin, 'duplex exsurgit homo, duplex religio, omnia in religione duplicia'. In opposition to it, in six arguments, he explained St Thomas' thesis on the natural desire to see God. He regarded it as intolerable to treat as erroneous a doctrine openly maintained by celebrated theologians in Rome itself and other Catholic regions with the explicit approbation of the sovereign pontiffs.[129] Seeking the origin of the thesis that he was opposing he observed that there was nothing about it to be found in scripture or in the Fathers; that just a few traces began to appear in the old Scholastics and that its inventor was Suarez,

[127] Other points against 'pure nature' on 27 February and 25 December 1779, 27 March 1780. On 10 April 1779, in an account of theses defended for a chair of theology at the University of Toulouse: 'M. Maignan in the discussion took up very thoroughly the abuse M. Bousquet continually made of the distinction between the natural order and the supernatural order; he took him to task for admitting two orders of duties, two last ends and so on. As M. Bousquet put up a very poor defence on this point, . . . one of the Sulpician teachers, probably to encourage him, said aloud that M. Maignan was somewhat ignorant since he did not know a distinction familiar to the weakest student in theology. But M. Maignan pointed out that he was well aware of this distinction, since he opposed it to such purpose, and that this Sulpician was blinded by prejudice for not appreciating the strength of his objections.'
[128] *Tractatus theologicus de gratia Christi salvatoris et de praedestinatione*, vol. 2. No author's name. Cf. above, p. 111.
[129] Pp. 339-405.

who himself admitted as much.[130] Going to the heart of the problem he put forward an idea that is not without weight, although,
as so often happened, it is unfortunately mixed up with a Jansenist spirit:

> Observandum est quaestionem non esse de natura quadam
> humana, quae alterius generis aut speciei foret quam nunc
> est; quae scilicet alias haberet inclinationes naturales,
> aliamque intelligendi et volendi capacitatem (utrum huius-
> cemodi natura humana sit possibilis, otiosis discutiendum
> relinquimus); sed de natura humana, qualis reipsa est, sum-
> mum et infinitum bonum appetente, mortemque et alias
> molestias naturaliter refugiente. Cum enim naturae purae
> assertores doceant naturam puram non aliter a natura lapsa
> differre, quam ut nudam a nudata, consequens est easdem
> ab ipsis inclinationes naturales, eamdem mentis capacitatem
> naturalem, easdemque repugnantias naturales attribui
> naturae purae, ac naturae lapsae.[131]

In 1787 the famous Jansenist Council of Pistoia was held. Pius
VI in his Bull *Autorem fidei* condemned its errors but without
affecting the teaching of the Augustinians. He confined himself
in paragraphs 16 and 17 to recalling the doctrine already contained in the Bull of St Pius V.[132] The theologians of the nineteenth century, although the majority of them had adopted the
modern thesis, continued nevertheless to put it forward as an
opinion of the schools for which there was a considerable *consensus*,[133] but from which it was not forbidden to depart. In 1800,
the *Acroases* of the Dominican Albertinus introduced the question

[130] P. 341 : 'Nonnulla certe eius semina in veteribus Scholasticis occurrunt;
sed nonnisi diuturno temporis lapsu absolutum evolutumque est, opera
praesertim Iesuitarum, qui pronis ulnis illud amplexi sunt. . . . Certe
fictitium illum statum excogitatum fuisse fatetur ipsemet Suarez, Proleg. IV
de statibus humanae naturae, c. 1.' We saw above what is to be thought
of this.   [131] P. 343.

[132] *De statu innocentiae et de immortalitate spectata ut naturali conditione
hominis*. Text of no. 16 in F. Litt, *op. cit.*, who exaggerates and, it seems to
me, even falsifies the implications of this document.

[133] Thus, for example, the *Institutiones theologicae ad usum seminariorum*
by Bouvier (vol. 2, 3rd ed., Paris, 1839), pp. 282 and 284.

of pure nature in these terms: 'Audacissimam vanamque quaestionem dirimendam assumo, quae tempus inutiliter terit, blasphemias fovet, animosque scindit.'[134] The new edition (1817) of Pluquet's *Dictionnaire des hérésies* still says simply: 'The state of pure nature, held by most orthodox theologians . . . as possible, must not be attacked as being a dream, empty imagination, a mere fancy. . . .'[135] As can be seen, this in an entirely defensive position. The Augustinian teaching is mentioned usually with deference (if not always with entire accuracy) and writers felt obliged to acknowledge that the Holy See had constantly refused to allow it to be condemned in any way, and that it would be wrong to confuse it with Baius' ideas.[136] In 1846 there appeared the *Institutiones theologicae* by Michael Marcelli (d. 1804) of the Hermits of St Augustine, which were mentioned above; this book popularized in unadulterated form the traditional teaching of the order.[137]

When the time came for the Vatican Council (1869-70) the debate, which had never quite died down, again became lively. But faithful to their principle of not dealing with what was an opinion of the schools, the Fathers were careful to leave the question alone.[138] A *schema* for a constitution, prepared by Franzelin, *Schema constitutionis dogmaticae de doctrina catholica*, contained in its sixteenth chapter ('De ordine supernaturali et

[134] G.-M. Albertinus, O.P., *Acroases de Deo creatore* . . . (Venice, 1800), p. 219.

[135] Vol. 2, under 'Quesnel'.

[136] Thus once more in the 1819 ed. of the *Praelectiones theologicae* by Pietro M. Gazzaniga, O.P., vol. 4, pp. 234-5: 'Neque multum laborant huius sententiae patroni, ut eam a damnata Baii doctrina toto caelo distare ostendant. Et primo, perquam facile est id ostendere evidentia facti: cum nemo ignoret, eamdem sententiam in scholis catholicis palam et ubique defendi, non reclamantibus summis Ecclesiae Pastoribus. . . . Multi insuper ex iis ipsis, qui statum naturae purae possibilem esse mordicus defendunt, fatentur ingenue, contrariam sententiam, prout in scholis catholicis defenditur, ab apostolicis fulminibus intactam hactenus remansisse.'

[137] Vol. 3 (Foligno, 1846), pp. 344-58: *An possibilis sit status purae naturae.*

[138] On 7 January 1870, in the first session of the 'Deputation of the Faith', the fathers, beginning the examination of the schema 'de doctrina catholica', were unanimous in deciding to leave aside anything that was only 'an opinion of the schools' (Granderath).

de supernaturali statu originalis iustitiae') the affirmation of a possible natural 'beatitude'.[139] But this schema was sharply criticized. The fathers of the Council were far more anxious to assert against the errors of rationalism, the possibility of a supernatural knowledge of God.[140] In the three canons dealing with the supernatural order, which follow the *Schema constitutionis de praecipuis mysteriis fidei*, all mention of pure nature is avoided.[141] As we know, the sudden interruption of the Council prevented the examination of the *schema*. The encyclical *Pascendi* (1907), provoked by the Modernist crisis, in one passage recalls that any claim of nature in respect to the supernatural must be ruled out. In this way the traditional assertion concerning the absolute gratuity of the supernatural was strengthened. But no more than the preceding documents issuing from the *magisterium,* such a passage does not provide even the beginning of an argument for the theory which would place this assertion in a logical and necessary connection with the modern idea of 'pure nature', and still less with the denials by which it was then often accompanied. Two years later, in 1909, Canon J. Paquier, the author of a work on Jansenius, noted carefully that 'it is really theologians, and not the Church, who speak to us of a state of pure nature'.[142] In 1910 there appeared the second edition of the great *Tractatus de ordine supernaturali* by Fr D. Palmieri. In it he shows a certain impatience that some still appeal 'ad communem quemdam consensum veterum Scholasticorum' to foster the idea of an innate desire for the supernatural, the sign of an ordination or rather of an essential capacity, which they call a 'claim';[143] but he does not

[139] Mansi, vol. 50, col. 71. Cf. Granderath, *Histoire de Concile du Vatican,* French trans., vol. 2, part 2, p. 10, and H. Rondet, *Vatican I* (1962), pp. 57-8, 96-102.

[140] That was the object of the 3rd canon of the new schema. Cf. Granderath, *op. cit.*, p. 20.

[141] Canones, 3: de hominis elevatione et lapsu. (*Collectio lacensis, Acta et decreta SS. Concilii Vaticani,* col. 566.)

[142] *Le Jansénisme* (1909), p. 16; p. 19: 'The Church has never given a dogmatic definition on the state of pure nature. And so it would be rash to include among our dogmas any of the dissertations of theologians about this. In their discussions with their opponents, Jansenius, Arnauld and others did not fail to point it out with some bitterness.'

[143] P. 66 (Thesis XI).

feel that he has the right to qualify their thesis as erroneous.[144] Thus no steps were ever taken against the old opinion. A spiritual undercurrent continued unobtrusively to give life to the fields which seemed to have been dried up by the wind of the new theses. A day was to come when the weakness of these theses would be seen in their fruits—or rather their fruitlessness. Then the needs of apologists, combined with a stronger spiritual growth, a better knowledge of tradition as well as a revival of theological ambition, started a movement in reaction against the whole system, and this is still going on.[145] As a matter of fact this movement was on occasion to cause scandal: 'adeo in oblivione devenerat antiqua doctrina Scolasticorum!' And yet its promoters usually spoke 'multo minus explicite minusque audacter ac antiqui theologi'.[146] This is hardly suprising: the most timid seem still too daring when naïvely they rediscover the simplest truths.[147]

---

[144] *Op. cit.*, p. 160: 'Quia (eorum) modus explicite ab Ecclesia reprobatus non est, etsi theologice defendi nequeat, nolumus ullam censurae notam eorum doctrinae inurere.' (This concerned the doctrine of the Augustinians.) This was a remarkable admission by an opponent who only made it under constraint. The insinuation in 'explicite' should be noticed.

[145] Among more recent indications, cf. Fr Richard Defrennes, *Essai de synthèse de la Théologie dans la Charité* (Congress of the lectors of the French Franciscan provinces, Brive, 1932, 1933, pp. 18-19, n. 3): 'Incidentally, we shall be able to say what we think of those who philosophize on the purely natural and human level, outside the supernatural and divine level, and as a result reason in unreality. We are right to regret this secularization of thought, whoever are the authors to whom it may be traced back, and we may well wonder what responsibility lies upon it for the present confusion in thought and morality.' Another indication is the great change in the exegesis of the 'foundation' given by the commentators on the Spiritual Exercises of St Ignatius of Loyola.

[146] Victorinus Doucet, O.F.M., 'De naturali seu innato supernaturalis beatitudinis desiderio iuxta Theologos a saeculo XIII usque ad XX' in *Antonianum*, 1929, pp. 202-3. Concerning Blondel, the author adds: 'Quidquid est autem de vera interpretatione philosophiae actionis, saltem certum est quod M. Blondel meritum habuerit theologos modernos ad Scolasticorum doctrinam de appetitu verae beatitudinis revocasse, et nunc erit forsitan eius vindicta, videre theologos plus naturae erga supernaturalia concedentes, quam ipse unquam ei tribuere ausus fuerat.'

[147] Joaquin Maria Alonso, C.M.F., 'Lo natural y lo sobrenatural' in *Revista española de Theologia*, Madrid, 1953, pp. 55-68, review of J. Alfaro, S.J., *Lo natural y lo sobrenatural, Estudio historico desde Santo Tomas hasta Cayetano*, Madrid, 1952, p. 68; see the passage quoted above, p. 127; the

The encyclical *Humani generis* in 1950 showed the same prudence as the earlier documents. In recalling that it is contrary to the 'real gratuity of the supernatural order' to claim that God 'cannot create beings endowed with intelligence without ordering them to, calling them to the beatific vision', it repeated in especially clear terms the fundamental truth that must be respected by theological investigation above all, but without canonizing any system.[148] In setting before us once more the angelic doctor as our guide, by this very fact the encyclical calls all, not to a servile conformism, likely to cause the same kind of abuse as Baius' or Jansenius' Augustinianism, but to an effort at renewal that will hardly be able to leave the system of pure nature intact, at least in its prevalent form.

The historian of theology ought, none the less, I repeat, to do justice to this system. However untraditional it was, and especially, dare we say, unreligious, the dualism engendered by an obsessive notion of 'pure nature' was not without its uses. We have seen the part it played. It would not be enough merely to acknowledge the kind of 'popular usefulness' that not so long ago a theologian was willing to grant, with somewhat scornful condescension, to the theory of 'average knowledge'. It not only served to 'save' the freedom of God in the anthropomorphic imagination of many, just as Molinism served to save the freedom of man, and without compromising the activity proper to nature, as Molinism again flattered itself that it did not compromise divine causality. Perhaps in addition, for some at least of its promoters, by this rejection of the supernatural into the background it was a way of seeking to guarantee the mysterious character of our destiny, and of expressing at the same time by the duplication of the orders the heterogeneous and immeasurable character of religion in relation to morality. We should have better grounds for assurance on this point if we could be certain that the genesis of the theory owed

author concludes: 'Pero sin obvisar que el Magisterio ha determinado igualmente que *ese apetito y esa imagen de Dios no constituyen la unica, posible y necesaria metafisica del hombre, ni del ser intelectual en cuanto tel.'*

[148] Cf. Aug. Trapè, *loc. cit.*, p. 3.

a little more to contemplation and a little less to controversy. In any case, one thing is certain: the movement that has begun to take shape in reaction against the theory, if it is not itself to deviate, must fulfil these conditions. Far more than the system whose weak points it has shown, it must proceed from the twofold intention, humanist and theocentric, that this system meant to serve, and better than it, the new movement will have to defend the dogmas which Baianism destroyed. It will also have to take into account a problem recurring, not only in the far-off days of St Augustine, St Thomas or Suarez, but even quite recently. In other words it cannot avoid a considerable effort of thought which cannot be provided by one man and cannot be conceived as a mere return to one or another of the former positions. If theology like dogma knows no irreversibility of time, nevertheless, again like dogma, it cannot tolerate archaism.[149]

From this effort at renewal the great doctors of the past must assuredly benefit—and first of all St Augustine. For from the confusions caused by the Augustinianism of Baius and Jansenius, as well as by the defensive system organized in opposition to their error, he emerged the first victim. Even today how many feel obliged to say bluntly that Augustinianism is incapable of distinguishing nature and the supernatural? From the sixteenth century onwards not only was St Augustine, like St Thomas himself, subjected to a series of 'falsifying interpretations', he was mistrusted. Without always daring to say so, many simply dismissed him. This was a misfortune like that suffered three centuries earlier by his doctrine of illumination. This was compromised on two scores at the time when Arab philosophy invaded

[149] The naturalist deviation that can be symbolized by the name of Baius and which assumed so many other forms since the sixteenth century, obliges theology to make progress. It calls us to a new effort of reflection. Far more than in the past, the gratuitousness of the supernatural needs to be made plain and to be explained; we must achieve a greater awareness of it and explain it more rationally. The mere vital possession of dogma no longer suffices after the denials of heresies and the questions raised thereby. Once the innocence of spontaneous thought has been lost, the methodical labour of reflective thought is required. Precautions of a kind that our ancestors never imagined, are also necessary. The soundness of theology depends on it.

the West, by the resemblance of several of its formulas to the extrinsicist theories of certain Islamic sects and by its translation into Aristotelian terminology which, under the influence of Avicenna, was made by William of Auvergne. This latter had thought to compare the relationship between God and man, between the eternal light and the mind which it illuminates, with the relationship between the passive intellect and the active intellect. It proved disastrous. This was to present an advantage to the opponents of an already shaken philosophical tradition and provoke distrust among the undecided. 'Avicennian Augustinianism', which was a falsified Augustinianism, was inevitably rejected. Was the real Augustine to be rejected with it? The option from which Thomist philosophy emerged can probably be explained in part by this.[150] But St Thomas, as we know, contrived to preserve within his new framework more of 'Augustinian spiritualism' than might have been expected. But now, pending the Cartesian and ontologist denaturations,[151] it was the turn of theological Augustinianism, to which St Thomas had remained substantially faithful, to be falsified. Those who were clear-sighted enough to denounce the error beneath the Augustinian formulas under which it hid, were not sufficiently so to restore the original teaching and restate it in its original sense. To refute Baius and Jansenius they appealed to different ideas, some of which, in their developments and ramifications, finally

---

[150] Sertillanges, *Les grande thèses de la philosophie thomiste*, pp. 195, 196. E. Gilson, 'Pourquoi saint Thomas a critiqué saint Augustin' in *Archives d'Histoire doctrinale et littéraire du moyen âge*, vol. 1, 1926. See in Ephrem Longpré, *Studi Francescani*, 1922, n. 3, the protestations of a disciple of Olivi, Peter de Trabibus, *In II Sent.*, dist. 24.

[151] Jacques Maritain, 'De la sagesse augustinienne' in *Revue de Philosophie*, 1930, pp. 728-9: 'Philosophical Augustinianism seems . . . naturally bound up with an excessive philosophism. . . . The Cartesian *Cogito*, the ontological argument, ontologism, occasionalism . . . far from being the least authentic forms of Augustinian spiritualism are only the residues of its rational disintegration. Already a process similar to materialization had come to be felt in theology when Jansenius transformed into the dense substance of his theological pessimism and hedonism the diaphanous but difficult text of St Augustine, together with his racy language that was too divinely human concerning grace and freedom, Adam's innocence and fallen nature, the delights of the senses and of grace.'

came to weigh heavily—though not, as was said of Augustinianism, with a 'majestic weight'—on the progress of theology. The need to answer, and to answer quickly, with the precarious means at hand, hastened a development which was already beginning to take shape, but which by no means proved fatal. In this way on the foundation of the old concept of the 'pura naturalia' originated the modern system of 'pure nature'.

Doctrinally there would be nothing to be said against the idea; it would be enough to point out it deficiencies[152] and we should have no objection to accepting its terms had it not increasingly been established on the ruins of the traditional and most central idea of Christian philosophy. To this idea St Thomas, after St Augustine, bears witness in his teaching on the 'desire to see God'. In the sixteenth century a provisional agreement between it and the new viewpoints imposed by circumstances was reached in St Robert Bellarmine. It is for the purpose of achieving a more durable agreement that I have endeavoured to work, doing my modest share in the wake of those who, for the past century or so, have set themselves to the task, by my other book, *The Mystery of the Supernatural*, which is the companion volume to the present work.

---

[152] For this theory 'on its own could not by any means resolve all the questions which arise concerning the relationship between' nature and grace 'in the present order of humanity'. Pieter Smulders, 'De Oorsprong van de Theorie der zuivere Natuur, sommaire' in *Bijdragen*, 1949, p. 127.

Index

Adam, A., xivn
Agaësse, Paul, 23n, 31n
Agnes, Mère, 101n
Aiguani, Michael, 124, 125
Al-Gazali, 183n
Albategni, 183n
Albert the Great, St, 108n, 178n, 214n, 242
Albertinus, G.-M., 272n, 303-4
Albizzi, 40n
Albumazar, 183n
Alcuin, 68
Ales see D'Ales
Alexander, 183n
Alexander VIII, 263n
Alexander of Hales, 21n, 113, 116, 144, 242, 248, 249, 249n
Alfaro, Juan, 20, 123n, 124, 124n, 126n, 127n, 131n, 132n, 133n, 141n, 142n, 183n, 217n, 218n, 219n, 229n, 306n
Alfragani, 183n
Alix, C., 133n
Alkindi, 183n
Alonso, J. M., 127n, 306n
Altenstaig, John, 150-2 and notes
Alvarez, Diego, 11n, 125-6
Alverny see D'Alverny
Amann, E., 21n
Ambrose, St, 112n
Amici, Francesco, 222
Anavalpetras (Ibn-el-Bitrodji), 183n
Anaxagoras, 183n, 239n
André, Valère, 3
Andrew of Crete, 190n
Angers see D'Angers
Annat, François, xiii, 60, 70n, 256-7, 263, 267
Anselm, St, 241, 242, 269n
Appolis, Émile, 299n
Arenas, 170n
Argentan see D'Argentan
Aristotle, 5, 5n, 13, 132, 145, 146, 160, 160n, 162, 162n, 174n,

177-8, 178n, 183n, 184, 189, 190, 190n, 209-11, and notes, 212, 212n, 214, 215, 238, 239n
Armellada, Bernardino ab, 141n
Arnaud de Bonneval, 242n
Arnaud, Joseph, 102n
Arnauld, Antoine, xiii, 36, 38, 39n, 40-1, 42, 43-4, 47-8, 47n, 48n, 50-1, 52n, 73, 77, 79, 86, 105-6, 106-9 and notes, 110, 255-6, 256n, 257, 266, 266-7, 305n
Arriaga, 129-30, 180, 181, 181n, 203
Arrubal see Pedro de Arrubal
Aquinas see Thomas Aquinas
Athanasius, St, 171
Auer, J., 244n
Auriole see Peter of Auriole
Averroes, 183n, 239n
Avicebron (Ibn-Gebirol), 183n
Avicenna, 183, 183n, 187n, 208, 215, 215n, 216, 216n, 238, 309

Bachelet see Le Bachelet
Baehrens, 190n
Bail, Louis, 16
Baillet, 258n
Bainvel, J. V., xvn, 128
Baius, xi, xin, xii, xiin, xiii, xiiin, xv, xvn, 1-33, 34, 35, 36, 39, 39n, 40n, 41, 42, 44, 45, 45n, 46, 53, 59, 69, 70, 71-2, 75n, 85n, 86, 87, 87n, 88n, 92, 92n, 97, 105, 118-22 and notes, 133, 134, 144, 144n, 147, 147n, 149, 150-1, 153, 153n, 162, 165, 166, 166n, 167, 168, 169, 170, 171, 174-5n, 202, 206, 240, 241, 247, 252n, 257, 258, 259, 261-2, 262n, 263, 264n, 265-6, 265n, 269, 278, 284, 287, 288, 288n, 289, 291, 297n, 298n, 301n, 307, 308, 308n, 309-10
Balthasar, H. Urs von, 67n, 80n, 177n

Spaemann, Robert, 7n
Spicq, 114n
Stegmüller, J., 134n, 155n, 158n, 162n
Suarez, Franciso de, 120, 125, 128, 129, 163n, 164, 176-8, 180, 181n, 182, 182n, 189, 199, 201-3, 204, 220, 221, 233, 254, 254n, 255, 255n, 257, 259, 302-3, 303n, 308
Suso, Henry, 43n
Swerts, 26n
Sylvester Maurus, 27, 222
Sylvius, 39n, 116n, 203n

Taine, 195
Talota, 289n
Tapper, Ruard, 45, 45n, 164, 164n, 166, 167, 170n, 176
Tauler, Johann, 67, 244n
Tavenaux, Réné, 80n, 278n
Tayard, Pontus de, Bishop of Chalons, 239n
Tencin, Cardinal de, 299, 299n, 300n, 301n
Tenerus, 166
Themistius, 183n
Theophrastus, 183n
Thomas Anglicus, 126, 127
Thomas Aquinas, St, 9, 24n, 31, 39, 49n, 56, 56-7n, 61, 79n, 95-6, 112, 113-7 and notes, 119n, 119-20, 123, 126-33 and notes, 135, 136, 138-44 and notes, 146, 147n, 148, 150, 152, 154-7 and notes, 159-62 and notes, 167, 168, 169, 172-3, 174, 174n, 177, 178n, 180, 181n, 182, 185n, 186-9 and notes, 191-7 and notes, 199, 199n, 200, 202, 203, 203n, 205, 207-39 and notes, 240, 243-4, 244n, 246-7 and notes, 251, 251n, 253, 255, 258-9, 267, 272-6, 279, 281, 281n, 288n, 289, 302, 308, 309-10
Thomas of Jorz, 126n
Thomas of Lemos, 148n, 205, 221, 224n, 250, 250n, 251n
Thomas of Strasbourg, 123n, 137n, 218, 218n, 246-7
Thomas of Sutton, 126n, 130, 138
Thomas of Wylton, 126n

Thomas, Jean-François, 38n
Thomasius, xii
Thomassin, 60, 72, 74-5, 74n, 106n, 262n
Thonnard, P.-J., 71n
Tiberghien, Canon, 128
Tiletanus see Ravestein of Tielt
Tinctor, John, 131
Tissot, G., 112n
Tobac, E., 36n
Toletus, Francis, 129, 152-63 and notes, 166, 168, 173, 178, 178n, 199, 199n, 200, 202, 203n, 204, 220n, 229-30, 292n
Tonquédec, Joseph de, 181
Torres, Bricio, 125n, 134n, 135n, 144n, 146
Trapè, Agostino, 92n, 283n, 307n
Trombetta, Antonio, 142, 185
Turmel, xivn
Turrianus, Luisius, 255n
Tsé see Wang Tang Tsé

Urban VIII, 40, 120, 153n

Vacant-Mangenot, 151
Vallière, G. de la Baule le Blanc de la, 43n
Vallisoleti, 205n
Van Crombrugghe see Crombrugghe
Van Dooren see Dooren
Van Eijl see Eijl
Vasquez, Gabriel, 51n, 178, 182, 189, 203, 232n, 254
Vaux, Réné de, 208n
Vermeil, E., 293n
Verrièle, A., 203-4, 222n
Versor, John, 131-2
Vianey, J., 296n
Vicenza, 141
Victoria see Vitoria
Victorianus, 287n
Viel, Aimé-M., 134n
Vignaux, Paul, 14n
Villavicentio, Fr Laurent, 17n
Vitré, Antoine, 47n
Vitoria, Francesco de, 123n, 124-5 and notes, 134n, 135n, 136, 143-4
Viva, Dominic, 180, 222n
Vooght, Paul de, 116n, 131n, 232n

Wang Tang Tsé, J., 10n
Whitehead, A. N., 238n
Wiggers, John, 179
Wilberforce, Bertrand, 132n
Willaert, Leopold, 39n, 68n
William de la Mare, 123, 243
William of Auvergne, 208n, 309
William of Auxerre, 241, 242
William of Ockham, 9, 9n, 13-4, 14n, 123n

William of Saint-Thierry, 91n, 112n, 115n
Wulf, Maurice de, 142n, 240-1n

Ysambert, 129-30, 236
Yves de Paris, 271n

Zaccaria, Francesco Antonio, 47n, 61, 79n, 299n